D0419196

SANCTITY VERSUS SOVEREIGNTY

THE POLITICAL ECONOMY OF INTERNATIONAL CHANGE
John Gerard Ruggie, General Editor

Sanctity Versus Sovereignty

THE UNITED STATES AND THE NATIONALIZATION OF NATURAL RESOURCE INVESTMENTS

Kenneth A. Rodman

COLUMBIA UNIVERSITY PRESS

New York   1988

Columbia University Press
New York   Guildford, Surrey
Copyright © 1988 Columbia University Press
All rights reserved
Printed in the United States of America

Library of Congress Cataloging-in-Publication Data

Rodman, Kenneth Aaron.
  Sanctity versus sovereignty.

  (The Political economy of international change)
  Bibliography: p.
  Includes index.
  1. Investments, American—Developing countries.
2. Raw materials—Developing countries. 3. Government ownership—Developing countries. I. Title. II. Series.
HG5993.R63 1988   332.6'7373'01724   87-24970
ISBN 0-231-06448-9

TO MY PARENTS

Contents

THE POLITICAL ECONOMY OF
INTERNATIONAL CHANGE
John Gerard Ruggie, General Editor

Preface

While this book began as my doctoral thesis in the early 1980s, it was strongly influenced by my learning experiences about world politics in the 1970s. Two events, and the controversies surrounding them, stood out in particular.

The first was the Vietnam War and the debate as to the motivations behind United States involvement. Politically heated arguments with friends were mirrored by debates in the classroom between realists and radicals. Were interventions in the Third World a function of ideology and misperception? Or were they guided by corporate interests and the needs of American capitalism? The debate was often a "dialogue of the deaf," as realists dismissed economic interpretations as conspiracy theories while radicals saw security and ideological rationales as little more than legitimations of economic imperialism.

The late 1970s saw a degree of convergence between the two schools as scholars enriched their models to incorporate each other's core insights. One work of particular interest, Stephen Krasner's *Defending the National Interest,* was both illuminating and problematical. The argument was illuminating in that it not only made a realist defense of the autonomy of the state; it also accounted for economic motivations by acknowledging that the state saw business as a prop of national power. The argument was problematical in that it left unanswered important questions: If overseas corporate expansion is defined as an instrument of foreign policy, is the state compelled to subordinate other interests and values to the need to create an environment in which business can "perform"? And if the answer to that question is yes, how autonomous is the state in pursuing initiatives which might challenge corporate preferences?

The second event was the OPEC price increase in late 1973. As an undergraduate, I was struck by how much attention policymakers and academics devoted to traditional arenas of national security (the nuclear balance, containment in the Third World) while the most serious setback to the United States in the postwar period came from this wholly unexpected source. It seemed as if U.S. foreign policy were building Maginot Lines while ignoring more likely economic challenges to national security. Even today, witness the attention this administration gives to issues such as Nicaragua and the Strategic Defense Initiative relative to that of the debt crisis which may be America's real "window of vulnerability."

Yet American policymakers did have a conception of national economic security which they equated with an order protecting the sanctity of foreign property rights against nationalization. The OPEC challenge seemed to foreshadow a major threat to this conception since it coincided with other developing countries nationalizing resource investments within their boundaries. Outside of OPEC, however, Third World producers have been unable to translate the assumption of formal sovereignty into real economic clout, either through control over prices or the ability to lessen dependence on foreign firms. In fact, many of the dispossessed foreign owners continue to manage their old concessions and market their resources.

The question that then emerges is how much change

did nationalization really represent? It was a small step to the study of international regimes to examine the sources of order and change in relations between Western business and Third World hosts. What were the factors which enabled developing countries to challenge American-sponsored rules? And what forces set limits on their ability to pursue resource-based nationalization strategies?

In wrestling with these issues, I have benefited from a continuing dialectic with friends, teachers, colleagues, and students. I was fortunate to have as mentors at M.I.T. scholars whose approach to the discipline was different from mine. In particular, each member of my dissertation committee, Nazli Choucri, Hayward Alker, and Steve Kobrin, was invaluable to my intellectual growth and the final product. John Freeman went above and beyond the call of duty as a nonreader in carefully reading the manuscript and providing important advice, particularly concerning the "sorting device" in the conclusion. John Ruggie made valuable suggestions for revising the manuscript for publication.

My research in Washington was funded by the Institute for the Study of World Politics. I am grateful to Ted Moran of Georgetown's Landegger Program in International Business Diplomacy and Gary Hufbauer of the Georgetown International Law Center for allowing me to use their facilities. The many archivists and information and privacy officers deserve recognition, particularly Bonnie Baldwin and Judy Howard at the National Archives.

Finally, I would like to thank my parents for having weaned me on politics, taught me the value of knowledge and scholarship, and showed me nothing but support throughout this long endeavor. It is to them I owe my greatest debt.

Abbreviations

AID	U.S. Agency for International Development
AIOC	Anglo-Iranian Oil Company
Alcan	Aluminum Company of Canada
Alcoa	Aluminum Company of American
AMFORP	American and Foreign Power Company
Aramco	Arabian-American Oil Company
Asarco	American Smelting and Refining Company
BP	British Petroleum
bpd	barrels per day
CFP	Cie. Française des Pétroles (French state oil company)
CIA	U.S. Central Intelligence Agency
CIEP	U.S. Council on International Economic Policy
CVP	Corporación Venezolana del Petroleo

EB	Bureau of Economic and Business Affairs, U.S. Department of State
ENI	Ente Nazionale Idrocarburi (Italian state oil company)
EPB	U.S. Economic Policy Board
ERAP	Enterprise de Recherches de d'Activités Pétrolières (French state oil company)
FDI	Foreign Direct Investment
FPC	U.S. Federal Power Commission
GAO	U.S. General Accounting Office
GATT	General Agreement on Tariffs and Trade
GSP	Generalized System of Trade Preferences
IADB	Inter-American Development Bank
IBA	International Bauxite Association
IBRD	International Bank for Reconstruction and Development (The World Bank)
ICSID	International Center for the Settlement of Investment Disputes
IFI	International Financial Institution
IMF	International Monetary Fund
IPC (Iraq)	Iraq Petroleum Company
IPC (Peru)	International Petroleum Company
ITT	International Telephone and Telegraph Company
LDC	Less Developed Country
LNG	Liquefied Natural Gas
MDB	Multilaterial Development Bank
MNC	Multinational Corporation
NEPCO	New England Petroleum Company

NIEO	New International Economic Order
NSC	U.S. National Security Council
NSDM	National Security Decision Memorandum
NSSM	National Security Study Memorandum
OAS	Organization of American States
OECD	Organization of Economic Cooperation and Development
OFE	Office of Fuels and Energy, U.S. Department of State
OPEC	Organization of Petroleum Exporting Countries
OPIC	Overseas Private Investment Corporation
Pemex	Petróleos Mexicanos
P.L. 480	Public Law 480 (Food for Peace)
Socal	Standard Oil of California
SPCC	South Peru Copper Company
UAE	United Arab Emirates
UFCO	United Fruit Company
USG	United States Government
YPF	Yacimientos Petroliferos Fiscales

SANCTITY VERSUS SOVEREIGNTY

Introduction

The transformation of the relationship between raw material investors and developing countries stands out as one of the most visible arenas of change in contemporary North-South relations. In the past, foreign firms owned and marketed a resource under concession contracts which favored them with minimal liabilities and a long time frame. The stability of these arrangements was legitimized by Western international law which held that they were binding and that nationalization or any other infringements were illegal without full compensation. To ensure compliance, parent states reserved the right of diplomatic protection—the use of official representations of economic and even military pressure to protect the sanctity of the acquired rights of their nationals.

To developing countries, this system amounted to a derogation of their sovereignty. The concessions were often the result of colonialism, gunboat diplomacy, or unequal bargaining power. They were seen as forms of extraterritorial privilege which left the host little control over a nonrenewable natural resource. Compounding this, the resources controlled by the firm were often the "commanding heights" of the economy, representing an inordinate share of its export earnings. Finally, diplomatic protection implied great power intervention, an affront to the principle of sovereign equality embodied in the United Nations Charter.

As a result, less-developed countries (LDCs) supported doctrines, such as Permanent Sovereignty over Natural Resources, that legitimized their right to redefine the traditional property rights of foreign investors free from international law or parent-states pressures. Yet, for the first two decades after World War II, this new norm represented little more than a long-term aspiration. The bargaining power of the multinational corporation (MNC) and the spectre of diplomatic protection inhibited LDCs from exercising what they believed to be a sovereign right.

Over time, developing countries were able to translate principle into practice. By the 1970s, almost all producer states had nationalized or assumed effective control over natural resource stakes within their boundaries. A contract was no longer a guarantee etched in stone, but an "obsolescing bargain" in which the initial agreement was continually renegotiated to enable the host to capture a larger share of the benefits.[1] In effect, a tight system of contractual sanctity gave way to a more flexible system in which sovereign states were less bound to the acquired rights of foreign investors. Corporations and their home states initially tried to stem the tide of change, but ultimately adapted.

From the vantage point of the mid-1970s, this appeared to be a dramatic change. To Third World elites, nationalization ended a system of neocolonialism and finally allowed economic self-determination to complement political independence. OPEC's success in nationalizing the oil industry and quadrupling prices seemed to foreshadow the success of nationalization strategies elsewhere. Many Western observers extended a comparable analysis, arguing that the balance of bargaining power had "cumulatively" and "irreversibly" shifted from firm to host. As one business historian noted, "By 1970, it was clear that the survival of all American enterprise would be on terms set by the host government."[2]

Yet, by the early 1980s, it was clear that the terms set by hosts confronted new limits. To capture export markets, state-owned enterprises still depend upon resources provided by foreign economic actors, namely technology and market access from multinational firms and capital from the international financial community. To maintain this access, most LDCs have offered some compensation and an ongoing contractual relationship to the dispossessed owner which allows the firm to manage its former concession and market its crude oil and mineral ores. In some cases, the need has been acute enough to compel LDCs to retreat from more ambitious strategies of economic nationalism toward policies more congenial to MNCs.[3] Despite the demise of the concession system, the ability of LDCs to assert sovereignty over natural resources still faces serious constraints.

This process of systemic change placed stresses on U.S. foreign policy. The concession system had been an integral part of the world order the United States had sought to preserve after World War II. To maintain it, the United States pursued a deterrent strategy which insisted upon the sanctity of contracts through diplomatic and economic pressure. As these instruments were no longer able to stem the erosion of the system, it was compelled to reconstruct its anti-expropriation policy. A more pragmatic strategy emerged which adapted to Third World economic nationalism. While traditional ownership rights could no longer be defended, the adverse consequences for corporate profitability and national economic security were mitigated by facilitating a post-expropriation relationship between firm and host and by encouraging the diversification of sources of supply.

This study examines the learning process through which the U.S. government and corporate actors resisted or adapted to Third World economic nationalism in raw materials. In so doing, it will address two important theoretical issues relating to (1) the sources of order and change in relationships between extractive MNCs and LDC hosts, and (2) the relative importance of economic factors in U.S. foreign policy.

Part 1 examines the evolution of the international "regime" governing the resolution of nationalization disputes, that is, the changing norms and practices to which actors adhered above and beyond the legal theories they espoused.[4] By focusing on behavior, the analysis goes beyond abstract legal debates to ask questions about the sources of adherence to particular types of order: Why were the rules of the concession system relatively well obeyed until the late 1960s? What were the factors that undermined the system and sustain current arrangements?

Part 2 sheds light on debates between radical and statist models about the centrality of corporate interests in U.S. foreign policy in the Third World. Anti-expropriation policy provides a useful arena to examine these models because it is an area where the defense of corporate prerogatives often collided with the diplomatic objective of maintaining constructive relations with Third World regimes. These tradeoffs became more acute over time as nationalization became more prevalent among nonradical regimes and as the efficacy of traditional investment protection strategies diminished. Finally, the issue has been the subject of two theoretically sophisticated works—Stephen Krasner's *Defending the National Interest,* and Charles Lipson's *Standing Guard*—that come to opposing conclusions about the appropriateness of each model.

Testing these models, however, runs into two problems. First, the debate is often framed over the relative importance of state and corporate preferences in motivating foreign policy. But how does one disentangle these factors when protecting investments and preserving a climate favorable to the expansion of foreign capital are defined by policymakers as part of the broader national interest? Second, more sophisticated recent scholarship from each school has enriched its framework to account for the core insights of the other model. While this increases the models' ability to explain a greater number of cases, it also serves to circumvent challenges posed by anomalous evidence.

The objective, then, is not to test or falsify either approach, but establish a typology spelling out the conditions under which each model's dominant explanation is most appropriate. To accomplish this, part 2 will comparatively analyze case studies over a forty-year period with an eye toward the role of corporate interests and regime considerations in public decision making. In the process, the debates over the sources of foreign policy behavior will be integrated with the study of regime dynamics to examine how changes in the international system affect the applicability of the radical and statist models.

Regime Dynamics and the Transformation of the Concession System

The term "international regime" has been used by scholars to analyze the degree to which world politics are characterized by patterns of rules and norms rather than pure anarchy. Regimes have been defined as "governing arrangements constructed by states to coordinate their expectations and organize aspects of their behavior in various issue areas."[5] They are "islands of order in a sea of anarchy" which add a degree of predictability to the international environment. As such, they enable states to pursue their long-term interests through cooperation or norm-governed behavior rather than short-term self-interest.[6]

Regime analysis provides both an alternative to and an enrichment of more traditional institutional and legal approaches to the study of international governance.[7] Rather than focusing on the constitutional provisions of international organizations or the formal obligations of international law, a regimes approach focuses on behavior. That is, it attempts to complement traditional approaches by establishing the conditions under which state practice converges or diverges from formal rules and institutions.

The dominant explanatory model in this field is the Theory of Hegemonic Stability, which attributes order to the relative capability of states in the international system. According to Keohane, the theory posits that "hegemonic structures of power dominated by a single country are most conducive to the development of strong international regimes whose rules are relatively precise and well-obeyed."[8] The dominant state will act to provide the "public good" of a stable regime because it identifies its interests with the system it manages and possesses the ability to shape and dominate its environment.

The devolution toward a more polycentric order presages regime erosion. The leader's rule-enforcing capabilities are increasingly frustrated. Its share of economic resources lacks the concentration to coerce others to comply. Nor does it possess the economic surfeit necessary to either co-opt compliance through side payments or absorb the short-term material costs of regime enforcement. As a result, priorities are eventually redefined away from economic milieu goals toward short-term material ones. Without a manager to vouchsafe the system by sanction, bribe, or sacrifice, short-term self-help replaces norm-governed behavior.[9]

Much of the critical discussion of this model has focused on North-North economic relations. American hegemony may have been necessary to create liberal economic regimes after World War II. Yet even neorealists have conceded that once regimes are in place, perceptions of shared interests from economic interdependence may be both necessary and sufficient to sustain cooperation even as power becomes more diffuse. The persistence of a relatively liberal trade regime (albeit with more "cheating" in labor-intensive and technologically mature industries) since the decline of American preponderance in the 1970s provides the most frequently cited example.[10]

But when the focus shifts from a North-North to a North-South axis, a number of key differences emerge which raise doubts about a parallel analysis. The former is characterized by conditions of interdependence and relative consensus on "embedded liberal" norms.[11] The latter is characterized by relations of dependence and much sharper normative dissensus. First, LDCs had no say in the creation of a liberal economic order into which they were supposed to fit and prosper like everyone else. Second, they argued that this order stunted their economic development and imposed severe constraints on their national autonomy.[12]

North-South arrangements, therefore, conform more closely to what Oran Young called "imposed regimes"—orders that are "deliberately fostered by dominant powers or consortia of dominant actors." Such actors achieve compliance by punishing defection to the point where potential violators reevaluate the costs and benefits of self-help. Since such orders are based upon restraints rather than "the explicit consent of subordinate actors," Young speculates that the hegemonic model may more appropriately explain regime stability and decay.[13]

My argument is that the concession regime largely conformed to Young's model of an "imposed regime," since its rules were enforced by the bargaining power of a small number of vertically integrated MNCs, reinforced by American economic power when necessary. The weakening of those actors altered the regime, but did not eliminate it, since, there remains a recognizable pattern of norms and expectations. The persistence of order can be attributed primarily to international markets and financial systems which continue to impose less centralized constraints on LDCs. To understand how the rules and norms governing resource investments in the Third World evolved, it will be useful to examine: the contours of the traditional concession regime and the interests and power that undergirded it; the role of cognitive and structural changes in the international system in contributing to regime erosion; and the sources of order under the contemporary system.

THE COGNITIVE AND STRUCTURAL BASES
OF THE TRADITIONAL CONCESSION REGIME

While the hegemonic stability model has been faulted for its state-centric bias,[14] it does highlight the key role the U.S. government played in sustaining the concession system. To the architects of the post–World War II order, foreign direct investment (FDI), and the concession system under which it operated, were important components of the liberal vision of world order. Encouraging the flow of natural resources to the Third World would serve the American national interest as a guarantor of stable access to critical raw materials, and a catalyst for economic development and social stability in the Third World. As a result, U.S. outward investment policy sought to preserve the concession system under which multinational corporations (MNCs) owned overseas resources and had complete discretion over their disposition. Expropriation and other LDC state incursions into the concessions were categorized as threats to the flow of private capital to the Third World and to the development of foreign sources of supply.

In order to protect existing investments and encourage new ones, the United States sponsored an international regime in which alien property rights were protected from sovereign encroachments such as expropriation. It supported the traditional international law principle of *Pacta Sunt Servanda,* which held that the terms of a contract between an alien and a sovereign are binding throughout its life and that any infringement is justiciable under international law. The United States conceded the sovereign right of a state to expropriate foreign property under the principle of eminent domain, but circumscribed this right with the legal requirement that the action be nondiscriminatory, pursued for a public purpose, and accompanied by "prompt, adequate, and effective" compensation. American statecraft, in effect, sought to extend the U.S. Constitution's Fifth Amendment protection of property to the rest of the world.

The stability of this system rested on a number of

cognitive and *structural* bases.[15] The former refer to principles and norms derived from neoclassical economics, the economic lessons of the 1930s, and the Lockean precepts about private property.[16] The latter refer to the configurations of power and interest in the international system that sustain a particular type of order.

The cognitive bases equated the regime with the provision of a public good and identified concrete U.S. national interests with its defense. They served a twofold function as a coherent system of beliefs to guide American strategies of regime maintenance, and a means of legitimizing American preferences to the larger world community.

The cognitive bases can be broken down into normative assumptions (the values underlying the regime) and instrumental assumptions (the concrete interests supported by regime maintenance). The normative rationale can be spelled out as follows: First, as with free trade, decision makers perceived a "harmony of interest" between the relatively unbridled operation of FDI and the economic interests of all parties. Encouraging the flow of investments into the Third World would serve not only corporate profits, but also the American national interest in access to raw materials. In addition, by transferring scarce factors of production to the poor countries, it would stimulate economic progress and political development, thereby serving American containment objectives.

Second, expropriation and other state interference with alien property rights were pejoratively labeled "economic nationalism," direct descendants of the "beggar-thy-neighbor" policies of the 1930s, and condemned as economically wasteful and politically conflictual. If prevalent, they would deter the flow of FDI to the Third World, and undermine the goals of both resource and development diplomacy.

Finally, the global rule of law—in this case, the sanctity of contracts—was equated with the provision of a public good. Stable and calculable expectations in contractual and property rights would create a climate in which firms

could make investment decisions on the basis of economic criteria without fear of political risk. All would gain from arrangements that give the freest possible rein to market forces.
The resultant stimulus to investment would increase corporate profits, spur LDC economic development, and promote
U.S. economic and foreign policy aims. As Robert Packenham
observed with respect to a similar logic underlying U.S. foreign aid policy, "all good things come together."[17]

Rules, however, need an enforcer. Domestically, rules
protecting property and contractual rights are guaranteed by
the state. The international system has no supranational authority to perfrom the same function. Decision makers feared
that contractual agreements might wither in an anarchic
world. Each state would have an economic or political incentive to squeeze private investors for short-term parochial advantage. The end result would be a spiraling diminution of
private capital flows as investors drew back from exposed positions abroad. This, in turn, would lead to an undercon-
sumption of the "public goods" associated with a strong regime, a condition harmful to all parties. Therefore, property
rights had to be protected from arbitrary sovereign encroachment if a market-oriented international system was to function efficiently.

Since self-help might work against the public good
of a stable property regime, the United States assumed the
role of putative sovereign to enforce the rules. The primary
instrument was economic pressure. Among the means available were formal sanctions, such as the Hickenlooper Amendment, which Congress enacted to mandate the cessation of
aid to any country that seizes American property and does
not take steps toward paying "full" compensation within six
months. Although that legislation was invoked on only two
occasions (Ceylon in 1963 and Ethiopia in 1979), informal
sanctions—delaying new aid authorizations, deferring consideration of the multilateral development bank (MDB) loans,
or quietly impeding access to credits and markets—were uti-
lized or threatened more frequently. On paper, sanctions

strategy was motivated by an economic "domino theory," which held that any successful defiance of American standards, even an intrinsically insignificant one, would set a precedent for others to follow. Therefore, economic pressure was employed or threatened as part of a strategy of regime maintenance to punish or deter deviant behavior.[18]

The instrumental assumptions represented American decision makers' calculation of the tradeoffs to be expected when sanctions are threatened or employed. The calculation encompassed three separate considerations: (1) the estimated *value* of punishing a deviant act, i.e., the public good of systemic order and the ancillary interests it supports (security of supply, capitalist development in the Third World, liberal world order, domestic prosperity); (2) the estimated *probability of success,* i.e., the ability to force the target state to give in or suffer sufficiently to signal others that expropriation does not pay; and (3) the estimated *costs* associated with sanctions, i.e., retaliation against immediate economic interests, disruption of host country growth, undermining democratic or reformist regimes, and souring bilateral relations.[19]

The normative assumptions underlying the policy were widely shared throughout the bureaucracy, but the instrumental ones were not. There was consensus on the desirability of promoting foreign investment and discouraging expropriation. But the logic of regime maintenance often compelled the state to pay a short-term concrete price for a symbolic victory which left the regime intact. How high a price was it willing to pay? Differences in bureaucratic mission and expertise predisposed particular agencies to answer this question differently. Not surprisingly, intragovernmental disagreements arose as policy choices posed questions of the best means of advancing the regime and the acceptable level of costs incurred in doing so. But prior to 1970, because of the strength the regime, the costs and risks of regime maintenance were usually minor. As a result, bureaucratic differences were relatively muted.

To understand the sources of regime strength, one must turn to the structural bases of the regime, the configurations of power and interest that buttress the system. The hegemonic model would point to the preponderant position of the United States, with a near monopoly over relevant economic resources, e.g., aid, credits, markets. As the primary contributor to international financial institutions, the United States also possessed the clout to use those institutions to further its vision of world order. The United States could successfully punish or deter deviant behavior by negative sanction—inducing compliance by denying needed resources; positive sanction—dispensing rewards (aid, sugar quotas) for correct behavior; and (3) utilizing its surfeit of economic resources to absorb the costs of and/or co-opt medium powers into regime enforcement.[20]

The analysis of international structure, however, need not be limited to state actors.[21] State power was not the primary vehicle through which the concession regime was directly maintained. More important were corporate bargaining advantages which public pressures would occasionally reinforce. Therefore, the material bases of the regime can be broadened to subsume factors other than American hegemony, i.e., (1) the structure of the early bargaining relationship between firm and host, and (2) the concentration of private economic resources in specific commodity markets.

First, the bargaining relationship between firm and host during the early phases of a concession severely limited the host's ability to renegotiate. Given the high fixed cost and uncertainty of exploration, large multinationals possessed considerable advantages because of their access to capital markets and technology and their ability to compensate for risk through exploration and development in several countries. LDCs were obliged to offer highly favorable terms or forego development. Even when production was in place, the host's options were further limited by its complete dependence upon the firm's technology and specialized information to develop and market its resources.

Second, corporate bargaining power was accentuated by the concentration of a small number of large, vertically integrated (mostly American) firms in most natural resource industries. Corporate cohesion facilitated the maintenance of the concession regime through its bargaining power vis-à-vis a large number of uncoordinated host countries. In instances of more serious threats, such as nationalization, it could impose discipline to implement effective economic sanctions. The oil company boycott of Iran for its 1951 nationalization of the Anglo-Iranian Oil Company provides the most dramatic example of this capacity.[22]

SOURCES OF REGIME EROSION

Until the late 1960s, the combination of American economic dominance and corporate bargaining power provided a strong regime. By the end of the decade, however, the concession system was faced with the environment that was increasingly dissonant with its cognitive and structural bases. Systemic stress and pressures for change were brought about by (1) Third World rejection of regime norms and (2) changes in the international system which increased host country bargaining power.

First, from the vantage point of much of the Third World, the liberal premises underlying the regime were conservative and antinationalist—little more than a euphemism for continued dependence. Most LDCs perceived a conflict between their interests and those of the MNC on both historical and structural grounds—historical, in that many of the concessions were by-products of colonialism, gunboat diplomacy, or nominally independent and unresponsive local elites; structural, in that the objectives of the multinational firm, which are globally oriented, often diverge from the aims of the host country, which are nationally oriented.[23] Since MNCs were political (power-maximizing), as well as economic (profit-maximizing) actors, their superior bargaining power would often tilt an agreement to their predominant, if not exclusive, advantage. State intervention, from this perspective, was not a malign or irrational force, but a potential source of countervailing power to rectify an existing imbalance and redirect the benefits.

To LDCs, a world order that sanctified property rights above the prerogatives of sovereignty ignored the degree to which alien property rights have been a lever of domination and control. While insuring a stability of expectations for the firm, they often produced instability for the host by subordinating national planning for the life of a contract to the global objectives of an integrated multinational network. If maintaining such an order can be said to have provided a collective good, it was one that is consumed asymmetrically. In Oran Young's terminology, it produced not a "negotiated regime" where states mutually agree to act with restraint in order to achieve common ends, but an "imposed regime" designed to rationalize an unequal status quo.[24]

Developing countries, increasingly aware of these inequities, rejected the moral authority of the traditional system. They sponsored alternative regimes (the Calvo Doctrine in Latin American and Permanent Sovereignty over Natural Resources in the United Nations), which took the issue of nationalization out of the realm of international law and placed it under the exclusive competence of the host country. At the heart of these schemes was the assertion that a state's sovereign right to promote the general welfare took precedence over the sanctity of property rights acquired by foreign investors. The question of compensation for the dispossessed owner was subject only to the national laws of the host, not international law. Diplomatic protection and international arbitration were condemned as offensive to national sovereignty.[25]

Second, changes in the structural bases of the regime enabled LDCs to supplement rhetoric with action. Most important was the effect of transnational processes and non-state actors in weakening corporate bargaining advantages.

First, the LDC state increased its bargaining power through what has been called the "obsolescing bargain" process.[26] As state companies gained expertise with respect to the economics and technology of the industry, they were better situated to renegotiate on more favorable terms. And, as the firm was committed to a large fixed investment, its threat to exit in response to state demands was far less credible. Second, the emergence of new entrants in most natural resource industries weakened tight oligopoly structures. This reinforced the obsolescing bargain by increasing host country options and undermining the efficacy of industry-wide sanctions.[27]

The decline of American economic hegemony also played a role. With the economic recovery of Western Europe and Japan, alternative sources of aid, trade, and credits opened up, thereby diminishing the effectiveness of unilateral economic pressures. But hegemonic decline was secondary to the decline of corporate bargining power as a determinant of regime decay. Its primary consequence was that public policies were unable to compensate for the loss of bargaining clout by MNCs.[28]

The dynamics of change enabled LDCs to challenge regime rules with less vulnerability to retaliation. Consequently, by the early 1970s, most LDCs were able to nationalize industries and renegotiate contracts, offering, at most, partial or deferred compensation. A striking feature of this trend toward national control was its pervasiveness throughout the entire developing world. Even such "open" economies, such as Liberia, Malaysia, and Papua-New Guinea have removed foreign control at the primary level.[29]

Nonetheless, the end result was a loosening rather than an elimination of the regime protecting overseas resource investments. Despite some loss of autonomy, the MNC remained an important actor because of its control over financial, technological, and marketing resources. For the extractive multinational, the key to success was no longer ownership, or even compensation, but guaranteed access to primary products to feed downstream operations (i.e., refining, smelting, fabrication, and distribution), an access that could be assured through a post-expropriation contractual relationship.

Since most LDC development strategies were still tied to export performance, and this performance was, in turn, still dependent upon services and factors of production provided by the MNC, corporate bargaining leverage persisted. If demands went too far, even the most risk-taking MNCs and banks would no longer proffer new investments and credits. LDCs that tried to exclude or excessively restrict the MNC would often become suppliers of last resort as they steadily lost their share of the market.[30] As a result, host countries were no longer constrained by the direct coercion of an oligopolistic industry, but by the more impersonal requirements of the international market system.

Therefore, despite the erosion of a tight regime, a discernible pattern of norms, rules, and expectations persisted. What emerged was a more flexible quasi-regime where the modal outcome was nationalization, or its functional equivalent, accompanied by something less than full compensation and an ongoing contractual relationship for the dispossessed owner. It was a far cry from the era when the MNC operated as a "state within a state," with freewheeling immunity from local law. But it was the end of neither capitalism nor foreign investment in the Third World. Though MNCs lost some measure of control, they were generally able to adapt to the activist state and continue to operate profitably.

ESTABLISHING A SORTING DEVICE FOR MODELS
OF FOREIGN ECONOMIC POLICY

The case studies in part 2 address the relative merits of competing models as to the role of overseas economic interests in the conduct of American diplomacy. U.S. foreign policy has been characterized, on the one hand, as quixotic and predisposed to pursue "grandiose principles at the expense of a cool assessment of national interests," and on the

other hand, as a malign force coercively attempting to forge
a world receptive to its economic interests through a policy
of nearly continuous intervention. These conflicting interpretations, usually made in the political context of the containment doctrine, can be extended to foreign economic policy
in general, and anti-expropriation policy in particular.[31]

Critics within the statist tradition have labeled U.S.
policies toward expropriating countries more as "Pavlovian
reactions against communism" than as policies of economic
self-interest. Robert Gilpin and Stephen Krasner see U.S. foreign policy as guided by a national interest autonomously defined by the state and not reducible to the interest of any
particular societal group. These interests are defined primarily in terms of the security and ideological aims of the
Cold War. Corporate interests and economic milieu goals are
clearly secondary, promoted primarily for their contribution
to larger political aims. When conflicts emerge between the
state's diplomatic goals and corporate or other economic interests, the tendency is for the broader interests of foreign
policy to prevail.[32]

Consistent with this model, Krasner makes the point
that the United States intervened in expropriation cases only
when it perceived (or, more often, misperceived) the seizure
as part of a radical or communist takeover, thereby supporting what the state autonomously (and often erroneously) defined as the national interest. But support for international
property rules often conflicted with more general foreign policy ends:

> Since American private investors are often at odds with
> host country governments, the desire of central decision-makers to
> strengthen ties with such countries (or at least prevent them from
> deteriorating) in order to enhance the territorial and political se-
> curity of the U.S., can bring conflict between American officials
> and corporate objectives.[33]

Therefore, in the absence of this perception of communism,
the United States generally relaxed regime rules and adopted
a policy of accommodation. This became increasingly true as

American power declined and the diplomatic costs of regime maintenance escalated. Krasner concludes that the state's general reluctance to exercise its power on behalf of aggrieved firms ultimately shaped and redirected corporate strategies toward accommodation with nationalization.

In contrast, radical critics attribute anti-expropriation policy to the structural relationship between the imperatives of the MNC and American foreign policy. The American attempt to make the world over was not a millennial vision divorced from reality; rather, it was a "rational" attempt to create an international environment congenial to overseas economic expansion.

In this view, an expanding American capitalism required that the United States try to preserve what Magdoff calls the "Global Open Door," that is, a world order in which "American business could trade, operate, and profit without restriction."[34] Expropriation and other Third World strictures against foreign capital were real challenges to this imperial structure, and to leave them unanswered risked its progressive erosion. As a result, the United States pursued a relentless policy of intervention to "satisfy this hunger of the multinational corporations for maximum *lebensraum*" free from socialism or economic nationalism.[35]

In a more qualified recasting of the radical approach, Charles Lipson adopts a corporate preference model: "Government policies, to protect foreign investment including the passage of laws and their enforcement, conform to the predominant preferences of the largest U.S. multinational corporations."[36] Unlike most proponents of the radical model, Lipson confines its explanatory power to anti-expropriation policy. In other issue areas, he notes that competing public and private groups are more active and numerous and the corporate community has "a less coherent and influential voice." In contrast, corporations more strongly influence investment protection because they are more directly affected and generally agree on its desirability.[37]

Lipson traces changes in public policy to the evolution of corporate beliefs concerning the efficacy of sanctions. The hard-line policies of the 1960s reflected business concern about expropriation in the wake of the Cuban revolution. The business community successfully influenced Congress to legislate tough foreign aid sanctions to deter seizures. Executive decisions to invoke sanctions or use informal pressures conformed to this aim. In contrast to Krasner, Lipson attributes the shift to more "pragmatic" U.S. policies in the 1970s to changes in corporate strategy, i.e., the need to adapt to economic nationalism in a more hostile and less malleable world.[38]

The debate between the statist and radical models has usually been framed over the question of whether state or corporate preferences shape foreign policy. But this poses a knotty definitional dilemma because FDI and the creation of a favorable climate for it were defined by central decision makers as part of the "broader interests of foreign policy."[39] For example, Krasner asserts that the state was generally unwilling to subordinate its public preferences to the particularistic interests of threatened firms.[40] But the protection of specific firms was designed to assist not only the firm in question, but the stability of a system that was seen as integral to general foreign policy goals.

This problem can be understood by extending Lindblom's theory of "the privileged position of business" from the domestic to the foreign policy sphere.[41] In domestic politics, Lindblom argues, discretionary corporate decisions have serious public consequences on national income, wages, and the allocation of resources and labor. Broad areas of policymaking are thereby removed from public control and depend upon corporate "performance." The state, therefore, is not wholly autonomous. Its success in achieving public goals is symbiotically tied to business confidence and it must frequently defer to corporate preferences to induce "performance."

In foreign policy, private economic actors, through their independent actions, also assume many of the functions of governments. Private decisions about capital investment in the Third World have a significant impact on important foreign policy aims, such as secure and low-cost access to raw materials or the flow of private capital to supplement development initiatives, such as Kennedy's Alliance for Progress or Reagan's Caribbean Basin Initiative. Private noncooperation can effectively thwart those state initiatives, as witnessed by Carter's human rights policy in the Southern Cone dictatorships in Latin America or Reagan's economic warfare strategies against the Soviet Union.[42] While the state can often assert its priorities over private economic actors, it is dependent upon their autonomous behavior to achieve important outcomes. The state, consequently, must be somewhat solicitous of corporate concerns about expropriation and a secure investment climate to preserve an environment in which MNCs can confidently venture their capital. Through this relationship, state preferences can be shaped and redefined by the more expansive corporate definitions of regime requirements.

Incorporating Lindblom's insight into the analysis complicates efforts to devise tests to falsify the paradigms through case studies. It is difficult to specify the evidence that would lead to the rejection of either because both can account for economic and noneconomic motivations, the chief difference being their causal direction. As Bobrow and Kudrle note, it is difficult to distinguish between a "state that is pursuing its view of the national interest and one that is consciously or unconsciously serving the ends of the capitalist order."[43] That distinction can only be determined by the researcher's larger philosophical assumptions concerning the relationship between politics and economics or the inherent tendencies of capitalism toward monopoly, disequilibrium, and crisis.

Lindblom's thesis raises other unanswered questions: How solicitous must the state be of corporate preferences and economic milieu goals? To what extent has business's "privileged position" precluded the state from pursuing options that subordinate corporate "indulgences" to other interests? How constrained is the state by corporate prefer-

ences and the structural relationship between business confidence and national security? Under what conditions might
it be more insulated from corporate aims?

Each formulation sets forth a different answer to these
questions. In Krasner's model, the state is relatively unconstrained by business.[44] Despite the U.S. verbal commitment
to economic milieu goals, such as the free market and the
sanctity of contract, the state possessed considerable freedom
of action to subordinate them to diplomatic objectives. "When
there was a clash between more general political aims . . .
and creation of a more open international order in which individual initiative could flourish, it was the latter that was
sacrificed."[45] In effect, the state was successful in placing diplomatic objectives over corporate preferences or regime maintenance.

Lipson posits a model that in many ways resembles
a pure structuralist approach.[46] The U.S. government assumed responsibility for maintaining a regime protecting FDI
because the United States, as the world's foreign investor,
par excellence, had the most to gain from such an order; and
in alliance with established industries, it possessed a concentration of resources sufficient to regulate a world order conducive to its preferences. Since the expansion of foreign investment was conceptually linked to national power and
domestic well-being, regime-governed behavior was pursued
to maximize national economic advantage within the incentives and constraints of the international system.

A third approach can be added, one that sees policy
less as a function of a coherent decision rules, ideological or
economic, and more as the disjointed outcome of the fragmentation of power within the state and the society. The bureaucratic politics model traces anti-expropriation policy to
bargaining and compromise among different agencies, each
with its own parochial perspective.[47] The pluralist model views
policy as heavily influenced, if not determined, by the particularistic interests of competing societal groups.[48] Policy,
through these lenses, is less the outcome of a coherent and

purposeful actor than of the competition and compromises between diverse governmental and private interests engaged in bargaining and compromise.

Each approach sets forth a parsimonious explanation of the decisive causal locus of policy determination. Each is also successful in illustrating several key features of U.S. anti-expropriation policy. But none successfully explains all the cases. There is ample evidence to support, challenge, or amend each approach.

The search for explanatory completeness can lead to a kind of descriptive anarchy producing nothing more than a diffuse set of ad hoc observations concluding that everything matters. No theory can be expected to explain all the cases. Moreover, each of the models explicitly recognizes this. While they all set forth a modal explanation of the determinative cause of state behavior, they are also sufficiently laden with "escape clauses" to explain anomalous outcomes.

Krasner accomplishes this through categorizing the United States as a "weak state" where economic and political power is fragmented and dispersed. Since the state cannot command MNCs to behave in specified ways, the latter can use "negative power" (the refusal to act in ways preferred by the state) to influence state policy.[49] As a result, Lindblom's insights are fully compatible with this enriched version of a statist model.

Lipson's corporate preference model "side-steps the confounding diplomatic issues that affect all expropriation controversies, allowing us to concentrate more precisely on anti-expropriation policy."[50] But it is precisely these conflicts between diplomatic objectives and regime goals that Krasner examines to build his thesis. The intensity of the state's commitment to economic milieu goals can only be measured by the other interests it would sacrifice to promote them.

In sum, both Krasner and Lipson concede the other model's explanatory power through establishing residual categories. Yet neither sets forth a "typological theory" that specifies the conditions explaining the variance among the cases.[51]

In reconciling their competing claims, this study will inductively establish just such a typology. The aim is not to demonstrate the superior explanatory power of particular works or paradigms. Rather, it is to discover the boundaries of their explanatory domains.[52] For example, when is decision making conducted in the insulated world of statism and when do corporate preferences substantially limit executive discretion? When do the diplomatic consequences of hard-line policies make regime-oriented strategies unacceptable? How has this varied with changes in political leaders, regime strength, interest group coalitions, or geographical setting?

The findings will be drawn from a systematic comparison of case studies over a forty-year period. The cases will examine bureaucratic battles over public decision making, scrutinizing the learning process through which the U.S. government resisted or adapted to regime change. As noted earlier, U.S. anti-expropriation policy was guided by a well-formulated system of beliefs—normative assumptions of the beneficence of FDI and instrumental assumptions spawned during American hegemony. However, these beliefs confronted an international milieu which progressively undermined their premises. By focusing on the degree of institutional learning that took place vis-à-vis various expropriatory precedents, one can analyze the degree to which corporate preferences and regime considerations were paramount in decision making over time.

This focus on learning is pertinent for reasons other than reconciling the competing models. Recent stresses in the international economic system have demonstrated that the liberal economic paradigm conveys, at best, a partial view of the world. While the market still plays an important role, state intervention and planning have become an increasingly prominent feature of Western and Third World economic strategies. For the most part, this trend has not necessarily been an economically "irrational" force, but an attempt to control the adverse consequences of unconstrained market forces and economic interdependence on social stability and national vulnerability.[53]

Continued adherence to a doctrinaire liberalism in such a context represents an attempt to impose upon the world an American vision of political economy at a time when others are amending this vision, and American clout to arrest this trend has eroded. Anti-expropriation policy can thus be seen as a microcosm of foreign economic policy wherein one can measure the flexibility of the liberal world view in an increasingly pluralist world.

PART ONE.

REGIME ANALYSIS: THE COGNITIVE AND STRUCTURAL DYNAMICS OF THE POSTWAR ANTI-EXPROPRIATION REGIME

1.

United States Support of an International Property Regime: Principles, Norms, Rules, and Enforcement

The United States emerged from World War II as the dominant political and economic power in the non-Communist world. With its core interest in security relatively unthreatened, it used its preponderant position less to respond to immediate threats or pursue short-run material aims than to promote what Arnold Wolfers called "milieu goals," i.e., to shape the norms and rules of the international environment in which nations operated.[1] These norms and rules were designed to protect the international system from the excesses of nationalism that fractured it during the interwar period. The containment doctrine, which opposed the spread of revolution and communism, was the political expression of this initiative. Its economic counterpart was the Bretton Woods system, which endorsed the free market and private ownership with minimal state intervention.

With respect to foreign investment, the United States

supported the traditional international "regime" protecting the property and contractual rights of overseas business from seizure:

> The United States recognizes the rights of sovereign states to nationalize or expropriate foreign-owned property provided that such takeovers conform to international law standards which require that takeovers be for a public purpose, do not discriminate against U.S. citizens, and are accompanied by prompt, adequate, and effective compensation.[2]

In the 1940s and 1950s, this policy was confined, with a few notable exceptions, to legal suasion aimed at ratifying these rules in international forums and bilateral treaties. In the early 1960s, after a number of prominent expropriations, beginning with Castro's wholesale eviction of American business, the United States initiated a more coherent policy of formal and informal sanctions. The aim was to maintain the regime by deterring or punishing precedents in violation of its rules.

The concept of an international regime has been used by scholars, who examine the degree to which various arenas of international relations are characterized by rules and norms rather than pure self-help. In a recent anthology on regime analysis, Stephen Krasner defined the term as

> sets of implicit and explicit principles, norms, rules, and decision-making procedures around which actors' expectations converge in a given area of international relations. Principles are beliefs of fact, causation, and rectitude. Norms are standards of behavior defined in terms of rights and obligations. Rules are specific prescriptions and proscriptions for action. Decision-making procedures are prevailing practices for making and implementing collective choices.[3]

For the purpose of the exposition of an anti-expropriation regime, Krasner's definition will be modified as follows: (1) The *principles* of the regime refer to the instrumental and philosophical beliefs underlying U.S. sponsorship of an anti-expropriation regime. That is, what concrete American interests does it serve and how does it fit into American conceptions of how the world economy should be ordered? (2) The regime *norms* establish legitimate and deviant behavior by confirming alien property rights and imposing specific obligations upon any host country contemplating expropriation. (3) The *rules* reflect the codification of the regime norms into legal obligations. (4) *Decision-making procedures* will be redefined as *regime enforcement*. Maintenance of the rules and norms of the regime was not the responsibility of an explicit institutional apparatus with formal decisionmaking procedures. The system was policed instead by the less formal coordination of U.S. government and private economic actors using sanctions and incentives.

Regime Principles: Instrumental and Philosophical Beliefs

The main objective of American diplomacy since World War II has been the maintenance of a Pax Americana—a stable and prosperous international order free from communism and Soviet influence. To the architects of this order, the value of an anti-expropriation regime was measured in terms of the contribution FDI made to this order, i.e., as a guarantor of access to critical raw materials at reasonably stable prices; as an engine of growth in the developing world, encouraging stability and democracy and inhibiting revolution and communism; and as an assist to the American economy. Policymakers, therefore, identified the American national interest with support for the concession system and the provision of a climate favorable to foreign investment. Expropriation of alien property, as well as other threats to international contractual rights, were seen as threats to both the security of existing investments and the prospects for future ones.

These *instrumental* beliefs about common interests were embedded in deeper *philosophical* beliefs emanating from neoclassical economics and Wilsonian internationalism. They held that a world in which national borders are open to the free flow of goods and factors of production leads to the greatest good for the greatest number. If private enterprise makes economic decisions according to market criteria, investment will flow to the most productive projects. This, in turn, leads to an efficient international division of labor which allocates scarce resources efficiently, maximizes global welfare, and minimizes international conflict. Acts of economic nationalism, such as expropriation, thwart the harmony of interests and engender waste and conflict.

INSTRUMENTAL ASSUMPTIONS

The Investment Climate. A leitmotif of U.S. outward investment policy after World War II was the promotion of an international order that facilitated the transnational movement of capital and preserved the concession system under which most Western investors operated. Establishing rules that buttressed corporate ownership against sovereign intervention was considered instrumental in creating an environment conducive to the expansion of foreign investment. This was particularly true in the developing world, as the Randall Commission noted, to compensate for the disadvantages of an unskilled labor force, small markets, and political instability.[4] A strong regime gave the investor the order he needed to offset political and economic risk.

Conversely, an environment in which expropriation was endemic would discourage overseas investors. As one State Department official put it, "Private investors come from environments in which property rights are recognized and assured and will not continue to put their assets at risk in countries in which these rights are not respected."[5] The Paley Commission report, *Resources for Freedom* (1952), concurred, observing that "a principal deterrent in [developing countries] is the investor's doubts about whether or not bargains once made are kept."[6] Without reassurance, resources firms will look elsewhere and capital and technology will not flow to the LDCs.

Security of Supply. Traditional U.S. raw material policy aimed for self-sufficiency to maintain national freedom of action and protect domestic producers. Blessed with a resource-rich continent, the United States' dependence on foreign sources of supply was minimal. The importance of FDI for material security was first recognized when World War I diminished domestic reserves of copper and oil. World War II placed an even heavier drain on domestic resources and the United States began to perceive itself as a "have-not" nation in many important raw materials.[7] Reflecting this perception, a 1947 study by the National Security Resources Board concluded that "prompt development of urgently needed sources of supply by the application and utilization of American private investment, management, technical skills, and equipment, should be encouraged."[8] With the mounting resource demands of a globalist foreign policy and domestic economic growth, the Truman administration decided that the United States must more aggressively look outside its borders to augment declining domestic reserves.[9]

The Korean War brought the issue to center stage. A National Security Council (NSC) study in 1951 emphasized the critical importance of the overseas petroleum concessions for the prosecution of the war and the success of the Marshall Plan. It was then that the Truman administration decisively moved away from a strategy of national self-sufficiency to one of encouraging reliance on foreign sources of supply.[10] This policy was supported by the Paley Commission, which rejected national self-sufficiency as too costly—"a self-imposed blockade and nothing more." The report concluded that "private investment must be the major instrument for the increased production of raw materials abroad."[11]

The issue then was to actively encourage private capital to go abroad to develop the lowest-cost source of supply. A key to this aim was preserving the concession system, in which American corporations owned outright the natural resource production facilities, as well as the output, and enjoyed exclusive rights to explore, mine, and drill. This system had the advantage of leaving little actual control in the hands of the host countries, overcoming the fear that the security of supply would hinge on the political vagaries of newly

emerging (and inherently unstable) nations. Protecting it
would give investors the security to venture their capital and
develop the lowest-cost sources of supply. As Bergsten, Horst,
and Moran put it, the concession system offered "effective exercise of sovereignty by the companies over their foreign operations and the ability of the home governments to compel
or persuade the companies to put that sovereignty at the service of home-country goals."[12]

Expropriation posed a two-pronged threat to resource diplomacy: the loss of control over existing concessions, and the vitiation of the climate for future investment.
First, the Paley Commission emphasized the importance of
corporate ownership of primary extraction; loss of control
through expropriation could place national economic security
in the hands of an LDC host potentially susceptible to Soviet
influence.[13] This was particularly acute in oil, where nationalization could lead to supply cutoffs or other interruptions
if control fell into the hands of groups "hostile to participation in the world economy." The ultimate fear was that "if
the United States or the United Kingdom [oil] companies were
for any reason expelled from Venezuela and the Middle East,
the oil from those areas would to a serious extent be lost to
the free world."[14]

Second, decision makers hypothesized that an environment in which expropriation was rampant would induce
resource firms to back off from overseas development. The
Randall Commission observed that "investors in the development of new foreign sources of raw materials must be assured against frustration of their ventures."[15] In the absence
of host country constraints, investors would develop the
cheapest alternative sources of supply according to market
forces. Conversely, an international order that tolerated the
flouting of contracts would discourage such ventures, thereby
leaving the United States more vulnerable to domestic shortages.

Development Diplomacy. A strong regime accelerat-
ing the flow of FDI to the Third World was also seen as a

counterforce to the appeal of revolution and communism. U.S. policy endorsed overseas business expansion in the belief that it would stimulate growth in the Third World. The liberal credo on which this policy was based implied a progression from economic growth to political stability to political democracy (and conversely, an avoidance of a retrogression from poverty to chaos to communism).[16]

In post–World War II Europe, the Marshall Plan achieved these objectives through a massive infusion of public funds. But Secretary of State Marshall observed that a comparable effort for the LDCs was "beyond the financial capacity of the U.S. Government." Nor was Congress likely to accept large-scale economic commitments. Postwar decision makers came to see foreign investment as a Marshall Plan of sorts for the developing world wherein the capital would be provided by private enterprise instead of the public sector.[17]

The belief that MNCs were catalysts for growth in the Third World was based upon the traditional "liberal" theory of economic development, namely that MNCs were purely economic actors, transferring resources from locations of abundance to locations of scarcity. In so doing, they brought to the LDC resources that the latter could not produce itself except at prohibitive cost (e.g., capital, technology, marketing and management skills) and thereby enabled the LDC to overcome balance of payments constraints on development plans.

Foreign investment in extractive industries was seen as crucial in promoting a policy of export-led growth. The Paley Commission, which provided the justification for an internationalist materials policy, observed:

Materials production for world markets makes possible a more rapid expansion of industry, agriculture, and public utilities by providing foreign exchange that can be used to buy equipment for industries and farms, and to construct irrigation, hydroelectric, and transportation systems.[18]

In effect, export-oriented extractive firms would bring in foreign exchange and the tax revenues necessary for a diversification of the local economy.

The resultant economic growth was linked to social stability and the development of participatory institutions. It fended off the poverty and chaos that render developing countries susceptible to Communist influence and Soviet penetration. One State Department official reasoned that "misery bred revolution, whereas economic growth, political democracy, and social justice would reinforce one another."[19] In addition, State Department anlaysts accepted prevailing social science theories that the differentiation of social structure (the creation of a middle class) that accompanies economic development was a necessary precondition for stable modern political institutions. Finally, private ownership was tied to political democracy as a counterweight to the domestic centralization of power.[20] A strong regime, almost by definition, spurs economic development through private enterprise, fosters political democracy, and limits Soviet influence in the Third World.

Conversely, expropriation seriously impedes the process of economic development. Unless accompanied by "full" compensation, seizures increase the level of noneconomic risk for foreign investors. In such a climate, officials reasoned, "it could hardly be expected that foreign capital will continue to be attracted."

Undermining the investment climate was likened to "killing the goose that lays the golden eggs." One Treasury official testified: "If these people want to grow, if they want to advance, if they want to develop, they have got to understand what makes capital flow and what makes it not flow. . . . Fellow, you are not going to do it by scaring off private capital."[21] The flow of private capital needed by LDCs will not be forthcoming if "recipient countries are pushing national policies that make private investment precarious and unrewarding."[22]

Even if compensation is paid, additional economic burdens fall upon the host:

The wisdom of any expropriation is questionable, even when adequate compensation is paid. The resources diverted to compensated investments that are already producing employment and taxes often could be used more productively to finance new investments in the domestic economy, particularly in areas of high social priority to which foreign capital does not always flow.[23]

Since most LDCs suffer from serious capital and foreign exchange shortages, the funds required to pay compensation and run the operation will deplete scarce reserves in sectors where private capital was willing to do the job.[24]

Expropriation, it was feared, would also promote the growth of statism in the Third World. State companies were seen as woefully inefficient when compared to private enterprise. Undisciplined by the competitive market, they allocate resources according to political, rather than economic, criteria. One State Department official warned that when states "intrude to operate or excessively control undertakings normal to private enterprise, inefficiencies, extravagance, and disorder inevitably ensue."[25] An ambassador to the United Nations told the General Assembly: "Nothing is easier than to build the wrong factory in the wrong place for the wrong product in the wrong market."[26]

Economic nationalism, in general, and expropriation, in particular, were seen as "irrational" in economic terms. As one influential academic saw it:

Confiscation feeds the political excitement new governments need, and satisfies latent nationalism and the desire to be master in one's own house. . . . The fact that confiscation either postpones or retards the economic expectations of a growing population is lost in the revolutionary excitement.[27]

Expropriation, in sum, was defined by the United States as an "affective" policy pursued at the expense of economic growth and technical advancement.

Benefits for the U.S. Economy. United States decision makers equated regime stability with the health of the American economy. Expropriation would hurt the U.S. balance of payments by (1) decreasing the profitability of U.S.

overseas firms, (2) lowering tax revenues from overseas operations (3) increasing the need for foreign public expenditure by deterring private capital flows, and (4) threatening domestic price stability.

1. In so far as expropriations threaten the profitability of overseas affiliates of American firms, they adversely affect the U.S. balance of payments. A General Accounting Office (GAO) study states that reinvested earnings and a subsidiary's repatriated capital "help allay concerns over the effects of investment capital outflows."[28] Gilpin notes that the United States saw this as an increasingly important means of financing its overseas position in the 1950s and 1960s as its balance of trade surplus steadily diminished.[29]

2. Increased nationalization would eliminate an important source of revenue for the U.S. Treasury. When a profitable operation shuts down, tax receipts are correspondingly stricken. United States tax law, moreover, allows overseas firms to write off expropriation losses where compensation falls below book value. One Treasury study pointed to a direct contribution of strong regime enforcement to the U.S. balance of payments: "If the U.S. Government could redress the bargaining disadvantages so that investors reached better settlements, its revenue would increase, because the company might realize taxable gain rather than deductible loss."[30]

3. A stable foreign investment regime eases budget and payments deficits by allowing private investment, rather than public funds, to be the primary vehicle for transferring resources from rich to poor. The Randall Commission noted:

> The United States Government should make clear that primary reliance must be placed on private investment to undertake the job of assisting economic development abroad. It shoud point out that *United States resources for public loans are limited and inadequate in relationship to total investment needs,* and that public lending or any other form of public finance will not be a substitute for private investment.[31] (Emphasis added.)

American policymakers recognized that public funds for development were limited. If private capital is welcome in LDCs, the Gray report argued, it will place "a minimum net demand on our national wealth."[32] Eisenhower saw the use of private investment for development assistance as a long-run solution to the balance of payments problem because it was "our best chance for the reduction and final elimination of government-to-government loans and grants."[33] A strong regime aids the U.S. economy by removing a measure of the burden placed on the U.S. Treasury by development diplomacy.

4. A strong regime helps keep domestic prices stable; a weak one contributes to inflationary tendencies by raising raw material costs for domestic industry. Firms are less inclined to develop overseas resources, thereby increasing domestic scarcity and the price of these vital inputs. A weakened regime thereby undermines the objective of finding the lowest-cost alternative sources of supply. State control also increases the prospects for cartelization and other nationalistic manipulations of trade and investment, the outcome of which would inevitably be higher commodity prices.

PHILOSOPHICAL ASSUMPTIONS

The policy of encouraging overseas private capital was predicated on the classical liberal theory of the "harmony of interests." As with free trade, an "open door" for foreign investment permits the free flow of capital and other factors of production to produce an equilibrium beneficial to all. As noted by a former Undersecretary of State for Economic Affairs:

A liberal international economic system permitting broad flows of capital and other factors of production according to economic forces offers the best hope for stable economic growth—in the Third World, in other developed countries, and in our own society.[34]

In effect, "mutual benefit is the *sine qua non* of successful foreign private investment."[35]

To the planners of the postwar order, the market was a politically neutral arbiter of economic decisions. A regime that supported investment through private enterprise rather than state companies placed economic decisions outside the realm of politics and the decreased probability of international conflict. Furthermore Secretary of State Cordell Hull argued, "the economic dissatisfactions which breed war must be eliminated."[36] The immense productivity of a world order that maximized foreign investment would, through the creation of abundance, eliminate national conflict bred by a condition of scarcity.

Akin to its support for FDI, American antipathy toward nationalization was conditioned by liberal internationalism and the economic lessons of the 1930s. Just as a policy of laissez-faire toward the transnational flow of capital would promote a "harmony of interests," state manipulations could only lead to the waste and conflict produced by the beggar-thy-neighbor policies of the advanced industrial states in the early 1930s. Economic nationalism, in brief, was inconsistent with worldwide economic interdependence. States should relinquish sovereign power in their economic affairs so as to maximize world welfare. The realm of power and politics should not impinge upon the separate realm of economics and welfare. In this context, nationalization was a "throwback to a bygone era when states were not concerned about encouraging foreign investment or with the ability to improve the lot of the common man."[37]

Regime Norms:
The Sanctity of Contracts

U.S. support for anti-expropriation norms must be seen in the context of overall U.S. policy toward FDI. Officials were aware of investor reservations about ventures in developing countries, namely, small markets, an unskilled labor force, currency depreciations, xenophobia, political instability, etc.[38] Therefore, the United States strove to encourage investment into the Third World by increasing the incentives and decreasing the risks faced by potential investors.

A number of techniques were used to promote FDI. The Investment Guaranty Program, established under the Economic Cooperation Act of 1948 to cover the risk of inconvertibility in Europe, was extended to cover expropriation in 1950. The Mutual Security Act of 1951 extended coverage to LDCs.[39] The program was transferred to the Agency for International Development (AID) in 1961 and the Overseas Private Invetsment Corporation (OPIC) in 1969. The United States also negotiated several bilateral tax treaties that would relieve investors of the burden of double taxation.[40] The foreign tax credit gave international companies the right to use taxes paid to one country as direct offsets against taxes owed to another.[41] Finally, the Economic Cooperation Act of 1948, and later, the Export-Import Bank were given enlarged lending powers to finance foreign ventures.[42]

By the late 1940s, investment protection was considered as important as, and complementary to, investment promotion. To Harriman and Marshall, the threat of expropriation was the most serious risk facing the foreign investor. If contracts between firm and host could be easily flouted, prospects for large-scale investment would measurably diminish. Therefore, policymakers considered it necessary to establish norms of international conduct regarding the expropriation of alien property.[43]

In promulgating regime norms, the United States pressed for adherence to traditional international legal standards. As put forward by Cordell Hull during the Mexican expropriations in the 1930s, it admitted "the right of all countries freely to determine their own social and industrial programs. This right includes the sovereign right of any government to expropriate private property within its borders in furtherance of public purposes."[44] The right of nationalization is implicit in the sovereign power of eminent domain. But this exercise of sovereignty is not absolute and must be consistent with international law.[45]

The relevant international law principle governing contracts between sovereign states and alien investors is *Pacta Sunt Servanda,* that is, contracts entail binding reciprocal obligations. They are acquired rights that can not be modified without the consent of both parties. Any unilateral termination or modification of a contract is not illegal, per se, but is subject to fair compensation.[46] Contracts can not be avoided by municipal legislation alone because "any state seeking to avoid the necessity of making payment . . . could avoid all pecuniary responsibility simply by changing local law."[47]

The American position was that regardless of national law, any expropriation must meet an international minimum standard. In other words, it must be nondiscriminatory, pursued for a public purpose, and accompanied by "just" compensation. The nub of the issue has been compensation. As Hull stated, "the taking of property without compensation is not expropriation. It is confiscation."[48]

The standard of compensation, that it be "prompt, adequate and effective," was also established by Hull.[49] The requirement of *promptness* addressed the inadequacy of deferred payment or the issuance of long-term bonds unless accompanied by compensatory interest.[50] Intention to pay at some later time was not acceptable either. As Hull remarked, "It is not less confiscation because there may be an expressed intent to pay at some time in the future."[51]

To meet the criterion of *adequacy,* compensation must reflect "fair market value." While the United States admitted that "in many cases, there is not a market for nationalized property," it also asserted that an assessment of a company's value should take into account its earning power. Book value—the difference between a firm's assets and liabilities for tax purposes—is an inappropriate measure because it fails to take into account future profits.[52]

For compensation to be *effective,* it has to be of "real economic value to the recipient." The *Foreign Relations Law of the United States* stipulates that it must be in "an effectively realizable form . . . in the form of cash or of property readily convertible into cash."[53] Also, it must be "withdrawable" without any requirement to reinvest in the host country because "once he (the investor) has lost his investment, it would be inequitable to require him to keep his funds in the territory of the state that has deprived him of it."[54]

In adjudicating disputes, the United States requires that foreign investors first exhaust local remedies. But if companies believe that they have suffered a "denial of justice," avenues beyond the local courts must be available. Compensation should not be determined solely by the laws of the nationalizing state, but rather through international arbitration.[55] Acceptable mechanisms include third-party arbitration, the International Court of Justice, and the International Center for the Settlement of Investment Disputes (ICSID) established by the World Bank in 1965.

The United States maintains that international strictures take precedence over national law when the two collide. Since the failure of a state to pay compensation or go to arbitration is wrongful under international law, the United States reserves the right to intervene under the "Right of Diplomatic Protection."[56] This right is predicated on two tenets of traditional international law: (1) The Law of State Responsibility for Injury to Aliens—"a State is responsible, under International Law, to injury to an alien caused by conduct subject to its jurisdiction"; and (2) *Enrichissement Sans Cause* (Unjust Enrichment)—by enriching itself unjustly at the expense of an alien, "a State would be depriving a foreign community of the wealth represented by that investment."[57] These, in turn, are based on Vatellian theory than an injury to the material interests of a citizen abroad is an injury to the home state and that such an injury engages a right to intervene if the treatment of its citizens falls below a certain minimum standard.

Codifying the Rules
of the Game

The next step in establishing the regime was to codify the
"rules of the game" through multilateral forums and bilateral treaties. The objective was to gain consensus and legitimacy for regime rules. However, the U.S. position ran into
a direct collision course with the regnant doctrines in the Third
World—the Calvo Doctrine in Latin America and the principle of Permanent Sovereignty over Natural Resources at
the United Nations.

The Calvo Doctrine, originally expounded in 1868 by
the Argentine diplomat Carlos Calvo, represented the Latin
American position on investment disputes and diplomatic
protection. Calvo posited that aliens are entitled to be treated
on a plane of absolute equality with local nationals, but they
can not ask for more than that regardless of international
law standards. Contracts between aliens and host states are
subject to local municipal, not international law. Investors
are required to use the local judicial system as the final and
authoritative arbiter in any dispute. The foreign contractor
also waives his right to diplomatic protection from his home
government.[58] To Latin American nations, sensitive to colonialism and gunboat diplomacy, diplomatic protection smacked
of extraterritoriality—a pretext for continued violations of
the territorial sovereignty and judicial independence of the
weak by the strong.

The principle of Permanent Sovereignty over Natural Resources established by the developing countries at the
United Nations endows the Calvo doctrine with international
status. That most states should have exclusive jurisdiction
over foreign investment within their boundaries is inherent
in their sovereignty. As a result, states have a right to nationalize, expropriate, or alter the terms of contracts to promote their conception of the general welfare. The require-

ment of compensation is unilaterally determined by the nationalizing state in accordance with local legislation.[59]

Both doctrines repudiated the Vatellian principles espoused by the United States. A normative "tug of war" was fought between these two positions as the United States sought multilateral ratification of its version in international forums. The results were, at best, tenuous compromises between theoretically unbridgeable positions.

In 1945, at the Chapultapec Inter-American Conference, the United States successfully sponsored a resolution condemning barriers to trade and investment flows, but not without Latin American qualifiers reserving the right of state intervention.[60] Article 25 of the Act of Bogota (1948) stipulated that "any expropriation shall be accompanied by fair compensation in a prompt, adequate, and effective manner." Its meaning, however, was clouded by formal Latin American reservations along the lines of the Calvo Doctrine. The final resolution was so riddled with contradictions and ambiguities that it was ratified neither by the U.S. Congress nor by a sufficient number of Latin American countries to come into effect. The Havana Conference to establish an International Trade Organization was fragmented by the same conflict and came to the same inconclusiveness.[61]

The United States met similar obstacles in the United Nations. General Assembly Resolution 626 of December 21, 1952 asserted the right of all states "to freely use and exploit their natural wealth and resources wherever deemed desirable by them for their own progress and economic development."[62] The United States, in the minority, voted against the resolution. Its major defect from the U.S. viewpoint was its omission of any reference to respect private property or oblige compensation. According to the American representative, it was a license to expropriate without compensation.[63]

In General Assembly Resolution 1803 on Permanent Sovereignty over Natural Resources (December 14, 1962), a tenuous compromise was reached between these contradic-

tory regime alternatives. The resolution affirmed "the inalienable right of all states freely to dispose of the natural
wealth and resources in accordance with their national interests." But it also implicitly accepted *Pacta Sunt Servanda*
and the obligation to pay compensation:

> In [cases of expropriation], the owner shall be paid *appro-
> priate* compensation, in accordance with the rules in force in the
> State taking such measures *in the exercise of its sovereignty in ac-
> cordance to international law.*[64] (Emphasis added.)

The ambiguity of the resolution made for divergent interpretations. The United States interpreted "appropriate" compensation as "prompt, adequate, and effective," while the LDCs
did not. The references to principles of sovereignty and international law did not explain which prevails when they were
in conflict. The LDCs accepted some obligations with regard
to takeovers, but whether these conformed to American standards was a matter of interpretation.[65]

The LDCs fully rejected the U.S. position in 1974 in
the Declaration for the Establishment of a New International
Economic Order and the Charter of Economic Rights and Duties of States.[66] These resolutions set forth an unqualified
sovereign right to expropriate. Compensation was to be unilaterally determined by the expropriating state; no reference
was even made to international law. Any form of "diplomatic
protection" was an infringement on sovereignty.

Having failed to achieve anything but ambiguous
compromises in multilateral forums, successive administrations fell back upon bilateral arrangements to legitimize regime rules. The technique for this was the Treaty of Friend-
ship, Commerce, and Navigation. These treaties contained
clauses that defined the terms of compensation if expropriation occurs, and provided for arbitration in cases of dispute.
The program to negotiate such treaties in the developing
countries began with the Economic Cooperation Act of 1950
and was broadened by the Mutual Security Act of 1954.[67]

A 1977 GAO study, however, reported that many

treaties are old and do not cover expropriation. Those that do are either riddled with escape clauses which allow national interest waivers on the payment of full compensation, or involve countries for which the guarantees against expropriation are largely unnecessary.[68]

An absence of consensus prevented any formal institutionalization of the regime rules. As a result, enforcement came to rely on U.S. government and corporate economic power.

Regime Enforcement

While U.S. policy labored to put the issue of expropriation within a legal framework, it developed no coherent strategy for enforcement until the early 1960s. Despite LDC rejection of regime norms, the threat of widespread expropriation before that time was more hypothetical than real. From 1945 until 1960, major expropriations were limited to Communist nations (Eastern Europe and China) and those regimes perceived as pro-Soviet (Nasser's Egypt and Sukarno's Indonesia). Other incidents, closer to the American sphere of influence (Arbenz in Guatemala and Mossadegh in Iran), had culminated in the overthrow of the "offender" government (with a covert assist from the CIA). The American imperium had brought a measure of tranquility to investors.

Many MNCs felt capable of fending for themselves, and they preferred a lower-profile U.S. policy with fewer political strings.[69] American policymakers, moreover, believed that in a dispute they could do little save legal jawboning. As the Paley Commission observed, "There are strict limits to what the U.S. Government can do. In the last analysis, it is the private investor himself, and the government of the host country, who are the principle parties of direct interest."[70]

The situation changed dramatically in the early 1960s. The most traumatic experience took place in Cuba, where American companies had operated for decades with freewheeling immunity from local interference. Castro's wholesale eviction of American business came as a rude shock. Both the corporate community and the U.S. government feared that the Cuban precedent could jeopardize all investment in Latin America. This fear was compounded in 1962 by an uncompensated seizure of a Brazilian subsidiary of ITT in the state of Rio Grande do Sul, as well as serious investment disputes in Argentina, Honduras, Ceylon, and Indonesia.

These events stimulated widespread corporate agitation for a tough anti-expropriation posture. The overseas business community, now uncertain of its footing, believed that state support was necessary to maintain the inviolability of the concession system. Companies such as ITT, United Fruit, Texaco, and Standard Oil of New Jersey, pressed the U.S. government to punish violator nations. Corporate reasoning was based upon a theory of deterrence—that inadequately compensated expropriations were challenges to the "regime" and, unopposed or unpunished, would become precedents for others to emulate.[71]

At the urging of the business community, Congress legislated a vast arsenal of formal sanctions to punish or deter offenders. The Hickenlooper Amendment to the Foreign Assistance Act of 1962 mandated an automatic cessation of bilateral assistance to any country that has

nationalized or expropriated or seized ownership or control of property owned by any United States citizen . . . [and] fails within a reasonable time (not more than 6 months . . .) to take appropriate steps . . . to discharge its obligations under international law toward such citizen or entity, including speedy compensation for such property in convertible foreign exchange, equivalent to the full value thereof. . . . Such suspension shall continue until *the President is satisfied that appropriate steps are being taken,* and no other provision of this chapter shall be construed to authorize the

President to waive the provisions of this subsection.[72] (Emphasis added.)

Unlike its predecessor, the Johnson-Bridges Amendment (1959), which contained a national interest waiver, the sanctions were designed to be mandatory, depriving the President of any discretion in implementation.[73]

In 1963, the Hickenlooper Amendment was broadened to encompass nullifications and repudiations of contract.[74] It was also extended to embrace discriminatory taxes, as well as other forms of "creeping expropriation" which "have the effect of nationalizing, expropriating, or otherwise seizing ownership or control of property so owned."[75]

The variety of sanctions was also augmented. To reinforce the Hickenlooper Amendment, the Sugar Act of 1962 stipulated the suspension of the sugar quota to violators.[76] In 1965, the Hickenlooper Amendment was extended to cover loans from the Inter-American Development Bank (IADB).[77] The Gonzales Amendment (1972) committed the Treasury Department to vote against any multilateral development bank (MDB) loan to offender nations.[78] Section 502(b)(4) of the Trade Act of 1974 denied beneficiary status for generalized system of trade preferences (GSP) to nations that "have not taken reasonable steps to compensate the former owners."[79] In sum, the extensive web of U.S. assistance to developing countries was brought into play to maintain the regime by the threat of withholding preferential benefits.

The congressional rationale behind the stiffened policy was that seizures in violation of American standards were threats to the regime. Such acts must elicit sanctions from the U.S. government in order to maintain the credibility of its implicit commitment to protect foreign investors. Legislators were guided by an economic "domino theory" wherein success in defying American interests in one area, no matter how insignificant, would be interpreted as a sign of "weakness of will," and embolden others to take similar action. The metaphor invoked was a "prairie fire" which, if not contained, would lay waste to American property rights throughout the Third World.[80]

Successful deterrence, Congress reasoned, demanded that sanctions be both overt and mandatory. First, if the United States were publicly protecting the interests of investors, "it will make other governments think twice before taking them."[81] Second, congressmen were convinced that presidential flexibility encouraged countries to believe that they could "get away with" expropriation. Automaticity, it was argued, would more successfully deter violations by making reprisal the inevitable result of a specific proscribed action. It would say unequivocally, "There is nothing we can do about it; the law requires it."[82]

While successive presidents and the Department of State have traditionally opposed the Hickenlooper Amendment and other related measures, they shared a common apprehension about expropriation and investment security. In testimony before Congress, Secretary of State Rusk stated that the United States must uphold the sanctity of contract. Failure to do so, he reasoned, could decrease the flow of private capital to the LDCs, to the detriment of American interests.[83] Another State Department official noted that "the US has a particular interest to avoid damaging precedents involving excess profit deductions, confiscatory taxes, and unreasonable settlements."[84]

The State Department's objection to Hickenlooper was a matter of means rather than ends. It centered on different *instrumental* beliefs about the effect of public mandatory sanctions on the *probability of success* and *cost* of this kind of regime enforcement. First, Rusk contended that automatic public sanctions "would arouse nationalist feelings and exacerbate rather than ease the problem at issue."[85] That is, it would render the dispute more intractable by increasing the value a target might attach to noncompliance by linking it to resisting imperialism, or making it impossible for the target to comply or compromise without suffering fatal political damage.

Second, Hickenlooper-type sanctions imposed potentially serious costs on U.S. foreign policy, such as vitiating bilateral relations; destabilizing reformist regimes or pushing them toward the USSR; general confrontation with the Third World; and assisting Communist propaganda by identifying the American aid program with the interests of "big business." "All U.S. interests in other countries," Rusk argued, "should not be tied to a particular investor in a particular situation." FDI is only one of many interests the United States should consider in relation to a particular country. The President should be given discretion to "balance the many factors which serve the national interest."[86]

In fact, the Hickenlooper Amendment has been invoked only twice—in Ceylon in 1963 and in Ethiopia in 1979. Successive administrations have found it too unwieldy an instrument and found a loophole to bypass its mandatory requirements. While the legislation tended to be mandatory, a presidential finding that the expropriator was not taking "appropriate steps" toward compensation was required to invoke the amendment. Through a liberal interpretation of what constitutes "appropriate steps," the Executive got around the mandatory nature of the law.[87]

Nonetheless, the State Department has found the amendment useful as a latent statement of intent. After ratification, Rusk termed it "useful" in sending a message to potential expropriators.[88] Shortly after its passage, satisfactory settlements were reached in disputes in Brazil, Argentina, and Honduras.[89]

Even without formal sanctions, the government could induce a favorable resolution through a panoply of informal measures. The most common technique—pursued against Argentina, Brazil, Peru, Jamaica, Guyana, and Bolivia—was the withholding of all new aid authorizations pending a settlement (without touching aid already in the pipeline). While rarely invoking the Gonzales Amendment, the United States used its clout in MDBs so that loans to violator nations did not come up for consideration.[90]

The key difference between State and its congressional protagonists was tactical—informal pressures were better suited for reaching settlements and minimizing costs. But the approach still accepted a policy of principle and precedent. The objective was to enforce a regime in which contractual rights are not easily flouted. The United States used its extensive foreign assistance programs with "carrot and stick" implications to send a message that "confiscations" would not be permitted. The ends of the Hickenlooper Amendment were often pursued with measures of greater flexibility and lower profile.

In sum, American support for an anti-expropriation regime derived from the perception of the role foreign investment would play in overall American foreign policy. Since expropriation ran counter to these interests, the United States adopted a policy of "deterrence" by establishing explicit rules governing conditions for expropriations, and effective sanctions if those rules were violated. Differences within the government centered on instrumental assumptions, i.e., tactics for enforcement, the expansiveness of regime requirements, and the level of costs to be absorbed in implementation. There was no significant questioning of the normative ideal of the regime, its economic "rationality" for all parties, or its association with the protection of vital national interests.

In one sense, it is misleading to speak about an evolution of U.S. investment protection since the official contours have remained unchanged for many years. Inquiries to the State Department's Office of Investment Affairs are still referred to President Nixon's 1972 policy statement and Cordell Hull's 1938 pronouncement.

Since the early 1970s, the real changes have taken place in the *implementation* of policy. Developing countries have become more aggressive in challenging the regime and more successful in assuming control over natural resource investments. Consequently, U.S. policy has evolved away from a more stringent application of deterrent actions toward a looser approach which "fudges" on regime rules in order to ensure a mutually profitable post-expropriation relationship between firm and host. This adaptation is not a rejection of the principle that nations must make good for deprivatory wrongs against aliens. Rather, it is a redefinition of what is considered wrongful. In other words, it is a retrenchment to a weakened quasi-regime with more tenable parameters.

Policy adaptation was conditioned by changes in decision makers' perception of three critical variables: (1) the decreased *value* or necessity of a "tight" regime (given the firm's maintenance of access through contractual relations) to support foreign policy and national economic security interests; (2) the increased *costs* of regime enforcement policies; and (3) the decreased *probability* of successful enforcement. To understand the evolution of elite perceptions, along these lines, it is necessary to turn to the erosion of the normative and material bases that supported the regime until the 1970s.

2.

The Erosion
of the Cognitive Bases
of the Regime

> Power goes far to create the morality convenient
> to itself, and coercion is a fruitful source of consent. But
> when all these reserves have been made, it remains true
> that a new international order can be built up only on
> the basis of an ascendancy which is generally accepted as
> tolerant and unoppressive or, at any rate, preferable to
> any other alternative.
> > E. H. Carr,
> > *The Twenty Years Crisis*, p. 236.

> Economic theory, when heedless of the political
> dimension, tends to be either irrelevant or a self-seeking
> ideology of power.
> > David Calleo and Benjamin Rowland,
> > *America and the World Political Economy*, p. 253.

Every attempt to construct a world order is compromised by the immediacy of its origins. Its founders justify its existence through a "vocabulary of the general good," assuming the identity of its interests with those of the international community as a whole. But, as E. H. Carr notes, this "turns out on inspection to be an elegant disguise for some particular interest."[1] As the parochial nature of such an order becomes evident to those disfranchised from its benefits, it loses its claim to legitimacy. Its continued viability comes increasingly to rely on coercion.

The American commitment to an "open door" policy for foreign investment (and opposition to expropriation) was couched in a liberal vision of world order which would provide a "harmony of interests" for all members of the international community. The sponsorship of "free trade" was the quintessential expression of this vision and its underlying world view can be summed up in three propositions. First, free trade promotes an international specialization which maximizes global efficiency and increases the "size of the pie" for all parties. Second, economic nationalism—state intervention to manipulate the free flow of goods—thwarts the harmony of interests and produces waste and conflict. This was exemplified by the experience of the 1930s when the protectionist policies of the advanced industrial states sharply reduced the volume of world trade. Third, "beggar-thy-neighbor" policies flourish in an environment where accepted rules of conduct are absent. The way to ensure international collaboration and avert economic warfare lies in international institutions, such as the General Agreement on Tariffs and Trade (GATT), and the viability of such institutions, in turn, is based upon American leadership.[2]

When these "lessons" were transferred from trade to investment relations, three parallel premises emerged. First, foreign investors were purely economic actors whose unhindered activity promoted a "harmony of interests" between the profitability of the firm and the economic development of all, especially those least developed. Second, nationalist policies inhibiting FDI, such as expropriation or the unilateral modification of contracts, retarded the free flow of investment and injured all parties. Finally, rules and institutions for investment relations, parallel to those of GATT for trade, were

necessary to extend the sanctity of contract to the world at
large and offer firms the degree of security deemed necessary
to venture capital.

While these lessons may have some relevance to trade
relations between advanced industrial states, they inaptly
describe investment relations between powerful multinational corporations and countries emerging from colonialism
and dependence. First, structural differences between the
globally oriented MNC and the nationally oriented host engender significant divergences of interest. The firm's superior bargaining power (at least in initial negotiations) tilts
the incidence of benefits to its predominant, if not exclusive,
advantage. Second, host state intervention is not necessarily
malign or irrational, but a potential source of countervailing
power to redirect the benefits. Finally, to insist on the immutability of contracts between host and firm when the latter was in an overwhelming bargaining position would be to
freeze a status quo born of power.

While the rationale for the mutual beneficence of FDI
was stated in universal terms, its material embodiment served
American interests. The elevation of property over sovereignty benefited the United States as the world's foremost
exporter of capital and downplayed the importance of power
and dependence in foreign investment relationships. The implication of trying to impose a laissez-faire liberalism on an
illiberal world forged by power limited the ability of LDCs
in using the countervailing power of the state to redress the
situation. In effect, it was conservative and antinationalist.

Premise One:
The Harmony of Interests

The traditional American approach to expropriation was nurtured by liberal economic theory. Economic actors pursuing

their own individual interests serve the interests of the community. Transactions operate according to the market mechanism, an "unseen hand" which impartially promotes a "harmony of interests" if unmolested by the state.

From this perspective, the multinational corporation is a "benign force in world politics."[3] Its activities enrich both firm and host as it plays a purely economic role in transferring resources from areas of abundance to areas of scarcity. Private foreign investment is the "most prolific source of capital" for the developing countries.[4] In addition, "private foreign investment carries with it management and technical skills" enhancing the host's productivity.[5] In effect, FDI contributes to economic growth by providing LDC hosts with factors of production that they could not reproduce except at prohibitive cost.

Foreign investment in the export-oriented natural resource sector is especially important for economic growth. The Paley Commission noted that new technologies and access to marketing networks expand productivity and trade. This, in turn, yields "government revenue and foreign exchange earnings [which] can provide the financial basis for a domestic development program."[6]

Second-order dynamic effects also accrue from FDI, in addition to the first-order increments of revenue and trade.

> To appreciate its contributions, we must analyze its whole impact on the domestic economy in terms of such things as the training of labor, the development of local related industries, the growth of new and existing cities and towns, the production of commodities that otherwise would have been imported—in short, all the things that go to make up national prosperity and economic strength.[7]

The diffusion of the firm's technical skills and specialized knowledge improves the quality of the host's factors of production and stimulates other sectors of the economy.

The MNC is, as a result, regarded as an apolitical, anational force promoting increased interdependence of the global economy, and furthering worldwide specialization and optimal efficiency. The integration it imposes upon the international system is conducive not only to world prosperity but to world peace as well. This ethos of business internationalism was succinctly captured by Adlai Stevenson: "The sun never sets on the American business empire. An empire without a capital, colony, or ruler, it flourishes everywhere because it renders its customers greater satisfaction at lower costs than they receive elsewhere."[8] The world view derives from what one historian called the "productivist view of America's post-war vision"; the sheer productivity of economic forces could create an abundance that would eliminate the need for power and coercion.[9]

In sum, American support for an open investment policy is deeply rooted in the liberal imagination. The advantages of foreign investment are characterized as "axiomatic" and "self-evident."[10] It is always beneficial; more is better. Even the metaphor for the source country as a "host" implies that the firm is a guest who is freely invited at the former's pleasure. One State Department official went so far as to declare that "the self-reliant and virile principle of private enterprise" and the "institution of private property ranks with those of religion and the family as a bulwark of civilization."[11]

The liberal approach describes the potential benefits FDI can confer upon a developing country by introducing resources that were previously scarce or unavailable and by assisting exports. At the root of the theory is the assumption that outcomes derive exclusively from market forces, neutral rules that optimally allocate resources.

But the beneficial impact of foreign investment can not be assumed a priori. The assumption of an automatic harmony of interests derives, in part, from the misconception of FDI as an international capital movement in a perfectly competitive market. As Stephen Hymer discovered, direct investment can better be explained by the theory of monopolistic competition.[12] Investors enter foreign markets because they possess some advantage—technology, managerial expertise, or sources of finance—which they can exploit to earn a higher rate of return than local competitors.

This is particularly true in natural resource extraction because of the high fixed cost and uncertainty of exploration. Large multinationals are best suited to assume such risks because of their greater access to capital markets and expertise. Moreover, their international spread enables them to compensate for failures by repeating the gamble in several countries, something difficult for smaller national companies.[13] As a result, foreign investors in resource extraction tend to be vertically integrated global enterprises from oligopolistic industries.

The imperfect competition of natural resource markets means that there is "no presumption that left alone the firm will act in the best interest of the host."[14] The liberal vision of harmony ignores (1) the structural differences between firm and host that lead to divergences of interest, and (2) the extent to which the firm seeks to maximize its economic and political power to ensure that when conflicts arise its interests will prevail.

First, the interests of the MNC, which are structured globally, are often difficult to reconcile with the interests of the host, which are structured nationally. The classical model, which assumes that firms act to maximize returns to a given subsidiary in a given country, is inapplicable to the transnational enterprise. As Richard Robinson notes, "Any time a subsidiary utilizes a resource from which a larger profit (or more power?) could be extracted by an associated firm elsewhere, it does so at the expense of the corporate family."[15] For the transnational firm, the "bottom line" is not the level of profit in a single affiliate, but its effect on the corporate system as a whole. Such corporate objectives can lead to results that are dissonant with the host's interests in economic development, particularly in the areas of defensive investment and transfer pricing.

There is no assumption of automatic common interest between firm and host regarding the desirability of maximizing returns to a given subsidiary. Firms from oligopolistic industries seek to control most known deposits as barriers to entry against new entrants. The transnational firm may treat a particular stake as a defensive investment, maintained less to make a profit than to prevent other companies from utilizing it so as to discourage competition or restrict supply.[16] A case in point is the Iraq Petroleum Company after the 1928 Red Line Agreement. The companies in the consortium acquired exclusive exploration and production privileges for all of Iraq and thereafter kept production at a nominal level. The reason for "sitting on the concession" was to restrain competition and avert a glut which could undermine the industry's oligopolistic position.[17] One need not impute malevolent intent on the part of the major international oil companies. This was sound business strategy from the perspective of an oligopolistic industry. Intention aside, the policy's implications were not at all sound from the perspective of the economic development of Iraq.

A second area of conflict is the issue of transfer pricing. Since most natural resource firms are vertically integrated, primary production usually moves not through markets, but intrafirm trade. To maximize overall revenues, corporate bookkeeping can shift profits to areas with low tax rates and reexport more finished goods at market price to their final destination. For example, there is little in the way for an open market for bauxite ore outside the integrated multinational network. Prior to the 1970s, the aluminum companies transported bauxite at cost to their refineries and smelters outside the Third World host.[18] For the firm, this is an economically "rational" strategy. But for the host, it minimizes the tax base and frustrates export-oriented development strategies.

The gravity of these issues for LDCs is compounded by their dependence on a single commodity for a large proportion of their foreign exchange and government revenue.

For example, in 1979, bauxite comprised 52.9 percent of Jamaica's foreign trade; copper, 90.6 percent of Zambia's. The oil industry in Venezuela provided 65.5 percent of that country's foreign exchange in 1975.[19] Theodore Moran noted that "all the Fortune 500 do not play the role in the United States that Anaconda and Kennecott play in Chile."[20] Given this level of economic dependence, "private" corporate decision making had enormous consequences for strategies of resource-based growth.

Second, the liberal approach, by ignoring the issue of power and focusing exclusively on market forces, is an incomplete conceptual reference. Concessions often originated in unequal bargaining. Many were the by-products of colonialism or gunboat diplomacy and became investment enclaves designed as extensions of the industrial policies of the imperial powers.

Even in the absence of overt coercion, the firm enjoyed a superior bargaining position vis-à-vis the host at the outset of a concession. This was a function of the considerable differential in vulnerability between the protagonists. The firm controlled factors of production, such as finance, technology, and specialized information, upon which the host was dependent. The single-resource nature of its economy heightened the host country's vulnerability. Since most extractive firms operated in oligopolistic industries and could relocate in response to better terms, the dependence was not mutual.

These asymmetries in vulnerability were not naturally offset by the diffusion of technology, as presumed by liberal economic theory. The firm has no commercial interest in the dissemination of its specialized information. Rather, it has an interest in suppressing technology transfer to protect itself from domestic competition and to maintain the host's technological dependence. For example, the foreign oil companies in Venezuela built their refineries in the nearby Dutch colonies of Aruba and Curacao to keep this technology from the Venezuelans.[21] If not compelled to do otherwise, the firm pursues what one scholar calls a "policy of silence" to inhibit or tightly control local knowledge creation.[22] This, in turn, will weaken the linkages that liberals predict will stimulate other sectors of the economy and will maintain asymmetries of vulnerability and power between firm and host.

These differentials in vulnerability permitted firms to dictate and maintain one-sided concession agreements. It would not overstate the case to conclude that the MNC gained its stake and sustained its presence through its overweening power, not the free interplay of market forces.

In sum, structural differences between the MNC and host imply, as Vernon observed, that the two "respond to different principles and operate in different dimensions."[23] Given the imperfect competition of natural resource markets, the self-interest of the global corporation often diverges from the national economic interest of the host. And the firm's superior bargaining power (at least during the initial phases of a concession), means that when the interests of the firm and host collide, the former will invariably prevail. Once assumptions about FDI as a purely economic actor are relaxed and realities of power are factored into the equation, assumptions about a "harmony of interests" must be called into question.

Premise Two:
Nationalism as Retrograde

In the liberal internationalist's lexicon, the MNC epitomizes the trend toward interdependence and an integrated world economy which transcends power politics and the nation-state. The workings of the market, it is reasoned, impose an order and stability on the world that is conducive to peace and economic progress. Therefore, the economically "rational" policy for any host country is one of relative laissez-faire, allowing the benign forces of private capital investment to increase the "size of the pie" for all concerned.

Those who looked upon the MNC as the harbinger of a new world order hold the corollary view that the nation-state is "out of touch with the essential evolution of modern times." A former Undersecretary of State for Economic Affairs, George Ball, wrote that "the nation-state is a very old-fashioned idea and badly adapted to the needs of our present complex world."[24] This outlook emanates, in part, from the liberal view that the spheres of politics and power should not interfere with the autonomous spheres of economics and welfare.

Acts of economic nationalism, such as expropriation, are characterized as "irrational," contrary to the "harmony of interests," and productive of waste and conflict. Nationalizations are as indefensible as the tariff wars and competitive depreciations of the 1930s. Henry Kissinger, addressing the Group of 77 at the United Nations, echoed these sentiments: "History has left us the legacy of strident nationalism—discredited in this century by its brutal excesses of a generation ago, and by its patent inadequacy for the global needs of our time. The economy is global."[25] A proliferation of nationalizations will precipitate mirror imaging in which "each nation seeks to achieve its goals at the expense of others, thereby leading to the demise of the system."[26] "Governments would be free to take property far beyond their ability and willingness to pay, and the owners thereof would be without recourse."[27] Just as interventions in trade relations reduced the level of global economic intercourse, state interposition into the terms of contracts will reduce the incentives for investors to go abroad to the detriment of all.

According to the liberal *Weltanschaung*, expropriation can be explained not in terms of economic interests, but of affective impulses—what C. P. Kindleberger calls "world populism."[28] Expropriations are variously defined as an emotional reaction to past wrongs, real or imagined; a function of "frustrated irrational politics and misguided nationalism"

and "xenophobia," often cultivated by populist regimes in order to compensate for domestic political weakness; and an au-
tarkic policy aimed at reducing vulnerability to the world
economy.[29]

Whether pursued for reasons of national autonomy,
political favor, or psychological satisfaction, expropriation
policies entail an economic cost. One economist defines economic nationalism in terms of the "theory of the second best":
"Economic nationalism figures as a collective consumer good
that can be invested in by sacrificing real consumption in
order to increase the collective consumption of nationalism."[30] Echoing this reasoning, Ball wrote that if LDCs nationalize foreign investments, "they must be prepared to pay
a great cost in delaying their own economic development."[31]
In effect, there is a zero-sum game between ending dependence, on the one hand, and economic and technical advancement on the other.

Therefore, the United States contends that expropriations inflict the deepest wounds on the host countries
themselves. They poison the investment climate and dry up
the inflow of private capital. In addition, they are "wasteful
from the resource standpoint," using up scarce local capital
where private foreign capital is available.[32]

The United States' position against property seizure
was phrased in terms of the self-interest of the host country.
To refuse or oppose expropriation, one Senator remarked,
would be to act "as the parent who gives money to his child
to buy food staples at the grocery, and does nothing about it
when the child buys candy instead of the bread of life."[33] Less
blatant, though no less paternalistic, is the conclusion of a
U.S. government study: "It is largely because the United States
has wanted to assist the development of the underdeveloped
countries that active means have been taken to discourage
expropriation."[34]

The MNC, as previously remarked, is not exclusively an economic institution; it maintains its position and
prerogatives through the exercise of power. It is through power

that the firm seeks to promote the global objectives of the home office over the national objectives of the host. It is only through countervailing power that corporate actions can be restrained and redirected toward the host country. The only locus of countervailing power to do the job is the LDC state.

The role of the state in regulating or modifying foreign investment agreements is designed, as Bergsten notes, to "increase the likelihood that the subsidiary will respond positively to the national policies of the host country."[35] As the bargaining power of the state increases relative to the firm, it tries to renegotiate the agreement, increasing its share of the revenue through increased taxation, profit-sharing innovations, or restrictions on profit repatriation. It can increase the benefits to the domestic economy through expediting the transfer of skills and technology. Finally, it can curb activities detrimental to the economy, such as transfer pricing and defensive investment strategies, through nationalization, majority participation, or tighter regulation. In this context, nationalization and other restrictions on foreign investment are not necessarily malign or irrational forces; rather, they can be self-interested attempts to redirect the incidence of costs and benefits.

Liberal antipathy toward an activist state has deep roots in American political mythology. In opposing nationalization, one congressman asserted that it is not "something we do here in the United States, and therefore, it is not something that should be done in any other democratic Latin American nation."[36] Ironically, this view contradicts much of the nineteenth-century international and twentieth-century national experience of the United States with regard to the role of the state in the economy.

During the nineteenth century, the United States held aloof from Great Britain's advocacy of "free trade." The United States practiced protectionist trade policies and restricted foreign investment to avoid vulnerability to external domination. To do otherwise, it was thought, would have placed American industry and national autonomy at the mercy of the more advanced and economically developed United Kingdom.[37] Echoing a similar theme, a Department of State study in the 1970s justified curbing foreign ownership of critical sectors of the economy that "could encumber military and diplomatic policy."[38]

This antistatist bias also rubs against the evolution of liberal thinking on the role of the state in the domestic economy. Classical liberalism, in its devotion to laissez-faire, based its position on the assumption of an atomistic, perfectly competitive world. As industrial concentration and private economic power came to characterize industrial relations in the nineteenth century, liberalism's prescription degenerated into an apologia for corporate privilege. With the New Deal, liberalism evolved into a theory of affirmative government and the welfare state, which endorsed state intervention in "private" economic activity if it served important social interests.[39]

But, as Alan Wolfe observed, "while Franklin Delano Roosevelt and the New Deal were dismantling laissez-faire liberalism within the United States, Roosevelt's Secretary of State Cordell Hull was creating laissez-faire for the world at large."[40] Like its domestic counterpart, a global laissez-faire, blind to private economic power and the positive role of the activist state, provides only a fictitious equality of opportunity which leaves corporate privilege unchallenged. The liberal vision of world order has yet to make the transformation to the welfare community that its vision of the social order has made to the welfare state.[41]

It is true that many expropriations have been enacted for affective or political reasons, accompanied by disastrous economic consequences. Foreign concessions have often been associated with unpopular local regimes or the coercive diplomacy of an imperial power. This history has bred a massive residue of ill will toward many firms. Companies such as United Fruit and W. R. Grace have achieved notoriety as villains within the folklores of the countries in which they have operated. Public sentiment has invariably called for a rectification of past wrongs regardless of the economic consequences.

Nationalism, however, "feeds not only on the psychological hunger for collective identity, but also on the powerful urge to assert collective control over a chaotic environment."[42] The demand for the renegotiation of previously agreed-upon contracts does not flow primarily from anger, ignorance, or greed, but from the circumstances under which those agreements were negotiated. To call it irrational, Kobrin argues, is "to confuse the long-term politico-economic determinants of the propensity toward forced divestment with the short-term political factors affecting timing and form."[43] While a particular expropriation outcome may not conform to a model of pragmatic self-interest, there is, nonetheless, a built-in dynamic "rational" to the foreign investment process which propels the state to intervene and change the terms of investment agreements.

In disparaging acts of economic nationalism as irrational, liberalism presumes an idealized world where the MNC is solely an economic actor. Such an analysis may accord with neoclassical models of efficiency, but the never-absent power factor is missing. The omission deprives its prescriptions of real-world credibility, particularly in the developing world. The firm has often used its superior power to achieve objectives that conflict with the needs of the host. The interventionist state is the only logical candidate to redress that situation. Increasing national control is, if not rational according to the liberal economist's calculus, often intelligible in terms of the political and economic interests of the host.

Premise Three:
The Sanctity of Contract

The economic and political traumas of the interwar period were ascribed by American policymakers to the absence of accepted international principles and mechanisms to support those principles. State sovereignty collided with international order, and the unchecked pursuit of national interests produced world disharmony. The failure to see the need for collaboration and the inability to prevent violation of liberal economic principles led to a breakdown of international intercourse, and finally of international peace. Law must regulate the dealings between nations, and international institutions must uphold the law. In international economic relations, all nations could then take advantage of maximized production and the unimpeded flow of wealth across national boundaries.

American officials, spurred by this vision, labored to establish a legal framework protecting the sanctity of overseas contracts. The United States supported the traditional international law principle of *Pacta Sunt Servanda*—that investment agreements between foreign investors and host countries are binding and subject to international jurisdiction. Any expropriation or alteration of a contract must be nondiscriminatory, pursued for a public purpose, in accord with due process of law, and accompanied by "prompt, adequate, and effective" compensation.

The rationale was that universal recognition of the sanctity and immutability of contracts was necessary for all parties to realize the mutual benefits of FDI. Contracts clarify and particularize the rights and obligations of parties. Once conferred, they become acquired rights. The expectation that contracts will be kept provides the stability necessary for investors to go overseas. Cordell Hull expressed this view in the context of an orderly international society:

> The whole structure of friendly intercourse of international trade and commerce . . . rests on the respect of governments and peoples for each other's rights under international law. The principle of prompt, adequate, and effective compensation is part of that structure.[44]

Sanctity of contract has been characterized as a "cornerstone of international intercourse," because it is "essential for the welfare of every nation, and without its protection, no commercial or financial intercourse could be safely carried on."[45]

The United States opposed Third World principles such as the Calvo Doctrine and Permanent Sovereignty over Natural Resources because they subordinated contractual rights to national sovereignty. "In the guise of liberalism," one State Department legal advisor argued, the developing countries "reassert the ancient theory of unbridled sovereignty that states are responsible only to themselves."[46] Sohn and Baxter note that these doctrines suggest "that compliance with contracts is a matter of expediency, and that no moral opprobrium attaches to the violation of the pledged word."[47] They transform the international community from a world of law in which property rights are protected from arbitrary state power to a world of force where the weak are at the mercy of the strong.

This position rests upon the view that, in a condition of anarchy, states can coercively alter the terms of contracts to suit their own short-term national interests without regard for the effect of their actions on the international system. Hence, a structure of internationally recognized and enforced property rights is necessary, says Schwebel, to "lend a degree of stability to the process of foreign investment, which is not notably stable or secure."[48] This is especially important for the poorest countries because without that investment, Becker states, "economic development will be slow to come."[49]

Third World countries, on the other hand, argue that they are not bound by traditional rules of international law which were formulated prior to their independence. Principles regarding alien property rights were fashioned to provide complete security for foreign investors against the encumbrances of host government sovereignty. These rules, as Jorge Castaneda wrote, "were not only created against the will of small states, but even against their desires and interests."[50] Another Third World scholar noted that "a rule which confers absolute security to capital is not a neutral rule, given the present distribution of property and wealth among nations."[51]

An examination of the basic tenets of international

contract law, and the premises that underlie them, reveals a high degree of parochialism in the American position. The principle of *Pacta Sunt Servanda* affirms the immutability of contracts between aliens and states. State Department lawyers argue that the investor's vested rights take precedence over the state's sovereign power to promote the general welfare because aliens are subject to international, not national, law and do not share in the "general welfare." Underlying this principle is the assumption that "states are free to enter or not to enter contracts," and bargains are freely entered into by two informed and equal parties, each of which knows what it wants and knows what it is getting.[52]

This assumption ignores the history of the early concession agreements, which were hardly the result of symmetrical bargaining positions. In colonial and nominally independent areas, alien investments were designed as extensions of the economy of the parent country. Parent nations, as needed, backed up arrangements with "big stick" diplomacy and economic pressures. Even in the absence of overt coercion, the firm usually enjoyed an overpowering bargaining position. If, as was often the case, the firm was part of an oligopolistic industry, its bargaining leverage was enhanced by its ability to choose between several investment sites and its formidable capital and technological resources. LDCs were obliged to outbid each other in generosity as they competed for investments in a seller's market.

The terms of contracts reflected this disparity in vulnerability. Concessionaires were granted exclusive prospecting rights over large tracts of land, sometimes an entire country, for fifty years, ninety-nine years, or in perpetuity. The investor paid nominal taxes, and suffered few, if any, restrictions on profit repatriation, the import of technology, or the use of expatriate help. The host government had no effective control over the company. In order to prevent subsequent state encroachments, concessions usually contained "stabilization clauses" proscribing nationalization or other forms of state intervention. In effect, the terms of concessions were designed to promote and protect the firm's long-run profit position. As a consequence, the contribution of FDI to host country economic development was minimized.

Carr observed that the doctrine of the absolute sanctity of treaties has been used as a "bulwark of the *status quo*" by the powerful to "maintain their supremacy over weaker nations on whom treaties have been imposed."[53] Like the terms to which the vanquished submit after defeat in war, contractual conditions accepted under the compulsion of economic necessity are neither voluntary nor neutral.

This absolutist view of contract and its impermeability to state intervention is at variance with United States constitutional law. In the *Charles River Bridge Case* (1837), the Supreme Court reversed John Marshall's position on the immutability of contract, and declared that the state can not divest itself of the power of eminent domain. This was expanded in *East New York Savings Bank vs. Hahn* (1945), when the court asserted that the state had the right to modify vested rights in the public interest even if such modifications violated the stipulations of an earlier grant. To argue otherwise, the Court continued, would pervert the Constitution's contract clauses into "an instrument to throttle the capacity of the State to protect [its] fundamental interests." Since the New Deal, intervention to regulate and modify contracts to protect the weaker party in industrial relations, consumer protection, environmental issues, and race relations has achieved widespread legal approval. A similar standard is absent in international contract law.[54]

In international dealings, states have used the doctrine of *Clausula Rebus Sic Stantibus* to terminate treaties. This principle presumes that the context in which a treaty was signed will not change. A nation may opt out of a treaty if new conditions arise that make performance injurious to its national interest. Developing countries have often cited this principle as a justification for renegotiating initial bargains with investors.

The State Department recognizes this principle as

valid in dealings between sovereign nations, but not in agreements between private aliens and states. The terms of a contract, even if granted in perpetuity, are sacrosanct: "Nothing can prevent a state from binding itself irrevocably to the provisions of a concession and from granting the concessionaire irretractable rights."[55]

The Law of State Responsibility for Injury to Aliens and *Enrichissement Sans Cause* are the two main doctrines protecting alien contractual rights. These principles bar states from injuring aliens or unjustly enriching themselves at the expense of their property rights.[56] No correlative principle protects the state from injury or self-enrichment by private aliens at the expense of its society. In fact, Third World legislation providing for such remedies, such as Allende's "excess profits" deductions from compensation owed the copper companies, has been actively opposed.[57]

These principles reflect a Lockean vision of the negative state and private property. The alien investor is not a wielder of power, but a source of creative energy and productivity. His property, the fruit of his labor, is purely private, not a structure of control over others. Its effects are wholly beneficial to the welfare of all. The state, on the other hand, is an artificial creation, armed with the power to despoil, against which the individual and his property must be protected. Agreements between power-oriented nation-states can be changed if new conditions arise, but those between "tainted" nation-states and private individuals are sacrosanct. Since investors are, by definition, apolitical productive forces, it is inconceivable that a country would need protection against injury or unjust enrichment from them.

In the contemporary industrial age, however, property confers not only the power to enjoy, but also the power to control. There is vast private economic power in the world economy. The MNC competes as an equal with many states and, in some instances, is more powerful than the sovereigns with whom it contracts. By denying this reality, American international legal standards set themselves against the forces of change and align themselves with an unpopular status quo.

The American interpretation of these principles is again inconsistent with domestic practice. The Renegotiation Acts of 1942 and 1951 require that all government contracts conferred to private companies during wartime shall be revised following a war without any obligation to compensate contractors for future earnings lost. The rationale was the companies producing vital defense supplies could exploit a wartime emergency and collect excessive profits, causing injury to the "general welfare."[58] Given the changed circumstances of peacetime, the government had a right to redress its past bargaining disadvantage and revise the contract. Such a notion of corrective justice is disallowed for developing countries, whose economic conditions have been likened to the "moral equivalent of war."[59]

The Law of State Succession posits that a state is bound by the acquired rights granted by its predecessor. This is necessary, according on one government lawyer, so that a new government may not "pick and choose" those agreements with which it wants to comply.[60] As with the United States Constitution's prohibition of *ex post facto* laws, the repudiation of past obligations was viewed as deprivatory of legitimately acquired rights.

Independence, however, would be an empty pretense and a cruel hoax if a new government could not divest itself of obligations incurred by colonial or nationally irresponsible governments. Such a legal system amounts to an effective veto over a state's freedom to pursue its own course of economic development and social reform.

International law is not an isolated and self-contained credo deducible from unassailable premises and an inescapable logic; it can only be understood in political context. As aptly stated by one international legal scholar: "For any international law principle to survive, it must advance the common interest not of a limited ideology, but of the wider global community it purports to serve."[61] By this standard, the U.S. position on the sanctity of contract fails. It assumes a world in which firms are purely economic actors and bargains are freely negotiated by equal parties. State intervention, it is argued, should be subordinated to an impartial system of justice. When these assumptions are relaxed and private economic power is given its full weight, the position becomes a disguise for an inequitable socioeconomic structure. As Bergsten, Horst, and Moran state: "To argue that there should not be an ongoing process of adjustment—because of the sanctity of contract—is only to argue that agreements should be frozen on terms favorable to foreign investors."[62]

Through the lenses of economic liberalism, the United States sought to impose upon the world its conception of global interest. That conception was based upon an idealized world in which private economic power did not exist, and upon a negation of the positive role the state could play in harnessing economic forces toward constructive ends. The policy of deterring expropriations aligned the United States with a concession system on a collision course with Third World nationalism. As a result, investment security came to rest more on enforcement through sanction than on consensus through internalized norms.

3.

The Erosion
of the Structural Bases
of the Regime

If it is true *that the economy must be deferred to,* then there is a case not only for constraining the imprudent actions of the prince but for repressing those of the people, for limiting participation, in short, for crushing anything that could be interpreted by some economist-king as a threat to the proper functioning of the "delicate watch."

> Albert O. Hirschman,
> *The Passions and the Interests,* p. 124.

Just as within the state every government, though it needs power as a basis of its authority, also needs the moral basis of the consent of the governed, so an international order cannot be based on power alone, for the simple reason that mankind will in the long run always revolt against naked power. An international order presupposes a substantial measure of consent.

> E. H. Carr,
> *The Twenty Years Crisis,* p. 235.

In *The Passions and the Interests,* Albert O. Hirschman described how early proponents of capitalism likened the economy to a "delicate watch" which, to function effectively, must not be tampered with by capricious sovereigns (or anyone else). American diplomacy took a similar view of the global economy and the threats posed to it by economic nationalism. The protection of property and contractual rights which enable the entrepreneur to risk his resources and enjoy the rewards of his endeavors was a precondition for the functioning of an international market system. Herein lay the rationale for supporting a regime that repressed threats to these rights.

As noted in the previous chapter, LDCs assessed the assumptions underlying the anti-expropriation regime from a different vantage point. The premises of liberal internationalism, when applied to foreign investment relations between MNCs and LDCs, were seen as rationalizations of corporate privilege. LDCs, progressively dissatisfied with the distributional consequences of the regime, rejected its moral authority. In its place, they supported alternative doctrines that elevated sovereign rights over contractual sanctity.

American decision makers interpreted Third World assertions of economic sovereignty as threats to the "delicate watch" of a liberal world economy and assumed responsibility for enforcing regime rules. Dissatisfied with the absence of effective international adjudicatory and enforcement mechanisms, the United States reserved the right unilaterally to preserve behavioral norms and repress the threat that unbridled sovereignty posed to an "open door" for foreign investment.

Until the late 1960s, the United States, in coordination with established industries, was generally successful in enjoining deviant behavior. The susceptibility of a target state to economic pressure was the key to whether regime maintenance could be achieved through economic sanction. Galtung argues that the key concepts for the efficacy of sanctions are *vulnerability* and *concentration.*[1] If the sanctioner commands a concentration of public or private resources, it potentially has the power to coerce. If the target's economy is dependent upon a single industry that relies on resources from the sanctioner, that country is vulnerable to economic pressure. The probability of successful enforcement is a function of this structure of economic vulnerability.

During the early postwar era, such a condition existed with respect to the United States and most of the Third World. Developing countries were, for the most part, capital-poor economies concentrated in one or two foreign-dominated sectors for most of their export earnings. The hegemonic position of the United States conferred upon it a near monopoly over relevant economic resources, e.g., aid, markets, and export credits. As the primary contributor to international financial institutions, the United States possessed the clout to use those institutions to further its foreign economic policy ends. In addition, the predominance of large American firms from oligopolistic industries produced a concentration of private resources that could maintain a strong regime through overwhelming bargaining power, private boycotts, or investment curtailments.

This management of anti-expropriation norms conformed to what Oran Young called an "imposed regime," i.e., an order that is "fostered deliberately by dominant powers or consortia of dominant actors." The hegemonic coalition achieves compliance by raising the costs of defection to the point that potential violators reevaluate the costs of self-help.[2] Like Carr, Young notes that imposed regimes are characterized by the exercise of naked power and do not assume "explicit consent from subordinate actors." Hence, imposed orders are "unlikely to survive for long following major declines in the effective power of the dominant actor or actors."[3]

This pattern can be discerned in the evolution of the anti-expropriation regime since the late 1960s. With changes in the balance of bargaining power between firm and host and the decline of American economic hegemony, the concession system came under vigorous attack. LDCs were able to challenge regime rules and alter concession agreements without paying the price that would have been exacted in an earlier era. The end result was that by 1970, there was a "major shift toward host state control over the operations of multinationals."[4]

As a consequence, natural resource concessions have been rendered obsolete. Contracts are no longer ironclad agreements fixed in stone, but starting points in an unfolding relationship. As David Smith noted, "the concession must not be seen simply as a contract, but as a process in which the rights and obligations of both parties change over time as specific factors change."[5] The phenomenon of induced contractual renegotiation, of which nationalization is the most dramatic example, has become pervasive throughout the entire Third World. By the mid-1970s, almost all extractive industry at the primary level was at least majority controlled by host governments, even conservative anticommunist regimes such as Saudi Arabia, Indonesia, and Malaysia. As one study observed: "Regardless of political persuasion, host governments are seldom impervious to the appeal for increased revenue from the foreign extractive sector."[6]

Expropriation, however, is only one of many threats facing the foreign investor, and it is by no means the most debilitating to corporate growth and power. For most nationalizing hosts, expropriation more often reflects a dependent than it does a self-reliant model of development. To capture export markets, hosts still need the international corporate and financial community for capital, technology, and specialized information about markets. As long as this dependence persists, so will corporate leverage to maintain an ongoing relationship.

In addition, many firms have adapted to the new environment, acknowledging that majority-owned subsidiaries are a thing of the past. In nationalized extractive industries, opportunities are available for profitable operations based upon a contractual rather than a concessionary basis. The critical issue for the firm lies in its ability to buy back crude oil or mineral ores at reasonable prices for highly profitable "downstream" operations such as smelting, refining, fabricating, transportation, marketing, etc., which are outside the control of host countries. The trend has been most pronounced in petroleum, though evident in other extractive fields. The "delicate watch" of global capitalism was more resilient to sovereign interference than had been expected.

This chapter will examine the sources of regime transformation in international property relations, specifically, the factors that undermined the instrumental assumptions of U.S. anti-expropriation policy. The critical variable in explaining change was what many scholars call the "obsolescing bargain," that is, the shift in bargaining power from the firm to the host as a function of the firm's commitment to a large fixed stake and the host country's "learning curve" about the industry. In addition, the effectiveness of public and private sanction to shore up the investor's position was undermined by the weakening of the market concentration possessed by the major firms in most resource industries, and by the decline in the proportion of relevant economic resources (aid, markets, credits) controlled directly by the U.S. government. As a consequence of these changes, MNCs and their parent governments have been compelled, of necessity, to adapt to new forms of property relations.

The Obsolescing Bargain in Raw Materials

The disparity of power between host and firm at the time of the initial concession enabled the latter to impose asymmetrical conditions upon the former. The variables that made for the preponderant position of the firm related to differentials in the costs of severance for the parties. Power, however, is not a static quantity and, as its components vary, so does its balance. This process of the devolution of bargaining advantages from firm to host in raw material investments is termed the "obsolescing bargain."[7]

At the outset of a resource venture, the firm "holds all the cards." Exploration for minerals and petroleum requires a large amount of capital and entails considerable uncertainty and risk. Large MNCs are well suited to assume those risks because they can repeat the gamble in several countries. To compensate for the possibility of failure, these firms could only be enticed by contractual promises of substantial rewards and minimal liabilities if an investment becomes a winner.

The investor's bargaining advantages were accentuated by the cohesion of the corporate community in a given industry vis-à-vis the fragmentation of LDC hosts. The firm, invariably a member of an oligopolistic industry, could play one country off against another to obtain the best terms available. Its ultimate leverage rested in its option not to proceed. The host, facing a concentrated industry with relatively uniform investment strategies, was severely limited in its options. It was confronted with the choice of developing its resources in line with dictated terms, or foregoing development altogether.

Adding to this disparity of power was the host's complete dependence upon the technology and specialized information of the firm in developing and marketing its resources. The investor, at the outset, possessed a monopoly control over technology and skills. Many firms consciously restricted the diffusion of technology in order to perpetuate this dependence. Techniques included the international patent system; locating more advanced facilities outside the host country; and the use of expatriate help in the more skilled positions.[8] Dependence was not mutual since the resource of the host country was usually available elsewhere.

For all these reasons, the terms of the initial concession were skewed heavily in favor of the firm. They imposed, most notably, limited financial obligations upon the firm. The most common tax was the royalty, calculated from a certain percentage of physical units of output. This had the advantage for the LDC of being easy to administer, but revenues bore little relation to market prices.[9]

The concessions typically gave the companies unrestricted rights over extensive land areas (often larger than the investor could reasonably develop) for extended time periods. United Fruit, for example, was given exclusive rights over large tracts of land in Central America, only 10% of which was cultivated. The Liberian government gave Firestone Rubber exclusive rights over one million acres for ninety-nine years.[10] The areas demarcated for exploration became virtual corporate fiefdoms. The companies possessed the unilateral ability to find resources and develop them to whatever extent their global needs required. Little, if any, control was in the hands of the host state. Concessions, such as Union Miniere in the Belgian Congo, have been characterized "quasi-governmental."[11] Investors were insulated from sovereign control in most concessions by "stabilization clauses" ensuring that future changes in local law do not affect the initial contract.[12]

Attempts by the host to regulate the firm or renegotiate better terms were limited by its informational dependence—its lack of knowledge and experience with the technology and the economics of the industry. It was poorly equipped to know how hard to push in monitoring or taxing investment activity. Expropriation as a possible course of action was almost unthinkable because of the host's dependence on foreign capital, technology, and markets, not to mention the certainty of corporate and parent country retaliation.

However, as Raymond Vernon notes, "Almost from the moment the signatures have been dried on the document, powerful forces go to work that quickly render the agreement meaningless in the eyes of the government."[13] After the operation was successful, the host came to view the lucrative concession terms as exploitative. As Moran observed: "A gamble with large risks has been won, and the host government is unlikely to want to keep paying for long a premium that reflects those risks."[14] The stage was set for subjecting the contract for review.

Changes in the balance of bargaining power allowed developing countries not only to reject the legitimacy of the initial concession but also to do something about changing it. While the firm enjoyed the initial advantage, it became committed, over time, to a large fixed investment which can only be liquidated at considerable cost. Once an investment was sunk and uncertainty dispelled, assets became more vulnerable to adverse treatment, and the deterrent embodied in the firm's threat not to invest was reduced.

The bargaining leverage of the host was further enhanced by what Barnet and Müller called the "global redistribution of knowledge."[15] LDCs played upon the vulnerability of the firm's assets to compel the diffusion of specialized information through the training of local manpower and administrators and the standardization of some relevant technologies. The training of many host country nationals in Western universities of science, business, and economics reinforced this trend. International organizations, such as the United Nations Center for Transnational Corporations, also allowed the "fragmented" periphery to increase their bargaining position by pooling their collective experiences with foreign investors.[16]

The immediate result of this process was the growth of the technical and administrative capability of the LDC state in economic policymaking. The diffusion of knowledge stimulated the development of expert personnel to staff regulatory agencies and state companies which could better supervise investor behavior. The power of the firm was correspondingly reduced. As the host state added to its negotiating, operating, and supervisory skills, it assumed many of the functions that previously only the investor could perform. This placed the state in a better position to run the operation itself or contract with other foreign firms in cases of expropriation. As the host country moved up the learning curve, the costs of economic nationalism proportionately diminished.[17]

As the power of Third World governments grew vis-à-vis foreign investors, they enacted measures that increase the local share of economic benefits and placed limits on corporate discretion. Increased government revenue was usually the first order of business. The primary vehicle for this was a shift from a royalty system to either an income tax or a profit-sharing accord, both of which accounted for market prices. To prevent capital flight, reinvestment requirements and restrictions on profit repatriation were enacted. The next step was to compel the companies to pursue policies that promote linkages with the rest of the economy through requirements to "buy local," the indigenization of the work force, the transfer of more advanced levels of processing or refining to the host, or required investment in local infrastructure or community services.[18]

The strategy ultimately moved from increasing local value added through regulation to controlling corporate pricing and production policy. Because of structural differences between corporate and national interests in the operation of a local subsidiary, control figures as an area more important than the division of the revenues. Expropriation, equity participation, and other vehicles of state control, were logical outcomes of this process. As Smith and Wells observed, there has been a pattern leading toward a shift "to forms in which the government reserves substantial participation and control over the venture."[19]

These secular trends increased the power of the LDCs to challenge the traditional concession system in primary production. Host LDCs have been able to nationalize or renegotiate without seriously disrupting their economies. The result, as Moran notes, has been that firm and host are now engaged in a game of mutual accommodation and joint maximization:

> [A] process of on-going mutual adjustment in which for-
> eign investors act in accord with their own best interests when they
> are in the strongest position and accede to necessity when they are
> weak and exposed while host governments accede to necessity when
> they are weak and act in accord with their own best interests as
> they gain strength.[20]

Contractual sanctity has given way to a fluid process in which
the terms change in proportion to changes in the perceptions
of interest and bargaining power of the parties.

The Decentralization
of Private Economic Resources

The corporate community, concerned that the obsolescing
bargain process threatened its interests, employed countervailing power to abort its effect. Until the late 1960s, it was
generally successful in fending off (or co-opting) most challenges to its property rights. Such strategies were viable because relevant resources were concentrated in a small number of firms in oligopolistic industries. In recent years, with
the emergence of new entrants weakening the oligopolies, the
effectiveness of coherent strategies to arrest the obsolescing
bargain process has decreased.

International competition in natural resource sectors was severely limited during the early postwar years. Investment, except in colonial enclaves, was primarily American and limited to the largest corporations. Corporate access
to financial networks and control of modern technology and
world markets were potent bargaining chips. The concentration of these resources in a small number of firms only increased their effectiveness.

Mancur Olson observed that a concentration of resources in a small number of actors facilitates coordinated
group action to defend its collective interest. Each member

can more confidently subordinate its individual self-interest for the sake of common aims.[21] Corporate cohesion facilitated the maintenance of anti-expropriation norms through its bargaining power vis-à-vis a large number of uncoordinated host countries, and its ability to impose discipline for effective economic sanctions.

First, by putting a ceiling on the terms each would accept from a prospective host, the industry limited the options of an LDC in contract negotiation or renegotiation. As Smith and Wells note, "where the organization of the industry is such that the country is dependent on a small number of firms that do not bid against each other for the development of the resource, the bargain is likely to be favorable to the foreign enterprise."[22] Second, challenges to the rules of the property regime were met through private transnational economic sanctions against the transgressor. For example, when Mossadegh nationalized the Anglo-Iranian Oil Company in 1951, the major oil companies refused to do business with him and expanded their production elsewhere to compensate for the loss of Iranian oil. The result was a drastic decrease in Iranian export revenues, contributing to the overthrow of the government in 1953.[23]

The 1960s saw an increase in competition and a dilution of producer concentration in most extractive industries at the international level.[24] In part, increased competition from Western European, Japanese, and independent American companies was a function of technological advances in transportation and communication, as well as the standardization of technologies for exploration and extraction. It also reflected the economic reconstruction of Western Europe and Japan, whose firms began to go abroad and compete with established firms.

The process was expedited by American sponsorship of an open, nondiscriminatory international economic system. The United States firmly opposed tariffs and closed currency blocs which had traditionally worked to stifle global competition. Ironically, the very success of the United States

in promoting the "liberal" goal of an open economic order undermined the "illiberal" corporate power which enforced the
"liberal" regime protecting alien property rights.[25]

The attenuation of oligopoly structure undermined
private regime maintenance capabilities along the lines of
Olson's theory of large group behavior.[26] By creating conditions in which firms, especially those least established, had
a greater incentive to "cheat," it reinforced the devolution of
power toward the host country, and decreased the efficacy of
corporate sanction.

First, the decentralization of private investment resources opened up more alternatives for the host country.
While established firms opposed yielding to changes from the
traditional concessions for fear of a demonstration effect, new
entrants had no such fear, at least in the short run. Smaller
American firms and competitors from Western Europe and
Japan vied with the established multinationals for the same
"slice of the pie." Since the interest of these firms was to "get
in," rather than to preserve what they had, they had less of
a stake in supporting a tight regime and, unless co-opted,
more of an incentive to break ranks.

These "have-not" firms were willing to offer generous terms and novel arrangements to get their "foot in the
door." Japanese and European firms, to gain a foothold, were
among the first to enter the natural resource field on a basis
other than total ownership. For example, ENI (the Italian
state company), the Arabian Oil Company of Japan, and
Standard Oil of Indiana (an independent American firm) broke
ranks with the major oil companies and accepted local equity
participation. While the Libyan government was limited in
the deals it could strike with the major oil companies as to
the relinquishment of unexplored concessions, it struck a deal
in 1955 with American independents, such as Continental and
Occidental, whereby concession area would be progressively
reduced if no petroleum was developed in five years.[27]

The decentralization of private economic resources
reinforced the "obsolescing bargain" by providing the host

country with a wider array of alternatives. LDCs were better situated to negotiate and renegotiate packages that expedite the transfer of technical knowledge and production methods. Both of these outcomes, in turn, mitigated dependence on any particular foreign firm and placed it in a stronger position to renegotiate on more favorable terms that delimit corporate control.

Second, the proliferation of investors decreased the proficiency of corporate sanction. The oil companies were unable to impose a quarantine on Libya in the 1970s, as they did on Iran in the 1950s. The major oil companies refused to deal with Qaddafi's coerced "participation," but they could not enlist the cooperation of independent oil companies, such as Occidental, Continental, and Marathon. These firms, with few, if any other sources of supply, gave a higher priority to maintaining that source than to supporting the global concession system.[28]

In such a competitive situation, the individual firm is caught in a Prisoner's Dilemma. It may make common cause with competitors to punish an expropriation, thereby supporting the collective good of a stable regime. As the number of firms increases, however, so does the probability of members breaking ranks, especially with the presence of "have-not" firms whose immediate interest in a particular concession outweighs its interest in the "public good" of systemic order. As more firms behave this way, private enforcement of the regime becomes ineffective. The end result was, as Lipson notes, that "as expropriation risks have increased over the past decade, most corporations have responded flexibly and individually, rather than punitively and collectively."[29]

Olson notes that to realize collective goods, large group cohesion can only be sustained through externally imposed coordination. Lipson notes that the United States government, lacking direct control over economic actors, is ill-suited to prevent ad hoc adaptation.[30] In fact, the United States consciously attempted to play this kind of leadership role in the early 1970s when John Connally came to the Treasury

Department (see chapter 7). Its objective was to more consistently and punitively respond to violations of regime norms
to induce MNCs to redefine their interests away from accommodation. But, as will be shown in the next section, changes
in the international system reduced the power of the United
States to make LDCs pay for nationalization and limited its
ability to influence the decision calculi of private economic
actors.

The Weakening of U.S.
Government Sanction

Until recently, the corporate community generally was able
to regulate and enforce contractual stability through its own
devices. If these failed, public sanction by the parent country
was solicited. Over the past century, the main vehicles for
public sanction have been military (interventionary) force;
bilateral economic sanctions; and multilateral economic
sanctions. The efficacy of each relied on the dominance of
United States military and economic power.

MILITARY SANCTION.

The traditional means of deterring or reversing expropriations has been the use of interventionary force against
the violator nation. During the nineteenth and early
twentieth centuries, the major capital-exporting powers frequently used or threatened force against those who would
"despoil" the property of their citizens. Developing and colonial countries were neither able to resist this nor make the
costs of intervention prohibitively high.

Lipson suggests that military force is most effective
when interventionary capabilities are highly concentrated.[31]
But the United States possessed a near monopoly of power

projection forces after World War II and rarely used force in economic disputes such as investment protection. In fact, since Roosevelt's Good Neighbor Policy was enunciated in 1933, the United States abjured the right of military intervention to protect the property rights of its nationals. When force was used, it was done covertly, and its main thrust was generally political rather than economic. In the absence of a perceived association with "communism" or the Soviet Union, force was not considered a suitable policy instrument in dealing with economic nationalism.[32]

The main reason for the infrequent use of force has been the increased domestic and international costs of intervention. According to Bryce Wood, the United States wrote off military intervention as a means of investment protection after the landing of the marines and the occupation of Nicaragua (1927–1932), the duration and cost of which were out of proportion to the interests involved.[33] Since the Vietnam War, the United States has been reluctant to directly intervene even for political reasons because of the costs of popular disaffection and economic disruption attributed to extended military involvements.

Not only have the costs of intervention increased, its efficacy in achieving economic ends has also diminished. Military force is not a fungible resource transferable to any issue area. This is particularly true in the economic realm, as the OPEC experience has made clear.[34] To achieve "target compliance," intervention requires that the offending government be overthrown and clients be installed who respect traditional property rules.[35] This could be done only against the interests and desires of a socially mobilized population. It would probably require that the sanctioner accept the burden of occupation. In addition, such a return to "gunboat diplomacy" would probably inflame anti-American sentiment in other host countries with unforeseen diplomatic and economic side effects.

Due to its increased cost and decreased effectiveness, the use of force in pursuit of economic aims is no longer considered a serious option. As Ernst Haas observed:

Governments no longer dispatch their navies to collect foreign debts or open up ports to trade; they no longer conquer neighboring countries to gain access to oil, copper, or gold. They do not even use the threat of military force to foist an unwanted trade agreement on a weaker country. And, *the expectation that the stronger will not use violence in economic relations has given the weaker the courage to assert themselves in many international forums.*[36] (Emphasis added.)

It has also given them greater "courage" to assert themselves vis-à-vis foreign investors within their own borders.

BILATERAL ECONOMIC SANCTIONS.

The effectiveness of public bilateral sanctions in checking regime erosion has decreased due to the declining proportion of economic resources directly controlled by the U.S. government. This outcome was primarily a function of the economic recovery of Western Europe and Japan and the emergence of private firms and banks as the primary transmitters of capital to the Third World.

First, economically, as well as militarily, the United States emerged from World War II as the preeminent power. With Western Europe and Japan recovering from the devastation of the war, the United States was the only major source of public assistance for developing countries. It also held a near-monopoly in markets and export credits. The Agency for International Development (AID) and the Export-Import Bank would channel funds to states that complied with American norms for the treatment of foreign property, penalizing others by omission. The concentration of relevant public economic resources in the United States allowed the pocketbook to replace the gunboat as the primary deterrent to challenges to international property rules.

In the 1960s, the economic dominance of the United States receded with the economic reconstruction of Western Europe and Japan. The emergence of a multicentered global economy brought into being a decentralization of sources of aid, trade, and credits which, in turn, reduced the probability of effective public sanction.[37]

In addition, the Europeans and the Japanese were not inclined to absorb short-term material costs for the regime. As former colonial powers, their investments were either safe in client states (e.g., French investments in the Ivory Coast) or had been taken over following independence (e.g., French oil interests in Algeria, British mining interests in Ghana, or Dutch rubber interests in Indonesia). As later arrivals to overseas investment under the Bretton Woods system, these countries were more concerned with investment promotion than investment protection. Therefore, they did not identify their interests as closely with the international property order. Again, the very success of American foreign policy—in underwriting the economic recovery of Western Europe and Japan—worked against the goal of enforcing regimes enshrining contractual sanctity.

Second, since the 1970s, MNCs and private banks have come to far exceed public aid programs as the primary conduit for capital transfers to LDCs. Furthermore, these private institutions are not easily amenable to public control. Richard Feinberg notes that since these actors rarely alter their behavior to suit state preferences, the U.S. government's "ability to manipulate overseas events has been severely reduced."[38]

For example, U.S. aid designed to stabilize the "moderate" Salvadoran junta of October 1979 was more than offset by private capital outflows. President Carter's denial of aid to human rights violators in South America was dwarfed by the private credits extended by bankers who appreciated those regimes' "good investment climate." Despite the Reagan administration's sanctions against the Sandinista government, overseas affiliates of American corporations continue to do business there. The Nicaraguan debt is still being serviced through the Chase Manhattan Bank.[39]

With respect to anti-expropriation policy, a similar

pattern is discernible. From 1968–1973, informal public
sanctions were applied against Peru for its uncompensated
seizure of an affiliate of Exxon. But the aid cutbacks were
more than offset by the expansion of private capital flows.
Oil and mining firms, attracted by Peru's resource potential,
were keenly interested in exploration. Private banks, impressed by Peru's abundance of natural resources and conservative fiscal policies, helped finance these ventures.[40] As
a result, the self-interested actions of private economic actors
worked to blunt the effectiveness of coercive regime maintenance strategies.

MULTILATERAL ECONOMIC SANCTIONS.

During the early postwar period, the United States
was the principal contributor to IFIs, such as the World Bank
and the International Monetary Fund (IMF). While not ostensibly created to deal with expropriation, their insistence
on creditworthiness as a precondition for their programme
and project loans was used to "deter expropriations and ensure prompt settlements."[41]

Since influence within these institutions is weighted
according to contribution, the United States was able to shape
lending policies to coincide with its own precepts of economic
orthodoxy. Operational Policy Memorandum 101 of the World
Bank stipulated that

the bank will not lend for a project in a country if it considers that
the economic position taken by that country with respect to alien
owners of expropriated property is substantially affecting its international credit standing. Nor will it appraise projects in such a
country unless it has good grounds for believing that the obstacles
to lending will soon be removed.[42]

And, as one study noted, "confiscation of foreign property or
expropriation without adequate compensation can hardly fail
to affect adversely the credit standing of the expropriating

country."[43] During the 1960s and the early 1970s the IBRD
held up several loans to developing countries—most notably
Algeria, Indonesia, Iraq, the United Arab Republic, Zaire,
Peru, and Chile—to punish inhospitality toward foreign
investors.[44]

The recovery of Western Europe and Japan in-
creased those countries' contributions to IFIs, and hence their
influence over the implementation of policy. Krasner notes
that the United States no longer possesses a veto power over
specific loans from the IMF or the World Bank. Since the
1970s, it has occasionally stood alone in voting no or abstain-
ing on grounds of human rights, nonproliferation, or economic efficiency.[45] Attempts to use IFIs for anti-expropriation norms have met a similar result since Europe and Japan
do not share American strategies. During the 1970s, the United
States often stood alone in voting against (on expropriation
grounds) or unsuccessfully blocking loans to Guyana, Bolivia, Iraq, Syria, the People's Republic of the Congo, and
Ethiopia.[46]

Corporate Adaptation:
The Multinational Corporation at Bay
or a Capitalist Polycentrism?

MNCs were not oblivious to the changes taking place. They
naturally preferred the greater latitude for action and opportunity for profit they enjoyed when the ownership prerogative was unencumbered. For a time, they tried to stem the
tide of events through sanction, both private and public. This
only postponed the obsolescing bargain. The traditional system was under siege and its days were numbered.

Despite regime change, prognostications about entering an era of the "multinational corporation at bay" may
be as premature as those that predicted a similar fate for the

nation-state. Natural resource firms have adapted, in part, shifting new investments away from the developing world to "safer" areas with less economic promise, such as Canada, Australia, and South Africa. Over the past twenty years, the percentage of new direct investments in exploration that have gone to the Third World has diminished from 60 percent to 15 percent.[47] Part of this, however, is due to a shift in the strategy of overseas firms away from equity ownership. One United Nations study, *The Future of the World Economy*, projects a continued capital inflow to the Third World composed more of loan and portfolio investment rather than direct investment.[48]

Despite the erosion of its autonomy and power, the MNC has not disappeared from the developing world. Under the new conditions, it still retains considerable leverage from its control over technological innovation, financial resources, and most importantly, the transportation and marketing networks necessary for host country exports.

Most LDCs still want to do business with foreign firms, as evidenced by the plethora of "invest in our country" advertisements in the *New York Times Annual Economic Supplement*. The host still needs the resources provided by the transnational firm, but only under conditions where the latter functions as a paid contractor, not an equity owner. A twofold tension emerges: the LDCs are in the market for skills and resources that only the company can offer; the firms have to give a little more to get at the raw materials.

While the rhetoric of the Third World reflects a "meta-power" strategy seeking an insulation from or transformation of a liberal international economic order, its expositors recognize this as a maximalist position about whose achievement they have no illusions. In practice, the strategy has more often been one of "relational power," i.e., improving one's distribution of benefits within the system.[49] Even so unsympathetic a neoconservative critic of the "new egalitarianism" as Robert Tucker observed that "the outlook of the small states is, with few exceptions, nothing so much as the outlook of those who wish to preserve a system while securing a more independent and advantageous role in it."[50] In the area of natural resources investments, the strategy has not been one of ending dependence, but of pragmatically manipulating interdependence, enticing foreign investment while extracting a greater contribution from it.

MNCs are in the process of adapting to new realities, accepting the fact that wholly owned subsidiaries and the traditional concept of the sanctity of contract are artifacts of the past. In their stead, they have accepted induced participation, management accords, and production-sharing agreements, not as a matter of choice, but as the best option available. The result, as Peter Gabriel notes, is that the "basic function of the multinational corporation is shifting from the mobilization of capital, in which the company's reward is entrepreneurial for risks taken, to the sale of corporate capabilities, in which the reward is managerial for services rendered."[51] The companies offer expertise and run the day-to-day operations on a contractual basis and market the goods abroad. The trend has been most pronounced in petroleum, but is present in other areas, as evidenced by the iron industry in Venezuela, the bauxite industry in Jamaica, and the the copper industry in Zambia.

In extractive industries, the critical issue for the firm has been the ability to buy back primary products at preferred prices for highly profitable "downstream" operations, which are outside the territorial grasp of the expropriating host. When faced with expropriation, a firm will seek maximum compensation, but other considerations may be more important. One Treasury study showed that settlements in the 1970s averaged only between 50 to 70 percent of book value.[52] The key is the negotiation of service contracts permitting favorable access to raw materials.

Recent studies have found that overseas firms no longer consider expropriation a critical issue; in a 1972 survey by the Council of the Americas, only 10 percent of the respondents ranked it as one of their major concerns.[53] A 1975 survey sponsored by the U.S. Council on International Economic Policy (CIEP) demonstrated a parallel result. One interviewee claimed that "expropriation is really a non-issue. There are so many more subtle and less dangerous things a country can do to ruin your investment."[54] In both studies, expropriation was not ranked high because of the ability to operate successfully in its aftermath. The real threats to overseas operations came from other regulations in which the host state expropriates the profit rather than the property.

In addition, the change in ownership did not necessarily connote a transfer of real control. The nationalized firm often retained significant control after ceding equity ownership. For example, Zambia's 51 percent participation in the foreign copper industry did not impinge on corporate management authority and left the companies in a more remunerative financial position.[55] Conversely, OPEC members received 85 to 90 percent of crude oil profits before they even demanded equity participation in 1971.[56] The watershed experience in the erosion of the oil company position vis-à-vis the producers, Libya's unilaterally imposed increase in the posted price of crude oil, preceded by nearly three years that country's nationalization of the industry!

Some firms, making a virtue of necessity, have rationalized that their long-term interests might best be served by acceding to nationalist ascendancy and assuming a lower profile.[57] Ceding day-to-day extractive operations to the state or local nationals confers legitimacy, and hence stability, to the process at the primary level. This ensures an uninterrupted supply, though (usually) at greater cost.[58] It also co-opts the host state into accepting greater responsibility for labor problems by giving it a greater interest in the sector. Conversely, an attempt to maintain an unpopular stake in the face of nationalist resentment could lead to serious disruptions of supply and expose the firm to total expulsion.

Most firms have come to regard parent government intervention as counterproductive and advocate a minimal role for it. The abovementioned Council of the Americas study found that 76 percent of the respondents judged the Hickenlooper Amendment "inappropriate" and "ineffective." It was characterized as the "least effective means" for dealing with disputes. "It does not deter illegal expropriations or facilitate settlements of investment disputes once unjust takings of U.S. properties have occurred." State sanction was viewed not only as useless, but counterproductive as well. In the words of C. W. Robinson of Marcona Mining, the use of economic sanction is the "twentieth century equivalent of nineteenth century British gunboat diplomacy" and "out of touch with the realities of Latin America." Another company executive stated that through arousing public sentiment, it has "inhibited negotiations for successful solutions or compromises."[59]

These changes have not done away with a regime to protect foreign investment, but have reshaped it into a quasi-regime with more flexible parameters. Wealth deprivations, if accompanied by some compensation and a contractual arrangement, are no longer resisted. Arbitrary violations of contractual rights are no longer protected by concentrated public or private sanctions. But if a host country "goes too far" in restricting firms, deterrence will come about by what one businessman called "the economic laws of nature: Capital goes where it is wanted and well-treated."[60] Bergsten, Horst, and Moran concur: "The business climate is the most effective deterrent and response to expropriation."[61]

It is for this reason that the shift in bargaining power to the Third World has to be viewed tentatively and a discernible pattern of norms and expectations persists. LDC sovereign discretion is limited by its continued dependence upon MNCs for technology and market access and, to an increasing extent, on the international financial community for capital.

First, as Krasner notes, LDCs can assert formal sovereignty and set the terms of engagement, but cannot "compel multinationals to invest . . . or prevent their exit."[62] If they push their advantage too far, they may lose access to the corporate technology necessary to maintain long-term competitiveness or develop their resources expeditiously. The situation is even less favorable if the lowest barriers to entry exist at the extractive stage. State-owned enterprises may be selling a highly elastic good in a competitive market to an industry whose interest is to buy the commodity as cheaply as possible. If the host pushes prices or terms too high, it may become a supplier of last resort.[63]

Second, with the nationalization of MNCs, state companies have become increasingly dependent upon private capital markets and IFIs to finance exploration and production. In the past, MNCs, with solid financial reputations, were able to borrow easily. LDCs have a more difficult time demonstrating creditworthiness. To meet the performance criteria of lenders, they need to maintain a sound operating relationship with MNCs. As debt has increased with successive OPEC price increases, the need to maintain access to desperately needed foreign capital serves as a further constraint to driving a hard bargain.[64]

In sum, LDCs have been able to end this system of extraterritorial privilege and takeover of the "commanding heights," but important aspects of commodity markets are beyond their control. LDCs, therefore, have recognized the need to avoid a total alienation of foreign capital. They have generally paid some level of compensation (albeit below the U.S. standard) and concluded contracts with former owners to continue operations. These norms are accepted less as a duty than as a necessity to promote their exports and maintain their status as sites for new investments and borrowers from capital markets. Outright confiscation is prevented not by force, threat of aid sanctions, or concentrated boycott, but the the diffuse threat of corporate ostracism as firms decide which modes of property relations are compatible with their interests and which are not.

Implications for American Foreign Policy

In sum, the 1970s witnessed a shift in bargaining power between MNC and LDC which rendered the old concession system obsolete. As Smith and Wells note, "The signing of a concession is only the invitation to the ball. . . . The foreign investor may feel at times that he has entered into a contract to make concessions rather than a concession contract."[65] Nonetheless, the structure of commodity markets and the international financial system place limits on LDC sovereign discretion. What emerged was a looser set of norms which vary from sector to sector as a function of a state company's ability to provide itself with capital, technology, and market access. They still leave open a profitable ongoing relationship for the foreign firm.

MNCs have been in the process of adapting to this polycentric business climate in which the standard for the treatment of foreign contractual rights is set by a more autonomous host country definition of its public interest. Many have come to treat political risks, such as forced divestiture, like any other business risk. Some have adopted innovative arrangements to anticipate conflict and change, e.g., uncoupling the investment package, and automatic phased changes with respect to ownership, taxation, and relinquishment of concession areas, so as to institutionalize and facilitate change.[66]

A *modus vivendi* between firm and host is possible even after expropriation. It would also satisfy, notwithstanding the greater cost, the American national interest in stable supplies of raw materials and the viability of foreign investment in the developing world. A shrewd reading of history might have instructed American policymakers that irresistible changes were taking place which were not necessarily incompatible with U.S. overseas interests. The emerging scenario called for the United States government to play the role of moderator between MNC and LDC, making change more orderly through nudging the companies toward compromise.

Such a transformation would have required the shedding of a good deal of ideological baggage with respect to foreign investment and expropriation. The policy of containing expropriation, like that of containing communism, compelled nations to define their interests in terms of an externally imposed ideological framework (i.e., liberal internationalism or anticommunism). Departures from the norm were heretical challenges to the postwar order, not indigenous developments. Fearful of permitting a dangerous precedent, public decision makers often gave strong support to aggrieved firms without examining the merits of each case. This outlook contributed to a continued attachment to the status quo at a time when the Third World was determined to break up vestiges of the old order.

Though the policy persisted for a time, it was based on instrumental assumptions rendered obsolete by the dynamics of change in international property relations. The *probability* of successful regime enforcement was eroding because of the waning of American hegemony and the weakening of corporate oligopoly structure. Public and private coercion was too porous to arrest the "obsolescing bargain."

The diminished operational probability shifted the real (as opposed to perceived) *values* and *costs* away from regime enforcement. In effect, it reversed the direction of the traditional causal assumptions about the relationship between defending a tight regime and important national interests.

First, contractual flexibility did not necessarily debilitate the climate for foreign investment, although it might have appeared that way when compared to the early postwar regime. Nationalization of raw material investments may not have fatally injured corporate interests if it was accompanied by a satisfactory post-expropriation relationship which insured access to primary product. Continued dependence of the LDC on MNC expertise and decentralized corporate decisions about risk provided some level of order and predictability. The emergent order (quasi-regime) discouraged some firms, but others continued to invest, albeit on a nonequity basis.

Economic reprisal to defend the regime, on the other hand, undermined local social stability and/or aroused anti-American nationalism, diminishing the position of unaffected businesses, the prospects for compromise settlements and ongoing relationships, and the environment for future investment. In effect, intervention was nonreproductive of the looser level of stability provided by the quasi-regime. By projecting an image of toughness, it generated more resentment than respect and, in the process, vitiated the very investment climate it had been invoked to support.

Second, while regime change invalidated Hull's espousal of *Pacta Sunt Servanda* in his vision of a liberal world order, a new order evolved that was not wholly antithetical to an open world economy. The emerging system was based more on welfare state rather than laissez-faire norms. It permitted private sector involvement and the transnational flow of capital, but under closer sovereign supervision, if not control. In effect, it transferred internationally a conception of property and contract whose practice had, with the onset of the New Deal, become accepted domestically.

Attempts to arrest this change and reinstall the *ancien regime* would inflict the costs of continual confrontations with the Third World and a resultant diminution of international economic transactions. This would produce the opposite of what Hull intended—a world order where political conflict impeded transational flow of private capital.

Third, national economic security was still maintained within the quasi-regime, although a higher price was paid for it. First, extractive firms continued to invest in the development of overseas resources on a nonequity basis, although not as much as they did in the heyday of Pax Americana. Second, natural resource firms generally retained access through a contractual relationship, providing primary products to consumers through established marketing networks beyond the grasp of expropriating hosts. In fact, the devolution of formal ownership to the host assisted resource security by giving the producers an increased economic stake in the success of the operation and removing the foreign image, and hence legitimizing extractive operations.

Attempts to coercively defend the concession system threatened short-term security of supply and further increased commodity prices by producing confrontations that

complicated the environment for post-expropriation relationships, increased the possibility of supply cutoffs, and harmed
the climate for continued overseas development of natural
resources.

Fourth, Third World economic development was frequently assisted through the nationalization process as host
countries underwent a learning curve with respect to the industry, obtained a larger take from extractive operations, and
redirected affiliate policies away from the needs of the integrated corporate network toward national economic and social goals. Reprisal and confrontation, on the other hand,
impeded development diplomacy by undermining the economic base of the host and further retarding capital inflows.

Fifth, the effect of regime change on the United States
balance of payments was negative because firms wrote off
their expropriation losses against their tax liabilities and
passed on the increased costs of adaptation to the consumer
through higher prices. An obdurate policy of resistance, however, would have been ineffective in reversing these effects.
In addition, it would have impeded the adaptation necessary
to maintain continued corporate viability (thereby harming
the balance of payments) and the development of low-cost
sources of supply (thereby contributing to inflation). The adverse consequences on the American economy would have been
compounded.

As the stresses between the regime and the de-
compression of the concession system became more evident,
an uneven process of learning ensued as the shock of "un-
intended effects" revealed the anachronistic nature of policy.
The process by which various expropriatory precedents precipitated such an awareness in various levels of the bureaucracy is the subject of the case studies in part 2.

PART TWO.

CASE STUDIES

4.

Expropriation in Latin America, the Good Neighbor Policy, and World War II: Establishing the Rules of the Game

Traditional U.S. policy toward outward investment was based upon the principle of the "open door." Initially invoked in 1898 against the Great Power partition of China into economic spheres of influence, it called for equal access to trade and investment sites around the world. The policy was natural to an emerging power confronted with mercantilist practices overseas. This was particularly evident in raw materials where Europe treated its dependencies as exclusive fiefdoms to augment domestic self-sufficiency.[1] Even before it achieved the hegemonic position to implement its vision, the United States gave verbal commitment to rules and norms to unlock the imperial door to foreign investment.

By World War I, the United States emerged as the world's leading capital exporter, particularly in Latin America where it achieved economic and political dominance. As it was more successful in penetrating imperial enclaves, new challenges to the "open door" emerged within the host countries themselves. In Latin America, the primary threats to alien property rights were local instability or sovereign encroachment. Moreover, Latin American states sought to legitimize the latter prerogative through the Calvo Doctrine which made the national courts the final arbiter of disputes between aliens and sovereigns. For the United States, concerns about investment promotion were superceded by concerns about investment protection.

The United States, consequently, played a leadership role in extending traditional property rules to the inter-American system.[2] Successive Secretaries of State argued that sovereign states could not diminish the acquired rights of foreign investors without full compensation. They reserved a right to intervene to protect their nationals from such depredations. During the first third of the twentieth century, the Department of State was characterized as "a big international law office" and a "collection agency for investors and bondholders."[3]

In a prescient article written in 1927, Walter Lippmann predicted that strict application of this policy would lead to "an irreconcilable collision between the power of [the United States] and the will of its neighbors." There was, he reasoned, an inherent tendency in Latin America to overturn its *ancien regime* and the extraterritorial privileges associated with it. The acquired rights of foreign investors were an integral part of that structure. A policy of sanctifying those rights, reasoned Lippmann, was self-defeating: "Nothing would be so certain to arouse . . . ill-will as the realization in Latin America that the United States had adopted a policy, conceived in the spirit of Metternich, which would guarantee vested rights against social progress as the Latin American peoples conceive it."[4]

Until the 1930s, the military and economic dominance of the United States in Latin America shielded it from the consequences Lippmann foresaw. The Roosevelt Corollary (1904) reserved the right to intervene in response to disorder that threatened overseas economic interests. Gunboat and dollar diplomacy provided "diplomatic protection" and enforced a "regime" enshrining the sanctity of contracts in the hemisphere. Great Power consensus on international property rules begat tranquility to Western investors throughout the world. Only the Bolshevik Revolution in 1917 successfully challenged the system.[5]

A reassessment of the efficacy and cost of interventionary force in coping with economic nationalism occurred in the early 1930s. This began with the Hoover administration's intervention in Nicaragua (1927–1933), the cost and duration of which far exceeded the interests involved.[6] The lessons were given official pronouncement in 1933 with Franklin Roosevelt's Good Neighbor Policy which renounced the Roosevelt Corollary and abjured unilateral military intervention.

The nonintervention pledge did not, however, signify a lack of concern with international property rules or the rights of its investors. On the contrary, it coincided with the origins of U.S. support for liberal economic regimes on a global scale. The sanctity of overseas property and contracts was viewed as a prerequisite for a nondiscriminatory global market system. As a result, Undersecretary of State Sumner Welles stated that the nonintervention policy was based upon the "anticipation of reciprocity," namely that Latin America would uphold its obligation under international law to respect contracts and submit disputes to impartial arbitration.[7]

The Roosevelt administration did not initially foresee the policy's implications. Latin American nations placed the same value on freedom from foreign economic domination as they did on freedom from foreign intervention. The consequence of a shift that limited the means but proclaimed the same ends was almost foreordained. As Bryce Wood observed, "when the prop of armed force was withdrawn from the international standard of protection of nationals, the states against whom it had formerly enforced refused to accept the jurisdiction of arbitration tribunals."[8] The result was, as Lippmann had predicted, a proliferation of conflicts between the vested rights of investors and the sovereign rights of host countries. The most serious of these were the oil expropriations in Bolivia and Mexico and Venezuela's demands for an income tax for crude oil exports.

What was at stake in these disputes was not only the private interests of the oil companies, but the integrity of a system that policymakers equated with their economic security and vision of an orderly world. But a strategy of coercive regime maintenance implies that short-term costs have to be incurred to punish violators and deter others. This precipitated a bureaucratic debate over the desirability of economic pressure. In effect, this was a debate over the best strategy to protect American economic interests, i.e., through punishing violations of traditional norms or through accommodation and legitimation.

Ultimately, the hard-line position was overtaken by events. The imminence of global war made the short-term price of coercion too great. The United States pressed the oil companies to adapt to nationalization in Mexico and Bolivia and anticipate it in Venezuela through accepting an income tax.

This outcome conforms to Krasner's point that the state's reluctance to proffer support to aggrieved firms altered the preferences of private economic actors. Since decision making took place in the White House and Department of State, where private interests had minimal influence, "general foreign policy goals prevailed against the interests and pressures brought by private corporations."[9] Since corporate ownership strategies needed forceful state backing, they eventually had to adapt.

But the symbiotic relationship between business and government cuts both ways. Once the emergency of global war disappeared, so did the "political" rationales for accommodation. As the costs of economic pressure decreased, support for international property rules was elevated on the agenda. This was best exemplified by U.S. policies toward the Mexican state oil company after 1945.

The First Test: Bolivia's Nationalization of Standard Oil

The Bolivian government's seizure of a subsidiary of Standard Oil of New Jersey was the first major takeover of a non-agricultural natural resource investment outside of the Soviet Union. It also represented the first major test of the Good Neighbor Policy and the policy of pacific protection. Despite its minor holdings in Bolivia, the parent company called for a tough line lest the precedent be used against larger holdings in its worldwide network. The initial U.S. response downplayed Standard Oil's concern for the externalities of expropriation, and encouraged compromise. In line with the premises of the Good Neighbor Policy, Latin American nationalism was seen as a force to which the U.S. government and business must adapt in order to safeguard long-term interests.

BACKGROUND

Standard Oil obtained its Bolivian concession in 1922. With State Department leverage, the company was granted exclusive rights for exploration despite a 1921 law proscribing monopolies in resource extraction. The company entered Bolivia when oil prices were high, but the Great Depression softened the market and further production became uneconomical. In 1932 the company stopped looking for new oil and in 1936 it put its assets up for sale.[10]

Bolivian Standard was nationalized on March 13, 1937, by the "leftist" junta of Colonel Toro which had assumed power in a coup a year earlier after the Chaco War with Paraguay. The charges against the company were: a failure to pay surface taxes and an 11 percent royalty on production; falsification of production records; covertly shipping oil and refinery equipment to Argentina; and noncooperation during the Chaco War.[11]

Bolivia's Foreign Minister, Enrique Finot, argued that the company was not entitled to compensation because it had failed to live up to its contract and had forfeited its properties under a penal clause in the contract. Finot rejected international arbitration as a derogation of national sovereignty. Finally, he assured the American Embassy that the Standard Oil case was unique and foreign capital would remain secure.[12]

The immediate stakes for Standard Oil were trivial. Production averaged only 450 barrels per day. Nevertheless, the company refused to recognize the nationalization decree, claimed a market value of $17 million, and sought strong State Department pressure in support of its claims.

The company's primary concern was the symbolic effect of the Bolivian action. It did not want to convey to others the image that its properties could be taken over. If this occurred, the company reasoned, "a precedent will have been established for similar action in other countries."[13] The aim was to reverse or punish Bolivia's action as a deterrent to others who would challenge the "sanctity of contracts."

THE INITIAL U.S. GOVERNMENT RESPONSE: ACCOMMODATION

For the Department of State, this was the first major test of the Good Neighbor Policy—a challenge to its vision of reciprocity and international law. The threat posed by Bolivia's action was obvious—the possibility of a contagion that would threaten regime rules protecting foreign investments throughout Latin America and the long-term security of supply of raw materials. The central question was whether the renunciation of coercive measures was compatible with order in international property relations.

Despite these concerns, the immediate response of the State Department was moderate. It shied away from corporate preferences designed to punish Bolivia. Nationalism was viewed as a force that must be conciliated in the best long-term interest of foreign policy in general, and the longer-run status of overseas economic interests in particular. The case was initially dealt with on its own merits, not as a symbol of the larger dynamic of regime maintenance.

The American embassy in La Paz reported that the legal case was arguable from both sides and recommended that concern be expressed to the Bolivian government through a friendly representation rather than a formal protest. To revert to old policies of pressure, an embassy official argued, might "precipitate the downfall of the present military junta . . . [and] provide political capital to the opponents of the United States."[14] The cost of anti-American nationalism likely to ensue from strong-arm policies outweighed the precedent-setting cost of the takeover. Hence, State opted for the role of bargaining agent seeking negotiated compromise between disputants rather than its traditional role as lawyer for the companies.

State refused Standard Oil demands for diplomatic intercession to coerce Bolivia into rescission or arbitration. The company was advised to exhaust local remedies. Standard demurred, insisting that the junta had stacked the Bolivian Supreme Court and that it could not "expect an unbiased opinion."[15] Aware that governmental support would not be forthcoming, Standard Oil filed suit under protest.

Even when State convinced the Bolivians to accept the principle of compensation as a basis for negotiations, Standard Oil demurred. To have direct dealings with the Bolivan government without rescission of the nationalization

decree would "indicate that confiscations by a foreign government are merely private matters between the government
and its victim."[16] A compromise with principle, even if the
company received some compensation, was inadequate. As one
U.S. embassy official noted: "The Standard Oil Company pre-
fers to accept financial loss than to allow the impression that
it can be forcibly expulsed [sic]."[17] The company's strategy
was to bide its time until a more pliable regime came along.

United States policy in this case was a historic precedent; for the first time it had abstained from threat and
coercion in protecting the property of one of its nationals.
Despite the potential threat the Bolivan action posed to foreign investment in Latin America, the State Department defined the issue differently than did Standard Oil. Investment
security, it reasoned, would be better served by bending principle and adjusting to, rather than pushing against, Latin
American nationalism. Bolivia's action was treated as a dis-
crete phenomenon, amenable to diplomacy and compromise,
not a harbinger of future assaults to be suppressed for its
symbolic value. Events the next year in Mexico would challenge that assumption and precipitate a serious bureaucratic
debate over investment protection strategies.

The Mexican Expropriation
and the Stiffening of U.S. Policy

Mexico's expropriation of its foreign petroleum industry grew
out of its history. The initial concessions were obtained under
the dictator Porfirio Díaz (1876–1910), who had opened up
Mexico to foreign capital. The companies were granted rights
over the subsoil, in violation of Spanish law, and exemption
from all taxes except for a nominal stamp tax. Civil order
and labor peace were maintained by a national constabula-
tory which "made Mexico one of the safest places in the

world—except for Mexicans."[18] Under this permissive regime, petroleum development expanded rapidly from 10,000 barrels per day in 1901 to 12.5 million in 1911.[19]

The overthrow of Díaz and the Mexican Revolution gave rise to popular demands for social justice and revisions of the privileges granted in the Díaz mining laws. Article 27 of the Constitution of 1917 gave legal expression to the Calvo Doctrine. It stipulated that control over the subsoil and the right of eminent domain were sovereign prerogatives: "The nation shall forever have the right to impose upon private property the limits the public interest may require." Mexican leaders asserted that they were free to alter or repudiate laws; foreign investors must obey these laws and foreswear diplomatic protection.[20]

The State Department viewed this nationalization provision as a serious challenge to its economic interests in Mexico with possible repercussions elsewhere in Latin America. Recognition was withheld until 1923, when Mexican President Obregón signed the Bucareli agreements, affirming that Article 27 would not be applied to concessions granted prior to 1917.

During the 1920s and the early 1930s, the oil companies succeeded in blocking all attempts to change their concessionary status. The U.S. government reinforced corporate aims, brandishing a wide array of weapons, such as nonrecognition, arms supplies to rivals, and denials of access to credits and markets. The Mexican government, weakened by internal revolt, was too vulnerable to challenge U.S. government preferences.[21]

Mexico was in a stronger domestic position when Lazaro Cárdenas assumed the presidency in 1934. In that year, Petróleos Mexicanos (Pemex), the state oil company, was formed. In 1936, a nationalization law was passed, applicable to all foreign mining interests. In addition, labor unions, with the backing of the government, demanded increased wages and better working conditions. Mexico's Federal Conciliation and Arbitration Board gave the demands the effect of law.

The foreign oil companies, as a united front, considered this an unwarranted violation of valid contracts and appealed through the local judiciary system.[22] On March 1, 1938, the Mexican Supreme Court ruled against the companies. The companies refused to abide by the ruling and entered into direct negotiations with Cárdenas.

To coerce a favorable presidential decision, the companies withdrew large sums of money from Mexico. An obdurate policy was seen as necessary to hold the line against further nationalist encroachments against its interests both in Mexico and the rest of Latin America. The companies believed that this strategy would work because Cárdenas could not afford the economic consequences of nationalization.[23]

The companies seriously underestimated the degree to which Cárdenas found this challenge to Mexican sovereignty more threatening than the economic risks of nationalization. On March 18, the oil companies were nationalized for their refusal to comply with the full terms of the law. Compensation, at book value, was offered in the form of an immediate down payment, with the balance to be paid from future profits.

OIL COMPANY STRATEGY

The foreign oil companies, led by Standard Oil, pressed for extensive private and public sanctions. Standard's president, W. S. Farish, based his stand on principle and precedent:

The company attaches importance to the expropriation of its properties in Mexico *not because of the purely Mexican aspect of the matter but because of its effect on other countries*. . . . If the company accepts some arrangement which in effect is based upon some compromise of principles of international law, the company then considers it is lost since a precedent will have been established.[24] (Emphasis added.)

A retreat from principle would signify that there would be "no safety for American property elsewhere in Latin America."[25] The company was willing to settle for no less than immediate compensation based upon the value of its subsoil rights (an impossible figure given the state of the Mexican economy) or restitution.

Standard believed that a prolonged stalemate was preferable to a compromise with principle, even if it resulted in the total loss of its Mexican properties. Farish explicitly stated that he would "prefer to let things go than accept a proposal which compromises the principle of compensation." This policy was reinforced by the belief that time was on the company's side; the Mexicans could not operate the industry and would, of economic necessity, be compelled to give in or "drown in oil."[26]

The oil companies used their own resources to force such a choice on Cárdenas. Since the major oil companies controlled 95 percent of the world's marketing outlets, they effected a boycott of Mexican crude. Oil that did get through to North America or Europe faced legal suits for the handling of "hot" oil. Other private-sector sanctions debarred Mexico from securing tankers for the transportation of oil; procuring machinery and spare parts; and purchasing tetraethyl lead for gasoline production. One company went so far as to convince a chain of travel agencies to discourage Mexican tourism.[27]

The sanctions had a significant effect on the Mexican economy. Production declined from 4 million barrels in March to 2.1 million barrels in April and did not return to the March level until the mid-1940s. Petroleum exports declined by 40 percent.[28] The effect, however, was not catastrophic. Mexican oil production had been declining prior to nationalization and by 1938 accounted for only 12 percent of its foreign exchange earnings. Meanwhile, the proportion of oil consumed domestically increased from 43 percent in 1938 to 66 percent in 1942, the result of a conscious decision by

Pemex to steer away from exports.[29] In addition, Mexico was able to circumvent the boycott by selling to independent oil companies, such as Eastern States Petroleum, at 12 to 15 percent below the world market price. Far more ominous from the U.S. government's point of view, Mexico felt compelled to sell oil indirectly to the Axis powers.[30]

THE STIFFENING OF U.S. POLICY
IN MEXICO AND BOLIVIA

The Mexican nationalization gave rise to a reevaluation of U.S. policy toward expropriation. In Mexico, the stakes were larger and more extensive than they were in Bolivia. Mexico was a nation of greater prestige and its actions were more likely to be a source of emulation for other Latin American governments. Cárdenas' actions signaled to decision makers that expropriation was more than a passing phenomenon and posed the dilemma of how to guard against future incidents without reverting to the interventionism of an earlier era.

There was bureaucratic consensus on regime norms. All accepted Mexico's sovereign right to expropriate and the oil companies' claims for compensation. All ruled out the use of force and advocated arbitration as the preferred means of resolution. There were, nonetheless, sharp bureaucratic cleavages over the use of economic pressures to preserve regime rules. These derived from the lessons drawn from the Bolivian and Mexican experiences. The hard line, espoused by Cordell Hull and Sumner Welles at State, shared the companies' concern for precedent and principle and attributed Cárdenas' action to American equivocation with Bolivia. Ambassador Josephus Daniels and Treasury Secretary Henry Morgenthau favored compromise; expropriation was the result of corporate obduracy and sanctions could only arouse anti-American nationalism and push Mexico toward the Axis.

The implementation of policy reflected a bureaucratic stalemate between these two positions since President Roosevelt
did not become actively involved.[31]

Hull's preferred response was a stiff note of protest
and a withdrawal of the ambassador, to be followed by the
progressive constriction of economic relations. He reasoned
that the Mexican action had repercussions beyond the immediate interests involved, threatening the liberal world order he sought to construct; the health of the Mexican economy; the security of supply of raw materials; and domestic
economic recovery.

First, since the passage of the Reciprocal Trade Act
of 1934, the United States actively advocated an open multilateral world economy. Expropriation, to Hull, directly
challenged this vision of an "orderly world society."[32] Therefore, he responded to the Mexican "gauntlet" by formally
spelling out the parameters of an anti-expropriation regime.
Accepting expropriation as a right inherent in sovereignty,
its implemenation must be nondiscriminatory, pursued for a
public purpose, and accompanied by "prompt, adequate, and
effective compensation." Since the rights of foreign investors
were governed by international law, impartial arbitration,
not the local judicial system, was the legitimate forum for the
resolution of disputes.[33]

The Mexican takeover fell short of this standard;
payment was in the form of long-term bonds and only for the
value of the companies' assets, and was thus neither prompt
nor adequate. Refusal to submit the dispute to arbitration
was a clear violation of responsibility "at a time when law-
lessness is steadily expanding in many regions and when this
government is preaching to all nations the value of law and
order."[34]

Hull was most concerned about the long-term effects
of Mexico's actions on maintaining an international order
guaranteeing the sanctity of contract. Like the oil companies,
he was concerned about the externalities of expropriation:

When a great country like Mexico establishes a policy of taking over property without any serious plan or purpose to make reasonable payment, it would at once become known to all nations. . . . [I]f this country should acquiesce to the seizure of oil or any similar properties on account of the unpopularity of the owners . . . those who would seize it would unquestionably suspend all further law for the purpose of seizing other and all foreign owned property. Other nations would quickly follow suit.[35]

The Bolivian experience was thus redefined. Since laws limiting the rights of foreign investors had repercussions in other Latin American countries, the American response could no longer be seen merely in terms of bilateral relations; it must be a statement of symbolic significance.

Pressure, therefore, must be sufficiently great and the settlement sufficiently expensive to discourage similar actions elsewhere: "If these moves did not produce the desired results in Mexico, they would at least be a timely warning to other Latin American governments with covetous thoughts and sticky fingers."[36] Compliance in Mexico was secondary to setting an example for others; economic nationalists had to be put on notice that a price would be exacted.

Second, the hard-liners believed that expropriation would harm Mexico's economic, and hence political, stability. Welles "scolded" the Mexican Ambassador, saying that it was a "notorious fact" that Mexico would not operate the oil industry except at increased cost, lower profit, and lower wages. He pressed for rescission because the Mexican government "was not in a financial position where it could pay in cash for the properties expropriated."[37] In addition, Mexico would be harmed by the poisoning of the investment climate so that not "one penny of additional capital could be invested in Mexico except by persons residing in a lunatic asylum."[38]

This concern, in turn, affected a third interest—security of supply. Bernard Baruch warned Hull that Mexico and Bolivia may be unable to operate the oil companies, but will turn to others to do so: "Those others might be Japan, Italy, and Germany, who need these raw materials."[39] Hull came to link the issue of expropriation with the possibility of the disruption of wartime resource supplies. He warned the Bolivian Ambassador that "there was never so ripe a plum dangled before a hungry man" as the riches of Latin America before the Axis. Expropriation, he warned, would open the door to Axis penetration.[40]

Finally, there was a concern for the effect of widespread expropriation on the American economy. Foreign investment was part of the world economic order upon which American welfare relied. At stake was not only corporate profit, but the ability of the American economy to pull itself out of the Depression.[41]

Hull's main bureaucratic protagonists, Daniels and Morgenthau, challenged these assumptions. Daniels was sympathetic to the Mexican Revolution which he saw as a Latin American analogue to the New Deal. He supported the principle of compensation, but held the oil companies responsible for their own predicament. He wrote to Roosevelt: "They are as much against fair wages here as the economic royalists are at home." Hard-line policies would only embitter relations by replacing the Good Neighbor Policy with "big stick" paternalism. If American interests were to survive in Latin America there must be an accommodation with local sensitivities.[42]

In an ironic reversal of the role it would play in the 1970s, Treasury argued against sanctions because of their effect on foreign policy issues. Morgenthau feared that a position of intransigence might move Cárdenas toward the Axis or undermine his government, inadvertently promoting a profascist coup: "We are going to wake up one morning and find inside a year that Italy, Germany, and Japan have taken over Mexico." On the other hand, "with any kind of sympathetic treatment . . . we may be able to pull them through and have a friendly neighbor to the south."[43]

Daniels and Morgenthau voiced the "pragmatic" point that the political costs of maintaining a tight regime exceeded the likely benefits. American overseas interests, at this historical juncture, would be better served by compromise than confrontation. The bureaucratic division between Hull and Welles, on the one hand, and Daniels and Morgenthau, on the other, manifested itself in a disjointed policy of sanction, most notably with respect to economic sanctions, particularly the attempted boycott of Mexican silver, and strategies for negotiating a settlement.

First, in 1936, the U.S. Treasury negotiated a three-year agreement with Mexico to purchase nearly all of its newly mined silver. In response, Mexican silver production expanded to the point where it contributed more to government revenues than did oil. It employed 100,000 workers and provided 10 percent of government revenue. One historian concluded that an effective boycott could have "sent the Mexican economy crashing."[44]

Hull, through his economic advisor, Feis, pressed Morgenthau to suspend the 1936 agreement and boycott Mexican silver. To increase the pressure, Feis urged the sale of stockpiled silver to reduce the world price by one cent per ounce. Compliance would be achieved by diminishing Mexican government revenue and weakening the peso.[45]

Morgenthau reluctantly acceded to Hull's request. He opposed the use of silver as a weapon because it violated the spirit of the Good Neighbor Policy and rendered a settlement more difficult. Moreover, 70 percent of Mexican silver was mined by American companies. Daniels concurred, noting that it would "produce an impasse and prevent possible future negotiations for payment."[46]

Treasury, however, only halfheartedly enforced the measure. It continued to buy silver on the spot market, much of which was Mexican, without inquiring into its origin. When Feis approached Morgenthau about a further reduction of the price of silver, the Treasury Secretary refused. In April, Morgenthau rescinded the directive and the import of Mexican silver resumed.[47]

State was successful in implementing some modest punitive measures. First, while it took no absolute stand against independent oil company involvement with Mexico, it supported the private sector boycott by warning such companies that they were "fishing in troubled waters." Second, from 1939 to 1942, the U.S. Navy was barred from the purchase of all Mexican oil, even from non-nationalized fields. Third, Mexico was conspicuously omitted from general tariff reductions in 1940. Finally, U.S. government lending to Mexico was stopped until November 1941. State interceded to veto five proposed Eximbank loans.[48]

Second, bureaucratic divisions affected the policy of negotiating a settlement. A Treasury study in late March 1938 contended that Mexico could only pay compensation if it is assisted and that economic coercion could "result in driving Mexico to seek assistance elsewhere and/or into political and economic chaos."[49] Morgenthau, therefore, opposed a punitive policy. His preference, as the only means for settlement, was a large low-interest loan in exchange for compensation.

The State Department, on the other hand, placed greater emphasis on the maintenance of principle than on obtaining a compromise settlement. The Treasury plan, Feis argued, would serve as a precedent for other Latin American governments by showing them that expropriation is painless and that the United States will help finance it. Any settlement must recognize the companies' claim to the subsoil and leave the industry in private hands.[50]

The Mexican expropriation precipitated a hardening of U.S. policy toward Bolivia as that country's action was defined by the State Department less as an isolated event and more as a part of a larger structure. In March 1939, when the Bolivian Supreme Court turned down Standard Oil's appeal, State sent a formal note of protest calling for arbitration and charging a "denial of justice," since the company was entitled to compensation. From then until late 1940, the United States provided no loans, Eximbank credits, or technical assistance to Bolivia. Official policy stated that all assistance would be suspended until the Standard Oil question was cleared up.[51]

State was, however, only partially successful in dissuading other Latin American countries from buying "hot" Bolivian oil. Paraguay, lured by the prospect of Eximbank credits, stopped importing from Bolivia. Argentina, a much larger purchaser, refused these enticements.[52]

As expropriation loomed as a more prominent issue, the conciliatory tone of the Good Neighbor Policy gave way to a tougher policy of economic pressure. But even in the early phases of this policy change, there were indications that U.S. power to enforce tight regime rules was limited. The United States was unable to coerce rescission or full compensation. The end result was an acrimonious impasse. U.S. policy ultimately compromised when an increasingly threatening international system made such confrontations costly as well.

Accommodation in Mexico and Bolivia

Events in Europe compelled the State Department to give up its support for expansive corporate definitions of interest in favor of compromise to promote hemispheric solidarity and military cooperation. By 1940, almost all governmental actors recognized that Axis expansionism was a far more serious threat than economic nationalism. A common view emerged that an economically strong and politically stable Latin America was necessary to thwart German penetration. The United States consequently pursued a larger public assistance program to prevent its southern neighbors from succumbing to the "organized economic and ideological campaign of the Nazis."[53]

Officials noted that economic pressures against Mexico and Bolivia had been ineffectual. They had soured bilateral relations and made negotiations for compensation intractable. While the companies preferred a stalemate to any compromise settlement, that was a luxury the United States no longer believed it could afford given the increasingly treacherous international situation. Decision makers began to separate their interests from those of the oil companies as the value of regime considerations paled before the need to shore up hemispheric solidarity for the impending war.

Another factor inducing compromise was the defection of Sinclair Oil from the solid industry front. Sinclair, a smaller company with fewer sources of crude, had a greater interest in preserving its stake than in preventing a demonstration effect. In May 1940 it opted for a separate settlement. In return, it received $8.5 million in compensation, to be paid over three years, and a five-year purchase arrangement at less than world market prices.[54]

In June 1940, Cárdenas offered the United States an escape. He proposed a Mexican-American Joint Claims Commission, rather than arbitration, to evaluate the companies' property for the purpose of compensation. As an added "carrot" toward accommodation, he offered the use of the Mexican coastline for American air and naval bases.[55]

By this time, Hull and Welles were concerned about the effect of sanction and stalemate on Mexico's economic and political position. Without a settlement, economic conditions were likely to foment an anti-U.S. insurrection or increase German influence by forcing Cárdenas to move closer to the Axis. Strategic realities in Europe compelled the United States to redefine its interest away from corporate preferences for arbitration. It was more important to obtain a settlement, even if it compromised principle, than to allow relations to drift in the face of strategic exigencies. Hull retreated from insistence on binding arbitration and accepted Cárdenas' proposal.[56]

Standard Oil, conscious of its holdings outside Mexico, refused to participate. As Farish told Hull, the company was "not at liberty to give its assent to the agreement":

To turn the industry over to Mexico under the conditions proposed in the plan of agreement would sacrifice the material interest of every party concerned, to say nothing of the sacrifice of principles of international law by which the very safety of foreign investments against confiscation is assured.[57]

Any agreement that did not recognize the companies' claim to the subsoil, reinstate corporate management, and maintain the principle of arbitration, set an unacceptable precedent. Standard preferred to leave the issue unresolved "rather than . . . sacrifice the principle of property rights."[58]

Farish had sympathizers at State: Feis and the Petroleum Advisor, Max Thornburg. Feis saw the Joint Claims Commission as "an unfortunate precedent with respect to other states." He preferred "the Mexican oil question to remain unresolved until such a time as Mexico's needs for foreign investments were such as to induce Mexico herself to solve the controversy."[59]

Hull acknowledged these debits, but concluded that the costs of continued stalemate far outweighed the violation of principle. On November 19, 1941, the United States and Mexico announced the establishment of the Cooke-Zevada Commission. When the companies refused to participate, the State Department stepped in to negotiate for them. The Interior Department, at the request of State, conducted an independent study, valuing the companies' assets at just under $25 million, considerably less than the $450 million they had claimed. The agreement was signed on April 27, 1942. The Mexican government agreed to pay $24 million—a down payment of $9 million with the rest to be paid over ten years. This was more than offset by a peso stabilization loan of $40 million.[60]

A similar reevaluation occurred with respect to Bolivia. Late in 1939, Welles downplayed the importance of precedent as the world situation grew more ominous:

While I am entirely willing to concede that . . . [the] questions of basic principle . . . are sound and desirable, it would nevertheless seem to me that if Bolivia at the present time were to involve herself in arrangements of the kind proposed by Japan and recently by Germany, it would inestimably have a direct effect upon the political trend in Bolivia.[61]

Officials at State viewed Bolivian nationalism as too potent to allow a settlement on terms favorable to Standard Oil. The withholding of economic assistance could only undermine a relatively friendly regime or push it to the Axis. Germany had already sent a military mission and was offering development assistance. Upgrading the value of a stable pro-American (or at least antifascist) Bolivian government, key officials argued that development assistance should not be contingent upon the Standard Oil question.[62]

The overthrow, in 1940, of the "leftist" Busch regime and its replacement with the more pro-American Peñaranda provided an added incentive for accommodation. The new regime wanted financial and technical assistance, as well as closer relations with the United States. While willing to compromise on the Standard Oil question, it considered the company's demands for rescission as an affront to its sovereignty.[63]

The State Department recognized that the current government was friendlier than the alternatives and feared its overthrow if compelled to accede to Standard's demands. The American Minister to Bolivia argued that Peñaranda had to take a strong stand against the company because the issue was being used as a "political football" by the German-financed opposition. The denial of loans, he continued, gives "excellent ammunition" to anti-American agitation. The Standard Oil question should not be allowed to "remain open like a festering sore." Accommodation and compromise were necessary to "strengthen the hands of those friendly with the United States in the government and . . . to create a healthier atmosphere for American-Bolivian relations."[64]

The State Department and the Bureau of Mines were also concerned that tougher policies were harmful to wartime security of supply. First, the United States wanted a long-term contract for the purchase of Bolivian tin for the Reconstruction Finance Corporation's smelting industry. Second, it was feared that the estrangement of Bolivia portended a turn to Germany, which would then control its natural resources.[65] The perceived threat expropriation posed to national economic security came full circle. Whereas Hull, in 1939, feared that the United States should pressure Bolivia into reversing expropriation because in its inability to run the industry it would turn to Germany, the State Department in 1940 saw the pressure of sanction as the most likely factor to produce the same result.

The decision calculus of policymakers was redefined. The need to speed the economic development of Bolivia and smooth out bilateral relations was, in the context of the European war, more compelling than holding the line for Standard Oil. In July 1941, after an attempted Axis-supported coup, aid was resumed despite corporate opposition. State pressed Standard Oil to accept the fact of nationalization as the starting point in negotiations with Peñaranda.[66]

Standard Oil initially resisted State Department pressure for negotiations because it left the nationalization decree, which it saw as a violation of international law, unchallenged. It acceded to negotiations, however, when the State Department ended its policy of economic pressure.

A settlement was reached on January 12, 1942. The Bolivian government paid Standard Oil $1.5 million at an interest rate of 3 percent from the date of seizure—well below the company claim of $17 million. As in the Mexican settlement, the sum was more than matched by $25 million in economic assistance and a $5.5 million Eximbank loan for the development of the state oil industry.[67]

In deference to corporate strategy, the deal was labeled a "sale" rather than an "indemnity." By defending the settlement as a business transaction, Standard hoped to give the impression that it was voluntary and prevent an example that others might see as an invitation. However, given the pittance of compensation exchanged for substantial economic aid, deterrence could hardly have been achieved. The result reflected the U.S. government's subordination of regime enforcement to the wartime exigency of cementing political and economic ties. Through its refusal to support Standard beyond a certain point, state preferences compelled the firm to redefine its priorities and negotiate a compromise.

Lesson 1: Accommodation to Avert Expropriation in Venezuela

One lesson learned by the State Department from its Mexican and Bolivian experiences was that for American corporations to operate smoothly in Latin America, greater sensitivity was needed toward host country priorities. The immediacy of global war made compromise even more urgent. A regime that protected corporate ownership must rely more on achieving legitimacy through a *modus vivendi* with nationalism than on naked power. In deference to this lesson, the United States played a pivotal role in pressing oil companies toward conciliation when their status was challenged in Venezuela in the early 1940s.

BACKGROUND

The petroleum concession in Venezuela granted by the Gómez dictatorship (1916–1935) had a tainted history. Obtained through bribery, the concessions were one-sidedly favorable to the investors. The dictator even allowed the oil companies to write their own petroleum legislation and assisted them in quashing a series of strikes in the late 1920s. By 1929, the combination of concessionary stability and a quiescent labor force enabled Venezuela to become the world's largest exporter of oil.[68]

The death of Gómez in December 1935 unleashed long pent-up popular demands for change and denunciations of the oil industry. Gómez's successor, Eleazar López Contreras, though committed to the maintenance of oligarchic rule, responded to these pressures with a program of economic and social reform. Prominent in his plans was the goal of acquiring a larger take from the foreign-owned oil industry.

The Petroleum Law of 1938 legalized labor union activity and boosted taxes and royalties. López Contreras pursued a "sow the petroleum" policy in which the added oil income would be used to revitalize and diversify the economy and fund an ambitious public works program modeled after the New Deal. The oil companies, however, insisted on the legality of their rights under the Gómez oil laws and refused to pay increased royalties. To drive this point more forcefully to the government, they temporarily reduced production and stopped new investments.[69]

López Contreras' successor, Isaís Medina Angarita, accelerated the pace of economic and political liberalization. In 1941, the Medina government publicly committed itself to go beyond statutory regulation to the abolition and rewriting of the Gómez concessions. The objective was to increase government revenue through the imposition of an income tax and achieve greater participation in the administration of the concessions. In July 1941, government officials met with company representatives in New York and Caracas over demands for renegotiation, increased taxation, and managerial control.[70]

The oil industry saw these demands as serious threats. The renegotiation of contracts and income taxation were thresholds that had not yet been crossed by any other producer country. Jersey's Venezuelan manager, Herbert Linam, adamantly opposed any compromise, declaring, "It's against my principles to let anyone else run my business."[71] The talks reached an impasse and were suspended in November 1941.

STATE DEPARTMENT POLICY

While the State Department did not take an active interest in Venezuela until the dispute over the 1938 petroleum law, the imminence of trouble was discerned by the American Minister to Venezuela, Meredith Nicholson, as early as 1936. Nicholson cabled that popular agitation against the oil companies arose from the latter's "identification with a regime which is now anathema to the Venezuelan people and its responsible officials." The local managers were unwilling to make the compromises necessary to survive because they came from the "old school of imperialists" who believe that the marines "ought logically to follow American investors in foreign countries wherever required by the interests involved."[72] His recommendation that the parent company should be approached concerning the replacement of these "anachronistic presences" found a sympathetic hearing from Lawrence Duggan, Chief of the Division of the American Republics. But Duggan's superior, Sumner Welles, found such a policy "undesirable."[73]

During the 1938 dispute, Duggan again pressed for a more sympathetic approach toward Venezuela. He argued that it was necessary to balance the "sacred character of property rights" against Venezuelan demands because under Gómez, the oil industry "exercised enormous power and was in a position to secure whatever it wanted and practically on its own terms." As a result, "the companies were getting all the cream, the Government and the workers only skimmed milk." To avert a probable repetition of the Bolivian and Mexican nationalizations, the United States must "impress upon [the companies] the necessity of . . . adopting a more conciliatory attitude."[74]

In light of Hull's firm stand on the Mexican expropriation, the State Department was not receptive to Venezuelan demands to alter its oil concessions. In 1939, Hull lectured the Venezuelan Ambassador about the pernicious practice of "taking things that do not belong to us and not paying for them within any reasonable time."[75] While American words and actions were ostensibly aimed at Mexico, they served as an indirect warning to Venezuela.

By the summer of 1939, however, the State Department had been chastened by its failure to induce compliance in Mexico and Bolivia and by the imminence of global war. These factors precipitated a reassessment of the role of sanction and compromise in dealing with investment disputes, and an assignment of greater weight to the immediate costs of prolonged confrontation.

On July 22, 1939, Welles outlined a new policy echoing Duggan's recommendations to accept Venezuela's campaign to regulate the industry and nudge the companies toward compromise. He admitted that the company's position was of dubious legal and moral merit: "The arrangements under which the oil industry got its start in Venezuela and the conditions prevailing are no longer applicable to an established industry operating one of the richest and best proven oil fields in the world."[76] The new ambassador to Venezuela, Frank Corrigan, concurred, reasoning that intransigence in responding to Venezuela's demands would only "force the government to emulate Bolivia and Mexico."[77] Recasting its operational assumptions, the State Department concluded that expropriation emanated from corporate unwillingness to revise its status toward a fairer division of the bounty. The challenge, as one study put it, was whether "large scale business, particularly the oil business, can so arrange its affairs in one of the other American republics to avoid serious trouble and possible expropriation."[78]

Officials additionally believed that the immediate costs of a prolonged confrontation were too great in a time of world crisis. To Welles, conciliation averted the immediate costs of a "public controversy" with "international implications."[79] The United States was under a dual compulsion: to placate a wartime ally and arrest any drift toward the Axis; and to maintain the effective functioning of the industry so that "Venezuelan oil remains available for the war."[80] Venezuela, unlike Bolivia (whose output was minimal) and Mexico (whose output was declining, even before expropriation), was a significant exporter of oil with "astronomical reserves." It was also Great Britain's only secure source of supply and, by 1941, accounted for 80 to 85 percent of its imports.[81] The immediate potential costs of confrontation overwhelmed the symbolic importance of resisting challenges.

Moreover, Welles noted that this modest loosening of regime rules connoted neither nationalization nor a serious impairment of the national interest in maintaining secure and ample supplies of petroleum.[82] Duggan had reported that López Contreras and Medina were economic conservatives, not radical nationalists "hostile to the companies."[83] The challenge at hand was to encourage corporate adaptation to inevitable changes and to avoid a long and bitter standoff that would poorly serve all parties.

When Medina pressed for revision in 1941, Standard Oil, the leader in the industry, was divided between those who wanted to resist any change and those who favored compromise. Hard-liners, such as Linam, argued that the company had a valid contract which it had no obligation to alter. Standard had been the leader in opposing the rewriting of concessions. To accede to Venezuela's demands "would amount to a general weakening of concession contracts and would remove an essential safeguard of company interest, an action that might have serious repercussions elsewhere."[84] He feared that concessions granted by governments would no longer be as binding as contracts between private parties.

The pragmatic viewpoint was expressed by Vice President Wallace Pratt, who maintained that adaptation was necessary for survival. The hard line was pursued in Mexico, he said, with disastrous results. A similar outcome in Venezuela would be more devastating. Pratt reasoned that an operation will survive not through the strength of its contract, but through the mutual recognition of shared interest. The price of continued corporate ownership was an adjustment of the contracts to increase Venezuela's share of the benefits.[85]

The terms of the Mexican settlement indicated to the companies that there were limits to diplomatic support. In November 1942, Linam was recalled and Standard accepted the principle of renegotiation. On March 13, 1943, Venezuela enacted the Hydrocarbons Law, basing government revenue on the companies' income. This was the first income tax ever levied against a foreign oil company and it laid the basis for the fifty–fifty profit-sharing method enacted by Rómulo Betancourt in 1948.[86]

The Venezuelan case demonstrated how state definitions of interest veering away from rigid regime maintenance can constrain and redefine corporate strategy. For the State Department, the immediate political and economic stakes were too high, given wartime considerations, to focus on legal precedent. Moreover, the demands of the Venezuelan government left intact corporate ownership and control. In the Mexican case, the expansive interests of the oil companies were eventually subordinated to diplomatic aims, but only after their position had been irretrievably lost through corporate obduracy. The lesson learned was that firms must adapt to nationalism before the cycle of expropriation was allowed to run its course; laws are only as strong as the interests that underlie them. By refusing to support the oil companies in their dispute with Venezuela, national actors nudged them toward a pragmatic strategy of contractual flexibility.

Lesson 2: No Loans to State Companies

The American experience with investment disputes in the late 1930s led to a retrenchment of regime maintenance policy and an acceptance of some level of contractual flexibility. The accommodation with nationalism, however, was limited to the recognition that compromise was necessary to avert expropriation. Once the threshold of expropriation was crossed, concern persisted for arresting its demonstration effect. World War II had temporarily overruled, but not eliminated, that concern. The refusal of the United States to lend to Pemex, or any other state company, was a means to contain possible externalities from the prewar expropriations.

Through the end of 1943, the Roosevelt administration supported Eximbank credits to the Mexican state oil company, Pemex, to build a high-octane gas factory and repair obsolescent refineries. The policy was strongly supported by the Interior and Defense departments, which saw Mexican and Caribbean oil as "strategic reserves of the United States" for the war effort. The State Department had reservations that loans rewarded a violation of international property rules and might encourage similar action elsewhere. But it had to concede that "the political situation is of so serious a nature" as to make pursuit of such considerations futile and dangerous.[87]

In 1944, the American ambassador to Mexico, George S. Messersmith, impressed upon Roosevelt the detrimental effect of these loans on foreign investment in Latin America. Assisting Pemex in this way created the precedent of lending to state enterprises and eased the Mexican economic situation so as to obviate its need to let the companies back in. Regime considerations were more important than immediate benefits because Mexican production was oriented toward domestic consumption rather than export for the war effort. Lending should be made conditional upon Mexico allowing the companies back in. While neither Roosevelt nor Truman were fully persuaded by this logic, the State Department successfully delayed prospective loans to Pemex.[88]

After the war, the State Department was more successful in implementing its preferences for regime maintenance. The strategic imperative of compromise was not as compelling, especially after discoveries in the Middle East glutted what was previously a tight oil market. In line with these priorities, in 1946, the policy of not aiding state enterprises was generalized from Mexico to the entire developing world. The United States sought to "scruplously avoid undertaking loans that private investors are willing to make on reasonable terms." The World Bank, whose policies at the time were virtually dictated by the United States, attached similar conditions to its loans. The objectives were to induce LDC reliance on private foreign capital and deter expropriation by refusing to support alternatives to private ownership.[89]

No public funds were to be granted to Mexico's nationalized oil industry unless, at the very least, the private companies reentered on a contractual basis. One rationale for this was that oil could not be adequately developed without the participation of the companies. This was tied to national security concerns about the adequacy of foreign supplies of raw materials:

> Our opposition to any direct U.S. Government aid to Pemex results from our conviction that Pemex cannot be counted upon at best to do more than develop petroleum for Mexico's growing internal demands . . . and what the U.S. needs is oil in vast quantities.[90]

Ambassador Messersmith contended that loans would retard the development of Mexican reserves by insulating Mexico "from solving her own problems by maintaining a sound operating basis with the companies."[91]

United States policy was also concerned with the precedent of assisting an expropriated state oil company and its effect on the rest of the world. A 1947 State Department study argued that nationalization was contrary to the "open" hemisphere espoused in the Economic Charter of the Americas and should not be condoned through the advance of funds from any agency of the government.[92] To support the administration of the nationalized Mexican oil industry, Acheson reasoned, would demonstrate to others that nationalization entails no great cost:

It probably would be interpreted in other Latin American countries as United States approval in principle of state operation of the oil industry; this in turn would strengthen extremist elements in Latin America which advocate the application of nationalization and other restrictive measures to foreign industries.[93]

In effect, it would "consecrate the principle of expropriation," and weaken the overall position of American investments abroad. Whatever gains the United States could obtain through the increased production of Mexican oil would be offset by greater losses elsewhere. The aim was, in the words of one scholar, to "contain the agency in the expectation that it would die an almost natural death."[94]

The State Department, however, did not insist on a return to the status quo ante. The lessons of the past decade indicated that some compromises with the traditional concessionary contract were necessary for the companies to get in and maintain their stakes. Reflecting this view, one position paper recommended company acceptance of management contracts:

The rights of a foreign country under this type of contract may not seem as secure, to the legal minds representing that company, as those usually granted in the past under the concession type of contract. However, the history of expropriation of American capital by governments during the past ten years indicates clearly that no rights, not even concessional ones involving an interest in the subsoil, are necessarily safe. Consequently, it can be argued realistically now that the right to develop the petroleum resources of another country under a contract comprising operation, management, and participation . . . will probably be just as safe for foreign capital as the concessional rights used in the past.[95]

If the companies could get in on a contractual basis, the study reasoned, the adverse effect of nationalization on United States interests would be neutralized.

The Mexican governments of the 1940s were not averse to a *modus vivendi* that "attract[ed] a limited amount of foreign capital with a minimum of visibility and loss of freedom of manoeuvre." The Petroleum Law of 1941, while prohibiting direct investment, allowed for joint ventures between Pemex and foreign capital in oil exploration. In the early 1940s, a number of drilling contracts with smaller foreign oil companies were signed. While Pemex retained managerial control, the contractors were paid in crude oil.[96]

While the State Department was willing to accept a compromise basis for continued oil company operations, the major oil companies were not. Unlike Venezuela, where ownership remained unscathed, Mexico had nationalized the industry. The companies refused to compromise, fearful that going in on a contractual basis would create the appearance that nationalization was a success.[97] In addition, Mexico was only a minor producer, rendered unimportant by expansion in Venezuela and the Middle East. The immediate costs were minimal; the symbolic costs were potentially large. Willing to retreat to an income tax to prevent nationalization, the industry was not ready to adapt to its *bête-noire*, nationalization.

While State Department definitions of systemic order concerns were not as expansive as those of the industry, it could not compel companies to compromise and contract with Pemex. Its preferred outcome of a compromise contractual arrangement was effectively vetoed. This left decision makers with the alternatives of aiding Pemex and symbolically supporting a nationalized oil industry without private participation, and continuing the policy of containing nationalization. Given that the safety of foreign investment in the LDCs was considered a vital component of national security, state actors opted for the latter. Just as the state's refusal to intervene compelled a corporate redefinition of interest in Venezuela, the oil industry's refusal to compromise redefined State Department preferences on the issue of lending to Pemex.

Conclusion

The Latin American investment disputes of the 1930s and 1940s posed for the United States the question of whether overseas investment could continue to operate in an environment of economic nationalism. The Good Neighbor Policy abjured coercive policies and saw accommodation with nationalism as the best means for legitimizing U.S. hemispheric interests. In line with that reasoning, Bolivia's takeover of Standard Oil was treated as an indigenous phenomenon to be dealt with in Bolivian terms, not, as the company wanted, as a precedent to be suppressed. The State Department, despite oil company protests, pursued a neutral role and encouraged both sides to compromise.

Mexico's subsequent expropriation of its foreign oil industry called these assumptions into question and sparked a bureaucratic debate over the best method to ensure foreign investment in Latin America. Hull moved toward oil company definitions of interest by responding to the act as a threat to a liberal economic order. To deter future assaults on the sanctity of property, it was necessary to establish regime rules and economic sanctions for enforcement. Nationalization cases were no longer dealt with on their own merits, but for their symbolic value in a global context. Daniels and Morgenthau, on the other hand, eschewed sanctions and pressed for compromise with principle. The "colonial" mentality of business and the use of economic sanction were more likely to subvert the investment climate than any expropriatory precedent. Due to low-level presidential involvement, policy represented a disjointed compromise between a policy of sanction and one of negotiation.

The coming of World War II compelled State to subordinate investment protection to more urgent foreign policy aims and abandon its modest policy of pressure. Given the potency of nationalism, pressure produced not only stalemate; it threatened U.S. security interests by estranging and weakening relatively friendly regimes. While the companies preferred such an outcome to a compromise with principle, the government gradually came to view the risks of the weakening of the hemispheric relationships and possible German encroachments more pressing than tenuous regime considerations.

The final compensation settlements ran counter to the articulated interests of investors and, moreover, were funded by the U.S. Treasury. Krasner is correct when he argues that "despite the clearcut threat these nationalizations posed to American corporations, the official policy of the United States can only be explained by foreign policy concerns."[98] It took the imminence of global war, however, for American foreign policy to decisively make that choice.

Krasner's argument also explains the lessons drawn from Mexico as applied to Venezuela.[99] The Mexican expropriation was seen, in part, as a function of intransigent corporate policies. it could be avoided through prudent compromise. Some retreat from the absolute sanctity of contract was necessary to legitimize foreign investment. Therefore, the State Department pressed the oil industry to accept changes that enabled Venezuela to impose the precedent of an income tax. Through the state's refusal to subordinate this view to corporate preferences, the oil companies were induced to adopt a more flexible strategy.

In the case of lending to Pemex, state preferences were limited and constrained by corporate strategy. The U.S. government refused to lend to Pemex in order to induce Mexico to readmit the companies on a contractual basis. The objective was to maintain the parameters of a loosened regime which accepted nationalization with compensation and a contractual relationship with the former owners. Mexico, for its part, was not averse to private participation in a controlled environment. Nonetheless, the international oil companies, for fear of conferring upon the Mexican nationalization an image of success, refused to go in on such terms. To compro-

mise with Venezuela on an income tax was one thing; to do
so with Mexico on ownership was quite another. While state
actors did not have as expansive a definition of regime maintenance as did the oil industry, they could not compel corporate adaptation. This constrained perceived choices and
pushed public decision makers into the companies' corner.

5.

Redefining
the Parameters in the 1950s:
Oil in Saudi Arabia and Iran

With the coming of the post–World War II era,
American decision makers embraced a global definition of
national interest. The experience of the interwar years generated a belief in internationalism and collective security.
Peace was indivisible and aggression (defined as Soviet expansionism) had to be contained. America's first line of defense was moving further from its borders.

National security was also defined economically. The
1930s informed decision makers that closed economic blocs
worsened the Depression and fueled political rivalry and war.
An open multilateral system of free trade and convertible
currencies would eliminate conflict by maximizing world
product and assuring equal access to all. It would, no doubt,
assist American domestic prosperity by opening up trade and
investment opportunities. But it would also serve American
security interests by economically strengthening allies, making them more resistant to revolution or Soviet influence.

American foreign policy aimed not only at freeing world trade, but at stimulating foreign investment. Given its hegemonic political and economic position, the United States could now implement its vision of the "open door" on a global scale. Liberal economic regimes supporting free trade and currency convertibility worked to break down mercantilist enclaves and give foreign investors the predictability they needed to develop the lowest-cost sources of supply regardless of national borders. Such an order became an integral part of decision makers' definition of national security, providing an adequate resource base for domestic prosperity and military preparedness, inexpensive raw materials for the reconstruction of Western Europe and Japan, and export revenues for economic development in the Third World.

While the United States succeeded in creating regimes that promoted foreign investment, the immediate postwar environment posed a number of serious problems for the maintenance of a regime protecting those investments. The new Communist governments in Eastern Europe and China expropriated all foreign-owned property, forswearing any obligation to repay the former owners. The Mexican and Bolivian nationalizations, having gone unpunished, were feared as harbingers of future assaults on the traditional system. In other developing countries, there was a growing trend toward increasing the economic responsibilities of states, legitimizing more extensive public regulation and ownership of industry. Compounding these fears, LDCs, in the United Nations and other international organizations, proclaimed economic self-determination as a corollary to political independence and constantly maintained the prerogatives of sovereignty over those of property.[1]

To stem these challenges, the United States supported the protection of contractual rights embodied in the Hull Doctrine. But the Mexican precedent taught decision makers that the absolute sanctity of contract was no longer a tenable objective. It had already accepted nationalization with minimal compensation in Mexico and Bolivia and contractual change in Venezuela. A more feasible goal was to redefine the regime within more defensible parameters. Expropriatory precedents indicated that corporate intransigence to demands for increased host country benefits expedited the trend toward expropriation. Prudent changes that did not affect corporate ownership and control were necessary to legitimize the concession system. When expropriation did occur, the United States, referring to its Mexican and Bolivian experience, did not believe that it could be overturned by economic coercion. It would nonetheless intercede diplomatically with quiet pressure to ensure the payment of reasonably "adequate" compensation and a contractual post-expropriation relationship between firm and host.

Overseas investors, however, adopted a more expansive view of regime requirements, preferring stronger opposition to nationalization and unilateral contractual change. The limits and possibilities of state actors in redirecting corporate strategy toward its priorities are revealed in the first non-Communist challenges to the postwar international property order: Saudi Arabia's demand to renegotiate the Aramco concession along the lines of a 50 percent income tax, and Iran's nationalization of the Anglo-Iranian Oil Company.

Both cases demonstrate how the mutual dependence between business and government in the international sphere cuts both ways. Initial state preferences in the Saudi and Iranian cases differed from those of the oil companies. Along the lines of the statist model, the U.S. government displayed considerable reticence in applying pressure for fear of undermining or alienating non-Communist nationalist regimes. In the Saudi case, the state's refusal to offer decisively left Aramco few options other than accommodation.

But the state could not compel the oil companies to continue to invest. Nor could it easily prevent the "seven sisters" from their boycott of Iranian crude. Since continued oil development in the Middle East was equated with national economic security, the form of adaptation in Saudi Arabia, i.e., the foreign tax credit, reflected the state's perceived need to "indulge" corporate preferences. Since the industry's strategy of starving Mossadegh into submission contributed to serious social instability in Iran, the choices facing public decision makers were redefined, i.e., intervention or a situation which might portend a Soviet gain. In both cases, the importance of the oil industry for national economic security, and severe political consequences of private economic strategies, served as limiting factors on U.S. government autonomy.

Accommodation in Saudi Arabia: The Fifty-Fifty Formula

Influenced by the recent success of accommodation in Venezuela, juxtaposed against the Mexican experience, the State Department, in 1950, pressed Aramco to accept changes in its concession with Saudi Arabia to give the latter a greater share of the operation's benefits. The result was a loosening of regime rules protecting the sanctity of contract. This cost was balanced against the interest in the maintenance of the stability of King Ibn Saud's government and the legitimation of Aramco ownership and operation of the concession.

The state's refusal to intercede on behalf of Aramco succeeded in influencing corporate strategy toward compromise. But while the U.S. government could withhold support for corporate resistance, it could not compel specific corporate actions. Given the role that the international oil companies played in the U.S. government's definition of national security, the mode of accommodation—the fifty-fifty income tax formula accompanied by a foreign tax credit in which the U.S. Treasury covered the increased payments—was a function of corporate preferences.

BACKGROUND

The 1933 Aramco concession was typical of the era in which it was granted. The companies received a sixty-year grant of exclusive exploration rights over 50 percent of the country and preferential rights over another 30 percent. In return, the Saudi government received a 12 percent royalty. Stabilization clauses exempted the company from all direct and indirect taxes on income.[2]

The Saudis became increasingly dissatisfied with the modest royalty as output and earnings began to soar. In the late 1940s, they pressed the company for contractual changes providing revenue on the basis of income and profit. Moreover, the 1933 concession compared unfavorably with the fifty-fifty Venezuelan deal in 1948 and a comparable deal with Pacific Western in the Neutral Zone. King Ibn Saud consequently demanded changes in the concession and warned of a possible shutdown if revenues were not increased.[3]

Aramco, for its part, was reluctant to increase payments. If it agreed to Saudi demands, Aramco oil, it was reasoned, would not be competitive with other sources in the Middle East. The company was also wary of renegotiating its contract for regime considerations. The inviolability of contracts had not been broached elsewhere in the Persian Gulf. Acceptance of Saudi demands could have serious implications for its global position. Nonetheless, the company decided to negotiate with the Saudis.[4]

UNITED STATES POLICY

American policy makers saw significant immediate and long-term interests involved in the negotiations. There was concern for the effect of what, in the 1970s, would be termed "leapfrogging," on the regime. Acheson wrote:

Revision contemplated by [the] SAG c[ou]ld be expected to have obvious repercussions on other contracts in [the] area, particularly since [the] key issue appears to be Saudi Arab demand for [an] income tax for which [the] co[mpany] might obtain [a] US Treas[ury] tax credit. No N[ear] E[astern] concessionaire now pays local income taxes.[5]

It was acknowledged that a cost of accommodation would be the weakening of principle implicit in the unilaterally imposed change of the financial provisions of contracts.

Long-term regime considerations, however, were overshadowed by immediate threats to American interests in the absence of a settlement. The political and economic stability of conservative Middle East governments and the progressive development of their oil concessions had become crucial elements in America's expanded definition of national security. A confrontation and prolonged stalemate posed serious threats to those interests. Conversely, large-scale assistance to Ibn Saud in the form of increased payments from Aramco could support them. Decision makers were further pushed toward accommodation because they believed that they could not effectively oppose Saudi demands, and acquiescence would still leave the concession in American hands.

Official policy was summarized and justified in a memorandum prepared by Richard Funkhouser on September 18, 1950. While the precedent of an income tax was a significant consideration, he wrote, it paled before the immediate costs of confrontation. Middle Eastern, particularly Saudi, oil was vital to the maintenance of the economic and political stability of Western Europe. A confrontation and subsequent disruption of supply constituted a serious threat to national security. In addition, the Saudi government was internally vulnerable to communist propaganda because of local social inequities. Resistance to Saudi demands could only assist the "sources of Communism" in the Persian Gulf states by undermining their economies and projecting an image of Western imperialism.[6]

Funkhouser offered a prescient analysis of how resisting contractual changes ran against the secular trends in
investor/host country relations; "This movement toward increased national benefit and national control is ubiquitous."
Like the history of labor agreements as unions increased their
clout, "contracts do not stand up or satisfy oil producing states
indefinitely." To "hold the line" and resist, as happened in
Mexico, would only allow "the process to become more accelerated and explosive."[7] To survive, the companies must adapt
and change the financial provisions of concessions to provide
a more equitable sharing of the profits.

Aramco's adaptation would serve important American political and economic interests. First, it would preserve
and consolidate Aramco's ownership of the concession and
maintain a secure supply of petroleum. Second, it would contribute to the political and economic stability of Saudi Arabia
by giving it a larger share of the benefits. Local dissatisfaction with oil company operations would be removed, and the
ability of Middle Eastern allies to resist communism and anti-
Western radicalism would be proportionately increased:
"Economic progress, political stability, and Western orientation within the area were all critical to the containment of
communism and the oil companies are well positioned to contribute to this objective."[8]

While supporting increased revenue for Saudi Arabia, Funkhouser was ambivalent about the form preferred by
Aramco—an income tax to be offset by a foreign tax credit.
This option, he argued, should not be "actively pushed" because it would shift revenue away from the U.S. Treasury to
subsidize the company position. He predicted that such a payment provision would give the companies more of an incentive to "retreat" as they came to identify their interests increasingly with the host country.[9]

The preferred mode of adaptation was corporate relinquishment of those concessionary areas in which there was
no planned development in the foreseeable future. Aramco's

exclusive rights over Saudi exploration were considered inequitable:

> Both [the Iraq Petroleum Company] and Aramco concessions are approximately the size of the whole mid-Continental region and contain as much oil. Although the analogy is imperfect, to have the Texas-Oklahoma-Louisiana oil fields controlled by one company would have obvious disadvantages.

The Saudi government could increase its revenue from oil not only through increased royalties, but through increased production from opening up unexplored areas to other private oil companies.[10]

The State Department accepted the rationales and recommendations of the Funkhouser memorandum. As Assistant Secretary of State George McGhee summarized:

> From the standpoint of the stability of the regimes in the area and the security of the Middle East as a whole, the continued ownership of our oil concessions, and the ability to exploit them, the government of Saudi Arabia [should] receive an increased oil income.[11]

The immediate interests involved, especially in light of the Korean War and the logic of globalized containment, were more salient than long-term regime considerations. Saudi demands, moreover, did not challenge corporate ownership or control. The decision was made to invite the company executives to the State Department and urge them to stabilize the situation by satisfying Saudi demands for revising the concession.

On November 2, the Saudi government enacted a 20 percent income tax on Aramco—a technical violation of the terms of the 1933 concession. The companies were uncertain about their response. On November 6 and 13, representatives of Aramco and its affiliate companies met with McGhee and Funkhouser to coordinate strategy.

McGhee conceded the costs to contractual principles, but argued that the Saudis had a strong case.

[W]hile true as a basic proposition, that the United States Government must be concerned with the non-impairment of valid contracts, the government must recognize that long-duration contracts by their very nature result in inequities which cannot be approved by the Government and which should be removed by adjustments to changing circumstances.[12]

A strategy of deterrence was not feasible because the U.S. government was limited in what it could do and the Saudi demands were of "a scale that would remove the possibility of preventing strong reverbrations elsewhere throughout the Near East concessionary system." Most important, the proposed changes did not "threaten the ability of the companies to operate."[13] In the interest of equity and the legitimation of the concession, there was no compelling reason to resist the revision of the concession.

Some representatives from the Aramco companies were concerned about principle and precedent. R. G. Follis, the president of Standard Oil of California, argued that the Saudi action was

in direct violation of the contractual terms and left the company with the choice of either virtually tearing up their concession or standing on it. Such arbitrary unilateral action would create a precedent which struck at the very heart of all company contracts throughout the world.[14]

The contract was valid and should be respected.

McGhee responded that it was "extremely doubtful just what the Department could usefully do." Given the realities of the situation, there was "a practical need for horse-trading."[15] In effect, State redefined the regime pragmatically to more defensible parameters. Through its unwillingness to risk the costs of diplomatic protection, the companies were convinced of the necessity for retreat.

The form of adaptation, however, was conditioned by oil company preferences. Funkhouser's proposal to offer "relinquishment" to the Saudis was rejected by the companies. Aramco officials feared that such an outcome would increase competition and undermine the industry's oligopoly structure. Aramco's preferred line of retreat was an income tax, accompanied by a foreign tax credit.[16] Unhappy with the effect of such an outcome on the U.S. Treasury, but persuaded by the importance of maintaining the concession and its inability to dictate corporate strategy, State assented to Aramco's preference.

On November 28, Aramco began negotiations with the Saudi government. On December 30, an agreement was reached wherein Aramco would pay "an income tax of 50 percent of net operating costs." Other Middle Eastern governments followed suit shortly thereafter.[17]

Despite the loosening of international contractual rights, Aramco believed the settlement consolidated its position in Saudi Arabia. "With its 50/50 slogan, it is attractive alike to governments and to the public. Its central idea can be easily understood by the man in the street and it makes an immediate appeal as something essentially reasonable and fair."[18] The Internal Revenue Service decided favorably on the foreign tax credit and allowed the taxes paid by the companies to be written off against American tax liabilities. This eased the oil industry's change from a royalty-based system to an income-based one by transferring the additional cost to the U.S. Treasury. As a consquence, Saudi income from Aramco increased for $60 million in 1950 to $110 million in 1951. Aramco's taxes to the United States decreased from $50 million in 1950 to $6 million in 1951. In 1952, its liability was under $1 million and was completely offset thereafter.[19]

CONCLUSION

The contention that the preferences of central decision makers were critical in defining the utility function of private executives explains an important part of the picture.[20] State actors were more sensitive to the dynamics of nationalism and the need for corporate activity to adapt. Per-

ceiving Mexico and Venezuela as precedents, Funkhouser
wrote that producer country demands for contractual changes
were "rational" and not just a "scheme by local radicals to
kill the goose that lays the golden eggs."[21] They were also,
like decolonization, inevitable: "Concession contracts, like the
British Empire, will undergo surprise attacks and crises, and
like the British Empire, probably cannot be protected by guns
and governments but only by enlightened thought, understanding, and compromise."[22] The State Department decided
that maintaining the stability of the Saudi government and
the short-term supply of oil was more important than a modest (and inevitable) loosening of regime rules. By refusing to
support an intransigent bargaining position, it induced corporate strategy to serve its definition of national security.

There are limits, however, to the role of state preferences in swaying corporate aims, and hence limits to the
autonomy of public policy. The United States is not a command economy; policy goals often depend upon the autonomous behavior of private economic actors. While state actors
can shape corporate strategy through their "negative" power
to withhold support, the reverse process is also true. Since
the flow of foreign investment to the developing world, especially for oil in the Middle East, is defined as an important
component of national security policy, American diplomacy,
often against its initial preferences, is pushed into the companies' corner. While a pure statist model predicts the fact
of adaptation as a function of the dominance of state objectives, it underestimates the rationales and pressures for government solicitation of business.[23] Since the state could not
"positively" influence corporate policy, the scope and mode of
adaptation was largely influenced by corporate preferences.

State's decision to acquiesce to the fifty-fifty principle and the foreign tax credit provides a case in point. State
actors preferred relinquishment proposals to the tax credit
because the latter imposed an added cost to the U.S. Treasury. Aramco, on the other hand, saw relinquishment as a

threat to market concentration and preferred an arrangement that spared them the burden of increased costs. The U.S. government could limit some corporate options, but could not dictate negotiating strategy. Rejection of the foreign tax credit could have resulted in either a parent/host confrontation or decreased production of Saudi oil. The effect of these outcomes on Cold War calculations convinced decision makers to redefine their preferences and identify Aramco's priorities with those of the state.

In the longer term, State Department officials such as Funkhouser and McGhee saw an irreversible trend toward greater host country control. In an insightful analysis of the obsolescing bargain process, Funkhouser, in 1953, wrote:

> The equation may be that the nationalization date equals X (time for the present generation to develop Arab oil experts), plus Y (completion of large investments and installations needed to produce in quantity), plus Z (a hardheaded bargaining position on the part of oil company management.) Z is a dangerous variable, Y is probably here, and X is moving along fast.

Nationalization, moreover, may not be a crucial threat to United States interests: "The same oil may be available to the same countries and to the same oil companies at the same price." Sound corporate strategy should anticipate change "to make the retreat as beneficial and orderly as possible."[24] Funkhouser suggested that oil companies might consider changes from traditional ownership such as operation through management contracts.

Under the American political system, however, the government could not impose its long view of investment security on the activities of MNCs. Since foreign investment had become an integral part of national security, the United States was often compelled to support short-sighted rearguard corporate actions born of obstinacy. Nowhere was this process more evident than in United States policy toward Iran's seizure of the Anglo-Iranian Oil Company.

Nationalization in Iran

When Iran nationalized the Anglo-Iranian Oil Company (AIOC), an affiliate of British Petroleum (BP), the initial United States reaction was conciliatory. Drawing inferences from the lessons of the late 1930s in South America and 1950 in Saudi Arabia, the United States attributed the Iranian action, at least in part, to the inflexible bargaining position of AIOC. Urging Iran to accept an obligation for compensation, it also advised the British to compromise with principle and accept nationalization and a contractual relationship in its aftermath. This conformed to the "learned" view that accommodation with nationalism was necessary to avoid nationalization and, if nationalization should occur, compensation should be demanded and a continued corporate presence should be ensured.

BP, with the complicity of Great Britain and the other major oil companies, adhered to a tighter definition of regime rules. The Iranian action was a threat to BP's other oil holdings and had to be punished to minimize externalities. BP refused to negotiate and sought to coerce restitution through a concerted boycott of Iranian oil. The unwillingness of AIOC and the "seven sisters" to compromise redefined the situation facing the U.S. government. Public decision makers were eventually pushed into the companies' corner. They faced a disintegrating economic and political situation in Iran, and feared that a lingering dispute might have ramifications elsewhere in the Near East. While the decision to overthrow Mossadegh was ostensibly motivated by Cold War "political" considerations, the situation with which the United States was confronted was a function of the more expansive regime considerations of the international oil industry.

BACKGROUND

During the 1940s, the Iranian government pressed for a renegotiation of its 1933 concession with AIOC. The government's main complaints were low royalty rates, the lack of indigenization of the company's work force, and the absence of any participation in the management of the company, including the right to see its books. Moreover, the company's policy of limiting the distribution of dividends to build up its general reserve piqued Iran because dividends, as well as tonnage, were the basis for royalties. AIOC management consistently rejected these demands, citing stabilization clauses in which Iran abnegated its right to taxation.[25]

In 1948, AIOC relented to the point of opening negotiations with Iran to discuss methods for increasing royalty payments. On May 14, 1949, an agreement was reached in which the royalty payment was increased by four to six shillings per ton.[26] Before the agreement was presented to Iran's parliament, the Majlis, the fifty-fifty formula had already been accepted in the Neutral Zone and Saudi Arabia. Iran's Prime Minister pleaded for comparable terms. AIOC refused to consider any change in the 1949 agreement, resting squarely on the principle that once an agreement had been reached, it was inviolate. To act otherwise, the company asserted, would only encourage more Iranian demands and set a precedent undermining the validity of all agreements.[27]

In February 1951, the Majlis rejected the agreement on the recommendation of an eighteen-man commission headed by Dr. Mohammed Mossadegh. On March 15, the Majlis, on Mossadegh's recommendation, passed the enabling legislation authorizing nationalization. AIOC then declared its willingness to consider renegotiation, but it was too late. On April 28, Mossadegh was appointed Prime Minister and nationalization became effective on May 1. All of AIOC's fixed assets were transferred to a newly formed state company. Mossadegh acknowledged the obligation to pay some unspecified level of compensation, but rejected arbitration as a violation of Iran's sovereignty.[28]

AIOC rested its case squarely on the issue of principle. Iran had signed a business contract which it had a duty to uphold regardless of the terms. While the company had accepted voluntary changes in the interests of equity (though only after the Majlis proposed nationalization), unilateral action of the kind pursued by Iran established a dangerous precedent.

The company urged a policy of economic reprisal against Iran. AIOC halted all payments to the Iranian Treasury, stopped tanker shipments, and withdrew its British staff. More importantly, it implemented a worldwide boycott of Iranian oil, threatening prospective buyers with legal action. The objective was to coerce Iran into rescission (or topple Mossadegh in favor of a more pliable government) by undermining its financial position. If this action resulted in the loss of BP's Iranian holdings, this was preferable to acceptance of the principle of nationalization.[29]

The major international oil companies, in supporting BP's strategy, closed ranks in boycotting Iranian crude. As Standard Oil's president Howard Page told the Church Committee, "a corporation with its concessions in countries around the world is very unlikely to purchase oil from nationalized concessions of another company in fear of setting a precedent which might redound upon it."[30] Concomitant with the refusal to market Iranian oil, production was increased in Saudi Arabia, Kuwait, and Iraq to make up the difference. As a result, Iranian oil revenue decreased from $400 million for the year in 1950 to $2 million for the two years between July 1951 and August 1953.[31]

The British government, with a 51 percent interest in AIOC, gave its full support to the company position. Britain, unlike the United States, denied a host country's right to expropriation, even with compensation. It took exception to State Department "pragmatists" who, in Mexico and Venezuela, "consider[ed] no price too high to obtain long-term peace." Foreign Secretary Herbert Morrison emphasized that the essential point in the AIOC controversy was "the wrong done if a sovereign State breaks a contract which it deliberately has made."[32] Acceptance of the unilateral termination of a contract jeopardized foreign investments everywhere. The British refused to recognize the nationalization and insisted on restitution or the submission of the case to the International Court of Justice.

INITIAL U.S. POLICY: ACCOMMODATION AND THE STRADDLING OF OBJECTIVES

Events in Iran placed American policymakers in the dilemma of having to choose between seemingly irreconcilable interests. On the one hand, they recognized the fairness and inevitability of Iranian demands for change and were fearful that sanctions would facilitate Soviet penetration. On the other hand, they were concerned about the future of the oil industry and the consequence of nationalization for other overseas interests. Further, Britain was seen as their primary ally in Europe. Therefore, they devised a compromise formula straddling these objectives to move both parties away from polarized positions. NSC 107/2, approved by President Truman on June 17, 1951, recognized both "the rights of sovereign states to control their natural resources and the importance [the United States] attach[es] to international contractual relationships."[33]

The implications of the Iranian action on the property regime were considered. A State Department study written on June 28 stated:

It is very likely that present developments in Iran will be watched very closely by all governments in the area as a test case indicating to what extent a local government can repudiate a contract without risking forceful intervention on the part of the concessionaire's government.[34]

To offset the precedent of confiscation, State insisted that Mossadegh recognize AIOC's contractual rights and pay compensation. But even with compensation, the Iranian nationalization could have adverse international effects: "When higher benefits are paid to one government, the other governments usually demand equal treatment."[35] Any increase in benefits beyond the Saudi formula could undermine the recently negotiated fifty-fifty accord.

While the United States exhorted Mossadegh to accept the principle of compensation, it distanced itself from Britain's refusal to recognize the nationalization and was ambivalent about economic sanctions. In fact, its initial orientation was more sympathetic to Iran. A CIA study attributed the nationalization to "the unyielding attitude on the part of the British."[36] The experience in Mexico colored an official view that adjustment was necessary to forestall nationalization. In 1950, Acheson observed that AIOC would have had to pay more to keep its concession under the agreements prevailing at the time.[37] Later, in his memoirs, he held BP responsible for its own predicament, one that Aramco had avoided by "graciously granting what it no longer had the power to withhold."[38]

The State Department recognized that "the principle of nationalization must be carried out in fact."[39] The belief that nationalization could not be bludgeoned away grew out of the Mexican precedent. Iranian government prestige and popular sentiment were so heavily committed to the issue that retreat was politically impossible. Drawing a parallel to Mexico's attitude toward Standard Oil, Funkhouser observed that "AIOC and the British are genuinely hated in Iran; approval of AIOC is treated as political suicide."[40] A settlement had to square with local opinion; a return to the status quo ante was impossible.

The State Department was under no illusion that the Hull Doctrine could be fully implemented in such circumstances. Acheson noted that the call for "prompt, adequate, and effective compensation" was "only an introduction to a long negotiation . . . the defendant was usually without cash or transferable property on which to levy. If paid at all, it would have to be out of earnings from oil fields and properties."[41] The Mexican experience taught that some relaxation of regime rules was necessary to reach a *modus vivendi*.

The potential concrete costs of a confrontational approach also pushed the United States toward accommodation. A State Department study asserted that America's core objective in the dispute was "the maintenance of Iran as an independent country aligned with the free world."[42] Mossadegh's National Front Party was initially perceived favorably by American policymakers. The Prime Minister was seen as an Iranian nationalist who had played a leading role in cancelling the Soviet Union's 1947 concession. His ability to end corruption and implement land reform was compared favorably with that of the Shah.[43]

The AIOC dispute raised the specter of economic chaos, a Tudeh (Communist) Party coup, or Teheran's realignment with the Soviet Union. Accommodation was necessary because Iranian "nationalism, untainted by communism, was the best bulwark against Soviet encroachment."[44]

United States officials were ambivalent about U.K. and oil company sanctions. Given the weak state of the British and other European economies, a long-drawn-out confrontation threatened short-term energy supplies and the viability of the Marshall Plan. Moreover, it increased "the possibility that Iran would turn to the Soviet Union for technical assistance and increase the danger of Soviet satellization." Further, the prospect of undermining Mossadegh and replacing him with a more compliant successor seemed unlikely because Mossadegh was still very much in control, and the most probable alternatives to Mossadegh were either the Tudeh Party or xenophobic nationalists like the Ayatollah Kashani.[45] The concrete risks of a fight over principle appeared to be too great.

As a result, the United States tried to broker a settlement, urging Iran to accept an obligation to compensate, and AIOC to accept nationalization and management contracts. During the impasse, American economic policies reflected this ambivalence. On the one hand, American aid to Iran, under the Point Four Program, was increased from $1.4 million in 1951 to $23.5 million in 1952, primarily providing urban and agricultural services. The purpose of this aid increase was to provide foreign exchange, made scarce by the oil boycott, so as to provide services necessary to minimize local instability.[46]

On the other hand, despite ambivalence toward the boycott, the United States did nothing to prevent it. In fact, it abetted industry strategy by dissuading independent oil companies from buying Iranian crude and refusing to extend loans to assist the oil industry.[47] The reason for this apparent contradiction is that the United States was still concerned with the implications of the Iranian actions on the regime. If Mossadegh were successful in exporting oil and prospering after the company boycott, one official testified, it would "endanger the rights of everybody in the world."[48] Complete normalization could only be preceded by a negotiated compromise.

American efforts to mediate such a compromise, however, failed. In July 1951, Acheson sent Averell Harriman to Iran as a conduit between AIOC and Mossadegh. Harriman's proposed compromise formula was for Britain to accept nationalization and Iran to pay compensation and contract with AIOC for marketing and technical services. Mossadegh told Harriman that he agreed to retain the original AIOC staff on an individual contractual basis and offered compensation based upon the quoted (book) value of shares. Oil, he assured, would still be sold to the United Kingdom at prevailing international prices. Harriman himself was convinced that Britain's soundest policy was to accept nationalization and negotiate favorable contractual and compensation accords.[49]

The British and AIOC, however, refused to agree to a settlement that did not challenge the validity of the 1951 nationalization decree. At the very least, they argued, the validity of nationalization should be decided by international arbitration. But British attempts to have the case heard before the International Court of Justice and the United Nations Security Council were rejected for lack of jurisdiction. In the absence of an agreement on its terms, the U.K. tightened the economic pressure.[50]

It was not until June 1952 that the British and AIOC agreed to the fait accompli of nationalization and moved toward the long-term solution of management contracts.[51] By then, however, the damage was almost irreparable; compromise had come too late, rendering it politically unacceptable in Iran. Moreover, the situation in Iran had deteriorated to the point that it precipitated a rethinking of U.S. policy.

UNITED STATES POLICY:
THE MOVE TOWARD A HARD LINE

In late 1952, the Truman administration adopted a tougher stance toward Mossadegh, a policy transition that was consummated by Eisenhower's decision to support his overthrow. Administration officials placed the onus on Iran for the continued impasse after Mossadegh's rejection of the Truman-Churchill proposals of August 1952. These proposals represented a compromise to restore oil operations. Its components were British recognition of nationalization; submission of compensation (not the legitimacy of expropriation) to the International Court of Justice; the resumption of the flow of Iranian oil to world markets; an end to U.K. sanctions; and a $10 million loan from the United States.[52] Mossadegh rejected these proposals, decrying the call for arbitration as a violation of sovereignty.

The administration became increasingly convinced that no settlement was possible as long as Mossadegh was Prime Minister. Acheson regretfully concluded of Mossadegh that "the passions he excited to support him restricted his freedom of choice and left only extreme options possible."[53]

There was also increased trepidation about the effect

of the prolonged dispute on the political situation in Iran. Whereas earlier studies found Mossadegh to be in complete control, NSC 136/1 (November 20, 1952) opined that the present trends were unfavorable to the maintenance of control by a non-communist regime for an extended period of time.[54] The inability to reach a settlement, which was now blamed exclusively on Mossadegh, made more imminent a Tudeh assumption of power or a cozying up to the Russians. American aid was viewed as insufficient, in the absence of a resumption of oil exports, to maintain Iran's staggering economy.

Concern was heightened when Mossadegh declared a national emergency and assumed dictatorial powers in January 1953. A State Department study warned of a "trend toward an authoritarian, socialistic state." Moreover, the State Department's Office of Intelligence and Research reported that two members of Mossadegh's cabinet had Tudeh affiliations. Ambassador Loy Henderson characterized Mossadegh as "naive on the subject of communism."[55]

The new Eisenhower administration, less tolerant to Third World nationalism, pushed for a harder line. Truman and Acheson were convinced from the Mexican, Venezuelan, and Saudi Arabian cases that economic changes were inevitable and the task of American diplomacy was to direct them into channels consistent with national interests. Eisenhower and Dulles looked more skeptically on reformist nationalism as a disruptor of stability and a precursor of communism.[56] Eisenhower wrote to Churchill that genuine nationalists "will soon find out that we are their friends and that they can't live without us."[57] It then is self-evident that those who nationalize Western oil companies and try to "live without us" are not genuine nationalists, but misguided demagogues or worse.

One last attempt was made to settle the dispute in early 1953. The British accepted a compromise formula in which AIOC would be paid out of oil revenues over a time span of twenty years. After initial optimism, the talks broke down on March 20 over valuation of the properties. Mossadegh refused to consider AIOC's loss of business as a result of the nationalization a legitimate claim.[58]

Mossadegh, to bolster his deteriorating position, appealed to Eisenhower for more assistance on May 28. He cited the necessity of aid to alleviate Iran's financial hardship and arrest the trend toward economic and political chaos. Implied in his message was a warning that the alternative to American assistance was communism.[59]

Eisenhower's negative reply to Mossadegh on June 29 signaled the abandonment of the policy of mediation. The solution to Iran's economic problems, he told the Prime Minister, was to meet its international obligations to "strengthen the confidence throughout the world in the determination that Iran fully adheres to the principles which render possible a harmonious community of free nations." It would be unfair to lend to Iran, he added, "so long as Iran could have access to funds derived from the sale of oil." He went further than Acheson in insisting that "reasonable" compensation comprised fair market value, not the mere price of physical assets.[60]

The decision to send Kermit Roosevelt on a covert operation to overthrow Mossadegh and promote a pro-Western alternative was actually made on June 22. Economic chaos, the CIA argued, was creating a "maturing revolutionary situation." The situation was exacerbated in July when the Soviets sent an aid mission and Mossadegh accepted Tudeh Party support. Eisenhower felt impelled to arrest what he saw as Mossadegh's "downhill course toward a communist-supported dictatorship." The relevant analogy was no longer Mexico and the need for compromise, it was China and the need to avert another loss.[61]

With the fall of Mossadegh and the return of the Shah on August 19, Eisenhower and Dulles moved to shore up the position of the new regime. It first provided a loan of $85 million. More importantly, it took the lead in restructuring Iran's oil industry to restore oil exports and build a stable

base for the new regime. As early as the Truman administration, United States officials realized the intensity of anti-
British sentiment and ruled out the restoration of full AIOC
ownership. In 1952, the United States government decided
that it was necessary to widen ownership of the concession
into a consortium which included American major and independent oil companies. The American companies were initially reluctant to join, but acceded after the Department of
Justice agreed to downgrade antitrust proceedings against the
industry. The decision was eventually implemented after the
fall of Mossadegh. In effect, it sought to assuage Iranian nationalism through preserving Iranian state ownership of the
oil fields and refineries, and through a corporate contractual
presence whose provisions were comparable to concessions
elsewhere in the Middle East.[62]

CONCLUSION

The CIA intervention against Mossadegh has been
cited by a number of radical analysts as a textbook example
of the pernicious effects of the United States trying to impose
a global "open door" for its multinational corporations. Through
its manipulations, Washington succeeded in killing two birds
with one stone. First, through "egging the Iranians on" to
nationalize, it succeeded in dislodging the British monopoly
in Iran and in carving out a 40 percent share for the American oil companies. Second, in destabilizing and toppling
Mossadegh, it responded to oil company fears about the precedent of nationalization. The strategy was not based upon
misperception. Rather, it was a stunning success in overcoming the two main barriers to a world order conducive to its
economic interests—European imperial privileges and Third
World economic nationalism.[63]
       Krasner makes a strong case in refuting this argu-
ment. He correctly observes that in its decision to intervene
against Mossadegh, "U.S. leaders were moved not by eco-

nomic considerations associated with either security of supply or the interest of private corporations, but rather their unease about the domestic political structure of the Iranian government."[64] Consistent with its core objective of keeping Iran out of the Soviet orbit, the State Department initially urged AIOC and the British toward compromise, advocating acceptance of the fact of nationalization and something less than "full" compensation. The political costs of tough regime maintenance—economic chaos in Iran or Mossadegh's realignment with the Soviet Union—exceeded its gains. The decision to intervene came not from commercial ambition, but from the perceived effect of the stalemate on Soviet penetration of Iran.

But while United States policy was not a function of obeisance to the oil industry, the choices with which it was confronted were constrained by the more expansive regime strategies of the oil multinationals. America's policies were initially ambivalent: an attempt to reconcile containment objectives with international property rules. It urged Britain and AIOC to compromise with nationalization and it increased aid to keep Iran afloat. But to avoid the appearance of condoning the precedent of state control, it made no effort to assist Iran's oil industry nor to impede the boycott. The aim was not to resolve the conflict, but to straddle contradictory objectives as a holding operation while the parties negotiated a compromise.

While state policies were ambivalent and tentative, corporate strategies were not. Nationalization was not to be accommodated, but overturned by an industry-wide boycott. Given the concentration of corporate resources, ostensibly neutral public policies to mediate a compromise supported corporate strategies by default.

While the immediate interest propelling the CIA intervention was avowedly "political" (averting a Soviet-aligned regime) and a function of state preferences, the situation that confronted state actors—the choice between intervention and chaos—was conditioned by corporate unwillingness to accept the state's looser definition of regime requirements. To avert such a stark choice, the State Department urged AIOC to adapt. AIOC and its American "sisters" refused to compromise with the principle of nationalization. Because the state could not "positively" modify the corporate strategy to starve Iran into submission, the state was eventually driven into the latter's corner.

Although state actions were aimed at politico-ideological ends, the intervention blended nicely with the oil industry's objective of deterring incursions into the regime beyond the Saudi formula. Such an outcome, they reasoned, would prove to other oil-producing countries that they could not effectively control the industry without the cooperation of the companies. Any attempt to do so would be prohibitively costly. Funkhouser, writing in 1953, thought differently:

It may be a false conclusion to consider that the Iranian catastrophe will deter others from following suit. On the contrary, it might be argued that other Middle East states (a) strongly sympathize with what they consider a courageous defiance of the West; (b) now more clearly recognize the extent to which the oil companies and Western governments can and will penalize the oil states by boycott; and (c) will consequently move carefully but more relentlessly toward breaking this "foreign control" of their countries and their resources.[65]

Time would bear out this prediction.

6.

The Decline and Rise of Investment Protection During the Alliance for Progress: Business Asserts Its Privileged Position

The oscillation in the U.S. government approach toward expropriation in the early 1960s demonstrates the influence of domestic actors in constraining and reshaping the executive initiatives. The Kennedy administration, drawing upon its reading of Castro's revolution in Cuba, promulgated the Alliance for Progress, which prescribed economic growth, social reform, and political democracy as the soundest antidotes to Latin American revolution. The strategy of insisting on a "good investment climate" and admonishing against expropriation—hallmarks of Eisenhower's development advice—was downgraded. Policies aimed solely at protecting foreign investors in an era of social ferment, it was reasoned, would only produce the kind of revolutionary situation that existed in Cuba prior to 1959. A more flexible strategy of reform and accommodation would better serve American containment objectives and legitimize the long-term security of overseas investments.

The performance of American diplomacy during the Alliance years belied its articulated goals, especially when the prerogatives of American investors collided with the objectives of social reform and political democracy. In Brazil, Argentina, and Peru, informal economic pressures on behalf of "aggrieved" companies undermined the economic base and political standing of democratic reformist governments, indirectly contributing to their replacement by military dictatorships. One critical study concluded that "during the Alliance, United States business interests, and in several cases the interests of a particular corporation, have taken precedence over the United States national interest in Latin America."[1]

The ability of the state to give operational meaning to its "lessons of Cuba" was limited by the potential non-cooperation of domestic actors whose independent actions were defined as an integral part of Alliance objectives and who drew different lessons from the Castro experience. To the business community and its supporters in Congress, Castro threatened to infect the hemisphere less with revolution and more with his example of taking over American business. Administration emphasis on social reform could only undermine the ideological foundations of private property and expand the scope for state intervention. The need was for greater, not diminished, vigilance against unwarranted interference with private property.

The Kennedy administration, to achieve the economic targets of the Alliance, needed substantial appropriations of foreign aid and increased flows of private capital to Latin America. Resurgent economic nationalism threatened not only the private interests of American investors, but these two bases of development diplomacy. First, it inhibited the flow of private capital to Latin America, placing a larger burden on the foreign assistance program. Second, Congress, under a concerted corporate lobbying effort, threatened to limit the scope and flexibility of the aid program in response to what it saw as State Department equivocation on expropriation.

Given the threat these outcomes posed to the administration's definition of national security, anti-expropriation was elevated on the Alliance agenda. The United States moved closer to corporate preferences for a more tightly policed regime. Policymakers did try to minimize the costs of such strategies through using informal rather than public pressure. Formal sanctions were only invoked once during this period—against Ceylon, a country whose minor strategic and economic importance ideally suited it to pay the costs of a symbolic demonstration of resolve. The modal response was more discreet: the exertion of pressure sufficient to obtain compliance without the kind of public arm-twisting that would make a settlement politically impossible for the host and produce collateral damage to other interests.

The Johnson administration extended this process to its logical conclusion with what became known as the Mann Doctrine. Economic growth through private capital inflows became the overriding criterion for development diplomacy. Political democracy and social reform were abandoned as core concerns because they often spawned economic nationalism and soured the investment climate. The United States government looked more favorably on conservative military dictatorships for their ability to provide internal order and make their countries attractive sites for foreign investment.

This outcome conforms most closely to Lipson's corporate preference model or Lindblom's theory that the "privileged position of business" constrains state options. The initial design of the Alliance was insufficiently "indulgent" of corporate fears of economic nationalism. In order to prevent capital flight and elicit corporate "performance," stronger investment protection strategies were seen as necessary. The end result was that initial Alliance priorities were reversed and policy implementation more closely resembled the preferences of overseas investors.

The Lessons of Cuba:
The Alliance for Progress
and the Deemphasis
of Expropriation

Under Eisenhower and Dulles, American diplomacy toward the Third World emphasized the maintenance of the status quo and the enlistment of military elites as the vehicles for containing communism. Growth and development were best served by the canons of economic orthodoxy—balanced budgets, deflationary monetary policies, and a "good climate for foreign investment." The Eisenhower administration eschewed public assistance, exhorting developing countries instead to "clean up their act" and make themselves attractive hosts for private capital. Economic nationalism, like its political counterpart, neutralism, was considered "immoral."

The 1950s was a period of relative investor tranquility with few assaults upon the prerogatives of corporate ownership. The few incidents that did occur were limited to countries such as Mossadegh's Iran and Arbenz's Guatemala that were perceived as communist or anti-American in orientation. Since it was assumed that only communists would challenge the axiom that American enterprise and values benefit the world, Arbenz's seizure of United Fruit only further confirmed his heresy.[2] The threat of widespread expropriation, however, was more hypothetical than imminent and United States policy was generally limited to sermons on the gospel of private enterprise and the sanctity of contract.

Castro's establishment of a communist regime in Cuba and his wholesale expropriation of $1.5 billion dollars in American investments was a deep psychological blow to American decision makers. The incoming Kennedy administration was initially concerned with the Cuban precedent less for its effect on American property than as a first blow in Khrushchev's call for "wars of national liberation." While Kennedy continued to quarantine and seek the overthrow of Castro, he differed from his predecessor in retreating from economic orthodoxy in a search for some common ground with Latin American economic nationalism.

Kennedy officials found fault with the Eisenhower administration for its obsession with ephemeral stability in the face of social ferment. Revolution, they believed, was a response to very real social inequities within Latin America. Change was inevitable and to "stabilize the dying reactionary situations" would only make the coming upheavals more violent and anti-American.[3] As points of evidence, recent rebellions had just swept away a number of military dictators previously hailed as champions of anti-communist stability. In a race against time, liberal reform was presented as the alternative and antidote to Castroism.

The Alliance for Progress, outlined by President Kennedy in March 1961, sought to reverse the priorities of the previous administration by offering the hand of "alliance" to Latin American nationalism. Development diplomacy was reoriented toward building stable, democratic, responsible national governments through public aid and social reform. The Alliance was designed to recast the image of the United States from an advocate of the status quo and oligarchic privilege to a supporter of reform and democracy. This would prevent communism from exploiting the misery of the "have-nots" and "divorce the inevitable and necessary Latin American social transformation from connection with . . . overseas communist power politics."[4] Kennedy summed up this sentiment declaring that "those who make peaceful revolution impossible will make violent revolution inevitable."[5]

At Punta del Este, in August 1961, the United States veered away from its traditional emphasis on orthodox economic theory.[6] Kennedy promised an unprecedented level of public assistance: $20 billion over a ten-year period. Latin America's share of aid appropriations would increase from an average of 7 percent from 1946–1960 to 25 percent for fiscal year 1962.[7] The development model put forward by the "Kennedy men" stressed greater public sector guidance in the spirit of the New Deal. Balanced budgets or deflationary policies should not be pursued at the expense of infrastructure improvements or redistributive justice. Arthur Schlesinger, a key Kennedy advisor on Latin America, reasoned that "if the criteria of the International Monetary Fund had governed the United States in the nineteenth century, our own economic development would have taken a good deal longer."[8]

Social reform and political democracy were also touted as core objectives of the Alliance. Participatory institutions, the soundest bulwark against revolution, required steady economic growth and a citizenry enfranchised in the benefits of the system. An entrenched oligarchy clinging to its privileged position was a roadblock to economic modernization and a source of political instability. Inequitable social structures, such as traditional systems of land tenure, must be reformed.[9] These aims implied an activist role for the state vis-à-vis vested economic interests.

The Alliance also distanced itself from what Schlesinger called "the theory of economic development as an act of immaculate private conception."[10] The maintenance of a "good climate for foreign investment" was no longer the sole criterion for development. Changing inequitable social structures took precedence over a near-term insistence on laissez-faire and the "open door." American political and economic interests were compatible with a wide variety of relationships between private enterprise and the state. In line with this reasoning, Kennedy ended the long-standing policy against Eximbank loans to state companies.[11]

Another reason for the demotion of the foreign investment issue at Punta del Este was Latin American sensitivities. A memorandum to Kennedy from a group of prominent Latin Americans warned that the Alliance was doomed if it allowed itelf to be seen as an entering wedge for American investors. Kennedy administration officials were also aware of the dominance of American capital in Cuba and the resentments against it which contributed to the rise of Castro.[12]

Although removed from its centrality and downplayed in rhetoric, foreign investment was still considered an essential ingredient for economic development under the Alliance. Private capital was necessary, Kennedy argued, "because there isn't enough public capital to do the job." Large-scale private investment was seen as the only way to diversify the single-commodity economies of Latin America. For 1962, the State Department set a goal for the private capital inflow to Latin America of $300 million.[13]

The administration's emphasis on social reform was not seen as incompatible with maintaining a hospitable environment for foreign capital. Latin American social and economic progress would provide long-term political stability, the sine qua non of a "good investment climate." In the short term, the administration assumed that business would come to terms with Latin American political pressures.[14]

Genuine revolutions, however, touch every aspect of a society, remaking its basic structures. The property rights of American investors were firmly grounded in the Latin American status quo, and any attempt to build a meaningful "alliance" required, as a first step, a direct confrontation with the legacy of U.S. government and corporate activities in the area and their bearing on the host. Ideally, such a policy would admit to many of the inequities of the concession system and accommodate Latin American attempts to redress the situation. The contradiction between supporting foreign investors and encouraging a development process that impinged on those same investors was obscured by what one scholar called "the theory of non-disruptive revolution," the notion that change can easily be achieved through pragmatic tinkering with the existing social structure.[15]

This contradiction did not go unnoticed by the business community and its allies in the Congress and the bureaucracy. Business was invited to Punta del Este only as an observer and felt excluded from the Alliance. It decried the scant reference to the role of private enterprise in the Alliance charter. Writing in *Foreign Affairs,* Emilio Collado of Standard Oil criticized United States policy because it tacitly supported "statism" and displayed "no conviction in the productive superiority of private enterprise."[16]

The overseas investment community drew different lessons from the Cuban experience. Castro's wholesale nationalization undermined the assumption that foreign investment in Latin America was generally safe. Alarmed at the trend toward increased state ownership and regulation, business feared the Cuban action as a model for emulation. It demanded protection from confiscation so that others would not follow Castro's example. The lesson drawn was that greater vigilance was needed to guarantee investors against expropriation or arbitrary intervention, a concern patently downplayed in the Alliance's initial priorities.[17]

From businessman's standpoint, the Alliance not only ignored expropriation, but abetted it by encouraging conditions that made it more likely to take place. The main impediment to Latin American growth was intensified state intervention in economic matters with "a consequent neglect of the [economic] bases on which social improvements fundamentally depend."[18] With its emphasis on social reform, American policy would open the door to populists and leftists whose radical economic experiments would lead to inflation and capital flight. The Kennedy administration's willingness to lend to state companies and aid nations that expropriate American-owned property only encouraged such economic folly.[19]

The corporate critique of the Alliance was shared by many in Congress and by the "traditionalists" at State. These groups preferred Dulles' emphasis on stability and saw social reform as disruptive to the maintenance of order. Growth and development were bulwarks against revolution, but they responded best to Latin American policies that encouraged and safeguarded foreign investment. Inter-American diplomacy should have encouraged such policies with unambiguous support for property rights.

During the early years of the Alliance, executive branch policy reflected the preferences of the "Kennedy men"—"scholars and professionals interested in inter-American relations with a personal or ideological stake in promoting democracy"—rather than the traditionalists. Kennedy gave reform a high priority, defining it as vital to the security of post-Castro Latin America. The high level of presidential attention given the issue "stacked temporarily [the bureaucratic and political process] to weight the influence of persons generally sympathetic with the Alliance's stated goals."[20]

This balance of bureaucratic forces was only temporary as powerful forces shifted it to the other side. The unwillingness of domestic actors—Congress and the business community—to cooperate presented the executive branch with the prospect that laxity on investment protection would produce a threat to the public assistance program, and capital flight from Latin America. Since decision makers cognitively related these outcomes to a failure of the Alliance, hemispheric security was ultimately redefined.

Congress and the Hickenlooper Amendment

THE CATALYST: BRAZIL AND ITT

While Cuba increased congressional concern over the expropriation issue, Brazil provided the catalyst for tougher action. On February 16, 1962, Governor Leonel Brizola of the state of Rio Grande do Sul took over a public utility affiliate of ITT. Brizola offered book value compensation of $400,000, although the company's claim was in the vicinity of $6–8 million. Brizola had, in 1959, nationalized a subsidiary of the American and Foreign Power Company (AMFORP), a case still unsettled in 1962. What distinguished the ITT case was that Brizola labeled it a first step in a national campaign by the left for the nationalization of all public utilities.

Harold Geneen, the president of ITT, immediately cabled Kennedy that there was a Cuban overtone to Brazil's action and its "specious gesture of trivial compensation." He urged Kennedy to "take an immediate personal interest in the situation" and act firmly to prevent a "chain reaction" adversely affecting the company's interests throughout Latin America.[21]

The State Department was not indifferent to this concern. It criticized the Brazilian action as "a step backwards in the mobilization of available resources for the success of the Alliance for Progress." The compensation formula was termed "so far below book value that the evaluation appears to have been made unilaterally."[22] Ambassador Lincoln Gordon was instructed to give the "fullest possible support to [the ITT] effort [to] obtain 'prompt and adequate' compensation, utilizing in this regard [the] full weight and influence [of the] USG."[23]

A preliminary settlement was reached on March 3 through the intercession of Ambassador Gordon. Brazilian President João Goulart, who did not support Governor Brizola's takeover, agreed to pay $7.3 million in compensation over twenty five years, 75 percent of which was to be reinvested in nonutility sectors within Brazil. As word of the formula leaked to the public, ambitious state governors proposed nationalization bills to state legislatures expecting that the federal government would pick up the tab. Goulart, faced with the prospect of fiscal chaos, postponed the offer.[24]

The Kennedy administration, viewing Brazil as the most important country in Latin America and a test case for the Alliance, sought accommodation. Kennedy received the Brazilian President in April for the purpose of resolving outstanding issues and building Goulart's domestic and foreign standing. At the meeting, Goulart suggested the purchase of Brazil's privately owned public utilities with compensation to be stretched out over time and reinvested in Brazil. This would allow American investors to withdraw from politically sensitive ventures, avoid a repetition of the ITT confrontation, and not deprive Brazil of foreign capital. Kennedy saw merit in the proposal and decided to work with Goulart. A $338 million aid package was subsequently released.[25]

Kennedy went on record opposing business and congressional suggestions that Alliance funds should be denied Brazil until full compensation was paid.[26] Rusk, testifying against punition, argued that Goulart did not approve of Brizola's actions and that the matter should be treated in Brazilian terms with an understanding of the political constraints under which Goulart was operating. The issue of expropriation, he concluded, required "case-by-case" improvisation, not a rigid rule of retaliation for its symbolic value.[27]

THE PASSAGE OF THE HICKENLOOPER AMENDMENT

American business has traditionally mistrusted American diplomacy as overly solicitous of other countries' sensitivities at the expense of its economic interests. The skepticism was reinforced by State's handling of the ITT dispute. The United States refused to employ economic pressure after Goulart's postponement of a settlement. Business was wary even if Goulart's compensation formula were accepted. Collado wrote that "the terms of compensation—which provide for low valuation, partial downpayment, and decades for payment of the rest—can only excite the interest of nationalistic groups in other countries."[28] The *Wall Street Journal* editorialized that the State Department policy in effect said:

"Stealing is all right, provided the government is the thief."[29]

Geneen, discouraged by the equivocal U.S. response, appealed to Senator Bourke Hickenlooper (R–Iowa) to make treatment of foreign investment a quid pro quo of aid. A widespread corporate campaign for tough anti-expropriation legislation ensued. Most visibly active were ITT, Texaco, Esso, United Fruit, Kennecott, Anaconda, Alcoa, the American Petroleum Institute, and National Foreign Trade Council, and the United States Chamber of Commerce.[30]

Corporate alarm came from a perceived confirmation of a dangerous trend set in motion by the Cuban experience. The Brazilian action and a number of serious investment disputes elsewhere triggered the fear that expropriations might escalate rapidly. Corporate decision makers adopted an economic "domino theory" in which even minor seizures threatened the entire structure of overseas property rights.[31]

Influential members of Congress shared corporate anxieties and enacted legislative sanctions. Section 620(e) of the Foreign Assistance Act of 1962, known as the Hickenlooper Amendment, mandated a suspension of aid to any expropriating state that fails to take "appropriate steps" toward the payment of full compensation.[32] In theory, the executive branch was denied any national interest waiver and was required to treat every expropriation in terms of regime considerations. That this legislation conformed to corporate preferences is evidenced by the fact that it was drafted by Monroe Leigh of Steptoe and Johnson, the law firm that represented United Fruit against agrarian reform laws in Central America.[33]

Congress shared the corporate focus on precedent and principle. Senator Hickenlooper argued that

> success in expropriation in one country would stimulate expropriation in other countries by dissident groups. The success of expropriation in Cuba and Brazil will stimulate expropriation in other countries. Now it is coming in Honduras and Panama. There

are bills in the legislatures of Chile and Peru—to do what? To seize American property.[34]

He continued that a "wave of expropriations" was overtaking the world like a "prairie fire" and, if not put out, "the sanctity and security of American investors in Latin America are done and over with."[35] All cases must therefore be addressed for their symbolic effect on international property order.

The sanctions were made mandatory so that neither the Kennedy administration nor foreign governments would discount the seriousness of congressional intent. State Department insistence on negotiating flexibility encouraged the LDCs to believe that they could use evasion, counterthreats, and prolonged negotiations to indefinitely put compensation on the back burner. Continued aid, in light of this, amounted to a "countenance of confiscation" because it allowed "Brazil and other Latin American nations to use our aid to force American firms out of business in Latin America."[36] On the other hand, by practicing what Schelling calls the "art of commitment," the United States would be saying: "There is nothing we can do about it; the law requires it."[37] By persuading LDCs that retaliation would be automatic and unalterable, deterrence would be more effective.

Congress also saw a deterrent advantage from public sanctions. Even if publicity impeded a particular settlement, it would send a message to others that a price would be paid for violating the rules. Only such an approach could contain the externalities of any particular action on a system of international property rights.

EXECUTIVE OPPOSITION TO THE HICKENLOOPER AMENDMENT

The Kennedy administration publicly opposed the Hickenlooper Amendment. Overt mandatory sanctions would render the settlement of disputes more intractable; hamper presidential flexibility; tarnish the American image and abet communist propaganda; and discourage economic development and social reform.

First, Secretary of State Rusk testified before the Senate that the administration shared its concern for investment protection. "When governments make agreements about private investment . . . they should comply with those agreements." He continued that existing diplomatic channels were the best medium to support private investors. Mandatory public sanctions would only "arouse nationalist feelings and exacerbate rather than ease the problem at issue."[38] A settlement would be less likely because host country compromise would become politically suicidal.

Second, Rusk argued that legal authorization for aid termination already existed and would be used when appropriate. A single-minded dedication to investment protection, however, may conflict with the attainment of other foreign policy goals. The Hickenlooper amendment effectively tied the hands of the executive branch, placing it at the mercy of one unrepresentative host country official (Brizola in Brazil) or one intransigent American citizen "whose actions could provoke expropriation and whose obstinacy could prevent a reasonable settlement." Presidential discretion was necessary for a "balancing of the many factors" that compose the national interest.[39]

Third, Hickenlooper sanctions were opposed for recasting the United States in an antinationalist mold. It carried the obvious implication that "our aid programs are . . . in effect, tools of American capital."[40] The principal beneficiaries would be anti-American demagogues and communist propagandists, thereby defeating one of the Alliance's primary objectives.

Finally, the provisions of the Hickenlooper Amendment were potentially inconsistent with the social reforms for which the United States promised moral and financial support at Punta del Este. Rusk was aware that American property rights were often part of the *ancien regime* and the scope for far-reaching changes was limited if full compensation was required:

> Land reform may well require expropriation of existing estates, some of which are owned by United States nationals. . . . The danger is that some Latin American governments might avoid this type of reform, even though they intend to provide fair compensation, through the fear that the United States would unilaterally determine the compensation inadequate or the procedure unfair and, hence, cut off all aid.[41]

Before acting, he continued, the United States should "reassure [itself] as to the operations, the conduct, financial structure, and other aspects of those private investors" who want protection.[42] By requiring an automatic response, the United States might be inhibiting behavior it preferred to encourage.

In sum, the State Department preferred a flexible, low-profile approach to minimize near-term costs. To congressional and corporate "hawks," obtaining a settlement, much less a compromise one, was subordinate to fidelity to regime principles. A tough response was necessary, regardless of its effect on a specific dispute in order to make an example of the target to others. To State, such a rigid definition of regime rules was unnecessary for the security of investors. Moreover, it was too costly in terms of the diplomatic aims of the Alliance. Compromises were necessary to solve the conflict and get on with diplomacy as usual.

Accommodation to the Hickenlooper Amendment

The Kennedy administration drew certain lessons from the Cuban Revolution; business and the Congress drew others. The administration gave priority to social reform and political democracy over the deterrence of expropriation. Nonetheless, in the 1960s the Hickenlooper Amendment was applied against Ceylon and informal aid sanctions were used against other countries involved in disputes with United States investors. The executive branch was effectively constrained from deemphasizing the expropriation issue because of its perceived dependence upon the independent behavior of domestic actors for development diplomacy: upon Congress, for the flexibility and scope of the aid program, and upon the business community, for its willingness to venture private capital.

THE ROLE OF CONGRESS

Congress, through its control of the foreign aid appropriations, traditionally "expresses its sense of the world and seeks to keep the State Department or administering agency responsive to its judgment of United States priorities." It often uses the power of the purse to set limits on executive branch initiatives in new directions.[43]

The Kennedy administration fell under heavy congressional criticism for its refusal to retaliate economically against Brazil over the ITT dispute. The State Department got around the mandatory provision of the law by invoking the clause that required a "Presidential determination" that "appropriate steps" toward compensation be absent in order to invoke sanctions. Senator Hickenlooper termed these "weasel words," which "leave the gate wide open for the Executive or the State Department to say that the steps were reasonable or appropriate."[44]

Frustrated by Executive branch inattention to its concerns, Congress proposed a number of additional riders to foreign assistance legislation further restricting executive branch flexibility, such as proscriptions against loans to India, Indonesia, and the United Arab Republic. With respect to expropriation, it sought to extend Hickenlooper sanctions to Public Law (P.L.) 480 (Food for Peace) funds, the Inter-American Development Bank, the Export-Import Bank, and the Peace Corps. One proposal would have terminated aid to any country that refused to sign an Investment Guaranty Treaty covering expropriation.[45] Congress pushed for further money-cutting amendments against countries that "despise our free enterprise society . . . [and] stake out insolent claims on our foreign assistance." For fiscal year 1963, the House Committee on Foreign Affairs cut the administration's aid package by $1.7 billion dollars.[46]

The amendment process threatened to torpedo the whole Alliance program. AID director David Bell informed Kennedy that proposed cuts brought appropriations "below the danger point."[47] The administration had to take a stronger stand against expropriation in order to amass political currency with Congress to obtain long-term aid commitments.

When, in 1963, Congress proposed to extend the Hickenlooper amendment to the "repudiation or nullification" of contracts, the State Department planned no opposition. Bell informed Kennedy: "We have acquiesced in the Hickenlooper Amendment. . . . We hope we can draw the line against other restrictive amendments offered from the floor."[48] Administration officials changed tactics and praised the virtues of the amendment's deterrent effect. Rusk, in 1963, testified that "our experience thus far has meant that the amendment has been a good thing."[49]

THE ROLE OF CAPITAL FLIGHT
FROM LATIN AMERICA

Although initially downplayed, private foreign investment was expected to play an important role in the Alliance program for economic development. However, a net Latin American capital inflow of $214 million in 1961 was transformed into a net capital outflow of $32 million in 1962. A Department of State study summed up the dilemma for hemispheric policy:

> The flow of private capital to Latin America has diminished and there is strong evidence of substantial capital flight. . . . Taking into account the limitations to the availability of public funds, it is clear that the objectives of the Alliance cannot be achieved without full participation of the private sector.[50]

A Commerce Department study, echoing business definitions of interest, attributed this shortfall to the deterrent effect of political and social ferment in the region:

> The political menace of communism, with massive expropriation, as was the fate of private investment in Cuba when Castro took over, and the less violent but nevertheless equally crippling takeover of American investments by local expropriation as in the case of Brazil, are obvious destroyers of business confidence.[51]

Treasury Secretary Douglas Dillon, one of the original architects of the Kennedy program opined the problem arose because "private enterprise has not always been made to feel that it is part of the Alliance."[52]

The Kennedy administration could not be indifferent to the flow of private capital because of its perceived linkage to economic development. As private capital flows lagged, it succumbed to pressures to adapt policy to corporate preferences. The virtues of an attractive climate for overseas business were extolled more frequently in Alliance rhetoric. In his 1963 foreign assistance message to Congress, Kennedy declared that the *primary* initiative of that year's program would be "efforts to encourage the investment of private capital in the underdeveloped countries."[53]

There were also substantive changes as the Alliance downgraded its emphasis on social reform, especially when it impinged on the rights of foreign investors. For example, in 1961, President Villeda Morales of Honduras enacted an agrarian reform law, based on the Venezuelan model, to redistribute uncultivated United Fruit properties to landless peasants.

United Fruit, dissatisfied with compensation in the form of long-term bonds, retaliated by withholding investment and production in Honduras, creating serious unemployment. It also pressed Congress and the State Department for assistance. Although initially reluctant, the State Department instructed the embassy to warn the Hondurans of the serious implications of their action vis-à-vis the Hickenlooper Amendment.[54] Assistant Secretary for Inter-American Affairs Edwin Martin subsequently cited the necessity of closely monitoring each nation's land reform program because "unwarranted expropriations . . . under the guise of 'land reform' can change drastically the climate for private capital and thereby still further reduce the resources upon which a country can draw."[55]

These changes were officially endorsed in March 1963 by the Clay Report, a conservative study commissioned by Kennedy to adapt to and blunt domestic criticism of the Alliance. The study highlighted the critical role of FDI in reducing the strain placed on limited public resources on the aid program. The United States was instructed to use the aid program more judiciously to foster an environment conducive to foreign investment. Kennedy's reversal of the long-standing policy against lending to state-owned enterprises was criticized as a step in the wrong direction: "Latin America must be encouraged to see its essential choice between totalitarian, inefficient state controlled economies on the one hand and an economically freer system on the other."[56] Foreign assistance should not be proffered without evidence of self-help measures, such as anti-inflation and stabilization plans and congenial rules for foreign investment—in short, a return to Eisenhower orthodoxy.[57]

This reorientation also found expression in tougher investment protection policies. Although the Hickenlooper Amendment was employed only once in the 1960s (Ceylon in

1963), the Kennedy and Johnson administrations informally tied aid more strictly to expropriation issues. The difference between Congress and the executive branch devolved to a matter of tactics rather than strategy. Bell wrote to Kennedy:

> We seek the same objectives Hickenlooper does. But formal amendments of this type may arouse nationalistic feelings and exacerbate rather than ease the problem at hand. . . . Working quietly but forcefully behind the scenes is a far better way of bringing about the results we are after.[58]

A deterrence strategy was adopted, but applied covertly (aid reductions or the withholding of new authorization) to minimize diplomatic costs.

As the imminent danger of Castroite revolutions receded and incidents of expropriation increased, the objective of social reform took a lower position on the foreign policy agenda. The value given to containing challenges to American economic interests concomitantly increased. Operational lessons were adjusted toward greater vigilance against expropriation to prevent congressional cut in aid appropriations and business flight from Latin America. While the State Department generally resisted corporate demands for formal sanctions, the case studies below show how it quietly applied economic pressure in expropriation disputes regardless of the merits of the case or the costs of such action to economic development, social reform, and constitutional government.

Formal Sanctions: Ceylon and the Hickenlooper Amendment

The application of the Hickenlooper Amendment against Ceylon in February 1963 represented the only instance of its use until 1979. Although Ceylon hosted very few American investments and played a minimal role in the eschatology of the Cold War, it placed itself in a highly volatile issue area where its action was responded to for its linkage to other issues. The imperative for the U.S. government was to project an image to Congress, the overseas investment community, and other potential expropriators that the administration meant business on the issue of expropriation.

BACKGROUND

In 1962, the Government of Ceylon, faced with a severe balance of payments deficit, was presented with a tempting offer. The Soviet Union was willing to sell oil to Ceylon at a price 25 percent below what American and British companies charged and on six months credit. To sweeten the deal, the Soviets agreed to accept payment in Ceylonese rupees which it could use to purchase exports from Ceylon's lagging agricultural sector.[59]

The foreign oil companies refused to comply when the Bandaranaike government ordered them to process and distribute Soviet oil. In April, May, and June 1962, Ceylon nationalized 83 oil and gas outlets of Shell and two American companies, Esso and Caltex, and concluded an oil supply deal with Russia and Romania. The companies claimed compensation for a market value of just under $3.5 million while Ceylon accepted an obligation for only book value (roughly one-third that amount).[60]

The parent companies adopted a systemic view of the Ceylonese action and pressed for application of the Hickenlooper Amendment. Esso and Caltex had only minuscule holdings in Ceylon and, of those, only 20 percent was taken. Larger issues of principle, however, were at stake. These multinational giants operated worldwide. Transgressions against one affiliate, whatever its size, if unanswered, could threaten all the others. In the Ceylonese case, there were two damaging precedents: the inadequacy of book value compensation, which would make nationalization less costly, and the acceptance of cheap Soviet oil, which could threaten the industry's market structure.

The companies urged strong action to make the costs indelibly clear to others who might contemplate either nationalization or dealing with the Soviets. After meeting with company executives, Rusk noted their conviction that

> even if they lose all their investment in Ceylon they must continue their demand for payment of fair market value, not only because of their more substantial interests elsewhere, but also because of the interests of all United States business abroad.[61]

A hard-line position, even if it proved to be a stumbling block to resolution, was necessary because the symbolic value of showing that expropriation does not pay outweighed the material costs.

UNITED STATES POLICY:
THE RATIONALE FOR HICKENLOOPER

Following the oil nationalizations, the State Department sent a formal note of protest to Ceylon. Ambassador Frances Willis stood squarely behind company demands for "fair market value" and warned of the implementation of the Hickenlooper Amendment if "appropriate steps" were not taken by February 1, 1963. Sanctions were deferred when, the day before the deadline, Mrs. Bandaranaike sidestepped the cumbersome requirements of Ceylonese law and sent a personal representative to negotiate directly with the companies. The government was willing to compromise upward from book value, but the companies remained adamant on their position.[62]

Citing the failure of Ceylon to take "appropriate steps," the United States invoked the Hickenlooper Amendment on February 8. Ceylon lost its annual grant of $1.3 million and an approved $3.2 million loan for modernization of its railway and airport. Food for Peace allocations remained unaffected.[63]

Following the American action, the *Economist* noted that making "an example of little Ceylon . . . smacks of such disregard of local political consequences that the only fair inference is that Washington could not care less for what happens in or to Ceylon."[64] The immediate consequences of sanctions in Ceylon were indeed adverse to American interests. Bandaranaike canceled negotiations with the oil companies and subsequently took over the rest of their assets. Political repercussions in Ceylon undermined pro-Western groups to the benefit of the radical left.[65]

The State Department took these eventualities into account as the costs of regime maintenance. Rusk wrote to Kennedy that relations with Ceylon had deteriorated: "friendly elements . . . were weakened and the extreme left benefited noticeably." Rusk also predicted a deterioration in the position of the oil companies. "Eventual settlement of the dispute has become more difficult," he argued, and compliance on compensation was not evident in the foreseeable future.[66]

While a deterrence strategy requires the absorption of short-term costs, those incurred in Ceylon were remarkably small. The Bandaranaike government was viewed as leftist and anti-Western in tone and its relations with the United States had been deteriorating since 1956. Moreover, the Commerce Department ranked Ceylon as sixty-fifth out of seventy-three countries in terms of the quantity of American investments.[67]

If the action was of minor economic consequence, it had major symbolic value. Given the increased concern about overseas property rights, a strong response was needed to prevent the Ceylonese action from serving as a model for others. As Rusk saw it, the equation was

> whether the adverse political effects in Ceylon of aid suspension will be counterbalanced or outweighed by the deterrent effect that the suspension may have on other nations contemplating expropriations of American private interests.

Action was taken for its "salutary effect elsewhere."[68]

A second objective was to refute domestic criticism that the administration was soft on leftist governments that expropriated American property. Inaction, Rusk observed, would have produced "serious repercussions for the aid program in Congress and strong criticism from American businessmen." Instead, the government action was "applauded as a practical demonstration of our determination to protect US business abroad."[69] Ceylon, in effect, provided a political whipping boy which enabled the administration to maintain congressional support for the aid program and build investor confidence.

The sanctions contributed to the decline of the already troubled Ceylonese economy. While the magnitude of the aid suspension was minor (cut from $7.5 million in 1962 to $3.5 million in 1963 and $3.9 million in 1964, all in P.L. 480 funds), the much more significant World Bank lending completely dried up.[70] Adding to Colombo's economic woes, the Soviets did not follow through on their initial oil shipment while Esso, Caltex, and Shell colluded to deny oil supplies, tankers, and contracts for lubricating oil.[71]

The aid suspension intensified existing pressures within Ceylon. In 1964, its liquidity position dropped to a point where it had only forty five days worth of imports left. The sanctions did not create the problem, but aggravated an already bad economic situation. As one study concluded, coercion was employed through the "simultaneous intensification of the problem and the denial of the most obvious hope for a solution."[72]

In April 1964 the Bandaranaike government, concerned with the loss of aid, established a compensation tribunal. The government fell in parliamentary election in March 1965, before the tribunal had completed its work. The new government, Mr. Dudley Senanayake's United National Party, was more pro-Western and rapidly settled the dispute on terms congenial to the oil companies. On June 22, 1965, an accord was reached wherein Shell received $7 million, and Esso and Caltex, $2.3 million each, to be paid over five years. The United

States immediately offered a $14 million loan, which was supplemented by a substantial effort by international agencies.[73]

Informal Sanction: Denouement in Brazil

Although the case did not involve a natural resource venture, Brazil's expropriation of its foreign-owned utility companies provided the catalyst for a stiffened policy on expropriation. The Hickenlooper Amendment and related addenda were not invoked, as administration officials had made a finding that Brazil had taken "appropriate steps." However, Brazil's inability to settle the AMFORP case, as well as its refusal to submit to anti-inflation and stabilization programs, led to an informal withholding of aid from the central government. As a result, Goulart was weakened and overthrown by a military regime with the "political will" to enforce American economic demands at the expense of constitutional democracy and social reform.

By early 1963, economic conditions in Brazil had deteriorated to a dangerous point because of rampant inflation, an overwhelming balance of payments deficit, and an ominous debt burden. In March, Goulart's Foreign Minister, Santiago Dantas, arrived in Washington to discuss assistance for Brazil's $700 million debt, $280 million of which was overdue. The talks coincided with the release of the Clay Report which opposed bailout assistance unless accompanied by economic "performance," an area in which Brazil had been noticeably remiss. Under the Bell-Dantas agreement, the United States agreed to immediate stopgap assistance of $84.5 million with an additional $314.5 million contingent upon a cruzeiro stabilization program, deflationary policies, a balancing of the budget, and an opening up of the country to foreign capital.[74]

The creation of a favorable climate for foreign investment was a critical component of "performance." A CIA study argued that the most serious impediment to economic growth in Brazil was the drying up of private capital, which it attributed to "nationalistic policies that increasingly limit investment opportunity and security."[75] If Brazil would change its policies to attract foreign capital it would reduce its foreign exchange squeeze and its need for public assistance. The best way to restore investor confidence was to resolve the outstanding expropriation disputes.[76]

The ITT case was actually settled in February 1963. The company received $7.3 million to be paid over twenty two years with 75 percent reinvested in nonutility sectors within Brazil. A similar settlement was reached with AMFORP in April for $135 million. The settlment, however, was announced simultaneously with the stabilization plan. The stark contrast between a generous settlement for a foreign company and a domestic austerity program gave both the right and the left ample ammunition to term the deal a "sellout." Goulart, concerned with the erosion of his base of support in the labor movement, referred the award back to a reevaluation board.[77]

Goulart's postponement of the AMFORP settlement was read by the State Department as a failure of "performance." Ambassador Gordon warned that if the matter were not settled, investor confidence could not be renewed. Continued delay would jeopardize further release of the aid package because it raised a "question of [Goulart's] personal good faith."[78]

It would be inaccurate to attribute the growing American antipathy to Goulart solely to his unwillingness to act decisively on AMFORP. Goulart conveyed to American decision makers an image of fiscal irresponsibility. A State Department study, written shortly after the Bell-Dantas accord, commented that "Goulart's understanding of economic or broader political problems seems virtually nil and he appears to lack the capacity or organization to carry out an effective [stabilization] program."[79] The United States became progressively disenchanted with Brazil's failure to make a deal with the IMF and curb wages, subsidies, and credits.

While the AMFORP case was not the sole cause of the increasing antipathy toward Goulart, it triggered the process. Decision makers saw the issue as symptomatic of the Brazilian President's inability to move on other economic issues. Ambassador Gordon told Goulart that "if [there is] no compliance on this, [there is] no basis for confidence that other aspects of [the] program would be complied with."[80] Undersecretary George Ball concurred, arguing that "the AMFORP case, although not inherently the most important issue of US-Brazilian relations, has become a test case of Goulart's good faith and capacity to resist Brizola in the interest of future collaboration with the US."[81] Following the postponement, Gordon expressed grave concern that Goulart lacked the political will to implement unpopular but necessary measures and buck nationalists who "would never be satisfied with anything other than stealing the companies." Once again, he concluded, it "demonstrates [the] weakness and lack of decision of the government under Goulart."[82]

In August, due to Goulart's tabling of the AMFORP case and equivocation on the stabilization program, the United States quietly suspended virtually all new aid authorizations to Goulart except for P.L. 480 funds. The new policy, called "islands of administrative sanity," forwarded aid not to the central government but to selected state governments that conformed to American standards and served as a counterpoise to Goulart's "reckless populism." The sanctions were not made public so that Goulart could not rally additional support by casting the United States as the "collossus of the north."[83]

The policy had a damaging impact on Brazil's inflation-torn economy. Economic aid was reduced from $304 million to $174 million, although, in a pattern that would be repeated in Chile a decade later, military assistance was increased from $24 million to $33 million.[84] The sanctions did not create Brazil's economic problems, but in light of the government's obvious need for massive infusions of capital, the sums released were not close to the level required to sustain the economy. In effect, sanctions weakened an already tottering central government through exacerbating existing frustrations and diminishing its popular and institutional support.[85]

As the United States cut its ties with the federal government, Goulart moved closer to Brizola and the more militant left. As early as 1961, the CIA had warned that Goulart had a "long history of working with communists," but suggested that he could be dealt with since he was a "thoroughgoing opportunist whose inclinations are leftist and populist."[86] By late 1963, the United States had become alarmed at Goulart's unwillingness to crack down on alleged communist infiltration of the government and the labor unions. Ambassador Gordon warned that Goulart was moving toward a state of emergency, assuming dictatorial powers on a Peronist model, an eventuality that presented the prospect of "full Communist control."[87] American officials, in response to these fears, gave more serious thought to replacing what they viewed as a dangerously radical regime.

On March 31, 1964, Goulart was ousted in a military coup. Ambassador Gordon labeled the *golpe* a "democratic revolution" and a "great victory for [the] free world." He recommended as much support as possible to the new Castelo Branco regime.[88] President Johnson immediately recognized the new regime and released $50 million in aid. Castelo Branco, for his part, settled the AMFORP case, opened the country anew to foreign capital, effected a stabilization program, and ratified his dedication to "stability" by suppressing the Left. To reward this "performance," the United States not only released the package promised to Goulart, but increased it substantially.

The extent of American complicity in the coup is disputed. While there is no "smoking pistol" demonstrating direct involvement, the State Department and the embassy were well informed about the conspiracy, to the success of which they were sympathetic.[89] On the eve of the coup, the embassy developed contingency plans to supply the military with petroleum if Goulart's forces destroyed the refineries. The lack of direct involvement appears to have stemmed more from expedience than from principle. The State Department and the embassy concurred that overt involvement was unnecessary lest it give the "revolution" an American, rather than a Brazilian design, and "play into Goulart's hands."[90]

Regardless of the extent of direct participation, the United States consciously contributed to Goulart's downfall by reducing aid to the central government and diverting what remained to those elements of Brazilian society that eventually overthrew him. This was pursued not only for politico-ideological considerations—the aid decreases preceded and precipitated Goulart's turn to Brizola—but because of Goulart's insufficient regard for American definitions of development diplomacy, of which the AMFORP dispute was prominent. When respect for democratic institutions or economic diversity collided with more established notions of economic self-interest, the latter prevailed. The imperative of deterring expropriation belied Alliance support for its much-touted goal of political democracy, a fact that could only produce a "demonstration effect" for would-be *golpistas* throughout Latin America.

Informal Sanctions: Oil in Argentina

A second case of informal sanctions was occasioned in 1963 by Argentine President Illía's cancellation of the oil contracts granted by the Frondizi government in 1958. Economic milieu goals and the appeasement of Congress composed the central motivation. Although the United States was more favorably disposed to Illía than it was to Goulart, its actions had the indirect effect of undermining the political standing and economic base of a democratic reformist government, culminating in its overthrow in 1966.

BACKGROUND

In July 1958 President Arturo Frondizi, acting against traditional Argentine policy, entered into a series of contracts with foreign companies to develop Argentina's oil reserves. The terms given to the companies were more lucrative than those in current practice, in part because the state oil company, Yacimientos Petroliferos Fiscales (YPF), signed over areas in which favorable geological studies had already been made. Frondizi's objective was to reduce Argentina's staggering oil import bill which, in 1957, had cost it $272 million in scarce foreign exchange. The program was highly successful in stimulating oil production. Within five years, production had nearly tripled and the share of imported oil from domestic consumption decreased from 62 percent to 12 percent.[91]

In 1962, Frondizi was overthrown by the military, and in the 1963 election campaign the Frondizi contracts figured as the central issue. The winner of the election, Arturo Illía of the People's Radical Party, pledged to scrap the agreements in favor of new ones which better protected the country's economic interests. His arguments against the contracts were procedural and economic.

First, Illía charged that the contracts were unconstitutional because they were conferred through secret negotiations in the President's office rather than through public tender. Congress, which must approve such agreements, had been bypassed.[92]

Second, whatever balance of payments gains Argentina had made through the increased oil production was offset by the "exploitative" terms of the agreement. YPF was required to buy all the oil produced regardless of its needs or the price charged by the companies. That price was tied to the world market price of oil and safeguarded against domestic inflation. Since the companies were granted licenses over areas where YPF had already found oil, the price was not justified by the risks. Moreover, the companies were allowed unimpeded conversion of their receipts into dollars and unrestricted remittance of profits abroad.[93]

The contracts were canceled on November 15, 1963. Illía offered the companies $70 million in compensation for expenses incurred; the companies wanted to include loss of profits and claimed three times that amount. It should be noted that Illía's action did not project an elimination of foreign participation but a desire to renegotiate new arrangements under closer state supervision. The companies were given recourse to the Argentine courts and activity was allowed to continue pending settlement.[94]

The oil companies condemned the Argentine action as a unilateral breach of contracts which were properly negotiated and valid. Ambassador Robert McClintock noted that Esso, a worldwide concern, would stand on the legality of its contract and refuse to relinquish its rights: "it is more concerned about the principle than the money." An inflexible position would "show the public that the government cannot annul contracts at its whim."[95]

To limit the spread of economic nationalism to the oil industry, the companies pressured Argentina by curtailing production and new investments. The companies also appealed to the U.S. Congress to take an active stand in the dispute. Only a few days after Illía's action, Congress responded by extending the Hickenlooper Amendment to cover the nullification of contracts.[96]

UNITED STATES POLICY

The initial American response was to try to persuade Illía to reconsider his course of action. Averell Harriman was sent to Buenos Aires to impress upon Illía the threat nullification posed to the aid program because of the Hickenlooper Amendment. When Illía remained unswayed, Harriman suggested prompt compensation. Illía demurred, citing the serious political repercussions of compliance with oil company demands.[97]

The next step was the application of informal aid manipulations to induce Argentine compliance. Ambassador McClintock advised the State Department as follows:

> If the [Argentine] government persists in ill-advised policies and if it seems our continued assistance to Argentina will not serve our interests, we should be prepared to terminate the program. . . . While we should continue to honor commitments already made, any new assistance in the foreseeable future should be selective, providing for private enterprise and provincial governments, and avoid supporting the central government unless it changes certain policies and attitudes.[98]

As was the case in Brazil, the United States chose to withhold all new authorizations to Argentina, pending settlement, rechanneling its largesse to "islands of administrative sanity." Rusk accepted McClintock's rationale, agreeing to "quietly cut back aid . . . without formal invocation of the amendment."[99] The embassy confidentially informed the Illía government that all soft loans would be held up until the matter was settled. From 1963 to 1964, economic assistance to Argentina was reduced from $135 million to $21 million.[100]

The rationale for the informal aid suspension was fourfold: (1) the encouragement of "sound" economic development policies in Argentina; (2) the deterrence of precedents infringing on investor rights; (3) the development of support from domestic actors for broader foreign policy goals, such as the aid program; and (4) the minimization of damage to bilateral relations.

First, to McClintock, the oil nullification was characteristic of Argentina's "unfortunate excesses in the name of national sovereignty and national honor." The implications of this "hyper-nationalism" were adverse not only to

American interests but also to Argentine economic development. While the inflow of private capital was the only way out of Argentina's severe foreign exchange position, "prospective foreign investors are by and large scared off by the government's economic policies." Rusk concurred, arguing that the problem was the "apparent failure of the [Argentines] to realize there is any connection between a settlement of the oil problem and its avowed need for further private investment and outside financial and economic assistance."[101]

Second, concern was expressed for the externalities of the Argentine action on the global investment climate. In a cable that Rusk approvingly transmitted to Kennedy, McClintock warned that "actions which started in a purely bilateral relationship between an American firm and [Argentina] might eventually evoke reactions which would have repercussions of a continental and even a worldwide nature."[102] McClintock's successor, Edwin Martin, was more sympathetic to Argentine claims against the companies and acknowledged the probability of bribery. But he also agreed that unilateral termination set a dangerous precedent.[103]

Third, pressure was also employed to prevent domestic actors from subverting the public assistance program. Rusk wrote that the Argentine action could "materially affect both foreign assistance legislation and the US effort under the Alliance for Progress for Latin America as a whole." Inaction would result in pressures from Congress and American companies that could "threaten the whole Alliance for Progress."[104] To demonstrate a sense of resolve to Congress without invoking formal sanctions, Rusk constantly informed Senator Hickenlooper and others of the progress of informal sanctions and negotiations.[105]

Finally, the State Department was concerned about minimizing the costs of American actions. Rusk feared that the aid cutback might produce economic dislocations that would "contribute to political instability and undermine democratic institutions."[106] In bilateral terms, this was important because the Illía government was characterized as "liberal and democratic in approach" and "basically friendly to the United States." In hemispheric terms, Illía had just been reelected after his predecessor had been deposed by the military. His ability to see through the end of his term was viewed as an important test of democracy in Latin America.[107]

Although the Hickenlooper Amendment was not invoked, this last consideration prompted only a tactical adjustment in the application of investment protection policies. McClintock and Rusk urged the companies to "tread softly" and avoid publicity in staking their claims. Rusk argued that the sanctions should be discreet ("we should leave a token program or programs going as proof we have not applied sanctions") to minimize the cost to bilateral relations and avoid a polarization of positions which could render eventual resolution more difficult.[108] But despite ambivalence about the merits of the case and the threat the cutbacks posed to constitutional government in Argentina, the imperatives of property protection were deemed too valuable for inaction.

In October 1965, the Illía government signed out-of-court settlements with most of the oil companies at slightly less than company demands. Rusk subsequently urged a resumption of aid:

> They have proceeded with the oil negotiations in good faith. So far as I can see, the Hickenlooper Amendment is not now being violated in letter or in spirit. The oil companies . . . are making profits and repatriating them."[109]

The damage, however, had already been done. The effort to coerce compliance with regime rules undermined Illía through reducing aid amid a severe balance of payments crisis, and diminishing the government's political standing through prolonging the controversy and creating the appearance of the government's capitulation. In July 1966, Illía was overthrown by the military. Unlike the Brazilian case, the United States tried (unsuccessfully) to dissuade the conspirators.[110] But the conditions that led to the coup were influenced by the subordination of the goals of reform and democracy to that of opposing expropriation.

The Mann Doctrine:
The Consummation of American Policy

American policy toward Argentina and Brazil demonstrated a reversal of executive branch priorities and an acceptance of corporate definitions of interest regarding the threat Castro posed to hemispheric interests. The values assigned to the maintenance of an international property regime—i.e., deterring other expropriations, building investor confidence, and assuaging Congress—were elevated to a higher position on the agenda. Although the verbal commitment to political democracy and social reform remained, the executive branch's indifference to these goals when they conflicted with corporate prerogatives was evidence of their demotion.

While this process had begun under the Kennedy administration, it was consummated under Johnson, and given forceful articulation by his Assistant Secretary of Inter-American Affairs, Thomas C. Mann, who was appointed to wrest bureaucratic control away from the "Kennedy men." In what later became known as the Mann Doctrine, the Assistant Secretary delineated the four basic objectives of Alliance diplomacy:

1. To foster economic growth and be neutral on internal social reform.
2. To protect U.S. private investors in the hemisphere.
3. To show no preference, through aid or otherwise, for representative democratic institutions.
4. To oppose communism.[111]

The retooling of the political and economic priorities of the Alliance emphasized the critical value of nonradical stability, whatever its form. It represented the logical conclusion of the lessons drawn by the Kennedy administration in renewing its concern for foreign investment and expropriation.

Business regained its former status in the Alliance hierarchy. To Mann and the new administration, foreign investment and economic growth were synonymous. A 1964 CIA study observed that "one of the principal difficulties" in meeting Alliance goals was the failure of private capital to participate:

> One of the more pronounced adverse trends in the hemisphere . . . was the deterioration of the investment climate and a concomitant sharp drop in business confidence in many countries. . . . Unilateral political actions against private companies . . . have or may touch off extensive repercussions throughout the private sector in many countries and cause increased flight of capital and deter new investors. Statism (state socialism), is probably growing in the area despite the pronouncedly adverse experience of most countries with state economic enterprises and economic intervention.

The culprit pinpointed by the study was Castroism which, if successful, could "have an extensive impact . . . elsewhere in the area."[112] Statism and economic nationalism were categorized as the most serious impediments to increased levels of foreign investment, upon which the Alliance, under Mann, was increasingly dependent.

United States policy was reoriented to "get tougher" with Latin American governments that refused to pursue congenial foreign investment policies.[113] As a result, and as evidenced in Brazil and Argentina, the economic "screws" were tightened regardless of the intrinsic merit of a particular case or of internal political difficulties confronting host governments. No longer were investment disputes assessed with consideration of constitutional government, economic development, or social reform. The national interest was defined primarily in the context of the grievances of foreign investors.[114]

Indeed, the abandonment of social and political objectives, as measured by their negative impact upon economic growth through private enterprise, was no longer defined as a cost. Social reform, with its implicit connotation of state activism, deters foreign investors with the prospect of regulation and eventual nationalization. The CIA noted that state-sponsored reforms, by spawning unbalanced budgets and placing an unaccustomed burden on the economy, "set off an inflationary spiral that could imperil fiscal stability and discourage investment."[115] Economic growth, according to Mann, was more important than redistributional policies for poor countries:

It is necessary to think, first, of economic development—of ways to produce wealth—before theories of distribution of wealth become meaningful. Or, as we say back home, it is necessary to make a very big pie before one can distribute large pieces to every member of a very large family.[116]

In other words, the revision of feudal systems of land tenure and extraterritorial privileges would have to wait until capitalism was allowed to complete its Promethean task of creating abundance.

Second, the commitment to democratic institutions fell by the wayside as decision makers became progressively disillusioned with the democratic Left and more appreciative of the military. A Defense Department study defined the main threat to American interests in Latin America as "the internal disorder and political instability arising out of the social upheaval now underway in the area." A revolution of rising expectations was stimulating "endemic anti-Americanism." Democratic regimes, vulnerable to these pressures, succumbed to their dictates. In stimulating "popular aspirations which are impossible of attainment," they contributed to political volatility. The military, on the other hand, was immune to these forces and, hence, a guardian of internal order and a bulwark against communism.[117]

Given the return of the foreign investment to its

"rightful place," the United States increasingly emphasized the military's "positive development role." The democratic Left enacted reforms not only against local oligarchs, but against the acquired rights of foreign investors. A CIA study observed that Latin American politicians demonstrated "little understanding of the role of private capital and the factors which promote government-business confidence." Democratic leaders were pushed toward statism and intervention as they sought to assuage popular passions for change by using American investment as a "scapegoat."[118]

The military was constantly referred to as a restraining infuence on such populists as Goulart and Illía. In power, it provided stability, the sine qua non of a "good investment climate." It was more favorably disposed toward foreign investment and more insulated from popular pressures for policies such as nationalization, better enabling it to promote political stability and economic growth through a coalition of "apolitical" financial and technical advisors. As a result, military regimes were no longer viewed negatively as ephemeral orders trying to place a lid on a boiling pot, but positively for their willingness and ability to effect American standards of economic "performance."[119]

In sum, Alliance policy evolved in proportion to changes in the perception of the main threats to American interests in the hemisphere. As the specter of revolutionary contagion receded and that of economic nationalism increased, Alliance policy came to support short-term order over projections of long-term stability through "peaceful revolution." The goals of reform and democracy were subordinated to the fostering of orthodox development plans and the maintenance of international rules discouraging expropriation. However desirable the reformist goals, they made little headway because of the private interests with which they conflicted and the perceived relationship between those interests and larger diplomatic aims. In the Brazilian and Argentinian cases, pressures to protect overseas economic interests were employed even though their indirect consequence was the military overthrow of democratic and reformist regimes.

In the next case examined, the expropriation of the International Petroleum Company (IPC) in Peru, a similar pattern emerged. That dispute, however, became a watershed experience for government and corporate attitudes toward expropriation because the military junta that assumed power was more, rather than less, antagonistic toward the American company in question.

7.

Peru's Expropriation of IPC and the Elevation of United States Anti-Expropriation Policy

When the military regime of General Juan Velasco Alvarez, on October 9, 1968, seized the La Brea y Pariñas oilfield, a wholly owned subsidiary of the International Petroleum Company (IPC), the new government's popularity was assured. The conflict between firm and host arose from the IPC's tarnished history and privileged status. A protracted and bitter struggle ensued over taxation and control. The denouement was attributable to corporate refusal to accept the consequences of its weakened bargaining position. The Peruvian government, while acknowledging an obligation to pay compensation, more than offset its liabilities with counterclaims for illegal enrichment.

IPC's parent, Standard Oil of New Jersey (now called Esso), called for a punitive response lest expropriation, and the allegation of "past misdeeds" as a legal ploy to defray compensation, damage its global position. In contrast, the other members of the business community in Peru, although still wedded to a policy of deterring expropriation, opposed a hard-line response. They generally accepted Velasco's contention that IPC, as a gross offender, was a special case. With good reason, they feared that profitable local business could be undermined by the acrimony that would surely follow sanctions. If other expropriations took place, firms believed that they could best deal with them through their own resources. Peru represented one of many cases that stimulated a "learning process" which showed that accommodation with the growing power of economic nationalism was possible and still profitable.

The IPC affair was also a watershed in the evolution of U.S. anti-expropriation policy, which ultimately changed course from a deterrent strategy of principle and precedent to a pragmatic one of accommodation. The initial response in 1969 eschewed the Hickenlooper Amendment in favor of non-overt pressure, along the lines of earlier cases in Brazil and Argentina. The pressure was briefly relaxed in 1970, but tightened in 1971 as the Treasury Department attempted to give the issue a greater sense of urgency and focus. Over time, it became evident that no Peruvian government would publicly indemnify IPC. As a result, the Greene Settlement was signed in early 1974 to allow both sides to disengage without formally conceding their positions (see pages 288–290). This "fig leaf" arrangement coincided with a general deemphasis of anti-expropriation policy.

Both Krasner and Lipson cite the case as a vindication of their models. According to Krasner, the event precipitated a learning process whereby national elites became increasingly unwilling to use economic pressure when "general foreign policy interests were not at stake."[1] It was the state's greater sensitivity to nationalism and its unwillingness to aggravate relations with Peru in order to protect corporate prerogatives that "provided the impetus" for the corporate move toward accommodation.

Lipson, on the other hand, sees Nixon's nonappli-

cation of Hickenlooper consistent with the preferences of both
IPC (which wanted high-profile attention more than formal
sanctions) and the business community in Peru (which feared
exposure to nationalist fallout).[2] The ultimate demotion of
coercive regime maintenance reflected not state preferences,
but corporate redefinitions of political risk.

While Krasner's model predicts the general direction
of state policy, it neglects Treasury's stiffening of policy prior
to accommodation. Often, this stiffening took place against
the consensus of firms doing business in the target country,
particularly in Peru.

This also confounds Lipson's corporate preference
model. While it was true that the nonapplication of Hickenlooper conformed to corporate preferences, the use of non-
overt pressures did not. Tensions with Peru over the IPC case
complicated profitable ongoing relations for those firms less
adversely affected by Velasco's policies. This was particularly
evident in 1971, when the denial of Eximbank loans to
American mining firms placed them at a disadvantage vis-
à-vis European and Japanese competitors.[3]

Each argument minimizes the degree to which divisions within both business and government weaken its conclusion. In reality, systemic change was the decisive variable,
undermining the material bases of the regime. Regime erosion imposed dissimilar costs and opportunities on different
segments of the state apparatus and corporate community.
IPC, an event of negligible material but major symbolic importance, was a focal point for these debates.

Among the multinationals, established extractive
firms saw a need for tougher strategies to deter threats to
their global networks. On the other hand, new entrants saw
the obsolescing bargain as an opportunity to wean investment sites away from the major firms. And manufacturing
firms, less vulnerable to nationalization, feared the effects of
prolonged confrontations on their ability to conduct business
as usual.

The U.S. government was beset by similar cleavages. The State Department increasingly saw compromise as necessary to protect diplomatic aims and legitimize the long-term viability of foreign capital. The lesson drawn by Treasury, particularly after John Connally came on board in 1971, was not of the need to adapt, but that past policies had not been stringent enough. A more consistently punitive policy was necessary to prevent corporate self-interest in adapting to nationalization from undermining the regime.

Given these cleavages, it is difficult to assert the primacy of state or corporate preferences. Due to the uneven impact of systemic change and uncertainty concerning the capabilities of the parties, policymaking was increasingly embroiled in bureaucratic politics. From 1971–74, implementation generally reflected Treasury's preference for a tougher policy, though this was modified somewhat in interagency bargaining with State. It was not until systemic changes were made clear by the "oil shocks" that all segments of the state and business community opted for accommodation.

IPC in Peru: History, Negotiations, and Expropriation

THE ORIGINS OF LA BREA Y PARIÑAS

An understanding of the significance of the IPC affair in Peruvian politics is impossible without a knowledge of the bitter struggle between the company and successive Peruvian governments. The story began in the nineteenth century when the land, which was later to become the La Brea y Pariñas oilfield, was ceded by the government to a private citizen. The title, however, was no ordinary concession, but one that gave its bearer ownership of the subsoil. Such a title contravened Spanish law, and later the Peruvian

Constitution, in that subsoil was considered the inalienable property of the sovereign which could be leased, but not ceded outright, to private enterprise. The land and the claim were passed on to successive owners until IPC assumed them in 1914. The company claimed that its ownership of subsoil rights foreclosed the Peruvian government's sovereign right to collect taxes from it.[4]

In 1915, the La Brea oilfields became the subject of a dispute between firm and host when the latter passed a decree denying the company's claim to subsoil rights and tax exemption. IPC refused to pay the required taxes and, in collusion with the Canadian government, effectively denied oil to Lima and northern Peru by requisitioning Peru's only tankers (Canadian owned) for the war effort. This exercise in economic blackmail "brought the government to its knees." The tankers were returned only when Peru agreed to accept international arbitration. The government was subsequently overthrown by the military in 1919. In 1922, the new regime signed a *Laudo Arbitral,* a fifty-year accord which upheld IPC's subsoil claims, accorded it a nominal tax status, and exempted it from royalty or any other form of levy.[5]

The special status of the La Brea concession and its association with "dollar diplomacy" nurtured an acute popular sense of exploitation. Lacking the authority to tax or control the firm, Peruvians were cast in the role of sideline observers as a valuable natural resource was depleted. National sentiment considered IPC's title null and void—an insult to the nation—and clamored for a rectification of the historic injustice. But the combination of Peru's dependence upon IPC and U.S. embassy pressure deterred successive governments from making any significant changes.[6]

By the 1960s, the situation began to change. The conditions that validated IPC's stranglehold over Peru began to erode. First, the entry of independent oil companies such as Belco and Occidental ended IPC's monopoly over all facets of the nation's energy supply. Second, by the mid-1960's, the diffusion of technology had become sufficiently pervasive to allow Peruvian nationals to operate the oilfields without external aid.[7] These factors reduced Peru's dependence on IPC, and increased its leverage to renegotiate more favorable arrangements.

THE BELAÚNDE NEGOTIATIONS
AND THE EXPROPRIATION OF IPC

In July, 1963, Fernando Belaúnde Terry was elected President of Peru. Belaúnde, a democratic reformist leader supported by the military, was hailed by President Kennedy as a model of "reform without radicalism."[8] The new president's first promise, after taking office, was to settle the IPC question and recover Peru's national patrimony within ninety days.

The government launched a two-pronged assault on IPC's position. First, the 1922 award of subsoil rights violated Peruvian sovereignty and was declared invalid; the land was to be returned to the state. Second, a claim was made against the company for $144 million in unpaid taxes accruing from fifteen years (Peru's statute of limitations) of operation under an illegal title.[9]

While Standard Oil's holdings in Peru were minuscule, the imperatives of global strategy mandated an adamant opposition to Belaúnde's demands. The allegation of illegal enrichment against a private firm was unprecedented; its use as a device to offset pecuniary obligations could set a model for others in the hemisphere. Even when Belaúnde showed flexibility on counterclaims, the company refused to relinquish its privileged status without guarantees of exclusive access to Andean exploration and a lower tax rate.[10] The acceptance of contractual changes that limited managerial autonomy, IPC feared, would stimulate challenges elsewhere. Hence, the company continued to exalt itself as an extraterritorial entity, separate from and not answerable to its surroundings.

Not until 1968 did IPC, in belated recognition of the hostile local environment, reverse its position and give up its claim of privileged status. The Act of Talara, signed on July 28, 1968, returned the La Brea oilfields to the state and allowed the company to stay on under a management contract. In return, IPC received token compensation and Peru withdrew its tax claim. As a sweetener to the deal, the company was given permission to expand its refinery at Talara and join Mobil and Gulf in Andean exploration.[11]

These compromises came too late for Belaúnde, whose credibility had been tarnished by five years of failing to redeem his pledge. Shortly after the Act of Talara was signed, a scandal broke out over a "missing page" which allegedly specified the minimum price to be paid by the company to buy back crude from La Brea.[12] A crisis of confidence ensued, culminating in a military coup on October 3. The first act of the new military regime of General Juan Velasco Alvarez was the physical expropriation not only of La Brea y Pariñas, but of all IPC's Peruvian properties and the concomitant denial of any obligation to compensate a company that had so patently defrauded the nation.

THE ROLE OF THE UNTIED STATES GOVERNMENT,
1963–68

During most of the five-year stalemate between Belaúnde and IPC, the United States government deferred most new aid authorizations to induce a settlement on terms favorable to the company. The policy indirectly contributed to the military coup and the confiscation of IPC by encouraging an obdurate corporate bargaining position, and by undermining the economic base and political standing of the Belaúnde government.

New aid authorizations for Peru were first held up in 1963 under Kennedy's Assistant Secretary for Inter-American Affairs, Teodoro Moscoso. The intial intent was to exert temporary leverage on Belaúnde to settle within his ninety-day deadline. Under Moscoso's successor, Thomas Mann, the suspension became permanent. For the next two years, Peru lost much of its annual grant and received no new soft loans or credits. This informal rebuke was calculated to "persuade Belaúnde to be realistic" and negotiate terms favorable to IPC.[13]

The United States gave its unqualified backing to the claims of the company in its negotiations with Belaúnde. No weight was given to the Peruvian contention that a historic injustice had occurred because of the company's unfairly privileged position. The State Department made no independent study of the merits of the dispute. In fact, its only source of information was Standard Oil of New Jersey![14] The overriding objective of American policy was to dissuade Peru from "arbitrary action" against corporate prerogatives.

In bilateral terms, this stance was dictated by the need to maintain an "atmosphere of confidence" for investors in Peru. A CIA study noted that the threat of contractual abrogation in the IPC dispute posed a potentially serious deterrent to the continued flow of private capital to Peru. One official told Belaúnde that the aid reduction was designed to hasten a settlement and restore the investment climate, a necessary precondition for development aid: "The USG cannot supply [the] needs of [the] entire world. Therefore, we believe countries . . . should provide the confidence necessary for foreign capital" to be eligible for aid.[15]

In regime terms, Mann was concerned that a settlement "unduly favorable" to Peru would encourage other Latin American countries to break their contracts and impose extortionate settlements on American investors. A precedent in violation of traditional international law, a CIA study warned, would have "widespread adverse repercussions" elsewhere.[16]

Mann's successor, Lincoln Gordon, sought to reverse this policy because he believed that the whole Alliance program should not hinge on one company, especially since Belaúnde had renounced expropriation. Gordon was joined by cold warriors such as W. W. Rostow whose regional priority was the containment of revolutionary insurgency rather than economic nationalism. When a package of $19.5 million in project loans came up late in 1965, Rostow urged approval: "Our choice, then, is to do what we know to be right and intelligent in fighting communism in the hemisphere *versus* using this particular loan as an instrument in negotiations about US oil properties."[17] Aid was temporarily resumed in 1966, but suspended again in 1967 when Peru violated regional arms control objectives and purchased Mirage jets from France.[18]

United States policy contributed to the prolonged deadlock by supporting an uncompromising corporate position. The use of informal pressures and the brandishing of Hickenlooper, in the estimation of Richard Goodwin, "tended to strengthen the intransigence of the company knowing what a great weapon they had against Belaúnde," rather than nudge IPC toward compromise.[19] The settlement reached in 1968 was substantially the same one that Belaúnde had offered five years earlier.

The policy of informal sanction also undermined Belaúnde economically and politically, indirectly contributing to his downfall. First, by depriving Peru of $150 million in aid in 1964 and 1965, it precipitated a downturn in the economy. Second, it undermined Belaúnde's public and institutional support. The failure to achieve a speedy settlement cost him his popularity and, ultimately, his office. Goodwin was told that General Velasco's knowledge of the aid manipulations was a factor in his decision to overthrow the government.[20]

In bonding itself to the cause of IPC, U.S. policy demonstrated an indifference to political consequences. Belaúnde was prototypical of the democratic reformist leadership that the Alliance endorsed. His success was viewed as an important test for democracy in Latin America since he was elected after the military had negated the results of the 1962 election.[21] Officials myopically hoped for a continuation of constitutional democracy while confronting Belaúnde with the stark choices of a politically suicidal surrender to IPC's demands, or an erosion of Peru's economic base. Apparently, economic dominoes were more important in the American game plan than were democratic ones.

Moreover, the U.S. actions even went beyond the requirements of the Hickenlooper Amendment in that informal pressures preceded expropriation, an intention Belaúnde explicitly renounced. In a protest to the American ambassador, Belaúnde claimed that he was being "condemned to purgatory for a sin he had not yet committed."[22] In its unyielding defense of corporate prerogatives, the United States linked itself to a firm whose behavior had done more to undermine the legitimacy of U.S. overseas investments than any confiscatory precedent. In so doing, it contributed to the very action it sought to deter: the confiscation of IPC.

The Expropriation of IPC
and the Policy of Non-Overt Pressure

BACKGROUND

On October 4, 1968, President Velasco declared the Act of Talara "null and void." Within a week, he expropriated the La Brea y Pariñas oilfields and, within the next few months, the rest of IPC's Peruvian oilfields, refineries, and distribution outlets. A reflection of the widespread popularity of the action, the day of the expropriation was declared *Dia de la Dignidad Nacional,* the Day of National Dignity.[23] Even the traditionally conservative journal *El Commercio* lauded the takeover as a fitting conclusion to "this unsavory chapter in the history of our country."[24]

Although IPC was not paid for its assets, the Velasco government did not deny a theoretical obligation to pay compensation. On February 6, 1969, it placed a check for $71 million—book value for IPC's assets—in a blocked account. The payment was made contingent upon a claim against IPC for $690.5 million for tax delinquency since the arbitral award in 1922.[25] These maneuvers, Velasco hoped, would enable Peru to stay within the letter, if not the spirit, of American law, and thereby prevent the implementation of the Hickenlooper Amendment.

Despite the "confiscation" of the IPC, Peru did not effect a general socialization of the economy, although it did assume greater state control over foreign capital. Velasco repeatedly insisted that IPC was a special case and should not be regarded as symptomatic of a general attitude toward foreign investment. IPC was characterized as a bad company that had unfairly exploited Peru. State action was necessary to redress past misdeeds. A wholesale eviction of foreign business was not intended.

THE CORPORATE RESPONSE:
IPC AND THE BUSINESS COMMUNITY IN PERU

IPC took a strong stand on the expropriation, demanding full compensation and forceful diplomatic assistance. While the La Brea oilfields represented only a microscopic fraction of its parent's worldwide operations (the oilfields were reportedly "dry"), the issue transcended Peru. The unilateral repudiation of an arbitral award without compensation, if left unchallenged, would establish a precedent with global implications. Decisions must be made in the context of maintaining an international property regime. As one official noted, "Our flexibility is limited by our worldwide commitments."[26]

Esso lobbied for active diplomatic intercession and initially pressed for Hickenlooper. Nonapplication, it feared, would be interpreted as a sign of weakness and an invitation to others. The company, reticent about the potentially inflammatory impact of Hickenlooper throughout Latin America, later requested only informal pressures.[27] The objective, however, remained the same, namely, to obtain compensation and prevent challenges against holdings elsewhere.

The stance of IPC contrasted sharply with that of the rest of the business community in Peru. It saw Velasco's action not as a threat to foreign investment per se but as a response to a company that had repeatedly flouted national sovereignty. It opposed sanctions because they threatened to poison the environment for local business. When disputes arose, most firms believed that they could most profitably fend for themselves.

Initial fears that the IPC seizure would typify Peruvian policy was assuaged by subsequent events. *Business International* noted that the Velasco junta pursued substantially the same policies as its predecessor, most notably with favorable tax, tariff, and credit policies, as well as virtually unrestricted profit repatriation. In November 1969 the government placed a full-page advertisement in the *New York Times* soliciting foreign investments. In 1970, the Department of Commerce reported a favorable expansion of the private sector with lucrative opportunities for investment in copper.[28] The government did not close its doors to private foreign capital, but redefined its *modus operandi*.

Business generally accepted Velasco's contention that IPC was a special case, not symptomatic of a general hostility toward foreign investment. Shortly after the coup, companies such as Mobil, Sears, Coca-Cola, Cerro, Xerox, and ITT expressed satisfaction with the junta's policies. Evidence of Peru's favorable standing with at least some sectors of the business community can be verified by grants of mining contracts and joint ventures in phosphates, iron, and copper in the years immediately following the expropriation. The most notable new investment was the South Peru Copper Company (SPCC), a $335 million copper-mining joint venture between Asarco and Cerro.[29]

Even in the petroleum sector, the government left

open a significant role for private participation. While the treatment of IPC was unique, the role of the private companies was redefined. The Hydrocarbons Law of November 1968 stipulated that no further concessions be granted in petroleum exploration, exploitation, refining, and domestic marketing. A new state company, Petroperu, was established to assume monopoly control over these functions. An important role, nonetheless, was reserved for the private companies, which continued to exploit the oil under operating contracts from Petroperu. In effect, the system of concessions was replaced by a system of licensing and production-sharing accords.[30]

For the most part, the foreign oil companies adapted comfortably to this new scheme. Belco, IPC's main Peruvian rival, increased its investment by $15 million in 1969, and subsequently converted its concession into a thirty-year production-sharing accord. The firm received compensation only for equipment and installations; in return, one-half of its production volume was accorded tax-free status.[31] Occidental was the first foreign firm to obtain licenses from Petroperu for Andean and offshore exploration. It signed a three-year agreement under which it invested $50 million over a seven-year period in return for fifty/fifty production sharing. When, in 1971, it struck oil on its first five drillings, there was a "mad rush" on the part of other firms to sign similar accords.[32]

While there was no general socialization of the economy as was the case in Cuba, the Velasco government did take over several other American concerns. In such cases, however, some form of compensation was paid and no claim of illegal enrichment was inveighed to deny compensation. In fact, some firms fared handsomely in the aftermath of expropriation. The compensation paid to ITT for its utility holdings was used to construct a luxury hotel in Lima. The *Peruvian Times* noted that the substantial compensation paid for the takeover of Chase Manhattan showed how it was possible to "buy out foreign ownership . . . in a way that won't alarm other foreign interests." With the exception of W. R. Grace, and, of course, IPC, no other firms solicited help from the U.S. government.[33] Most believed that their interests were best served by direct, low-key, nonconfrontational negotiations with the Peruvian government.

While many firms still endorsed the principle of sanctions as a countermeasure against confiscation, most believed that the concept would be misapplied in Peru. Local business was generally unsympathetic to IPC's position and was not anxious to pay the price for defending it in an aroused nationalist reaction which might imperil all foreign holdings. C. W. Robinson of Marcona Mining led the fight against a punitive policy, warning that the greatest threat to foreign investment in Peru and Latin America was an escalating dispute fueled by an intemperate U.S. government response: "United States investors in Peru are now suffering and will continue to suffer from a continuation of this unsound policy which ignores the basic facts of life in Latin America."[34] The American Chamber of Commerce for Peru warned that sanctions could only produce a "disturbing reaction prejudicial to . . . U.S. interests."[35] In sum, business opposed a hard-line posture because it would be ineffective and disrupt "business as usual."

The IPC case was one of several events that triggered a corporate "learning process" toward nationalization. Its lesson was that neither public nor private sanction could reverse the trend toward increasing state control. Affronts to national sentiment could only make the trend more violent and disruptive. Expropriation moved across the spectrum of perception from unthinkable blasphemy to necessary evil and potential opportunity. In Peru, for example, raw material investors were allowed to stay on as contractors in the aftermath of expropriation. Some vertically integrated extractive firms, reconciled to the "handwriting on the wall," sought to expedite this trend. This would legitimize the process of primary production by ceding it to the host state and, through a post-expropriation contractual arrangement, maintain access to raw materials for their highly remunerative "down-stream" operations. They were willing to pay a short-run price, in terms of reduced profit and control, in order to consolidate a still-lucrative overall operation.

U.S. GOVERNMENT RESPONSE:
THE POLICY OF NON-OVERT PRESSURE

As shown in chapter 6, the United States in the 1960s pursued a policy of deterring "improper" expropriations by informally withholding preferential benefits to offending nations. The policy was relaxed only when punitive policies conflicted with Cold War objectives. In Latin America, such cases were few (e.g., the acceptance of Frei's Chileanization of copper to prevent the election of Allende),[36] because the region was not an area of high national security concern. Investment protection became a dominant regional priority.

Against this backdrop, many observers were surprised when, on April 7, 1969, the Nixon administration indefinitely deferred Hickenlooper sanctions against Peru for its "confiscation" of IPC. Some journalists attributed this self-restraint to the immunity of a conservative administration from criticism by business and the Right.[37]

Appearances, however, were misleading. The Nixon administration took a serious interest in the dispute because of the importance it attached to promoting foreign investment in the developing areas. In an early speech on promoting development in the Americas, Nixon endorsed the leading role of the private sector as the "crucial catalyst" for economic growth. He admonished that there would be a "serious impairment of [a country's] ability to attract investment funds when it acts against existing investors in a way that runs counter to commonly accepted norms of international law and behavior."[38] In this belief, Nixon was influenced by the findings of the Rockefeller Report and the Pearson Commission, which pointed to the rise of economic nationalism in neutralizing the dynamic benefits of foreign investment in the developing world.[39]

Given this view, Velasco's action was regarded as the most flagrant arbitrary act against American investors since Castro's eviction of American business in 1960. It clouded the investment climate in Peru and had ramifications for the rest of Latin America. The unilateral termination of a contract and the assertion of sovereignty over all business within its borders violated traditional precepts of international law. Most worrisome was the precedent of a nation withholding compensation by retroactively assessing alleged past injuries.[40] These challenges had to be met to forestall the groundswell of uncompensated takings.

Despite regime considerations, Nixon also wanted to avoid a major hemispheric crisis early in his administration. He recognized the regional unpopularity of the Hickenlooper Amendment and feared that its application in Peru might produce a "domino effect all over Latin America, presumably meaning more expropriations on a tide of anti-American feeling."[41] Basically uninterested in Latin America, Nixon wanted to solve the problem quietly and focus attention away from Peru. Consequently, the task of mediating the dispute fell to the Department of State.

State also opposed the invocation of Hickenlooper. It did want to protect what it saw as the legitimate claim to compensation of a company that had presumably operated in good faith. At the outset, however, the issue was not framed primarily in regime maintenance terms, but in the context of bilateral relations with Peru. It was not a test of American will, but a diplomatic problem to be solved to normalize bilateral relations. The new government was not ideologically hostile to the West and did not aspire to socialize the entire economy. State's objective was to achieve some kind of compromise compensation formula to prevent the escalation of the economic dispute into a political crisis that could radicalize Peru.[42]

The State Department dispatched John Irwin to Peru

to seek a compromise behind which the executive branch could circumvent the requirements of Hickenlooper. Irwin was instructed to get some level of compensation or have the dispute submitted to international arbitration. In Peru, Velasco told Irwin that the case was already settled. He labeled IPC an "immoral" company entitled to neither compensation nor U.S. government support. Arbitration was rejected as a violation of Peruvian sovereignty and the Calvo Doctrine. Irwin noted that the Peruvians were "not inclined to give up much if any of [their] theological and intricate web of logic." Ambassador John Wesley Jones regretfully concluded that the application of Hickenlooper was unavoidable.[43]

Nonetheless, on April 7, 1969, Secretary of State William Rogers announced that formal sanctions would be deferred until August. A decision was made in July to defer them indefinitely. The "fig leaf" used to justify noninvocation was the administrative process by which IPC was allowed to appeal the $690 million tax claim, a process about which Irwin and Jones were highly dubious.[44]

The nonemployment of formal sanction did not connote an acceptance of the Peruvian action. The United States sought to coerce compensation through what Jessica Einhorn called a policy of "non-overt pressure." Although there was no official announcement or explicit statement of linkage, the U.S. government took quiet action to hold up new bilateral aid authorizations without cutting aid already in the pipeline; deny Eximbank credits to firms seeking business in Peru; dissuade private bank lending; impede debt rescheduling; and prevent loans from coming up for consideration in the Inter-American Development Bank (IADB) and the World Bank. As a result, bilateral lending was reduced to $9 million in 1969 and MDB lending was completely shut off until major earthquake relief was needed in May 1970.[45]

The policy represented a bureaucratic compromise within State between advocates of regime maintenance and diplomatic strategies. It sought to reconcile two seemingly incompatible objectives: insisting on compensation for IPC, and avoiding an open confrontation with Peru. Administration officials opted for covert pressure as the optimal strategy to avoid a damaging precedent while minimizing political costs. Discreet pressure would also leave Peru a "way out" without a publicly humilating capitulation, and avoid the kind of public arm-twisting that might rekindle memories of "big stick" diplomacy in Latin America.

American sanctions, however, were applied from a diminished power position because of previous aid cutbacks to Peru and the trend toward the multilateralization of aid. Peru was also less vulnerable than Mossadegh's Iran to concentrated corporate sanctions. The Peruvians were better trained to run the industry without IPC's assistance. The major oil company domination of the market had been weakened by the emergence of new entrants, such as Belco and Occidental, which were more than willing to break ranks with the major companies and contract with Petroperu. Finally, a boycott would have been irrelevant because IPC, unlike AIOC, produced solely for the domestic market. As a result this "modest" policy of pressure succeeded only in bringing about a deterioration of bilateral relations, threatening the very interest it was designed to promote, the investment climate in Peru.

The Nixon-Connally "Presumptive" Policy: Expropriation as High Politics

American policy toward Peru shifted, in 1972, from non-overt to overt pressure. On January 19, 1972, President Nixon issued a public statement emphasizing a tougher line on expropriation:

> When a country expropriates a significant United States interest without making reasonable provision for compensation to United States citizens, we will presume that the United States will

not extend any new bilateral benefits to the expropriating country unless and until it is determined that the country is taking reasonable steps toward providing adequate compensation. . . . [The U.S. will also] withhold its support for loans [to offender nations] under consideration in multilateral development banks.[46]

The United States, he declared, would use its leverage to wrest compensation and state publicly what it is doing so that "there should be no uncertainty" about America's resoluteness to protect its overseas interests. Pressures against Peru were forthwith tightened and made explicit.

The change in approach from back room to up front was triggered by apprehension that the recent spread of investment disputes and expropriations would escalate and threaten national economic and security objectives. It also reflected the views of John Connally, the new Treasury Secretary, that the government should play a more activist role in foreign economic policy. Treasury criticized State for soft-pedaling expropriation disputes in order to smooth over bilateral relations. The failure to act unequivocally against Peru had left intact a precedent with explosive implications. At stake was the very survival of the traditional system of FDI. Anti-expropriation policy was elevated on the foreign policy agenda toward "high politics." The adverse trend toward host country control must be met and turned back.

TREASURY ACTIVISM ON EXPROPRIATION

1971 was a critical year for the process and substance of foreign economic policy. It witnessed the growth of the role of Treasury in advocating that concrete economic interests should no longer be sacrificed for diplomatic considerations. Decision making was removed from the State Department to the Council on International Economic Policy (CIEP), a new executive agency created to reduce the clout of officials at State and the NSC who inhibited "bold" economic action for fear of "political" costs.[47] This coincided with the appointment of John Connally as Treasury Secretary who, because of his close relationship with Nixon, became the chief spokesman on foreign economic issues.

This procedural realignment was quickly translated into substantive change. The United States withdrew from the leadership role it had played in maintaining the Bretton Woods trade and monetary order and enacted policies of economic nationalism, namely, a surprise devaluation of the dollar, suspension of the dollar's convertibility into gold, and a 10 percent import surcharge. The aim of this new "get tough" posture was to improve the American economic position vis-à-vis allies who, for years, had been taking a "free ride" on the United States. As presidential aide Peter Flanigan said, "In the past, economic interests were sacrificed when they came into conflict with diplomatic interests. . . . For the first time, the United States is putting its economic interests first."[48]

This aggressive mind-set was carried over into the administration's new approach toward expropriation. A number of expropriations and disputes gave impetus to the perceived need to toughen up. In Bolivia, in 1969, General Alfredo Ovando Candia, the man who hunted down Che Guevara, took over Gulf Oil's holdings, offering compensation from the future profits of the nationalized firm. In Chile, Salvador Allende revoked the concessions with the copper companies and refused to indemnify the companies on the grounds of "excess profits." More ominously, oil producers in Venezuela and the Middle East were demanding at least majority participation in foreign oil concessions, offering in compensation only the value of assets and equipment.

Treasury officials recognized that the traditional system was under siege. Undersecretary John Petty testified that

the day when a major international corporation has all the bargaining leverage against a foreign country is long gone. The history of the negotiations and analysis of expropriations and the payouts for compensation received over the past few years would suggest very clearly that the negotiating leverage is in the hands of the host country, or sovereign nation.[49]

The adverse consequences of this trend on Treasury's bureaucratic sphere, the U.S. economy, made a policy reevaluation imperative.

To Connally, the lesson learned from recent events was not that that old shibboleths needed rethinking and accommodation with economic nationalism was necessary; rather, it was that past policy had not been strong enough and that compromise would be interpreted as weakness and would further undermine the position of U.S. overseas investments. Treasury believed that Peru's expropriation of IPC had set the pattern. The State Department had been remiss in not exerting sufficient pressure to bring the Peruvian government to terms.[50]

Treasury insisted that "the U.S. government should be visibly protecting the interests of its investors" to "put the world on notice of the certainty of the American response."[51] This approach emphasizes the importance of communication in deterrence. Overt actions make credible verbal communications designed to influence not only the target state, but the world community. Credibility could be achieved only if LDCs knew with certainty that flouting the "rules of the game" would cost them dearly. Consequently, Treasury advocated a clearly articulated policy, enunciated in advance, and applied almost automatically.

State's policy of non-overt pressure had no deterrent effect because no admission of pressure or linkage was made. To State, the objective was to reach a mutually face-saving settlement with a minimum of political damage. To Treasury, success was defined less in terms of settling a particular case than in terms of the preserving of the system. Even if it was fatal to a workable arrangement, Treasury advocated a public stance to demonstrate resolve and deter others from following a bad example. The political costs of this "get tough" approach were minimized because, in Connally's words, "we don't have any friends down there anyway."[52]

The expressed objective was to reverse the trend toward host country control of natural resource investments and reduce MNC incentives to adapt. Testifying before Congress, Connally argued that unless the United States became more resolute in defense of its investors, the oil and mining companies would no longer be able to play their accustomed role in providing the United States with essential commodities:

The United States government should say, you don't just negotiate with American business enterprises, you negotiate with the United States government. I think we have come to that type of position. We're not there yet, but I think we have come to that. Otherwise, I think American business would be fairly helpless in its dealings with other governments around the world.[53]

The U.S. government, as a matter of necessity, must play an activist role in arresting the obsolescing bargain to prevent economic nationalism from engulfing American business.

EXPROPRIATION AND BUREAUCRATIC POLITICS

The bureaucratic struggle over the formulation and implementation of U.S. anti-expropriation policy began over the issue of multilateral lending to Peru. In May 1970, following a serious earthquake, economic pressure against Peru was eased for humanitarian reasons. AID quickly released a $10 million grant and a $16.4 million loan for emergency relief. This was followed by a $30 million loan from the World Bank and a few soft loans from the IADB. Those at State who considered informal pressures harmful to U.S.-Peruvian relations used the disaster to justify releasing previously held-up AID loans.[54]

In May 1971, a five-year highway construction loan came up for consideration in the IADB. State supported the loan; Treasury, which is authorized to vote on MDB loans, wanted to veto it. Treasury officials cited the incompatibility of the loan with the policy of deterring expropriation. American support for it would convince Peru that it no longer had to move on compensation, and tell Chile and the rest of the world that "expropriating U.S. assets and providing little or no compensation . . . would not necessarily foreclose bilateral or multilateral assistance."[55]

Treasury acquiesced to State on the Peruvian loan because of the intercession of Kissinger at the NSC. With a note of protest, Treasury voted affirmatively. The American representative publicly questioned the wisdom of continued American participation in the bank when loans were proffered to a country "whose credit is impaired by the existence of a dispute over . . . compensation for foreign owned properties which have been expropriated."[56]

While State won the bureaucratic battle, Treasury was maneuvering to win the "war" and shift U.S. policy away from "quiet diplomacy" to public pressure. Connally used his personal ties with Nixon to remove the issue from State to the CIEP, where Treasury could increase its influence and implement a tougher policy. The stage was set for a major interagency battle. National Security Study Memorandum (NSSM) 131 (June 23, 1971) called for an interagency study to "raise the priority of the objective of avoiding expropriations or, if they occur, achieving prompt, adequate, and effective compensation." Treasury won an initial victory in the drafting of the study memorandum in that all loans to countries in question were to be "held in abeyance" unless specifically approved by the President.[57]

Treasury quickly translated this directive into a tougher policy. In late June, the United States abstained on World Bank loans to two countries embroiled in expropriation disputes: Bolivia for its nationalization of American-owned tin mines, and Guyana for its taking of the Alcan bauxite mines. The loans were $6 million for a cattle project in Bolivia and $5.4 million to Guyana for seawalls to prevent floods which created heavy agricultural damage. Each loan was considered technically sound and was supported by the American embassies.[58] In August, the denial of credits to Chile to purchase Boeing jets represented the first time when Eximbank credits had been formally used in a case of expropriation. This action preceded by one month Allende's nationalization of Kennecott and Anaconda![59]

In all three cases, Treasury officials conceded that they "did not believe that sufficient facts were at hand" to determine whether compensation negotiations constituted "appropriate steps" within the meaning of U.S. law.[60] The actions conformed to Treasury's call for a presumptive policy on expropriation, namely, that even if talks were proceeding, there would be a presumption against new preferential benefits in the absence of an immediate commitment to full compensation. In effect, countries were presumed guilty until proven innocent. Treasury saw these actions as an illustration of a more stringent policy, demonstrating to governments that they must "tread lightly in using expropriation as a means to respond to domestic political pressure."[61]

The State Department opposed aid and credit restrictions because they complicated diplomatic relations and negotiations for compensation.[62] State disliked the rigid application of policy advocated by Treasury. This reflected its organizational "mission" to improve relations with other nations.

State was not monolithic on the issue. The regional bureaus (most notably the Latin American one) were the most "dovish," favoring negotiation and compromise in almost every instance. Each case required an ad hoc handling to minimize damage to constructive relations. The Legal Bureau, on the other hand, took a tough line against precedents in violation of *Pacta Sunt Servanda*. But it was the Economic Bureau that represented the department in its battle with Treasury.[63]

The Economic Bureau opposed both the ad hoc position of the regional desks and the automatic presumption of Treasury. It was concerned with the need to maintain principles of international law for overseas investment. But it also appreciated the difficulty of hinging all foreign policy on one issue. Conspicuous economic pressure, moreover, would poison not only bilateral relations but the investment climate as well. Reprisal should be a weapon of last resort, not the opening salvo. The bureau recommended that the United States refrain from employing pressure while a dispute is under adjudication.[64]

State, as compared with Treasury, drew a different set of lessons from growing nationalist restrictions of American investments. Although it advocated a stern approach to the most glaring seizures, it recognized a steady trend toward host country control. There was a growing recognition of economic nationalism as a *fait accompli* to which investors must adapt. Nathaniel Samuels, Deputy Assitant Secretary of State for Economic Affairs, told a group of businessmen that nationalism had deep historical roots in Latin America and was "not a device to despoil or irritate American investors."[65] Nor was it necessarily inimical to U.S. interests. The best security for overseas enterprise depended upon adapting to LDC regulations: "New modes of investment must be evolved; we increasingly have to take into account national sensitivities concerning natural resources and certain sectors of the economy."[66] Political risk was best minimized by lower visibility and good corporate citizenship rather than economic reprisal.

National Security Decision Memorandum (NSDM) 136 (October 8, 1971) enshrined Treasury's presumptive policy as official doctrine.

> In each case of expropriation of a significant US interest there will be a *presumption* that the US will suspend new bilateral economic benefits to the expropriating country unless and until it is determined that the country is taking reasonable steps to provide compensation . . . or that there are major factors which require the continuance of all or part of them.[67] (Emphasis added.)

It also established a permanent mechanism in the CIEP to coordinate interagency policy. NSDM 148 (January 18, 1972) extended this logic to MDB policy: "The US will attempt to have new loans deferred in multilateral instructions and if a vote is necessary will abstain or vote negatively." On January 19, 1972, President Nixon publicly endorsed this policy.[68]

The outcome predominantly conformed to Treasury's preferences. First, it upheld the presumptive policy that new benefits would be suspended until a reasonable commitment was made. Second, the public presidential statement reflected Treasury's belief that an overt stance was necessary to maximize the deterrent effect of anti-expropriation policies.

State suffered a temporary setback, though not a total defeat. It was able to dilute some of the language of the policy statement. The insertion of an "escape clause" in the case of "major factors" ensured some measure of flexibility. More importantly, it was allowed to chair the interagency group and, thereby, exercise control over the implementation of policy. By holding on to a substantial role in the deliberative process, State retained some leverage to temper the Treasury "hawks" and pick up the pieces after the eventual departure of Connally and the diminution of Treasury influence.[69]

THE APPLICATION OF THE
CONNALLY APPROACH TO PERU

The Connally approach reflected an intensification of past policy in that it rejected any compromise with economic nationalism. All challenges were to be taken seriously and dealt with stringently lest superficially innocuous compromises accumulate into a spiral of incursions against American enterprise. In the IPC case, the issue was no longer U.S.-Peruvian relations, but the deterrence of expropriation. The imperative was to make it clear that Peru "could not get away with it."

Although no formal amendments were invoked, economic pressure was intensified and its linkage to IPC was made explicit. The United States publicly asserted that aid and Eximbank financing would be withheld until expropriation matters were cleared up. It also made public its opposition to lending from the IADB and the World Bank thereby opening to full view a previously "behind-the-scenes" deliberation.[70]

The paramount objective was to convey to the world an image of resolve, whatever the political consequences. One remarkable 1972 CIEP memorandum conceded that it was insensible that "so tarnished an American interest as IPC act as a roadblock to good relations between the United States and Peru." On the other hand, it stated:

> However much we may be convinced that the IPC case is a bad set of facts on which to base a policy, *the rest of the underdeveloped world is unlikely to be sophisticated enough to treat IPC as discreet [sic!]*. In other words, *we would probably be deemed to have given in to the Peruvians* and thus to have undermined the President's expropriation policy to an unacceptable degree.[71] (Emphasis added.)

Short-term political and economic costs incurred were written off as inconsequential. Action was necessary, regardless of the merits of the case, to demonstrate the "credibility of the American commitment" to protect FDI and deter all others who might contemplate expropriation.

While sharing some of Treasury's concerns, relevant officials at State and the NSC sought to moderate (though not eliminate) the sanctions. This advocacy derived from a preference for short-run political and economic considerations over regime goals. These analysts recognized that IPC was a special case "deeply embedded in the Peruvian psyche."[72] Despite this case, there had been no pattern of uncompensated expropriations in Peru.

A 1972 State Department report indicated that Peru's "conservative fiscal policies" provided low inflation, a favorable balance of payments, and a reasonable climate for foreign investment. Profitable opportunities were available for American businessmen, particularly in mining, but under more restrictive "terms which include a larger role for the state." Treasury's extension of sanctions to Eximbank credits had only "hindered our export expansion program and our ability to compete in Peru with foreign competitors who enjoy ample, low-cost government-backed credits."[73] In other words, the economic analysts at State saw coercive investment protection working at cross-purposes with the goal of supporting the expansion of American mining enterprises within Peru.

This analysis was shared by the presumed recipient of government action—the corporate community in Peru. Several firms continued to do good business in Peru. Others disliked Velasco's nationalization directives, but feared that home government intervention would make reasonable accommodations politically impossible. Both the American Chamber of Commerce for Peru and the Council of the Americas came out strongly against a punitive policy. This position coincided with the beginning of a general corporate move away from tough regime maintenance policies toward a posture of flexibility.[74]

Moreover, the years from 1969–1972 were a boom period for American petroleum and mining investors in Peru. Occidental hit oil in its first five drillings and SPCC went ahead with its $335 million copper venture. There were reports that several copper companies appealed to Connally to relax the pressure. They wanted Eximbank financing for their operation in Peru which had, in their estimation, some of the most attractive unexploited mining properties in all of Latin America.[75]

Connally, however, was implacably opposed to any mitigation of the sanctions. The heart of the matter to him was the principle of full compensation for expropriated property, not the profits of a handful of corporations. The concession system was on the line. He conceded that some corporate "quislings" might want to continue to do business with violator states, but such behavior should be neither encouraged nor condoned because it undermined the policy of deterrence.[76]

Connally's position reflected a recognition of the game theoretical dilemma facing individual investors. Since the United States is not a command economy, it lacks the central authority to dissuade individual corporate adaptations that promote the firms's short-term interests, but undermine the system as a whole. To Treasury, the U.S. government must consequently play an activist role to punish violators to such a degree that the incentives no longer favor accommodation. This was seen as the only way to maintain the "collective good" of a stable property regime. Treasury's activism also marked the beginning of a separation between its interest in maintaining a tight regime to protect the U.S. economy and the overseas firm's immediate interest in accommodation, a divergence more explicitly articulated during the 1974–77 bureaucratic debate over expropriation policy.[77]

Despite this stance, the ability of the U.S. government to compel Peru, or most other LDCs, to conform to its will on expropriation issues was eroding. The threat to cut bilateral aid was becoming less potent because the United States had been phasing down its bilateral aid commitments. With the exception of the IADB, the United States could not unilaterally block loans from MDBs as in the past.

Finally, the effectiveness of other vehicles of pressure, such as the denial of credits and markets, had been mitigated by greater Latin American interaction with Western Europe, Japan, and the Eastern bloc countries. Barbara Stallings found that Peru was able to circumvent U.S. policy by raising $877 million on the Eurocurrency market from 1972 to 1973. As a result,

the Velasco government managed to maintain a "healthy" economy in terms of traditional economic indicators. Growth in Gross Domestic Product between 1969 and 1973 averaged 5.5 percent, while that in industry averaged 7.1 percent. Unemployment fell from 5.9 percent in 1969 to 4.2 percent in 1973. Real wages and salaries increased by an average of 6.6 percent, while inflation was held to an average of 7.2 percent.[78]

U.S. policy amounted to little more than ineffective posturing, producing the embitterment of relations with Peru and the rest of Latin America.

Given the trend toward state control of primary production, the important issue in terms of national economic security and corporate interests was not expropriation, per se, nor even compensation; rather, it was the assurance of a post-expropriation relationship between firm and host whereby the former operates through contract and is guaranteed access to crude oil or mineral ores. Such arrangements were not inimical to a continued MNC presence, secure U.S. access to critical raw materials, and the promotion of LDC development. In offering contractual arrangements to Occidental and others, the Peruvian government showed itself capable of reaching mutually beneficial arrangements. The Connally approach, in characterizing all acts as challenges, was at odds with a changing world. It was not until the divergence between theory and reality became clear after the "energy crisis" of 1973–74, that decision makers moved away from this mindset.

8.

American Foreign Policy and the End of the Concession System in the Middle East: The Conflict Between Theory and Reality

In the early 1970s, the rules for the traditional regime governing international petroleum operations in the Middle East were shattered as power shifted dramatically from company to host. Under the old system, firms operated under concessions wherein they owned and produced oil and dictated price and production levels to harmonize with their global strategy. The fifty-fifty profit-sharing accord with Aramco had served as a prototype for the area and provided two decades of stability. The system was perceived by U.S. public decision makers as a vital component of national economic security.

The first breach of the system occurred in 1970 when, by enforcing production cutbacks and threatening expropriation, first Libya, and later the rest of OPEC, gained a role in the determination of posted (tax reference) prices. Then came the assault on corporate ownership, either through phased "participation" agreements (an initial 25 percent, to be increased to 51 percent in a decade) with the Persian Gulf monarchies, or the "shotgun-style" expropriations in Algeria, Iraq, and Libya. The process reached its logical conclusion after the 1973 Arab-Israeli war when the producers assumed unilateral control over prices, which they increased 400 percent in just over two months, and the Persian Gulf producers advanced to 1974 the acquisition of majority (60 percent) control. The oil companies were transformed from owners to service contractors who provide technology and expertise for a fee, and buy back and market crude production for their "downstream" operations.

The "petroleum revolution" fulfilled many of the worst fears of public officials about the consequences of regime decay, e.g., state control over the production of natural resources, the use of oil as a political weapon, and a massive increase in the price of energy. With Treasury's bureaucratic clout during this period, a tough coordination of private and public resistance to this change seemed foreordained. But despite the enormity of the consequences and the solicitation of the oil companies for diplomatic support, the U.S. government made only token gestures of resistance. More often, it urged the companies to adapt to the eventual loss of their pricing and ownership prerogatives because accommodation would serve both the regional containment of Soviet influence and the short-term security of supply.

Treasury's ability to translate its strong bureaucratic position and its preference for an "aggressive" response into policy was limited by the bureaucratic coalition that opposed such a stance, and the declining economic position of the United States and the major oil companies, which made concrete strategies of resistance impractical.

First, while Treasury was successful in implementing a tougher policy vis-à-vis non-oil or minor oil producers in Latin America, disputes with major oil producers in the

Middle East brought into play more powerful bureaucratic adversaries. Kissinger and the NSC opposed any confrontation with Iran or Saudi Arbia because of their designated role as defenders of the Gulf against "Soviet surrogates" after the withdrawal of the British. The loosening of regime rules and the increased price of oil were acceptable costs to insure the stability of these conservative Middle East states and allow them to play their designated role in the Nixon Doctrine as regional "policemen." In this more critical regional theater, Krasner's view that containment objectives supersede the maintenance of traditional property rules is confirmed.

Second, the efficacy of diplomatic intercession was limited by the erosion of the U.S. worldwide economic position, a weakening of its fundamental resource base, and hence, its economic influence. Previously, as the world's foremost economic power and exporter of capital, the United States had been willing and able to absorb short-term costs to maintain the system. Its role as system manager was enhanced because it possessed a surfeit of economic resources. Shortfalls produced by the boycott of Iran in the early 1950s or the closure of the Suez Canal in 1956 could be offset simply by increasing domestic production. The capability to make good any losses incurred during regime enforcement made it possible to co-opt medium powers, such as Western Europe and Japan.

By the early 1970s, the United States could no longer play this role. The ever-increasing demand for energy depleted U.S. spare oil capacity and increased the West's dependence on Middle Eastern sources of supply. American influence was further diminished by the emergence of OPEC, which enabled members to learn collectively about the industry and erect a common front vis-à-vis the companies, and by the proliferation of "independent" (nonmajor) oil companies, ready to undercut the majors on prices and ownership because they were heavily dependent on single sources of supply and more susceptible to host country pressure. The confluence of these factors undercut the effectiveness of traditional diplomatic protection.

As a result, accommodation was pursued not only for containment objectives, but for national economic security as well. This position was made most forcefully by State's Office of Fuels and Energy. Given the decline in issue-relevant power, rearguard battles over traditional ownership rights were seen as futile and potentially disruptive of short-term supply. On the other hand, corporate adaptation to participation and the loss of the pricing prerogative could legitimize that aim.

In sum, what emerged was not only a triumph of political over corporate goals, but a redefinition of economic milieu goals regarding the petroleum system in the Middle East. The threat to resource availability came less from nationalization than from the market conditions surrounding it. In fighting higher prices, the United States should soften the impact of regime decay through domestic conservation, the development of new energy technologies, and encouraging the diversification of sources of supply.

All of this did not imply that the United States was no longer interested in setting the parameters of acceptable behavior. When radical Arab states, such as Algeria, Iraq, and Libya, sought to go beyond participation and expropriate the companies, the United States, under Treasury's influence, adopted a sterner approach. The United States tried to reinforce corporate cohesion by denying credits, voting against loans in MDBs, and making representations against the purchase of "hot" oil. In the tightened energy market of the 1970s, however, the United States had little leverage. The Europeans, more concerned with short-term supply than with regime considerations, opposed the United States in the World Bank. Attempts to block the sale of confiscated oil, even from the American market, were rendered unfeasible by market considerations. The sum total of these oppositional tactics amounted to little more than a posturing that was eventually overtaken by the oil "revolution" of October 1973.

Despite the bureaucratic dominance of Treasury over foreign economic policy from 1971–74, its influence over U.S. oil policy in the Middle East was constrained by the declining economic position of the United States in the international system. The United States maintained the pretension of leadership on expropriation issues, but it lacked the resources to absorb short-term costs or dissuade smaller actors from bolting. Rhetoric aside, its policies in practice reflected what Richard Rosecrance called "America as an Ordinary Country." The systemic orientation was abandoned as a guiding principle and the national interest was redefined in terms of short-run compromises with principle.

The Libyan Price Hikes and the Teheran/Tripoli Accords: The Loss of Corporate Control Over Posted Prices

The first major assault on the concession system in the Middle East was a challenge not to corporate ownership, but to one of its prerogatives—the ability to autonomously set the posted price of crude oil. Prior to 1970, oil companies had been free to orchestrate price levels in response to economic incentives without reference to the producers. Through production cutbacks and threats of expropriation, the Libyan government of Colonel Mu'ammar Qaddafi succeeded, first against the independents, and then against the majors, in making price levels a subject of government-industry negotiations, and revising the concessions to increase the tax rate beyond the fifty-fifty formula. In 1971, these gains were generalized throughout OPEC in the Teheran and Tripoli accords. The result was the most significant increase in world energy prices since World War II.

The major oil companies recognized the pricing and tax precedents as serious threats presaging an erosion of their overseas contractual rights. Motivated by regime considerations, they were determined collectively to resist, or at least blunt, the demands and sought diplomatic assistance.

The U.S. government did offer modest support to increase industry cohesion in bargaining with producers, e.g., the Justice Department issued antitrust waivers to allow a unified negotiating strategy. But despite corporate requests and the impact of price increases on the Western economies, it urged accommodation. The issue came to a head before Treasury's emergence as an advocate of a tougher economic stance. The State Department position held that there was little the United States could do to resist. The loosening of the regime and the resultant increase in energy prices were deemed a necessary price to be paid to legitimize oil company operations in the Middle East and promote the viability of conservative Middle Eastern regimes.

ROUND ONE: LIBYA

In early 1970, the Libyan government pressured the foreign oil companies to cede their uncontested right to set the posted price of Libyan crude. Qaddafi demanded an increase of 44 cents in the per-barrel price and of 8 percent in the tax rate. These demands were justified by the contention that the companies were extracting "excess profits" from Libya vis-à-vis Gulf crude because of the former's lower sulphur content and greater proximity to the European market.[1]

The first target of Libyan pressure, Exxon, resisted despite threats of production cutbacks. The thresholds of host country participation in the determination of price and a tax rate increase beyond the fifty-fifty formula had not been crossed by any other Middle Eastern producer. As the largest of the major international oil companies, Exxon feared that capitulation would invite more important producers to follow suit. Moreover, any shortfall resulting from Libyan cutbacks could be offset simply by turning on the spigot elsewhere.[2]

Unfazed by Exxon's refusal to give in, Qaddafi turned next to the nonmajor or "independent" oil companies. These companies, unlike the majors, were almost wholly dependent upon Libyan crude for their downstream operations, and hence more vulnerable to cutbacks or expropriation. Libya was well placed to exert pressure on them. Qaddafi's predecessor, King Idris, had awarded oil concessions in such a way as to avoid excessive dependence on the "seven sisters" and, in contrast to other oil-producing countries, many firms, rather than one or two, operated. By 1969, Libya accounted for 7 percent of world production and 27 percent of Europe's imports; of that, 55 percent was produced by the independents.[3]

Qaddafi singled out Occidental Petroleum as his next target. In May and June of 1970, Libya cut Occidental's production from 800,000 to 425,000 barrels per day (bpd) to coerce compliance on pricing and tax demands. The other independents—the partners in the Oasis consortium (Amerada Hess, Marathon, and Continental) and Bunker Hunt—were cut back from 15 percent to 31 percent.[4]

Occidental preferred to resist but was almost entirely dependent upon Libyan crude for its European refineries. To strengthen its bargaining position, it approached Exxon on the possibility of supplying replacement crude at cost in the event of further cutbacks or a shut-in. Exxon rejected this request, subordinating corporate solidarity to its natural instinct not to assist an upstart competitor and a disrupter of the market.[5]

Denied alternative sources of crude, Occidental caved in. On September 4, 1970, it agreed to an increase from $2.23 to $2.53 in the posted price and to 58 percent in the tax rate. The Libyans then moved to generalize the Occidental settlement to the rest of the industry, and on September 21, the Oasis partners complied. A September 27 deadline was set for the rest to fall into line or face a shut-in.[6]

The majors viewed the Libyan demands as a threat to the way they had traditionally conducted business and sought diplomatic assistance to coordinate a joint strategy of resistance. On September 25, John J. McCloy and representatives of the five American majors, BP, and Shell met with Secretary of State William Rogers, Undersecretary U. Alexis Johnson, and the Director of the Office of Fuels and Energy (OFE) James Akins.[7]

The majors' position was based upon the global implications of capitulation on the petroleum regime in the Middle East. First, giving the Libyans a voice in pricing would break an important symbolic barrier and would lead inevitably to a process of "leapfrogging" wherein each producer would repeatedly seek renegotiation to match gains obtained by others. Second, the imposition of a higher tax rate would undermine the fifty-fifty formula which had governed the industry for almost two decades.[8]

The private consensus was that a stand had to be made to retard the steady march toward increased host government control. One company representative argued that

> The dangers to our own and the consumer's interest lay much more in yielding than in resisting demands . . . being made upon us. . . . sooner or later, we, both oil company and consumer, would have to face an avalanche of escalating demands from the producer governments . . . we should at least try to stem the avalanche.[9]

The Libyan demands should be rejected out of hand even if a shut-in or nationalization ensued. Their stake in Libya was dwarfed by their stake worldwide. If Libya went so far as to nationalize the industry, the State Department was asked to consider the possibility of a boycott parallel to that employed against Mossadegh in the early 1950s. One industry representative even urged the government to "dare the Libyans to nationalize; if they did, the Europeans would be told to tighten their belts while Libya . . . would be forced to yield soon because it could not dispose of its oil."[10]

The officials from State, unpersuaded by this logic, urged the companies to compromise with principle and adapt to the Libyan demands. Akins contended that the Libyan situation could not be compared to that of Iran in the 1950s, when

> the United States was largely self-sufficient and had perhaps two million barrels a day of shut-in capacity. There was also substantial shut-in capacity in most of the major producing countries in the world, and major new discoveries were developed in

Africa. This surplus gave the oil companies a great deal of flexibility and a great deal of security.

Conditions had changed; energy demand had grown explosively and reserve U.S. capacity had disappeared. A hard-line stand, Undersecretary Johnson noted, would be "ineffective at best."[11]

At worst, it could provoke a confrontation accompanied by severe disruptions of supply and the possible eviction of the established oil companies. An industry boycott, Akins reasoned, was not feasible because it would hit Europe too hard, and if it were attempted, "the Europeans would have made their own deals with the Libyans . . . they would have paid the higher price the Libyans demanded, and . . . the Anglo-Saxon oil companies' sojourn in Libya would have ended."[12] Moreover, if the Europeans signed bilateral deals with Libya, they might have expropriated affiliates of the majors on the continent. Accommodation was necessary to avert this eventuality.

Akins contended that the Libyan demands could be lived with and did not warrant a hard-line response. A study he supervised at OFE showed that Libyan crude was indeed underpriced vis-à-vis Persian Gulf crude when adjustment was made for density, sulphur content, and transportation costs. Obdurate resistance would only create a perception of injustice, both in Libya and the rest of the Middle East, and delegitimize the security of supply.[13]

Diplomatic calculations also entered into the official calculus. Libya had not yet become the *bête-noire* of American policy in the Middle East. State viewed Qaddafi as a revolutionary nationalist who had replaced a corrupt, though pro-Western monarch. His anti-Western stridency, however, was balanced by anti-Communist rhetoric. He was someone with whom the State Department believed it could deal and his Islamic nationalism could serve as a barrier to Soviet penetration. Earlier in 1970, the United States agreed to pull out from Wheelus air base as a concession to Libyan national sensitivities. Similarly, legal niceties in the arena of petroleum politics gave way to the aim of salvaging a working relationship with the new regime.[14]

Without the prospect of diplomatic support, the companies swiftly conformed to the Occidental formula. Two companies, Gulf and Philips, preferred to surrender their concessions and leave. The rest continued to operate, although wary of the future in Libya; they cut back on new investment, exploration, and development.[15] They were painfully aware that their real vulnerability and the unwillingness or inability of Western consumers to take forceful action had been exposed to the world. The key question facing the industry was how best to stem regime erosion from the assaults that were sure to follow.

ROUND TWO: TEHERAN AND TRIPOLI

Industry predictions about escalating price demands were borne out almost before the ink was dry on the Libyan settlement. At the Caracas conference, in December 1970, OPEC resolved to generalize Libya's gains in pricing and taxation. Unilateral enforcement was threatened if demands were not met. The organization set as its ultimate goal full sovereign control over pricing and production. Shortly thereafter, Libya pressed for a second round of price increases.[16]

The industry decided that its only recourse to arrest the drive toward producer control was to bargain collectivley with OPEC, and, to this end, formed the London Policy Group and the Libyan Producers (Safety-Net) Agreement. The former was designed to establish terms of reference and coordinate bargaining with OPEC. The latter mandated that members replace, at cost, any shortfall suffered by an individual company that defied Libyan demands, thereby circumscribing Libya's ability to pick off the companies one by one, as it did with Occidental.[17] The policy reflected an appreciation of the real dilemma faced by individual companies in balancing the industry welfare as a whole against its immediate needs.

To prevent "leapfrogging," the companies insisted on comprehensive rather than regional negotiations with OPEC. Separate negotiations would encourage each producer to outdo the others, leading to an escalating spiral of demands. An OPEC-wide accord, McCloy argued, was the only hope of removing "the chain reaction inherent in separate negotiations."[18]

In January 1971, the Department of Justice cleared the London Policy Group and the Libyan Producers Agreement from antitrust prosecution.[19] On January 13, the London Policy Group published a "message to OPEC" which called for an "all-embracing negotiation" to establish long-term stability in financial arrangements. It took a firm stand against any increase in the tax rate, retroactive payments, and obligatory reinvestment, agreeing only to negotiate some revision of posted prices with modest annual adjustments.[20]

On January 15, company representatives met with Rogers and Johnson to coordinate strategy. They decided that the U.S. government could usefully exert its influence with the conservative producer states to moderate their demands. On January 17, John Irwin was dispatched to Teheran, Riyadh, and Kuwait, to place U.S. government support behind the industry strategy.[21]

The Shah of Iran and his Finance Minister, Jahangir Amouzegar, registered to Irwin their opposition to comprehensive negotiations. Separate regional negotiations, they contended, were necessary to prevent "radicals" such as Libya and Algeria from setting the tone of the agreement. To assuage fears of "leapfrogging," the Shah offered a five-year guarantee of stability.[22]

Irwin was persuaded that the exclusion of Libya from Persian Gulf negotiations would facilitate a more moderate settlement. The companies, he reasoned, should take advantage of the Shah's five-year offer. On January 18, Rogers accepted Irwin's recommendation and advised the London Policy Group to "open negotiations with the Gulf producers and conduct parallel negotiations with Libya."[23]

State's departure from the agreed-upon negotiating strategy came as a shock to the company representatives. The State Department, one representative noted, had impaired the "essence of the combined strategy." Separate negotiations would play right into OPEC's hands by weakening corporate solidarity; extravagant Libyan demands would inevitably be replicated by "moderate" Persian Gulf producers. Exxon vice president for the Middle East George Piercy expressed "disappointment" in State's position, and opined that it would make the problem "harder to solve." While expressing distaste for State's quick capitulation, McCloy recognized that if the Shah and Saudi King Faisal were not willing to go along with the joint approach, not much could be done about it. The real culprit, conceded Piercy, was "the economic situation we have got today that we have no alternative to this oil."[24]

The companies, bereft of choice, accepted separate negotiations in Teheran and Tripoli. On February 14, the Teheran accords increased the posted price from $1.80 to $2.18 per barrel and the tax rate from 50 percent to 55 percent. In return, the companies were offered five-year guarantees against renegotiated price and tax increases. The North Africans were given a free hand to up the ante. On March 20, the Tripoli accords hiked Libya's tax rate to 60 percent and its posted price to 65 cents above the 1970 increase.[25]

With respect to the Libyan and Persian Gulf price demands, the support extended by the U.S. govenment was tenative in tone and minimal in effect. It urged accomodation to the loss of corporate prerogatives over pricing and the violation of the fifty-fifty formula despite corporate warnings that these precedents would open a "Pandora's box" of cascading demands. Public decision makers realized that this weakening of the regime would propel energy prices higher, but concluded that increased demand, the disappearance of spare petroleum capacity in the United States, and the pro-

liferation of "independent" oil companies left no other options.

An increase in the price of energy was rationalized
as a necessary cost to buttress the national interest in security of supply and the political objective of containment.
First, the State Department hailed the "stability" and "durability" of the agreements in assuring the availability of oil
against the disruptions of shut-ins or expropriations.[26] The
cost would be mitigated in the long term by developing alternative sources of supply. In the short term, it was necessary to adapt.

Ironically, assuring security of supply was always
considered one of the bedrock benefits of supporting an international property regime. State officials, however, believed that given the world energy situation, stringent regime maintenance was no longer possible. To hurl the gauntlet
at minor producers, such as Peru and Argentina, for symbolic
value was one thing. To risk the availability of Middle East
oil was quite another. A tough stand would constitute a leap
into the unknown creating the prospect of far more serious
short-term consequences. The United States was willing to
absorb the cost of higher oil prices to avert this risk and legitimize the situation.

Second, accommodation served the diplomatic aim of
resisting Soviet infiltration of the region. Higher petroleum
prices promised greater revenues for the Shah and the Gulf
sheikhdoms, which would minimize the risk of political instability and enhance their economic viability and capacity
to suppress internal rebellion.

Moreover, Nixon and Kissinger believed that the
main threats to regional stability were "radical" forces, acting as Soviet surrogates, which destabilized local governments. With the U.S. experience in Vietnam and the withdrawal of British garrisons east of Suez, direct military
intervention was no longer seen as a cost-effective means of
dealing with this threat. Under the Nixon Doctrine, the United
States came to rely upon specific clients for the projection of

its power in "proxy" conflicts in the third world. In Kissinger's words, Iran and Saudi Arabia would "fill the vacuum left by British withdrawal, now menaced by Soviet intrusion and radical momentum."[27] Higher oil prices were not burdensome if they provided the wherewithal for these states to play their designated role.

Algeria's Nationalization of the French Oil Industry

The first major assault on the ownership structure of the Middle East oil concessions was Algeria's 51 percent nationalization of the local affiliates of Cie. Française des Pétroles (CFP) and Enterprise de Recherches et d'Activités Pétrolières (ERAP), France's two largest petroleum companies. The French, seeking full compensation, responded with economic countermeasures, including a boycott of Algerian oil and gas, and solicited U.S. government support in holding up loan in MDBs and preventing the approval and financing of a major U.S. liquefied natural gas (LNG) project in Algeria. The United States, with Treasury playing a more central role in foreign economic policy, responded positively. But in the petroleum market of the 1970s, the sanctions amounted to little more than posturing and a settlement was eventually reached on predominantly Algerian terms.

On February 24, 1971, following a prolonged impasse in negotiations over oil prices and the revision of the 1965 Evian accords, Algeria took over 51 percent of all French oil and natural gas interests. President Boumedienne established a commission to evaluate the companies' assets for compensation and deduct Algerian counterclaims. Algeria expressed willingness to resume negotiations to reach an accord for continued oil company operations.[28]

The French government vehemently protested Al-

geria's unilateral action as a violation of the 1965 Evian accords and threatened a boycott of Algerian oil and a withdrawal of its special relationship with its former colony. CFP
accepted the nationalization, but insisted upon a full indemnity, with the amount of compensation to be determined
by international arbitration, not a national commission. The
French government and its oil companies agreed to continue
negotiations despite their protests.[29]

On April 15, France walked out of the talks because
of Algerian actions on pricing and compensation. First, Algeria unilaterally increased the posted price of crude from
$2.85 to $3.60 per barrel, the highest in the world. Second,
it offered only $100 million in compensation, the sum to be
reduced by $43 million in tax arrears with the balance to be
reinvested in Algeria. France, which valued the companies'
assets at $800 million, termed the offer derisory.[30]

The immediate French response was to attempt an
economic blockade against Algeria. It stopped imports of Algerian wine, suspended its technical assistance programs, and
threatened not to renew an immigration pact that allowed
guest workers into France with the unimpeded right to re-
patriate their earnings.[31]

Most importantly, France tried to effect a worldwide
boycott of Algerian oil and gas exports. On April 26, CFP
pulled its employees out of Algeria, refused to load its tankers with Algerian crude, issued a public warning that it
claimed title to the oil, and threatened to sue any buyers of
pètrole rouge. The major oil companies, alarmed by the expropriatory precedent, respected the boycott. As a result, Algerian production fell by 55 percent.[32]

France also persuaded the World Bank to halt all
new lending to Algeria pending a settlement. In this, it successfully enlisted the support of a United States government
increasingly under the influence of Treasury's activist views
on expropriation.[33]

Paris also approached the Federal Power Commission (FPC) and Eximbank about holding up the approval and

financing of a major LNG deal with Algeria. The project in question was a massive joint venture between the El Paso Gas Company and the Algerian state company, Sonatrach, to liquefy and export 10 billion cubic meters of natural gas per year to the United States for twenty-five years. A $250 million loan from Eximbank was awaiting approval by the State and Defense departments. To allow the deal to go through, the French argued, would prejudice negotiations.[34]

Despite the French protests, State sent a letter of approval to the FPC citing no objections on expropriation or other foreign policy grounds. By the end of 1970, Algeria had compensated all the minor U.S. oil and mining interests that had been expropriated after the 1967 Arab-Israeli War.[35] The nationalization of the French companies was viewed as "an inevitable part of the process of decolonization." The United States should not intercede and prejudge the merits of a case with such deep historical roots. Moreover, the case was "only one part of a complex bilateral relationship."[36]

An important gain from the deal, State argued, was that national security "will be enhanced by maximum diversification of sources of supply." The United States suffered from a scarcity of natural gas and Algeria possessed enormous reserves. State's position eschewed a traditional regime maintenance policy in favor of one that sought to protect national economic security from the consequences of regime erosion. This was consistent with OFE's view that national economic security would be better served not by fighting unwinnable battles over ownership, but by developing new sources of supply of vital energy resources, mitigating excessive dependence on Middle East oil.[37]

On June 15, Peter Flanigan, a White House aide allied with Treasury on foreign economic policy, intereceded to delay and possibly block the El Paso deal. The issue was submitted to the NSC for high-level review.

This action reflected the administration's "presumptive" policy that economic benefits should be withheld pending settlement of a nationalization dispute. Treasury and

White House officials were concerned that approval of the loan prior to an agreement on compensation would be seen as approval of Algeria's action and encourage high-handed treatment of the oil companies elsewhere. From this point of view, the huge stake the United States had in averting a precedent outweighed the concrete economic benefits of the deal.[38]

Despite these pressures, France and CFP eventually accepted a "compromise" that in all but name was a capitulation to the Algerian position. On June 30, a settlement was concluded between CFP and Sonatrach. Compensation was paid, but substantially canceled out by retroactive tax claims. The boycott was called off and the company was given a ten-year buyback arrangement at something less than market price. In December, a similar deal was concluded with ERAP. On July 19, 1971, State Department letters of approval to the FPC were allowed to go through.[39]

The key factor in the failure of coercive policies was a reversal of the dependence relationships between consumer and producer. First, a boycott was successfully employed against Mossadegh's Iran, in part, because only one company operated there. In contrast, the French companies in Algeria accounted for only 65 percent of Algerian production. It was difficult to distinguish between crude from the nationalized French concessions and from other Algerian fields. Libya, moreover, offered to buy Algerian oil for resale, further undermining the boycott.[40]

Second, increased Algerian production had become more important to France and less important to Algeria. The *Oil and Gas Journal* calculated that with price increases for undisputed (non-French) oil and exports from the French fields to the Eastern bloc, Algeria made more money on petroleum exports than before nationalization.[41] France, on the other hand, was dependent upon Algeria for 30 percent of its imports; disruption was economically and politically costly. The United States could no longer be relied upon to increase domestic production to compensate a European shortfall, as was done during the Iranian dispute in 1951, the Suez crisis in 1956, and the Arab-Israeli War in 1967. American efforts to support the French were destined to fail because the economic bases upon which the regime had been maintained were eroding.

From Prices to Ownership:
OPEC Demands Equity Participation

Late in 1971, OPEC decided to extend its demands beyond pricing to ownership. It pressed for negotiations to achieve "participation"—the initial purchase of a minority share of a subsidiary's assets, to be gradually increased to a majority holding. The companies initially resisted. Treasury favored aggressive support but offered little in the way of concrete proposals. State's "pragmatic" assessment discounted any effective countermeasures and accepted the inevitability of eventual producer control. It urged accommodation to participation in a stable and gradual transition period during which the United States could develop energy alternatives to the traditional regime. At the same time, it sought to isolate those producers who urged immediate outright nationalization.

At the Beirut conference (September 22, 1971), OPEC resolved to enter into a new round of negotiations with the oil companies to discuss parity, or the readjustment of posted prices because of the devaluation of the dollar, and equity participation.[42] The latter referred to the gradual assumption of control by buying into the local assets of the oil companies. While each member was free to work out its own formula, a minimum acquisition of 20 percent equity was set as an immediate demand, to be increased gradually over a period of years to 51 percent. Following the completion of accords of parity, in January, 1972, Saudi petroleum minister Zaki Ahmed Yamani was designated to negotiate a settlement with

Aramco as a prototype for the other Persian Gulf producers.

Yamani's preference for participation over nationalization reflected his desire to gain the benefits of greater control without the costs of confrontation. He recognized that oil reserves were finite and that the national interest in conservation may not have been identical with the global interest of the multinational oil firm. At the same time, he did not want to alienate the private flow of finance and technology or the companies' marketing apparatus. Participation was an important interim phase to achieve some measure of control over the industry while gradually developing the expertise needed for a complete takeover.

A continued corporate presence, moreover, was deemed necessary for producers to share in the collection of oligopoly rents. Yamani abjured nationalization because it would "deprive the majors of any further interest in maintaining crude oil prices . . . like the consumer, [they] would try to buy it as cheaply as possible."[43] Without MNC assistance, he believed, state companies could not limit production and fix prices, the consequence of which would be the plummeting of prices toward marginal costs. It was essential to keep the companies as partners to "restructure the oil trade so as to give expression to producing country interests through the good offices of the oil companies."[44]

The companies initially looked upon participation as a greater threat than the loss of the pricing prerogative. Increased prices could be passed on to the consumer. The loss of a percentage of ownership translated itself into the loss of a proportionate amount of profit. As one official noted, "It was like labor union . . . when they've agreed about wages they go for codetermination."[45]

The OPEC demand, as the *Petroleum Press Service* noted, was a "claim for a change in the basic relationship between governments and companies."[46] The concession system featuring fixed rights to sell and produce for a long time period gave firms considerable latitude to harmonize a subsidiary's policies with global objectives. It also enabled the majors to reduce uncertainty through a strategy of vertical integration.[47] Acceptance of participation would upset these aims by opening the door to partial, then full producer control.

The majors set out to resist participation. Exxon, taking the lead for the industry, declared it to be "contrary to the word and spirit" of Teheran. The companies initially would not even consider the issue a subject for negotiation. In October, the Libyan Producers Agreement was extended to cover participation as well as pricing, and on October 19, McCloy obtained Justice Department approval of a concerted industry front for forthcoming negotiations on parity and participation.[48]

To assist resistance, the industry wanted the U.S. government to use its influence to bolster its bargaining power. Treasury preferred an "aggressive" government role. Secretary Connally stated that since American companies could no longer negotiate on a par with sovereign governments, the United States "should take a larger hand in [the negotiations], and I think we ought to express to the producing countries the fact that this is not just a matter for the oil companies themselves, but rather a matter of gravest concern to the Nation."[49] Despite this "call to arms," no specific proposals were spelled out.

While Treasury successfully sponsored a tougher investment protection policy toward minor producers in Latin America, it fared less well vis-à-vis major producers in the Middle East. This reflected a recognition (even by Treasury) that the United States had little leverage and the immediate political and economic costs of confrontation were too high. Implementation of the policy, therefore, devolved to State Department officials who, from the first, had urged accommodation.

These officials argued that the United States lacked the means to prevent participation or induce a settlement favorable to the companies. Akins noted that the combination of increased demand, the disappearance of spare capacity in the United States, the concentration of resources in the Middle East, and the strength and cohesiveness of OPEC doomed a strategy of resistance. The Connally approach, in the words of one official, was based upon a "Texas view of the world"—an illusion of muscle that no longer exists. Akins wrote to McCloy that one had to deal with "the realities of the world in which we live."[50]

State accepted the eventual shift of decision-making power from firm to host as "part of an evolutionary stage by oil producing countries concerned over the life of a depletable nonrenewable resource."[51] Given this analysis, the objective was to make the transition as orderly and nondisruptive as possible. A study commissioned by Akins at OFE, *The United States and the Impending Energy Crisis,* urged the companies to bend to participation and accept a substantial modification of their traditional role to avoid outright nationalization.[52] Another study characterized participation as a "promising (but not trouble free) antidote to the very real threat of nationalization."[53]

The critical feature of participation for national economic security was the assurance of long-term supply. This could be achieved if companies accept a change in their role from owner to one of "providing the production, development, and transportation capability necessary to bring to the market the huge quantities of oil which the world will need in the future."[54] The key issue, Akins testified, was for the companies to "develop new forward-looking relationships with producer governments" to "maintain their position as the major marketers of oil."[55]

Security of supply would also be enhanced by the promotion of an "interdependence" between producers, companies, and consumers. Nationalization and other arbitrary actions would be forestalled by giving hosts an economic stake in the status quo. Moreover, OPEC countries would invest surplus revenues downstream, giving them a greater interest in the stability and expansion of supply. An OFE study concluded that such an arrangement would provide stability even after the disappearance of corporate ownership: "As the OPEC governments get more stake and more experience in all phases of the oil business, the more likely it would be that they would be inclined to act on sound commercial rather than politically-inspired bases."[56]

Acceptance of participation was mainly seen as a means of "buying time," that is, taking advantage of the stability of an incremental participation formula while seeking alternatives to the regime in providing energy security. Irwin noted that the trend toward national control was inevitable; at best, the United States could only "brake the pace of takeovers and win reasonable compensation." Undersecretary William Casey saw participation as "an opportunity for a gradual, stable, and mutually beneficial transition to new arrangements in the oil industry."[57] The strategy was to accept the inevitable loss of ownership and use the interval provided by participation to attenuate producer country leverage through conservation, new energy technologies, and the development of alternative (including domestic) sources of supply.[58] In sum, rather than pursue regime maintenance, they sought to soften the consequences of regime erosion.

Confrontation, as suggested by Connally and some oil companies, was viewed as counterproductive to these objectives. Irwin noted that it would only "raise the old bogey of imperialism and create a backlash among other nations that might otherwise be sympathetic." This would undermine the goal of isolating the "radicals" from the "moderates" and of maintaining a satisfactory basis for continuing relations. Akins informed McCloy that "a blunt refusal to consider new forms of relationships might accelerate the nationalization trend rather than retard it." Another official testified that "we do not believe that drama is called for in this delicate stage of oil negotiations."[59]

In the absence of diplomatic support, corporate resistance to participation was short-lived. On March 10, 1972, the companies accepted the principle of 20 percent participation, implicitly reconciling themselves to the eventual loss of majority control. The bargaining focus then shifted to the method and timing of acquisition, the mechanism for compensation, and the arrangements for the disposition of participation crude.[60]

On compensation, the companies claimed that net book value was unacceptable; they must be fully indemnified for the loss of future profits that would have accrued to them until the expiration of their concessions in the twenty-first century. Yamani rejected this method of valuation as a negation of the objectives of participation. In its stead, he offered net book value because petroleum resources in the subsoil were the property of the sovereign. The State Department supported the corporate claim and labeled book value compensation as "confiscation."[61] There is, however, no evidence that its support went beyond verbal suasion.

The companies, however, did not press hard on compensation. Their investments had been amortized many times over. The critical issue was to "ensure that as the percentage of ownership of the Saudi government in Aramco increases, the partners would continue to have a preferential right to buy back the Saudi share of Aramco oil."[62] The firms wanted service contracts enabling them to obtain access to participation crude on terms better than those available to competitors on the open market. This would permit them to dispose of the oil without disturbing the structure of the market.

Negotiations were expedited by events in the summer of 1972. On June 1, the Iraqi government nationalized the Iraq Petroleum Company (IPC) after a prolonged dispute over production levels and compensation for an earlier nationalization (see pages 255–260). The act was a sobering reminder to the companies of the fragility of their position, especially on the heels of the Algerian action. In August, King Faisal brought the point home by intimating that if the companies did not soon accede to a settlement, he would consider unilateral action on the Iraqi model.[63] Despite these threats, the U.S. government limited itself to recommending greater flexibility on the part of the oil companies.

An agreement between Aramco and Yamani was concluded in New York on October 5. The companies were to cede an immediate 25 percent to be gradually increased to 51 percent by January 1, 1982. The compensation figure of $510 million was based upon book value updated to account for inflation, a formula somewhat greater than that originally offered but, with no recognition of subsoil claims, far less than Aramco had sought. The member companies obtained buyback arrangements for the Saudi share of the crude at 7 percent below the market price. Negotiations along similar lines followed in Abu Dhabi, Kuwait, and Qatar.[64]

The agreement heralded a drastic overhaul of the system. The State Department commended it as providing an orderly transition from one regime to another. By delaying reversion for a decade, the accords provided breathing space during which the United States could diversify its sources of supply and change its pattern of energy consumption to minimize the consequences of regime decay. Despite this accommodation, the United States was resolved to discourage more radical producer demands on ownership that might undermine the Persian Gulf participation accords. Challenges from Iraq (during the negotiations) and Libya (shortly thereafter) would quickly test its ability to make good on this commitment.

The Iraqi Expropriation of IPC

On June 1, 1972, in the midst of Persian Gulf participation negotiations, the Iraqi government nationalized the Iraq Petroleum Company, a joint venture of Exxon, Mobil, Shell, BP, CFP, and the Gulbenkian estate. The companies attempted to institute a boycott of Iraqi crude to contain the externalities of Baghdad's actions on the Persian Gulf accords. The U.S. government joined the private company initiative through public exhortation and its influence in MDBs. The common front fell apart almost immediately, however, when France and CFP broke ranks after the takeover. The Europeans, more concerned with uninterrupted supply than regime considerations, were unwilling to go along with the American position in the World Bank. The result was that there was little IPC or the United States could do except for posturing.

The historical roots of the Baghdad/IPC dispute go back to the refusal of the former to pay compensation for the 1961 expropriation of IPC's unexploited concession area. From 1958 until 1961, the Qasm government pressed the companies for 20 percent equity participation, an increase in the tax rate beyond 50 percent, and relinquishment of unexplored areas. IPC consistently rejected these demands because they exceeded terms prevailing elsewhere and could produce a spillover.[65] After a prolonged stalemate, the Iraqi government, on December 12, 1961, passed the "infamous" Law 80 which nationalized all of IPC's concession area not currently under production, decreasing its size from 168,000 to 748 square miles. The takeover included what the company claimed were proven reserves in North Rumailah.[66]

IPC demanded rescission or full compensation and called for arbitration. Regime considerations guided company policy. Any concessions to Iraq, the least important of the Middle East producers, would immediately be demanded by others. IPC decided to make Iraq pay a price for its impertinence and throughout the 1960s, its member companies increased their oil production in other areas at the expense of Iraq.[67]

The State Department reinforced this pressure by discouraging American independents and French and Italian firms (Dean Rusk called them "poachers") from producing in the areas that IPC had been forced to relinquish. As Harriman told the president of Sinclair, "We could not wish to give governments, such as Iraq, the impression that American oil companies can be pushed around."[68]

The dispute erupted anew early in 1972 during negotiations on participation. In February, with technical and financial assistance from the Soviet Union, the Iraqi state company began production from the disputed North Rumailah fields. The first exports of Rumailah oil to the Eastern bloc began in April.[69]

IPC responded with the threat of legal action against purchasers of oil to which it still claimed title in the absence of compensation. To pressure Iraq into arbitration, it reduced its Iraqi production in Kirkuk, Basra, and Mosul, from 1.1 million to 0.6 million bpd. As a result, the Iraqi Ministry of Oil and Minerals estimated a loss of over 50 percent of its foreign exchange receipts during the period of the cutbacks.[70]

Negotiations for participation were complicated by the dispute. IPC offered to increase production and export capacity, on top of 20 percent participation, in return for compensation for Law 80. Iraq countered that compensation for Law 80 was unthinkable and that it was entitled to compensation for discriminatory production policies. On May 17, it gave IPC a two-week ultimatum to increase production or be faced with "legislative measures to safeguard the national interest." IPC refused to comply unless Iraq accepted liability for compensation.[71]

On June 1, after the expiration of the deadline, IPC was nationalized (the smaller Basra and Mosul petroleum companies, with the same ownership structure as IPC, were untouched.) The Iraqi government acknowledged an obligation to pay book value compensation subject to outstanding claims against the company.[72]

The threat posed by the nationalization transcended the consortium's stake in Iraq because each member company had far more significant stakes throughout the Middle East. The offer of book value compensation with retroactive deductions presented a subversive precedent for the not-yet-completed Persian Gulf negotiations. No less ominous was the immediate assumption of total control. As IPC's managing director contended: "We could have done a deal but only by complete capitulation. We would have sold the pass on current industry talks on participation." If, instead, the companies opposed Iraq's imposed settlement, he reasoned, it would have little effect on the Gulf.[73]

IPC responded by imposing a major company boycott of Iraqi exports and threatening legal action against purchasers of "hot" Kirkuk crude. The boycott hampered somewhat the marketing of Iraqi oil, but a number of factors softened its impact.

First, OPEC convened an emergency meeting on June 9 to endorse the Iraqi action and set aside $400 million in financial aid for any shortfall it might suffer. On June 20, Iraq received an initial installment of $151 million from Libya, Kuwait, and Abu Dhabi. The action was motivated by a collective interest in producer solidarity and also by the self-serving desire to forestall Iraqi sales at discounted prices, which in a seller's market would have undermined the economic basis for price increases.[74]

Second, the Eastern bloc was willing to operate the nationalized oilfields and buy Kirkuk crude. Following the nationalization, Iraq signed a trade and economic agreement with the Soviets that included barter deals for oil. The Soviets, however, took only token tankloads to demonstrate solidarity. To do more, one State Department study observed, would "entail a diversion of Soviet tankers from the profitable hard-currency trade with Western Europe."[75]

Third, and most important, was the defection of France and CFP from the solid corporate front. Following the nationalization, Baghdad invited CFP to keep operating its 23.75 percent share of IPC on a contractual basis at prenationalization financial terms. France and CFP, with fewer sources of crude outside Iraq and a greater dependence on Iraqi oil (especially after the Algerian nationalization), had a greater interest in assuring the security of immediate supply than in containing the externalities of the Iraqi action from the Persian Gulf. On June 18, a general agreement was negotiated between Iraqi Vice President Saddam Hussain and CFP, allowing the firm to operate the fields and purchase its crude for ten years.[76]

In the absence of countervailing pressures sufficient to induce compliance, the other IPC members eventually accepted a settlement predominantly on Iraqi terms. On February 28, 1973, IPC agreed to pay $338 million in back taxes in exchange for 15 million tons of crude, valued at $320 million. The consortium increased its Basra and Mosul production, called off the boycott, and withdrew its objection of the 1961 law. This was followed by a long-term buyback arrangement along the lines of the CFP deal.[77]

In the Iraqi case, the U.S. government had an interest in containing precedents that exceeded the Persian Gulf participation formula. It tried to reinforce the efficacy of private efforts by supporting the boycott and blocking Iraq from alternative sources of capital. In this it was wholly unsuccessful. Its most significant action was to vote against a $129 million educational loan from the World Bank.[78]

The vote was designed as a concrete application of Treasury's "presumptive" policy. The Treasury representative at the World Bank had unsuccessfully tried to have the loan deferred because of the absence of the "tangible requirement of reasonable steps." To allow the loan to go through would be a "clear signal to Iraq of the lack of U.S. government interest."[79] State, while expressing consternation at the World Bank for allowing the loan to come up for consideration, preferred an abstention to a negative vote. The latter would be perceived as a "conclusion on our part that the Iraqi government would not pay prompt, adequate, and effective compensation" and produce "unnecessary confrontation with the Arab world."[80]

The episode evinced the structural constraints on Treasury's presumptive approach to the petroleum politics of the 1970s. No other World Bank member supported American efforts to defer or veto the loan. Western Europe and Japan, more concerned with maintaining short-term supply in a tightened energy market, were unwilling to risk a confrontation that might disrupt that supply in order to preserve the participation accords.

Treasury recognized the futility of its action, but

persevered to "demonstrate to the World Bank our dissatisfaction with the management's application of its own policy on expropriation."[81] That this was the most significant result of U.S. involvement testifies to the growing marginality of the U.S. policy in the conduct of petroleum diplomacy. As one State Department official noted, the United States, in its isolated position, would be perceived as "not merely anti-Arab, but ineffectual."[82]

The Libyan Takeover

A second and more serious threat to the durability of the participation accords was posed in the summer of 1973 by Libya's enforced acquisition of 51 percent of the foreign oil concessions. The first Libyan nationalization was of BP's 50 percent share in the Sarir oilfields on December 7, 1971. The motive was ostensibly political: Britain's alleged complicity in Iran's seizure of three small islands claimed by the United Arab Emirates. The nationalization decree provided for compensation (at depreciated book value) to be assessed by a Libyan committee whose decision was final.[83]

BP and the British government formally protested this action as contrary to international law because a contract can be changed only by negotiated settlement, not unilateral fiat, and because it was pursued for political reprisal, not a "public purpose." In addition, the method of valuation was inadequate. The company claimed a market value of $600 million, which included future profits until expiry in 2017. In the absence of binding arbitration, BP would protect its contractual rights by filing suits for writs of attachment against cargoes of crude oil from its Sarir fields.[84]

Convinced that Libya would next move toward full control of the rest of the industry, the oil companies refused to lift BP's Sarir crude. A clear demonstration of industry firmness was needed, as one executive testified, to stave off "accelerated nationalization fever."[85] The U.S. government aligned itself with U.K. representations to prevent a precedent that exceeded the principle of participation.[86]

With the exception of a few "leaks," BP was successful in shutting in 225,000 bpd from its Sarir fields. The fact that title to the oil was disputed deterred potential buyers and depressed the prices Libya could obtain for it.[87] In March 1972 the Soviet Union agreed to jointly develop and refine the oil, and in June the first tanker shipments were sent to the Soviet Union, Romania, and Bulgaria. However, only token quantities were lifted, and Qaddafi publicly expressed displeasure that they were only barter transactions.[88]

Until October 1972, the BP takeover was an isolated event. But with the Gulf arrangements settled, Qaddafi expressed dissatisfaction with the Yamani formula and pressed for immediate 51 percent ownership. The consequence of noncompliance, he threatened, would be shut-ins or expropriation. One company, the Italian state firm, ENI, accepted the terms. The rest, with an eye on the Gulf, refused.[89]

Pressure was next applied to one of the independents, Bunker Hunt, which owned the other 50 percent of the Sarir fields. Qaddafi demanded that Hunt lift from BP's share and cede 51 percent of its equity for depreciated book value. When Hunt refused, its production was halted on May 24, 1973. On June 11, Hunt was nationalized. While Libya acknowledged a pecuniary liability, this was more than offset by a counterclaim of $140 million in back taxes.[90]

Hunt joined BP in legal action to block the sale of Sarir crude. Suits were filed in Brazil, Italy, Greece, and Houston, Texas, although much of the oil went to Eastern Europe where it was safe from pursuit.[91] The State Department protested the takeover as an act of "political reprisal and economic coercion" contrary to international law. It used its influence to dissuade companies from buying Sarir crude to make it as difficult as possible for Libya to "profit by its unlawful acts."[92] Finally, the Libyan Producers Agreement came into effect to present a solid corporate front against a new round of "leapfrogging" demands on ownership.

The efficacy of these actions was weakened by the tightening oil market in the summer of 1973. First, there was a "flood of panicked buyers for expropriated oil, better enabling Libya to market the crude directly." This development was abetted by a February 1973 decision of a Sicily court that dismissed BP's ownership claims and allowed the entry of Sarir crude.[93] Second, market conditions rendered the Libyan Producers Agreement ineffective. Crude oil could no longer be set aside for deprived companies except at the expense of lost sales. The independents and crude-short Mobil fell far short of their obligations to Hunt.[94]

On August 1, the Libyan government issued a thirty day ultimatum for the companies to cede 51 percent or face nationalization. Occidental was the first to comply on August 11. Noting the failure of the industry to adequately compensate Hunt for its losses, Occidental was faced with the threat of full expropriation and exclusion from its only Eastern hemisphere source of crude. The settlement transferred 51 percent of Occidental's equity to the Libyan state company in exchange for a book value compensation of $135 million and a buyback arrangement at $4.90 per barrel.[95]

On August 16, a similar agreement was reached with the independent partners in the Oasis consortium. The other Oasis partner, Shell, refused to comply and was subsequently barred from lifting from its share of the concession. Libya next gave Amoseas—a joint venture of Socal and Texaco—an August 25 deadline to come to terms. The rest of the companies had until September 1.[96]

The majors subsequently informed the State Department that they would form a common front against Libyan demands. They cited three damaging precedents: the immediate acquisition of majority control; compensation based upon depreciated rather than updated book value; and a buyback price intended to push up rather than reflect the market price. Libya per se, was not the key issue. Acceptance would surely reopen the hard-fought Persian Gulf arrangements and precipitate a new round of demands. The majors resolved to "stand firm and risk the total loss of their properties" to provide a "sounder basis for protecting the Persian Gulf participation arrangements from the spillover of Libya's greater financial and operating control gains."[97]

On September 1, Libya announced the 51 percent takeover of the remaining companies. Compensation was to be set by a commission, selected solely by the Libyan government, at depreciated book value, and the buyback price was set at $6 per barrel. The companies were allowed to continue to operate their 49 percent share until they complied.[98]

The majors protested and formally demanded arbitration. On September 6, company representatives met in New York to coordinate a showdown with Libya. All agreed to stop lifting and each was free to "take such [legal] steps as it deems necessary to protect its rights." Representatives of Exxon, Shell, and Socal approached the State Department for an "embargo [sic!] of 'illegally' expropriated Libyan oil from the U.S. market . . . or at least a statement that the USG was considering such an embargo." Western consumers would be told that this was the only responsible strategy against Libya's "arbitrary use of sovereign power."[99]

The State Department concurred that the pursuit of "hot" oil was the best strategy available. On September 14, it published a note of protest to Libya for its "absence of indication of intent to pay prompt, adequate, and effective compensation." It urged customers of companies whose properties had been confiscated not to buy from Libya.[100] The policy was reinforced by a public statement by President Nixon:

> Oil without a market, as Mr. Mossadegh learned many, many years ago, does not do a country much good. . . . Responsible Arab leaders will see to it if they up the price, if they continue to expropriate, if they do expropriate without fair compensation, the inevitable result is that they will lose their markets, and other sources will be developed.[101]

The Iranian case, however, was an outmoded precedent for the petroleum diplomacy of the 1970s. In 1951, the loss of Iranian oil could be made up by increased production elsewhere. In the tightened energy market of 1973, Libyan oil was needed. This was implicitly conceded by the State Department, which rejected suggestions for a complete boycott and made only halfhearted attempts to block Libyan sales.

When European governments such as Germany, Spain, Greece and Italy were sounded out about a full boycott, the responses were uniformly negative. Western Europe was heavily dependent upon Libyan crude; it received 650,000 bpd from the nationalized fields, production that could not easily be made up elsewhere. One State official, conceding the logic of the European position, admitted that the United States could not compel them to boycott Libyan oil. As smaller powers "they do not try to shape the world as we do," but "roll with the punch" to protect short-term commercial interests.[102]

Due to the acute supply situation, State could not even prevent American refiners from purchasing Libyan oil and using it in the domestic market. Almost immediately after the takeover, the New England Petroleum Company (NEPCO), a refiner that supplies 60 percent of the oil requirements of Consolidated Edison, began lifting from the nationalized Texaco/Socal concession and transported several cargoes to its refinery in Sardinia. Texaco and Socal subsequently filed suit against these purchasers in Sardinia.

State's Legal Bureau interceded on behalf of Texaco and Socal. NEPCO was informed that the oil had been illegally seized and the companies held title to it: "Contracting to buy it weakens the hands of the companies now locked in difficult negotiations with the Libyan government . . . [and undercuts] U.S. diplomatic representations to other States, such as Italy and Brazil, not to buy hot oil." To open the door to the flow of "hot" oil into the United States would eviscerate the most potent enforcer of regime rules: "If foreign governments see that American investors cannot successfully pursue production seized in violation of international law, the security of much of some 80 billion dollars of U.S. investment abroad will be weakened."[103]

NEPCO was unmoved by the warning. It contended that in view of the tight supply situation, no other oil was available. The consequence of not lifting would be serious "brownouts" in New York City and major parts of New England.[104] Despite recommendations put forward by the Legal Bureau, State did not request the U.S. courts to consider the legality of the Libyan action, without which acts of a foreign sovereign can not be considered illegal for the purpose of pursuing "hot" products. Given the domestic consequences of a "principled" stand, it went only so far as to request firms not to buy, but would not allow the courts to move against firms with contractual obligations and no alternative sources of supply. As one official noted, "In 1973, getting oil was more important than filing claims."[105]

Although it recognized that countermeasures would not be effective, the Legal Bureau maintained a protest on behalf of legal principle because "actions by one state transgressing the rights of another which go unprotested may be tantamount to the latter state's acquiescence. Acquiescence can lead to rendering lawful that which was unlawful."[106] Despite words and documents that give lip service to time-honored principles, it was evident that the United States no longer possessed the surfeit of economic resources that could enable it to absorb the costs of defending those principles. Its behavior more closely resembled that of an "ordinary power" placing greater stress on short-term costs and benefits than on principle and precedent. All pretensions about "holding the line" were blown away the next month by OPEC actions following the 1973 Arab-Israeli War.

The October Revolution: Corporate Adaptation to Regime Change

OPEC policies during and after the Yom Kippur War marked the final blow to the traditional regime protecting the private petroleum concessions. The companies lost formal ownership and any input in setting prices and production levels. The Arab oil embargo enacted the worst-case scenario that had haunted U.S. policymakers in their hesitant attempts to stem regime erosion, namely, that host country control over natural resources would be employed as a means of political reprisal.

First, OPEC ended the fiction of negotiating posted prices with the companies. Expressing dissatisfaction with the Teheran accords, OPEC cited *rebus sic stantibus* (changed circumstances) and convened special negotiations with the industry on October 8. On October 12, the company negotiators adjourned to consult with their parent governments. An OPEC communiqué on October 16 unilaterally increased the posted price by 70 percent, from $3.01 to $5.12 per barrel. On December 23, the price was again raised to $11.65 per barrel, nearly a 400 percent increase in just over two months.[107] These decisions conclusively established the producers' ability to take whatever decision they liked on pricing without reference to the oil companies.

The pricing "shocks" reverbrated into the participation issue. On November 13, Yamani informed the companies that they must expedite the transfer of equity because of the "changed circumstances of the Libyan and Iraqi actions and the upheaval in world oil prices."[108] On January 29, 1974, Kuwait took over 60 percent of its Gulf/BP consortium and Qatar followed suit on February 20. Saudi negotiations with Aramco were next.

These changes ended the chapter on corporate efforts to fight off nationalization. In May, 1974, Aramco agreed to the 60 percent formula. One month earlier, Exxon and Mobil acceded to Libya's 51 percent takeover, although Qaddafi would not budge from his compensation formula. By the end of 1974, all of the companies had signed at least preliminary settlements with Libya.[109] The rationale for resistance—preventing a precedent that might stimulate "actions elsewhere"—was no longer valid. The "actions elsewhere" had already taken place.

The new order compelled the oil companies to modify

their strategy. The industry reconciled itself to host country ownership and the demise of the concession system, and fell back on its considerable assets that were not diminished by the changed scene. The hosts still needed their technology, expertise, and access to markets. In general, they were able to use these counterweights to obtain service contracts with the new state entities.

Expropriation and compensation became secondary issues. More important were the contractual terms governing the post-expropriation relationship. If participation crude was made available at something less than market price, the companies could still supply their downstream operations. As one oil company executive put it, "Ownership is a semantic issue; the underlying business issue is access and price." Or, as another justified his firm's staying on in Libya: "You don't walk away from Libya if there is any way to get a deal that assures supply at market prices." In 1976, 85 percent of the oil pumped in Libya was supervised by American companies.[110]

In sum, the companies saw their role transformed from big offtakers of owned crude to bulk purchasers of large volumes from state companies. Some firms even cited advantages in having the producers as partners because they would take a greater economic interest in the industry and would deflect popular antagonism against local economic conditions.[111]

With respect to these events, as with other incursions into the international oil industry, the U.S. government played a marginal role. Initially alarmed by the magnitude of change, the United States attempted to confront OPEC with a solid front of producers. But Europe and Japan were far more dependent upon Middle Eastern oil and were unwilling to accept the cost and risk of a confrontational strategy. Nor was the United States in a position to supply them with spare oil while waiting out such a confrontation. With the erosion of the economic bases of the regime, there was little the United States could do to prevent the loss of ownership or its prerogatives.

While regime decay imposed the cost of higher prices, accommodation to it served short-term diplomatic and national economic security goals. In this, there was a bureaucratic convergence between the Nixon-Kissinger "grand design" and OFE's strategy of accommodation. Kissinger hoped that the transfer of revenue to conservative Middle East governments would strengthen them vis-à-vis internal rebellion and "proxy wars." Financing these governments through increased oil revenues provided a seductive alternative to a controversial direct aid program. Akins and OFE labeled the concession system an "anachronism" and argued that security of supply was not incompatible with host country ownership: "There is abundant evidence that most producers want to retain the companies' technical expertise even after their present arrangements are terminated through production or exploration service contracts." Corporate adaptation to this role would allow Western consumers to "retain the orderly and efficient processing and distribution systems that the majors will continue to supply even if they are required to divorce their production activities from their marketing role."[112]

In many ways, the issues of oil and the Middle East are unique cases from which it would be difficult to generalize about the evolution of United States anti-expropriation policy. The United States would be less prone to provoke a confrontation over the former where the short-term costs of a symbolic victory risked the disruption of so indispensable a commodity. Nor was it well placed to succeed in the latter because of the region's decreased susceptibility to American influence and increased vulnerability to Soviet penetration.

Regime change, moreover, had a serious effect on the American economy and the oil embargo portended the possibility of future threats to stability of supply. The success of OPEC had spurred other Third World raw material producers to assert greater control over natural resource investments within their borders and attempt cartelization or other commodity stabilization schemes. The question then posed to American resource diplomacy was how applicable the lessons of nationalization of oil in the Middle East were to other resources in other regions. Were national economic and security interests better served by accommodation or resistance to the obsolescing bargain? Which sorts of change were inimical to U.S. overseas interests and which were not? These questions would be the subject of a policy review and bureaucratic debate in 1974.

9.

From Principle to Pragmatism: The Search for Détente with Economic Nationalism

In their call for a New International Economic Order (NIEO), Third World nations demanded a revision of the "liberal" rules and institutions that had governed the world economy since World War II. Prominent among their demands was the principle of Permanent Sovereignty over Natural Resources which proclaimed the right of host countries to nationalize or renegotiate the terms of raw material investments unimpeded by international obligations. The success of OPEC in restructuring the international petroleum industry became the paradigm for others to assume sovereign control over their natural wealth. The result was a transformation of the rules governing international property relations in the extraction of natural resources.

MNCs initially resisted challenges to the traditional concession system, but ultimately adapted to the new era of state control. They recognized that expropriation was not necessarily the most serious threat they faced. In most cases, nationalization policies were pursued within the context of a dependent, rather than self-reliant, model of development. National ownership foreclosed some corporate options, but allowed continued operation on a contractual instead of concessionary basis. Corporate objectives were redirected to the licensing of technical and managerial services and the buyback and marketing of primary production. Most firms opposed parent government economic reprisal because, as was evidenced by the IPC affair, it was ineffective and it vitiated the climate for ongoing operations.

The initial U.S. government response to the wave of nationalizations following the OPEC "revolution" was unequivocally hostile. It refused to budge from traditional economic and legal precepts at the United Nations. Confrontation with the Third World over principle was necessary to abort future assaults on the international economic system.

By late 1974, the State Department moved from confrontation to partial cooperation with the NIEO in order to reform and legitimize the system. Anti-expropriation policy was similarly reassessed and revised. The combination of materials shortages and inconclusive confrontations, such as Peru over IPC, altered the instrumental assumptions of American policy. The negative impact of coercive strategies upon the immediate investment climate and security of supply assumed greater importance. Prudence dictated a need to form a kind of ideological détente between the principles of national sovereignty and contractual sanctity. The new "pragmatic" approach downgraded principle and precedent and encouraged corporate adaptation in the interests of post-expropriation cooperation between firm and host and improved bilateral relations. Arbitrary wealth deprivations would be enjoined not by concentrated private or public sanctions, but by decentralized market forces (e.g., uneconomic behavior would exact its own price in the form of loss of markets, future investments, or credits).

This change was not unanimously supported throughout the bureaucracy and was, for a time, actively opposed by Treasury. Treasury read the recent spate of nationalizations as an argument against compromise. It preferred a stricter application of the presumptive approach which, in its view, had all too often been honored in the breach. In this, it saw a divergence between the firm's short-term interest in adaptation and Treasury's mission to protect the U.S. economy. Some firms took the line of least resistance to unreasonable demands in order to maintain "access" because they could pass on the added costs through higher prices and tax write-offs. In addition, such firms set precedents that redounded against others and increased state intervention in the world economy. By Treasury guidelines, an activist policy was necessary to restructure corporate incentives away from acquiescence.

Treasury was constrained from translating its preference into policy, in part, by bureaucratic factors, e.g., Kissinger's reclamation of foreign economic policy for State with the resignation of Nixon. Also, systemic factors—the decentralization of private and public economic resources and the obsolescing bargain process—rendered concrete activist proposals ineffective. Treasury, over time, recognized this constraint and retreated to advocacy of a multilateral approach, which, in turn, was destined to fail because Western Europe and Japan did not share the same perception of events. As a result, what began as a substantive bureaucratic difference with State devolved into a debate over incremental or marginal responses.

From an examination of the bureaucratic debate, and the implementation of policy against investment disputes in Peru, Venezuela, and Jamaica, the operational assumptions of U.S. anti-expropriation policy can be summarized as follows:

1. Nationalization can not be deterred by private or public economic sanctions and is, moreover, no longer a critical issue. Access to raw materials can be maintained by cementing a post-expropriation relationship between firm and host which allows the former to market the resources.

a. The real threat to U.S. economic interests, i.e., security of supply and price stability, derives not from expropriation, *per se,* but from the subsequent terms of agreement, i.e., posted prices or tax levies designed to increase world commodity prices. The ability of LDC hosts to impose such terms is more a function of market scarcities than of national ownership.

b. Corporate viability is threatened less by expropriation than by regulations, such as confiscatory taxes, repatriation limitations, production limits, multiple exchange rates, and inconvertibility.

2. The traditional standard of "prompt, adequate and effective" compensation is no longer ascertainable. It represents, at best, only a starting point in negotiations. In most cases, something less than book value compensation is paid. The gap between methods of valuation can be bridged by an ongoing relationship between firm and host which allows the former to operate profitably.

3. Measures of economic reprisal, formal or informal, are no longer effective because of the obsolescing bargain process, the multiplicity of sources of aid, the loss of veto power in many MDBs, and the willingness of newcomers to break ranks with established firms.

a. The climate for ongoing operations is best enhanced by amicable bilateral relations, corporate good citizenship, and a lower-visibility means of operation.

b. Where informal withholding of aid is employed, as in Jamaica and Guyana, the results are economically inconsequential and intended only as symbolic disapproval. Such policies are generally avoided because they heighten confrontation and vitiate the chances for mutually acceptable compensation settlements or ongoing relations.

c. Formal sanctions are applied only in the most egregious instances where Cold War issues are seen as involved (i.e., Ethiopia). In these cases, the suspension is primarily "political" in motivation and redundant in effect because it usually ratifies a prior termination of United States aid.

    d. Capricious refusal to proffer any compensation or
       tolerate a continued corporate presence is best con-
       strained by the diffuse sanction that even risk-tak-
       ing firms and lenders will no longer deem the host
       an acceptable site for future investments and cred-
       its.
    e. The arbitrary exercise of economic sovereignty in
       pushing up prices is best constrained by the market
       forces of supply and demand, which will inevitably
       shrink the market share of an overpriced product.
    f. The U.S. can best facilitate setting the parameters of
       the quasi-regime by encouraging diversification of
       sources of supply. This represents a reorientation of
       strategy away from traditional regime maintenance
       toward the protection of national economic and se-
       curity interests from the consequences of regime ero-
       sion.

Corporate Adaptation
to the Obsolescing Bargain

The success of OPEC, both as a model for emulation and a
prod through higher energy prices, initially expedited the obsolescing bargain process. At the United Nations, the Group
of 77 called for unencumbered sovereignty over natural resources, warning firms that they operate at the will of sovereign states. Producer countries moved more relentlessly toward nationalization or its functional equivalent. The trend
was most pronounced in oil, but was also evident in copper,
bauxite, and other minerals.

    Despite these developments, a number of studies and
statements by business organizations reveal that, although
uneasiness persisted about arbitrary confiscation and the absence of internationally recognized settlement machinery,
expropriation was downgraded as a concern among overseas
investors. These surveys found that apprehension about na-

tionalization was most pronounced among extractive firms because of their immobility and greater sensitivity to host country exactions. In that sector, however, firms have learned that adaptation even to worst-case scenarios is possible. After nationalization, firms have usually not been totally excluded. LDCs have continued to rely on technology, management, and marketing services which the firms supply through service contracts for a fee. This has enabled vertically integrated natural resource firms to maintain access to mineral ores or crude oil for their downstream operations.[1]

Overseas investors evidenced a willingness to come to terms with the obsolescing bargain process and economic pluralism in the Third World. *The Americas in a Changing World,* a study supervised by Sol Linowitz for the Commission of United States–Latin American Relations, a private organization with heavy corporate membership, noted that U.S. business could coexist with a variety of relationships between the state and the private sector.[2] Exxon, in its 1974 *Annual Statement,* demonstrated a certain equanimity uncharacteristic of its earlier attitude toward state involvement:

[A] sound basis for continued relationships between producing countries and the industry [exists], though the relationship will be different from those which existed when the companies were discovering and developing the oil and gas reserves from which those countries derive now their economic power.[3]

Isaiah Frank's study of foreign investors found that companies had moved away from a rigid adherence to contractual sanctity toward a more flexible attitude toward renegotiation. One respondent explained that "these are the facts of life which any company has to live with."[4]

Expropriation and state control were less important than the terms of the ongoing relationship. A Council of the Americas study found that investors were more concerned with restrictive economic policies, political instability, multiple exchange rates, remittance restrictions, inconvertibility, inflation, and political instability, than they were with expropriation.[5] In brief, corporate perceptions of political risk had been redefined.

A business consensus looked skeptically upon U.S. retaliatory actions as outmoded and ineffective. According to the Frank study, most favored a minimal U.S. government role, and in the CIEP study, a soft-line approach was preferred by a margin of two to one.[6] Reprisals were not only considered useless, but counterproductive as well. They fanned the flames of xenophobic nationalism and left the corporate community hostage to the ensuing reaction. The fallout often visited collateral damage upon firms not involved in a dispute (as was the case in Peru) and soured the prospects for compromise settlements and ongoing relationships between affected firm and host. In 1973, the Council of the Americas lobbied against the Gonzales Amendment and sought to make Hickenlooper Amendment discretionary.[7] Experiences such as that of IPC in Peru crystallized an awareness of the futility and costs of traditional investment protection policies.

Unless all foreign capital was under attack, firms generally opted for what Lipson called "a more self-reliant approach to political risk." Visible association with the U.S. government was seen more as a liability than an asset. For example, the South Peru Copper Company (SPCC) held aloof from U.S. foreign policy positions and never used diplomatic channels in its disputes with the government. When the Indonesian government demanded contractual renegotiations in the mid-1970s, the major oil companies did not even keep the American embassy in Jakarta informed.[8]

Most respondents to these studies contended that the key to greater investment security was lower visibility and the adjustment of international operations to local sentiment and host country priorities. In this, many saw national control as an opportunity to lower their profiles and legitimize their access to primary product. George Philip found that Gulf Oil actually encouraged the Ecuadoran government to nationalize it in 1976 because "the company had more potential control over exports than it had over taxation legislation." United Fruit sold off most of its agricultural lands to local nationals to play the role of middleman, marketing bananas under the brand name "Chiquita." As one foreign investor noted, "When in Rome, don't just do as the Romans do, but look like Romans doing it."[9]

Even with nationalization, investors believed that market forces would ensure some kind of reasonable opportunity. If a host country was excessive in its demands, deterrence would be achieved through "diffuse, uncoordinated sanctions . . . because it discourages new investments by raising the associated risks."[10] In other words, the ultimate sanction against the capricious exercise of economic sovereignty should not reside in public reprisals, which are viewed as clumsy and further poisoning the environment. Rather, correcting forces would come into play as the host became an unsuitable site for future lending or investment. The parameters of a new quasi-regime would be enforced by the decentralized threat of corporate ostracism.

Corporate accommodation to the obsolescing bargain was based upon the following syllogism:

1. National control over primary production could no longer be deterred.
2. Nationalization was not necessarily inimical to the firm's global strategy if it could obtain technology and managements service contracts which retain access to primary production for downstream operations.
3. Public economic sanctions, formal or informal, vitiate the local climate for profitable adaptation to change.

Extractive transnationals, therefore, tried to legitimize their presence by accepting some diminution of their traditional prerogatives. Unfortunately, these changes followed years of a noticeably less "progressive" outlook, the memory of which was not easily forgotten.

The Evolution of United States
Expropriation Policy:
Tailoring Principle to Practicality

FROM RESISTANCE TO ACCOMMODATION
AT THE UNITED NATIONS

In late 1974, U.S. anti-expropriation policy changed from a deterrent approach focusing on principle and precedent to a pragmatic one, sacrificing principle to facilitate an ongoing corporate presence and smooth over bilateral diplomatic relations. The development of policy can be understood within the context of the unfolding of United States policy toward the NIEO at the United Nations from 1974 to 1975.

Encouraged by the success of OPEC and the image of the West on the defensive, Third World nations contended that the so-called "liberal" international economic system hindered their full emancipation by maintaining unequal terms of exchange and conditions of economic colonialism. In the Programme for a New International Economic Order (May 1974) and the Charter on the Economic Rights and Duties of States (December 1974), they demanded revisions such as price indexation, commodity arrangements, a debt moratorium, technology transfer, and greater decision-making power in international economic institutions.

In the doctrine of Permanent Sovereignty over Natural Resources, they declared the inalienable right to "nationalize, expropriate or transfer ownership of foreign property."[11] The resolution overturned a 1962 compromise (see pages 43–44) that linked compensation both to sovereignty and international law. The new doctrine declared that states have an inalienable right to dispose of natural wealth within their boundaries freely and fully. Investment disputes with aliens over ownership of this wealth were within the exclusive jurisdiction of the host state's judicial system without any minimum standards of conduct for compensation imposed by international law. Parent country diplomatic protection was categorized as an act of economic aggression: "No State may be subject to economic, political, or any other type of coercion to prevent the full exercise of this inalienable right."[12]

The United States took exception to this doctrine as a license for theft and a challenge to the very foundation of the international property regime. Ambassador Scali opposed its adoption because it did not "couple the assertion of the right to nationalize with the duty to pay compensation in accordance with international law." It excluded hosts from any international obligation, offering no protection against an "arbitrary standard of compensation or . . . the capricious administration of compensation laws by a local tribunal."[13]

The general tone of the U.S. approach to the "revolt from below" reflected a persistence of the Connally-style "get tough" mentality. Third World demands, coming on the heels of the OPEC increases, were viewed as blackmail and theft. A passive response to them would be interpreted as "appeasement" and a "failure of will." The United States should be more forthright in upholding the principles it had traditionally espoused. The session ended in considerable rancor with Ambassador Scali decrying the "tyranny of the majority" and administration officials making veiled hints about the possible use of force.[14]

The State Department ultimately regarded confrontation as less a policy than an admission of frustration. With growing dependence on imported raw materials and increasing LDC bargaining strength vis-à-vis MNCs, some form of *modus vivendi* was needed to assure security of supply. In the fall of 1974, Kissinger had Undersecretary for Economic Affairs Thomas Enders conduct a major policy review of U.S. policy toward the NIEO. Kissinger's hand was strengthened when Nixon resigned. Under Ford, he was able to reclaim foreign economic policy for State by taking issues out of the CIEP and placing them within the NSC where Treasury's clout was diminished.[15]

To Kissinger and Enders, not all aspects of the NIEO were necessarily inimical to United States interests. The experience of OPEC and subsequent challenges to the international economic system created an awareness of the potentially disruptive power of the poor, who perceived themselves as disfranchised from the world economic structure. To remove the stresses on the system, some LDC grievances had to be addressed as valid. If the United States continued to respond with hostility or indifference, a further radicalization of the Third World was inevitable. At the Seventh Special Session of the UN General Assembly, Kissinger expressed a willingness to discuss a number of formerly taboo subjects: stabilization agreements for specific commodities, preferential access to Western markets, transfer of technology, and codes of conduct for MNCs.[16]

The Kissinger proposals were not designed to overturn the existing international economic system which, he noted, had "generally served the world well." Rather, they reflected a strategy of "preservative adaptation."[17] The stresses in the system emerged because of the growth in LDC economic power and a concomitant sense of disfranchisement from the benefits of the system. Tactical adjustments of interest were necessary to create a new "equilibrium" and stabilize the system. In some areas, the rhetoric of confrontation had to be rephrased to harmonize with new perceptions. An example of this was the attempt to span the doctrinal gap between the Hull Doctrine and the principle of Permanent Sovereignty in the area of expropriation.

EXPROPRIATION AND BUREAUCRATIC POLITICS,
1974–77

In August 1974 the Economic Policy Board (which had subsumed the CIEP) conducted a review of expropriation policy.[18] In the context of the rising number of takeovers without "adequate" compensation, recent OPEC actions, worldwide supply shortages, and the growing U.S. dependence on imported raw materials, a number of questions were asked: Should the United States more frequently impose economic sanctions; establish more explicit guidelines to set the boundaries of acceptable host country actions; develop an early warning system to anticipate expropriation; make another presidential statement; or establish a new cabinet-level department, like the Special Trade Representative (STR) for trade, to coordinate a more activist policy?

The bureaucratic lines were drawn between the "pragmatists" at State, who favored accommodation in order to avoid diplomatic confrontation and maintain access to supplies through post-expropriation arrangements, and the "activists" at Treasury, who urged a strengthening of policy to deflect the adverse consequences of expropriation from the American economy. The contest, which continued on and off until the first year of the Carter administration, was won by State. The "presumptive" policy was replaced by one of "benign neglect" which encouraged (or accepted) corporate accommodation and relied on market forces to ameliorate the consequences of regime erosion.

In part, this outcome reflected Kissinger's bureaucratic reclamation of foreign economic policy. It also reflected changes in transnational relations, such as the decentralization of private and public economic resources and the obsolescing bargain process, which weakened traditional regime enforcement capabilities. Treasury modified its position as, with increased involvement with the issue, it was exposed to the systemic constraints of unilateral actions. As a result, its differences with State became more incremental than substantive.

State Department officials generally opposed the use of economic reprisal, stringent guidelines, or the creation of a specialized agency. Retaliatory sanctions were eschewed except as a response of last resort in the most egregious cases. Repeal of the Hickenlooper and Gonzales amendments was high on the agenda. One official wrote that since they have scope for nonapplication and only mean something if the executive branch wants them to, "they have all the drawbacks of a threat and none of the advantages. They are not credible. Their presence on the statute books is . . . offensive to Latin America."[19] Another noted that the use of the IADB as an arm of short-term economic interests would only undermine hemispheric relations.[20]

In part, this stance was characteristic of the traditional State Department preference for flexibility to balance off the many factors that embody the national interest: "The individual nature of each dispute . . . militates for ad-hockery rather than either an established bureaucratic structure or preconceived guidelines and categories."[21] The approach, however, was not unrelated to corporate or U.S. economic interests. Rather, it was predicated on the belief that the climate for foreign investment would be enhanced not by reprisal and confrontation, but by a greater sensitivity to the priorities of LDC elites, corporate good citizenship, and a lower-visibility means of operation.

Officials recognized that security of supply was not incompatible with state ownership. While the gap between the principles of contractual sanctity and Permanent Sovereignty was theoretically unbridgeable, there was considerable variance between the principles espoused and the reality of negotiations between investors and hosts. Despite claims of absolute sovereignty over natural resources, LDCs had invariably paid some compensation and allowed companies to stay on as service contractors and marketers. As one official wrote, "a new reality is emerging in the handling of investment disputes . . . quite different from what appears on the verbal surface." The United States, another argued, should work to promote a "process of ideological détente."[22]

Events in the Middle East were read as solid evidence that a pragmatic expropriation policy supported national economic security. Firms could legitimate and ensure supplies by ceding ownership and providing services to develop and market the resources. In so doing, they "avoid the question of ownership and all the issues that stir up emotions in the developing world."[23]

Another argument against an active policy was the opposition of most private firms:

> In some cases, the firms were even less anxious . . . to invoke sanctions because they felt either they could cut a deal on their own, or they had interests in a particular country which went beyond the expropriation of a particular set of assets.

To support a "publicly announced standard which would rarely be ascertainable" would only heighten tensions and make it more difficult to "shape an acceptable compensation package or ensure a long-term supply agreement." In effect, the United States could be cast in "the role of the boy scout helping the little old lady who doesn't really want to go across the street."[24]

State's preference was for what one official called a "laissez-faire" approach in which investors and hosts pursue their own interests and assume all the relevant risks:

> Investors can and do treat "political risk" like any other business risk and seek a high enough rate of return to offset the risk or try to obscure the foreign image of the investment through joint ventures.
>
> Expropriating governments can and do assume the risk of decreasing capital flows which may be caused by some expropriations.

"The private market, particularly the banking sector, can and often does exert sufficient leverage" to assure some compensation or acceptable terms for ongoing relations.[25] Decision makers were aware that a minimum level of order was imposed by the latent threat of private-sector noninvolvement.

Support for a "laissez-faire" approach did not connote an indifference to host country actions. Rather, it reflected a recognition that formal ownership was peripheral to the issue of national economic security. The Arab oil embargo, after all, preceded the Persian Gulf states' acquisition of majority ownership. The real threat to American interests came from worldwide supply shortages and growing dependence on imported raw materials. Enders testified that the only viable means to alleviate the threat posed by Third World commodity power was to increase domestic exploration and "investment in alternative supplies starts on a large scale as consumers conclude they could no longer count on traditional suppliers."[26]

The United States could hasten the process of diversification through the Overseas Private Investment Corporation (OPIC), and Eximbank incentives. This approach paralleled OFE's during the oil negotiations, that is, accepting the inevitable devolution of formal control to the host country, maintaining short-term security of supply through service contracts, and encouraging long-term market forces that would soften the effects of regime decay.

Treasury, in contrast, read the lessons of the recent past as a spur to a more consistent commitment to the "presumptive" approach. It painted a grim picture of "an increasing trend toward nationalization of US-owned property abroad." The bleak outlook was a function of a number of forces which altered the host country's decision calculus for expropriation:

> In the past, expropriation on narrow economic grounds was to some extent self-defeating, i.e., discouraging future investment flows, and was costly either in compensation costs or because of reprisal action. Now, with stiff competition for LDC raw materials, decreasing real costs, and eroding international standards, the economic incentive structure may actually favor expropriation.

As a result, investors have been at a significant bargaining disadvantage vis-à-vis sovereign states, and settlements have only averaged 50 to 70 percent of book value, "a measure of value which generally understates the fair value of the property taken."[27]

State's pragmatic approach drew fire because of its inclination to "give the expropriating country the benefit of the doubt by liberally interpreting the statutes for the imposition of economic sanctions." State's bureaucratic predisposition led it to smooth over bilateral relations, "almost always favor[ing] inaction." U.S. policy, therefore, responded only to diplomatic interests while economic interests were insufficiently articulated.[28]

Treasury interpreted the trend toward nationalization and the investor's short-term interest in adapting to it as harmful to the American economy:

> The investor often has an aversion to protracted and uncertain negotiations and—as in the petroleum expropriations—frequently seems to prefer to take minimal compensation and to try to profit from a continuing relationship. He will, then, cushion the loss by taking a tax write-off.[29]

Consistent with Connally's opposition to the copper companies in Peru, Treasury saw accommodation as a threat to the regime and, in turn, to its main constituencies—the American consumer and taxpayer.

Foremost in Treasury's prescription to preserve the regime was the need to respond to all challenges:

> The investments may be insignificant from the point of view of U.S. economic interests, but a failure to respond to the pattern may invite later expropriatory action. To preclude expropriatory action, the U.S. should be visibly protecting the interests of its investors.

But while the "USG must be concerned with the 'precedent-setting' nature of a particular settlement . . . an expropriated firm need not be." That is, an individual firm, in order to retain access, had a material interest in capitulation to a settlement that could have a "spillover effect" and undermine the global position of other U.S. overseas operations.[30]

Corporate adaptation harmed the U.S. economy because firms passed on expropriation losses through higher prices, thereby generating inflation: "Companies may be willing to bear the costs of an expropriation and then 'pass them on,' adding to inflation and the burdens of the consumer. USG interests are the opposite."[31] Inflation was also fueled by increased state involvement in the international economic system. This invariably increased commodity prices because government decisions, based upon political rather than market criteria, were inefficient, and "investors back[ed] off from what would otherwise [have been] productive investments.[32] Adaptation worked against Treasury's mission to promote a more competitive and efficient world economy.

Pragmatism also translated into reduced U.S. Treasury revenue. Under then-current tax laws, fifty cents of each dollar lost in an inadequately compensated expropriation settlement was written off against domestic, as well as foreign income taxes. If the critical issue for the firm was access, the tax write-off added to its disincentive to negotiate a tough bargain. The end result was that companies negotiate less advantageous settlements, and take "deductible loss on expropriation," rather than "realize taxable gain."[33]

Treasury favored an "activist" policy on expropriation to redress the investor's bargaining disadvantages and increase its incentive to press for tougher settlements. It advocated stricter guidelines to set the parameters of acceptable host country action and a clear expression of intent to invoke sanctions once those boundaries are crossed.[34] To provide the institutional framework for a more systematic approach, it proposed the creation of a cabinet-level Special Representative for Overseas Investment who could provide "early warning" to anticipate expropriation or review settlements as a "control over a company which may be too anxious to settle."[35]

Treasury officials conceded that its approach would exacerbate confrontation with the Third World:

We recognize that a more active USG role might seem to put the USG in a position of "confrontation" against the expropriating government. *The dispute may not be over facts, but over matters of principle*; the expropriating government may be under political pressures to take an anti-U.S. stand. In some cases, such as

Libya, this will be of little consequence because confrontation is inherent and cannot be avoided. (Emphasis added.)

U.S. overseas economic interests are ill served by compromises which only whet the Third World's appetite for future assaults. Confrontation over principle may entail some short-run costs, but would aid U.S. economic interests in the long run after "our strength and constancy have been demonstrated."[36]

However, after involvement with the issue for a time, Treasury discovered that transnational forces undermined its ability to arrest change unilaterally. "Standing alone," one official noted, "the U.S. cannot successfully bring sufficient pressure to bear to deter expropriations." Treasury's main emphasis shifted to multilateral efforts to exploit a presumed community of interest with other capital-exporting states, e.g., a Hot Products Convention, or better coordination of contributors to MDBs. Europe and Japan, however, had long since downplayed concern over nationalization. Without their support, officials recognized that unilateral reprisals would only increase LDC hostility without "adding significantly to the investor's bargaining strength."[37]

As Treasury became aware of the systemic constraints on an activist approach, its differences with State devolved from substantive to incremental. In 1977, one high-level official took note of the limited utility of pressure and the loosening of guidelines:

> Instead of requiring that actual negotiations be in progress, we have asked only that a country indicate that it is or is willing to make "reasonable progress" toward settlements. . . . The threat of [Gonzales Amendment] sanctions is a technique to get settlements, but actual "no" votes are not particularly useful.[38]

Its differences with State were over issuing more principled rhetoric or tougher positions vis-à-vis the most flagrant cases in politically marginal areas (Ethiopia, Southern Yemen, People's Republic of the Congo) where aid cutoffs would have little meaning anyway.[39] As the limits of United States economic power became evident, interagency differences became more a matter of tone and bureaucratic turf fighting.

The Pragmatic Approach and the Resolution of Investment Disputes in Peru, 1974–76

The Greene settlement (which resolved a number of outstanding cases, including IPC) and the nationalization of Marcona's iron-mining facilities demonstrate the operation of investment protection within a loosened quasi-regime. In both cases, international market forces induced Peru to compromise with principle, offering some compensation and accepting U.S. government intercession, to obtain external economic assistance. The United States also compromised with traditional principles on compensation. The objective was not to bludgeon Peru into accepting the traditional standard, but to resolve the dispute and, in the Marcona case, ensure a satisfactory post-expropriation relationship.

THE GREENE SETTLEMENT

United States relations with Peru steadily deteriorated from 1969 until 1973. In addition to the unresolved IPC dispute, the Velasco government nationalized several other American firms, including the Cerro de Pasco copper mines, W. R. Grace, and the fish meal industry.

In the summer of 1973, the United States and Peru made a last attempt to resolve their differences. On August 9, James Greene, of Manufacturers Hanover Trust, was designated as a special emissary to negotiate a lump sum settlement on behalf of the companies. The United States in-

sisted upon the inclusion of IPC in the talks to meet legislative
requirements for the resumption of economic assistance: "Any
unresolved claim would have the same effect on future aid
relationships as leaving all such claims unresolved." Peru
contended that the case was closed and adamantly refused to
entertain any consideration of it. The preamble to the negotiations stipulated that IPC would not for any reason be a
subject for discussion.[40]

On February 19, 1974, an accord was signed that resolved all outstanding claims and counterclaims. $74 million
was paid directly to Cerro, Grace, and the fish meal companies. A lump sum of $76 million was to be held in escrow
by the U.S. government until it determined how to divide it
among the other aggrieved parties. The disbursement fell
"within the exclusive competence of the Government of the
United States without any responsibilities arising therefrom
on the part of the Government of Peru."[41]

After the United States received the lump sum, it
gave $23.1 million to IPC. The legal "sleight of hand" in-
volved two steps: no mention of IPC in negotiations, and exclusive U.S. responsibility to disburse escrow funds. The Peruvian government decried the action as a "distortion of the
spirit and letter of the agreement" but, despite the face-saving protest, it was well aware of what was going to happen
to the lump sum. The ritual denunciation was a "fig leaf" for
public consumption.[42]

The settlement was a victory of pragmatism over
principle for both the United States and Peru. For the latter,
economic conditions necessitated an acceptance of U.S. involvement, despite the Calvo Doctrine, and payment of some
compensation, despite IPC's history. Following the settlement, Peru was once again eligible for U.S. economic assistance. It subsequently received $55 million in Eximbank fi-
nancing and $175 million in private bank credits for SPCC's
Cuajone copper project, as well as new authorizations from
the World Bank and the IADB. The move away from a prin-

cipled opposition to compensation came from an awareness of the limits placed on nationalization by the need for external capital and credits.[43]

For the United States, the Greene settlement represented a retreat from traditional compensation norms. The State Department tried to underplay the precedent-setting nature of the settlement, claiming that it was a "special case."[44] But how faithful could the policy have been to the deterrence of expropriation if the only way to get the Peruvians to pay was through a legal fiction which allowed them to deny they were doing so! In reality, the policy was actuated by short-term political and economic objectives at the expense of principle. It demonstrated, as one scholar noted, that "the requirement of 'prompt, adequate, and effective compensation' would not be insisted upon . . . if a compromise settlement could be worked out, permitting the removal of a major irritant to relations with the country involved."[45]

The prolonged stalemate with Peru over IPC, in juxtaposition with events in the Middle East, demonstrated to many in State, and even Treasury, the futility of traditional investment protection strategies. That so small a country and insignificant a producer as Peru could hold out despite serious economic pressure demonstrated the need for new compromise approaches. The change was apparent in the Marcona negotiations the next year.

THE MARCONA SETTLEMENT:
A NEW STANDARD OF COMPENSATION

On July 24, 1975, President Velasco announced the last major Peruvian nationalization—the Marcona iron mines, refining facility, and pelletization plant. The action conformed to Plan Inca, which called for state control over the exploitation, refining, and marketing of iron ore. The takeover was also accompanied by charges of failure to maintain reserves, evading taxes by exporting ores through Panamanian and Liberian shipping subsidiaries, and noncompliance with contractual obligations.[46]

The action against Marcona was surprising for two reasons. First, the company had a reputation as a "good corporate citizen." Its former president had been prominent in opposing punitive sanctions over IPC. Moreover, the company had already offered to phase out its concession and operate contractually in exchange for compensation in iron ore pellets.[47]

Second, the takeover was poorly timed because it complicated the debt rescheduling and MDB lending necessary for recovery amid serious balance of payments deficits. The debt was incurred as Peru sidestepped U.S. economic pressure through heavy borrowing in international capital markets. The banks had considered Peru a good credit risk given its high growth rate, low inflation, and abundance of natural resources.[48]

The strategy worked well until the OPEC price increases imposed a staggering import bill and local oil production was far below what had been anticipated. By 1975, the economy was in a serious bind. The OPEC-induced recession also punched a hole in global commodity markets and decreased the price of raw materials, such as iron and copper, upon which Peru was heavily dependent for export revenues. The banks, fearful of their overexposure, were negotiating a stabilization program (without the IMF) to shore up Peru's balance of payments. A new nationalization, with unresolved questions about compensation and Peru's ability to move the iron, complicated the process of servicing the $3.7 billion debt.[49] As a result of the economic crisis, Velasco was deposed by the armed forces on August 30 and replaced by the more "moderate" government of Francisco Morales Bermúdez.

Preliminary negotiations between Peru and Marcona ended in an impasse, primarily over the terms of compensation. The company's initial claim was a market value of $230 million, Peru's, a book value of $9 million. In the meantime, Peru's financial dilemma was compounded by its inability to move the ore. With a depressed market for iron, Marcona successfully deterred potential purchasers with the threat of lawsuits. The cost to Peru was estimated to be $8 to $10 million a month in foreign exchange.[50]

In October 1975, both the Morales government and Marcona solicited U.S. government intercession to break the impasse. The United States accepted the invitation and sent a delegation to supervise negotiations. It was headed by Undersecretary of State Carlyle Maw and included lawyers from Treasury and State, and two influential academics at State, Luigi Einaudi and Albert Fishlow.

The delegation immediately took the unprecedented step of commissioning an independent assessment of the various claims and counterclaims at the Stanford Research Institute. Marcona's real worth was estimated to be within a $55 to $65 million range.[51] The objective, one State Department lawyer wrote, was to "reason not only with the government, but with the American company" to get "Marcona to take realistic positions during negotiations."[52] This was a far cry from the IPC case, when the State Department uncritically accepted parent company data as its only source of information.

To ease Peru's financial bind, the United States sponsored an interim accord in December 1975, allowing Peru to use Marcona's ships to transport iron from its nationalized concession.[53] The objective was not to make an example out of Peru until it rescinded its policy, but to obtain compensation while minimizing the adverse consequences for Peru.

U.S. officials understood that Peru's financial situation made "prompt, adequate, and effective" compensation impossible. Fishlow proposed an alternative means of valuation—"net book value plus an ongoing relationship." Officials accepted this scheme as a bridge between book value, which they considered inadequate, and fair market value, which was rarely ascertainable.[54]

On September 22, 1976, the parties reached a $61.4

million settlement that was a combination of cash and a long-term sales contract. A promissory note of $37 million was paid to the company. The sum was financed by a loan from a U.S. banking group to minimize the drain on Peru's payments position. The remainder was paid through discounts to Marcona for the price it paid in its sales contract for iron ore.[55]

Like the Greene settlement, the Marcona accord was another example of "pragmatic" host and parent country policies. Despite the Calvo Doctrine's pronouncement that nationalization was the exclusive domain of local courts, Peru not only accepted but welcomed U.S. diplomatic intercession. Its need to maintain creditworthiness to the international financial community—through welcoming foreign investments, earning foreign exchange through mineral exports, and remaining eligible for U.S. aid—promoted this compromise with principle.[56] Peru's dependence on continued investments and credits placed limits on the exercise of economic sovereignty.

Yet the United States did not exploit Peru's vulnerability to reaffirm traditional property norms. In fact, it went to great lengths to avoid confrontation. It played an active role as a mediating participant, not a surrogate of Marcona. Principle took a back seat to "a potentially profitable relationship between the company and Peru in the export of iron ore."[57]

This accommodation to state control can be understood in terms of the evolution of perceived threats to national economic security. In the past, corporate ownership had been conceptually linked to security of supply. But by 1975, it was clear that resource availability was less threatened by national ownership than it was by market scarcities. At the same time, as LDCs financed their surging oil bills through private capital markets, debt replaced nationalization as the primary concern. The precedent of a Peruvian default was weighted more heavily than the precedent of an inadequately compensated expropriation. Hence, a compromise formula on Marcona was necessary to facilitate the rescheduling of Peru's debt.

One State Department lawyer noted the precedent-setting ingenuity of the accord whereby

> the settlement consists not of cash alone but of a combination of cash and a continuing relationship (albeit more limited here than an ideal economic package would have produced), which generates foreign exchange, utilizes the foreign company's expertise, and helps to assure continued production of the resources under government management.[58]

In truth, it was less a precedent than an acceptance of a pattern already established by Middle Eastern oil producers. It ratified the ascendance of pragmatism in adapting to a changed environment.

Accommodation to Venezuela's Nationalization of the Oil Industry

Venezuela's nationalization of the petroleum industry, on January 1, 1976, the most significant transfer of assets in the history of the Western Hemisphere, was peaceful and relatively free of conflict. The oil companies accepted the verdict, not on the basis of compensation paid (which they considered inadequate), but because of a satisfactory future relationship which guaranteed them access to Venezuelan crude. Secretary of State Kissinger commended Venezuela for its prudence and publicly opposed any form of economic reprisal.

This attitude was in marked contrast to the private and public responses to President Caldera's Hydrocarbons Reversion Bill in 1971, which planned to transfer ownership of the companies' assets and reserves to the state after the expiry of the concessions in the early 1980s. The companies retaliated by cutting crude production levels; the U.S. government, by restricting the import of Venezuelan crude and fuel oil.

The contrast between the two approaches was a clear demonstration of a corporate and official "learning process" vis-à-vis expropriation from 1971 until 1976. Interim experiences—the stalemate with Peru over IPC and the OPEC price increases—had demonstrated the inapplicability of traditional precepts. Sanctions and boycotts were shown to be ineffective instruments of pressure, and host country ownership did not necessarily preclude a corporate presence or American access to critical raw materials. The Venezuelan cases reflected a reexamination of policy and an adjustment to the changed environment, as decision makers moved away from a presumptive policy of deterrence to a pragmatic one of accommodation.

PRUDENT AUDACITY: VENEZUELA'S TAKEOVER OF THE INDUSTRY

The Venezuelan takeover of the oil industry was the climax of many years of gradually increasing state regulation and control over its principal natural resources. Venezuela had been the pioneer in challenging the industry, the first to institute an income tax and fifty-fifty profit sharing in the 1940s.

The momentum for reform was temporarily stalled during the Pérez Jiménez dictatorship (1948–1959). When the civilian government of Rómulo Betancourt returned in 1959, the issue of controlling the industry reemerged. The government's primary complaint was the companies' practice of reducing posted prices without consulting producer nations. Taxation to increase government revenue was still an important consideration. But Betancourt and his minister of mines and hydrocarbons Pérez Alfonso, realized that increased taxation alone would not provide the maximum return. Controls over the determination of price and the setting of production levels were also necessary.[59]

In 1960, the Betancourt administration established a state company, Corporación Venezolana del Petroleo (CVP), and declared that no new oil concessions would be awarded. CVP would become the primary negotiator with foreign firms, opening up new lands through service contracts, and would regulate the old concessions, gradually assuming the functions of the companies. Through the regulatory process, it was designed to gain administrative and technical expertise to "provide the nucleus for a system that would replace the existing network of concessions."[60]

The inevitable became imminent with President Caldera's Hydrocarbons Reversion Law in 1971. The legislation stipulated that the private oil concessions would lapse when they expired in 1983. At that time, all assets and reserves in any phase of the operation would revert to the state without compensation. The law also required companies to relinquish all unexplored areas within three years; deposit 10 percent of their asset value in the National Bank of Venezuela as a security against damage to property; and accept a tax rate increase to 60 percent and CVP's unilateral authority to set posted prices.[61]

With the election of Carlos Andrés Pérez, in March 1974, the Venezuelan government decided to advance expiry to 1975. On August 29, 1975, the Venezuelan Congress passed a nationalization bill calling for the establishment of a new state company, Petroleós de Venezuela (Petroven), to assume control over the old concessions on January 1, 1976; book value compensation; and a continued contractual relationship with the former concessionaires.

Venezuela offered $1.014 billion in compensation to the companies. The sum was calculated on the basis of depreciated book value and was roughly 20 percent of company claims. The companies were given fifteen days to accept the offer or have the matter submitted to the Venezuelan Supreme Court. International arbitration was explicitly excluded.[62] Both the amount and manner of compensation were dissonant with traditional norms.

The nationalization bill also contained a clause allowing Petroven to "enter into agreements with private entities of limited duration and in terms which guarantee the full control of the State." The proviso reflected an understanding that despite the increasing sophistication of the state company, Venezuela still needed the technological, managerial, and marketing skills provided by the foreign firms. Foreign oil companies could still participate, but on a service contract, rather than an ownership basis.[63]

In the months immediately following the nationalization, eighteen companies signed service contracts with Petroven: two-year renewable accords for oil sales and three-year renewable contracts for technical and administrative backup services. In general, the oil companies were allowed to manage the same properties they once owned, and lift roughly the same amount of oil, but under the supervision of government officials in Caracas, rather than corporate headquarters in New York. The Venezuelan action, therefore, did not exclude foreign capital, but redefined the terms of its penetration to increase national control over a natural resource upon which the economy was dependent.

THE OIL COMPANY RESPONSE

The oil companies reacted to Venezuela's 1971 Hydrocarbons Reversion Law and its arrogation of the right to set posted prices as important symbolic threats to the concession system, going beyond the Persian Gulf pricing and participation demands. Oilmen labeled the bill "de facto nationalization" and filed suit in local court against its constitutionality.[64]

In a joint effort to compel Venezuela to conform to Persian Gulf practices, the companies reduced new investment to negligible proportions and cut back production sharply.

They also solicited diplomatic support in restricting Venezuelan oil imports. As a result, Venezuela suffered an 18.6
percent decline in output in the first four months of 1972;
and its share of the United States market declined from 25
percent to 15 percent.[65]

These measures had little coercive effect, especially
after the 1973 oil "shocks" which increased Venezuela's tax
reference price from $3.10 to $14.08 per barrel. Venezuela's
oil income increased from $2 billion in 1972 to $9.7 billion
in 1974.[66] This obviated the need for external financing and
invalidated the traditional threat of production cutbacks.
Recognizing this, Exxon, in January 1975, broke ranks with
the industry and increased its investment by $110 million.
Within the next three months, most of the other firms followed suit.[67]

By 1975, the foreign oil community was still appre-
hensive about nationalization, but saw state control as the
wave of the future. The consequences of holding fast to old
positions had been highlighted by IPC in Peru. If private and
public sanction could not force compliance from so small a
producer as Peru, what effect could it have on Venezuela?

Venezuela, moreover, proposed to redefine, not exclude, private participation in the oil industry. This was clearly
demonstrated, in February 1975, by its takeover of the iron
ore companies, Bethlehem and U.S. Steel. Book value compensation was paid over a ten-year period at 7 percent interest. More importantly, the terms provided for future ongoing ties between the American companies and the newly
established state company. Each firm signed a two-year renewable lease in which it could purchase, at discount, the
same quantity of iron ore it produced before nationalization,
and ship it to the parent company.[68] The *modus vivendi* was
based upon an appreciation of mutual dependence and interest. Venezuela needed management and technology to expand its exports; the American companies wanted cheap and
reliable access to iron ore.

Oil companies saw in the iron ore settlement an acceptable solution to their own predicament. Therefore, they chose to defer to national sovereignty and work out a favorable post-expropriation relationship. Since Venezuela was still dependent upon their expertise, it would need them on a service contract basis. Using this leverage, they could lock in the right to buy back crude at preferred prices to supply their downstream operations. In fact, the Economist Intelligence Unit noted that some firms believed that spinning off ownership would enhance the stability of crude production, and hence the parent's access to supplies.[69]

The *Wall Street Journal* reported that the companies were displeased with the amount and manner of compensation. First, the sum was dictated by a national commission whose decision was not appealable beyond the local judicial system. Second, the sum represented only depreciated book value, amounting to 20 percent of the company's claim. Of that, only half was to be released, and the rest to be held in escrow and eventually defrayed by counterclaims. But the companies were "treading softly as regards compensation."[70] This reflected the perception that the future relationship, not compensation or the deterrence of precedents, was their main concern. By November, all but one came to terms.

On January 1, 1976, the oilfields became the property of the state. The companies were offered contracts allowing them to become technical advisors to the old concessions and to lift and market the same quantities they did prior to nationalization. Ironically, the first company to sign a management and sales contract was Creole, the local subsidiary of Exxon (the parent of IPC in Peru).[71] Its local vice president lauded the virtues of the new arrangements: "The government has gained control of the oil industry without risk, and we have found an attractive income for technology that we would have to develop anyway. . . . This is the way the world is going and it is, in itself, a profitable business."[72]

Events in Venezuela demonstrated the extent to which the international oil industry had accepted loss of formal ownership as a *fait accompli* and reoriented its strategy.

No longer were autonomy in pricing, nationalization, or even compensation the decisive considerations. Ownership of assets was conceded to the host. Negotiating positions were targeted at obtaining the most profitable contractual terms for maintaining preferential access to primary products.

UNITED STATES POLICY:
FROM DETERRENCE TO ACCOMMODATION

When Caldera put forward the Hydrocarbons Reversion Bill in 1971, the United States was still wedded to the Nixon-Connally approach. With economic nationalism on the rise, Caldera's actions were viewed as a challenge against which the United States must take a stand. The embassy was instructed to protest the actions as "confiscatory" and warn the Venezuelans of the Sabbatino Amendment which would permit companies to bring legal actions in U.S. courts that might block Venezuelan exports to the United States. As a symbol of official displeasure, Treasury Secretary Connally was dispatched to Caracas to lodge an objection. The *New York Times* editorially noted the negative symbolism of sending this "practitioner of abrasive nationalism" on so sensitive a mission.[73]

The United States tried to reinforce corporate resistance by hampering the sale of Venezuelan oil in the domestic market. Secretary of State Rogers contended that the Venezuelan bill

could so adversely affect the investments of American companies in Venezuela as to limit or preclude additional investments needed to develop the resources and production which will be required if the petroleum industry is to be maintained in the longer run at satisfactory levels.[74]

State Department officials announced that Venezuela was "no longer a reliable producer" and rejected its request for preferential access to the U.S. market on a par with Canada and

Mexico. Venezuela was informed that the United States would look elsewhere for more secure sources of crude. In 1972, this point was hammered home when Venezuela was pointedly omitted from a portion of a 600,000 bpd increase in the oil import quota.[75]

In December 1972 the United States lifted hemispheric preferences for the import of No. 2 fuel oil from Venezuela. Caracas protested this as an act of reprisal. The State Department requested that the embassy explain to Venezuela that the suspension was temporary and related only to conditions of supply and demand.[76]

Despite this disclaimer, circumstantial evidence indicates more than purely economic considerations at work. The embassy conducted a study that could not find "any information on supply and demands that would sustain [the] need to eliminate [the] Western Hemisphere source requirement for imported heating oil." Termination of the agreement was opposed in the interest of "our overall relations with Venezuela, of developing detente between [the] Venezuelan government and [the] oil companies, and of our security requirements and hopes of working out arrangements that will further our own security of supply."[77] One State Department official, while refusing to call the suspension "pressure," noted that it was a "message" to Caracas that its actions brought into question its continued reliability as a supplier.[78]

In early 1973, officials at OFE, concerned about the impending energy crisis, favored increased reliance on Venezuelan oil. James Akins advocated granting preferential treatment on a par with Canada and Mexico to mitigate dependence on Middle Eastern oil. He estimated that there were approximately 700 billion barrels of crude in the Orinoco Tar Basin and proposed to exchange U.S. assistance in developing those reserves for the free entry of heavy oils into the United States.[79] This recommendation was consistent with OFE's preference for diversifying sources of supply over traditional regime maintenance.

Word of the recommendation got out and elicited strong corporate opposition. Creole protested the publicity, arguing that it would "only make us look foolish and do harm to our negotiating position."[80] In deference to corporate objections, the State Department vetoed the idea, "question[ing] the advisability of discussing the possible restoration of Western Hemisphere preferences in a way that would raise Venezuelan hopes that the waiver could or should be rescinded . . . whenever the Venezuelan situation warrants."[81] It would be remiss not to point out the irony of an official policy that would forego the opportunity to develop Western Hemisphere oil reserves in deference to the sensibilities of the oil companies on the eve of the world's worst energy crisis. This represented only another manifestation of the myopic world view that tied national security to the traditional interests of the oil companies without examining real vulnerability in the rapidly changing world of oil.

U.S. hostility to Venezuelan plans continued until the summer of 1974. National Security Study Memorandum 203 (June 10, 1974) called for a review of U.S. policy to seek a "constructive and comprehensive" response to Pérez's takeover plans that would "ensure the continued access by the United States to Venezuelan primary products."[82]

Under the influence of the "pragmatists" at State, the United States accepted the virtues of necessity and encouraged corporate adaptation to the Venezuelan scheme. The offer of book value compensation was well below the principles it had traditionally espoused. But it recognized that to the companies, "the importance of compensation [was] subordinate to the possibility of an ongoing relationship with [Venezuela]."[83] As one official subsequently wrote, "Clearly the compensation for the property by itself was inadequate. But the whole package was favorable."[84]

In this new era of economic nationalism, such arrangements were deemed necessary to insure security of supply. Venezuela was considered a safe Western Hemisphere source of oil. Evidence of its reliability as a supplier was demonstrated by its behavior during the oil embargo. President Pérez took pains to assure traditional customers that supplies would not be interrupted.[85] Nationalization was no longer the key consideration.

Moreover, officials recognized that Venezuela was still capitalist in structure and welcomed foreign investment. The Department of Commerce, in 1975, reported that there are "many opportunities for profitable foreign investment, but they will have to be made in the context of ever-increasing Venezuelan participation and direction."[86] One official noted the need to discriminate between "sectoral nationalization that redefines areas and terms of exploitation and nationalization that is inserted into an anti-capitalist development strategy."[87] Venezuela was clearly in the first category.

Not all bureaucratic actors shared this equanimity. Some Treasury and White House officials characterized the State Department's policy as "extraordinarily inadequate" and "woefully weak." A former ambassador to Venezuela, Robert McClintock, urged the government to step in and negotiate for the industry because "the oil companies [are] no longer a match for producer governments." The rationale was that a retreat from principle, so soon after OPEC extortion and UN demagoguery, would only encourage further expropriations. Some intimated that Venezuela should be made "an object lesson from which we could argue for fair value in later nationalization cases."[88]

But even the expropriation "hawks" conceded that there was little they could do. Treasury's convictions did not extend to the point of direct U.S. government involvement or confrontation. Its "activism" was limited to support for symbolic gestures of disapproval, such as denial of trade preferences or military sales credits.[89] The Legal Bureau at State put on record its continued fidelity to traditional rules by inserting this statement in a public note to Venezuela:

Foreign investors are entitled to fair market value of their interests. Acceptance by U.S. nationals of less than fair market value does not constitute acceptance of any other standard by the United States government. As a consequence, the United States government reserves its rights to maintain international claims for what it regards as adequate compensation under international law for the interests nationalized or transferred.[90]

Despite this show of face, even the most obdurate conceded that little could be done.

Kissinger placed the seal of approval on the take-over by visiting Venezuela one month after it took place. In Caracas, he commended Pérez for his "prudence" in allowing a continued role for the oil companies.[91]

Moreover, Ford, Kissinger, and the State Department publicly went on record against provisions of the Trade Act of 1974 which mandated the exclusion of all OPEC members, including Venezuela, from the generalized system of trade preferences. Officials lauded Venezuela's nonparticipation in the embargo and its retention of a role for the oil companies. The use of these provisions to deter nationalization or cartelization was "wholly inappropriate to the situation." Their effect could only be counterproductive:

> Latin American sensitivities to the exercise of economic leverage have been finely honed by history. Such sanctions are almost always harmful . . . they appear as a public ultimatum; by seeking to challenge the recipient's sovereignty, they harden positions, encumber diplomacy, and poison the entire relationship.

The proper way to deal with OPEC was not through retaliation, but through "develop[ing] alternative sources of supply."[92] In looking beyond expropriation to the economic arrangements and market conditions that would follow, these statements indicated a considerable change in policy.

The Jamaican Bauxite Industry: The Market as Enforcer

Almost immediately after the OPEC price increases, bauxite-producing countries posed a parallel challenge of national control and cartelization. In March 1974, representatives from ten major producers, comprising 75 percent of world output, met in Conkary, Guinea, to form the International Bauxite Association (IBA) and forge a united front. In May, Jamaica unilaterally imposed a new formula which increased taxes by 700 percent and moved toward 51 percent equity participation. Shortly thereafter, the other Caribbean producers followed the Jamaican lead.

U.S. decision makers took a dim view of the Jamaican action and, in line with its presumptive policy on expropriation, halted new aid authorizations in the summer of 1974. The action, however, amounted to little more than a token gesture of disapproval because Jamaica's much larger multilateral aid (which was not halted) and increased take from bauxite exports more than offset the small AID program. In the short-run, the aluminum companies adapted to the tax and participation formulas.

In the long-run, both the United States and the industry saw the critical issue as neither participation nor compensation, but the financial terms under which the companies were obliged to operate. Eventually, the bauxite levy was pushed down, not by concentrated private or public sanction, but by market forces which made it unsustainable. The role of the U.S. government was limited to encouraging diversification of sources of supply. The Jamaican case is a prototype of how the structure of raw materials markets operates within the quasi-regime to constrain the exercise of economic sovereignty.

JAMAICA'S DISPUTE WITH THE ALUMINUM COMPANIES

The operation of the bauxite concessions had long been a sore point with successive Jamaican governments. The aluminum industry was dominated by a small number of vertically integrated private MNCs who controlled all three phases of production—mining bauxite, refining bauxite into alumina, and smelting alumina into aluminum. The companies had moved their mining operations into Jamaica and the Caribbean to find cheap ores for their refineries and smelters in North America.[93]

Like most raw materials, the price of aluminum ingot and fabricated aluminum products was high relative to that of bauxite ore. This worked to the disadvantage of Third World producers, such as Jamaica, who had difficulty moving downstream given the energy-intensive process by which alumina is converted into aluminum. In 1972, Caribbean producers accounted for 38 percent of the world's bauxite production. The corresponding figures for alumina and aluminum are 16 percent are 0.5 percent respectively.[94]

Working further to the disadvantage of Jamaica was the fact that there was little in the way of an open competitive market for bauxite. Over 80 percent moved through intrafirm trade.[95] To keep payments low, ore was shipped at cost to feed downstream operations. Under the Jamaican system, the companies paid Jamaica a fixed royalty per ton sold. Such a scheme did not account for prices. As the price of aluminum increased with inflation in the early 1970s, Jamaican bauxite revenues actually decreased.[96]

In early 1974, faced with a dire need for foreign exchange after the quadrupling of oil prices, Jamaican Prime Minister Michael Manley announced an intention to rearrange the traditional ownership structure of the "commanding heights" of the economy. The bauxite concessions, which accounted for 40 percent of the island's foreign exchange and 12 percent of its gross domestic product were the first priority.[97] In March, Manley opened negotiations with the six firms operating on the island: Alcoa, Reynolds, Kaiser, Alcan, Revere, and Anaconda.

On May 15, Manley walked out of negotiations and, declaring that the changed circumstances of the energy crisis outweighed the sanctity of contract, introduced a bill in the parliament which would unilaterally impose a 700 percent increase in taxes. (The bill was ratified on June 5.) The new scheme established a levy of 7.5 percent (to be increased to

8.5 percent in 1976) based on the price of aluminum ingot (as shown by the U.S. Securities and Exchange Commission), retroactive to January 1, 1974. The formula was devised to avoid the shortcomings of the aluminum industry's transfer pricing policies, as well as the "secular decline" in the terms of trade. Manley subsequently wrote that the aim was to "lock in Jamaica as a beneficiary of worldwide inflation."[98]

Manley also tried to develop means to blunt corporate countermeasures. First, to prevent production cutbacks, the companies were required to maintain production levels or pay taxes for levels not maintained.[99] Second, Jamaica proposed joint ventures with oil-rich neighbors, such as Mexico, Venezuela, and Trinidad, to move into the more energy-intensive downstream phases of aluminum production. The objective was to prevent the industry from turning Jamaica into a supplier of last resort by establishing markets for bauxite and alumina outside the integrated multinational network.[100]

The aluminum companies protested the Jamaican action which, they claimed, would make Jamaican bauxite uncompetitive and lead to a domino effect against their holdings elsewhere. Led by Alcoa, they contended it was as a breach of contract which would prohibit "an increase in taxes and levies applied to mining processing, or export of bauxite unless . . . agreed to by both the government and the company involved." Unilaterally imposed taxes were clearly illegal and justiciable under international law. On June 22, the companies agreed to pay the first installment of the levy, but only after invoking a clause in their contracts which allowed them to challenge the legality of the tax at the World Bank's International Center for the Settlement of Investment Disputes (ICSID).[101]

Although Jamaica and the United States were parties to the ICSID convention, Manley denied its jurisdiction in this instance because a tax increase was not an expropriation, and natural resource issues fell under the exclusive competence of national authorities.[102] In addition, he expressed an intent to move forward in placing all bauxite lands and surface rights in state hands and obtaining a majority (51 percent) share in the companies' assets. In September, the Jamaican government began participation negotiations with the individual companies.[103]

Jamaica's challenge came on the heels of the first meeting of the International Bauxite Association (IBA). Like OPEC, the IBA sought to maximize national ownership and harmonize pricing policies so as to increase the value added of production within its borders. A number of Western observers in the mid-1970s predicted a successful bauxite cartel. The ten members of the IBA composed 70 percent of non-communist production and over 90 percent of U.S. consumption. Bauxite was also a price inelastic good whose consumption did not decrease significantly with increased price.[104]

Following the Jamaican action, the dominoes began to fall. The other Caribbean producers—Guyana, Haiti, the Dominican Republic, and Surinam—passed parallel tax formulas. Guyana went Jamaica one better in its 100 percent takeover of Reynolds, its only remaining bauxite company.[105] The history of the oil negotiations between 1970 and 1973 appeared to be repeating itself.

UNITED STATES POLICY
AND THE LOWERING OF JAMAICAN TAXES

The U.S. government indignantly protested the Jamaican action, imposed as it was on the heels of the oil price increases. Undersecretary of State Kenneth Rush deplored it as an act that "raises prices in a way that fuels worldwide inflation."[106] The manner in which the tax was imposed was of particular concern. American officials were sympathetic to Jamaica's case for greater revenue and participation, but through negotiations, not by unilateral fiat. The rejection of ICSID jurisdiction despite Jamaica's treaty obligation also represented a serious precedent:

The ICSID proceedings involves U.S. interests which go beyond bauxite issues—those of establishing a viable mechanism for the settlement of investment disputes and protecting the integrity of investment agreements and treaties.

If effective counteraction were not forthcoming, the convention would not be worth the paper it was written on.[107]

On June 14, representatives from the three major American companies—Alcoa, Kaiser, and Reynolds—met with Peter Flanigan at the White House to coordinate strategy. The companies, especially Alcoa, solicited diplomatic pressure to force Jamaica to retreat. Treasury officials concurred, on the grounds that the Jamaican formula was "creating a domino effect among bauxite producing countries." The State Department called for consideration of all "possible USG actions which could discourage other governments from following Jamaica's lead."[108]

In June, the CIEP interagency expropriation group decided to avoid formal sanctions, but withheld new aid authorizations to exert pressure on Jamaica to accept arbitration or rescind the tax. In July, the United States held up an already authorized $9.1 million rural education loan and tied the disbursement of all future loans to the outcome of the bauxite negotiations. The loan was not released until February 1977, after Jamaica settled with the last American company, Alcoa. Additionally, until the middle of 1975, the United States used its influence to defer consideration of loans to Jamaica from the IADB.[109] To continue to give aid, Treasury argued, would give "the wrong signal . . . to a country unilaterally ripping off American firms."[110]

The strategy was opposed by AID, State's inter-American bureau, and the American embassy in Kingston. Ambassador Sumner Gerard cabled that with Jamaica's increased bauxite revenues and alternative sources of aid, there was "little the U.S. could do to discourage" Jamaica or the other Caribbean producers. Pressure would only be counterproductive:

Obvious US actions like the curtailment of AID programs or the discouragement of soft loans by other international lending institutions will simply strengthen their determination, to the detriment of the companies' interests (at least in Jamaica), and be interpreted as another indication of developed country "economic imperialism." The ability of the companies to react in a creative and flexible way is probably the best insurance for the future.

Holding up the loan would only polarize positions between Jamaica and the companies and harm "political and social stability in Jamaica which could ultimately have unfortunate repercussions for US political and economic interests."[111] Corporate adaptation in an atmosphere free of confrontation offered the soundest prospect for resolving the dispute and assuring a satisfactory postscript.

Statistics reveal the insufficiency of aid curtailments in coercing a favorable settlement. Bilateral economic assistance was cut from $9.9 million in 1974 to $0.6 million in 1975 and $0.8 million in 1976, mostly in P.L. 480 funds. IADB lending, which amounted to $22.9 million in 1974, was put on the "back burner." World Bank lending, in contrast, was increased from $20.5 million to $26 million over the same period. Aid from Canada and the Netherlands was also increased. The net loss in external assistance was more than offset by the dramatic increase in bauxite revenues which, with favorable economic conditions because of soaring prices for copper and tin, soared to $170 million in 1975. IADB lending was reinstated in June 1975, an admission of the policy's insufficiency to influence Manley's bauxite strategy.[112]

Neither was pressure sufficient to dissuade corporate adaptation. The aluminum companies, with the exception of Alcoa, made a weak show of resistance before adapting to Jamaica's terms. On November 20, 1974, Kaiser received a book value compensation of $15 million in exchange for 51 percent of the company's assets and the withdrawal of its ICSID claim. Kaiser's nonbauxite lands were returned to the state for badly needed agricultural pursuits. The company continued to manage the mining areas it ceded under contract and was assured access to reserves for thirty years. The smaller producers and Reynolds accepted comparable deals by April 1975.[113]

Kaiser and Reynolds were inclined to settle early because they were dependent upon Jamaica for roughly 60 to
70 percent of the ores used in their American smelters. Uninterrupted access to produce was their overriding consideration. Alcoa, with only 15 percent of its bauxite in Jamaica,
held out longer. A larger and more diversified firm, it took
more seriously the precedent-setting implications of Manley's
actions. Finally, in January 1976, it also agreed to negotiate
on the basis of terms accepted by the other companies. On
October 6, it reached a settlement ceding a smaller amount
of equity in its bauxite operations in exchange for minority
state ownership of its alumina refinery.[114]

The companies reluctantly acceded to Manley's tax
and equity schemes because they lacked the leverage to directly overturn them. First, the degree of market concentration possessed by the six major firms had eroded. With the
emergence of new entrants, Japanese buying groups, and state-
owned enterprises, their share of worldwide aluminum
smelting capacity had fallen from 85 percent in 1956 to 57.5
percent in 1975.[115] Coercive strategies were less likely to
achieve dramatic results because Jamaica was better able to
find customers for its bauxite outside the traditional multinational network.

Second, the American and Canadian companies had
become increasingly dependent upon access to Jamaican ores.
They had sunk more than $800 million in Jamaica and were
not keen on walking away from it. Moreover, each alumina
refinery was geared to process a single type of ore. To turn
elsewhere would have required expensive technological modifications. In the short run, the firms were tied to their traditional suppliers.[116]

Accommodation also served the overriding interest
of the vertically integrated extractive firm: guaranteed access to primary product. The logic of acquiescence was suc-
cintly stated by a Kaiser spokesman:

What we seek isn't land, it's bauxite. Assuming we receive
a fair price for the land rights we now hold, and a long-term work-

able arrangement on all issues, we believe that Jamaican ownership of the bauxite lands could be good for both Jamaica and the
company, giving Jamaica a stronger self-interest in the success of
the operations and relieving the company of the administrative de-
tail that comes with landholdings offshore.[117]

In addition, coming from an oligopolistic industry, the companies were able pass on the tax increases to the consumers.
The short-run incentives strongly favored accommodation.

In the long-run, the companies possessed a number
of advantages. In aluminum, the main barrier to entry lies
not in extraction, but in processing ores into alumina and
aluminum. It is difficult for energy-poor LDCs, like Jamaica,
to move into these areas because of the huge amounts of cheap
hydroelectric power required.

In a prescient article written in 1971, Theodore Moran
noted that if there are no serious barriers to entry at the
extractive level, nationalization does not necessarily create a
position of strength. And if the strongest barriers to entry
exist downstream, companies from a vertically integrated industry will seek the cheapest sources of supply. Those LDCs
who push nationalization or price-indexing schemes too far
will find themselves "suppliers of last resort."[118]

This is precisely what happened as aluminum companies responded by redirecting their new investments away
from the high tax areas in the Caribbean. For example, while
Alcan and Alcoa cut back on production and new investment
in Jamaica, they correspondingly increased it in their joint
venture with the Guinean government. Alcan and Reynolds
invested heavily in the development of new Brazilian mines
in the Upper Amazon while Kaiser devoted its energies to
Australia.[119]

Corporate strategies were abetted by the fact that
other IBA members were willing to "cheat" on the Caribbean. Australia did not impose any new levy. Guinea and
Brazil were just emerging as major producers and were in
desperate need of foreign exchange to finance their soaring

import bills. Underselling the Caribbean afforded both the opportunity to break into Jamaica's market share. As one Alcoa official noted, "The divergent internal political and economic needs of each country have kept the IBA from becoming a pricing body."[120] They also protect the aluminum companies from excessive revenue demands on the part of producers.

What is ironic about this trend is that all of these countries required at least 49 percent local or state ownership.[121] But by 1975 it was clear that the ability to raise prices was not a necessary function of state ownership. Equity considerations were far less salient than diversification or the terms of access.

State Department officials entrusted with the issue understood corporate strategies. They realized that the aid curtailment could not deter the companies from adapting as Treasury had hoped. It was little more than a gesture of disapproval of Jamaica's flouting of ICSID, in no way obliging Jamaica to change course.

For the time being, Enders testified, the United States could exercise only marginal influence:

> In the near term, aluminum companies are locked in. They have little choice but to pay the higher levies because of the cost of disrupting established supply patterns during the current period of strong demand, structural dependence on Jamaican bauxite, and their investments in Jamaica.

But the levy would be "unsustainable over the long-term because of the availability of bauxite worldwide, the availability of close substitutes, and development of new technologies."[122]

"The economic response to the Jamaican action," a White House study recommended, "should be increased production from other sources at a price below the Jamaican objective." Enders noted that the U.S. government could play a facilitative role in this by offering OPIC and Eximbank incentives for the companies to shift to non-Caribbean sources.[123]

Ownership rights, in light of recent history, ranked well below diversification of sources and access on favorable terms to both the U.S. government and the aluminum companies.

In effect, the United States would pay the cost of short-term price gouging and use the interim to encourage firms to redress the market imbalance by corporate expansion into safer regions for alternative sources. Having concluded that the traditional regime was not sustainable, officials chose, on the one hand, to assure short-term supply by accepting the inevitable and, on the other hand, to stimulate market forces to mitigate long-term consequences for the U.S. economy. As one radical critic noted, the United States "could count on the forces of the international marketplace . . . to put a damper on radical trends."[124]

This was indeed what happened as market conditions eventually compelled Manley to reduce the tax rate, though not the method of valuation. In 1975, Jamaican bauxite production fell by 25 percent, and alumina by 21 percent, as the companies cut back on additional investment and production in Jamaica and turned to areas with more favorable tax laws (see tables 1 and 2). As the market tightened (global production decreased by 4.6 percent), Jamaica bore the brunt of market fluctuation. The cutbacks, however, had little initial effect because, with the higher tax rate, Jamaican rev-

Table 1.   Worldwide Bauxite Production (thousands of metric tons)

	Jamaica	Australia	Guinea	Brazil	Total
1972	12.3	14.2	2.0	0.7	63.9
1973	13.4	17.3	3.0	0.6	68.8
1974	15.1	19.7	7.5	0.8	77.0
1975	11.3	20.6	8.2	0.8	73.6
1976	10.3	24.1	10.8	0.8	76.1
1977	11.4	26.1	10.8	1.1	81.1
1978	11.7	24.3	10.5	1.2	79.8
1979	11.5	27.6	13.7	2.4	87.7
1980	12.3	27.6	13.8	4.0	89.9

SOURCE: United States Government, Department of the Interior, Bureau of the Mines. *Minerals Yearbook: Volume I: Metals and Minerals*, 1974, 1977, 1980.

enues increased from $30 million in 1974 to almost $200 million in 1975.[125] This windfall enabled Jamaica to successfully weather the first set of oil "shocks" in the mid-1970s.

The negative trend, however, persisted throughout the late 1970s, even as the demand for bauxite picked up. From 1975–79, while worldwide bauxite output increased 19 percent, Jamaican production only increased marginally. Its share of global production decreased from 19.6 percent in 1974 to 13.1 percent in 1979. The main beneficiaries of this drop-off were Australia, Brazil, and Guinea. From 1974–79, Jamaica's share of global alumina production fell from 10.1 percent to 6.6 percent. In the same period, Australia's share increased from 17.2 percent to 23.9 percent.[126]

A similar pattern is discernible in the structure of bauxite and alumina exports to the American market. In 1971, the Caribbean accounted for 98.5 percent of all U.S. imports of bauxite. In 1979 that figure was 62 percent.[127] From 1974–79, Jamaica's share of the American bauxite market decreased from 54.2 percent to 46.9 percent while Guinea's increased from 8.7 percent to 28.4 percent. Over the same period, Jamaica's share of the American alumina market decreased from 24.9 percent to 15.3 percent, while Australia's increased from 57.8 percent to 76.6 percent.[128]

Jamaica was not completely cut off. Its annual bauxite and alumina revenues stabilized around $170 to $200 million, but at a time when the price of aluminum was increas-

Table 2. Alumina Production (Metric Tons)

	Jamaica	Australia	Total
1974	3165	5401	31437
1975	2489	5642	28715
1976	1793	6841	29586
1977	2048	6659	29643
1978	2111	6776	29600
1979	2074	7415	31067
1980	2478	7247	32983

SOURCE: U.S. Government, Department of the Interior, Bureau of the Mines. *Minerals Yearbook. Volume I: Metals and Minerals,* 1974, 1977, 1980

ing. These earnings were insufficient to cover a spiraling import bill for food and energy, and Jamaica fell more heavily into debt. The situation worsened in 1979 with the second round of oil price increases and an IMF-mandated devaluation.[129]

In order to regain its market share, Manley was compelled to revise the tax formula downward to find a level that would create an incentive for increased production and investment. While maintaining the nominal levy, he devised an incentive scheme of rate reductions from 25 to 50 percent depending upon the quantity produced. In 1980, the industry responded favorably to the new scheme. Bauxite and alumina exports reached their highest levels since the period before the levy.[130] The next year, with the election of the more conservative Seaga government, the Reagan administration moved to shore up the Jamaican economy with large-scale purchases of bauxite for domestic stockpiles. But the retreat from earlier policies preceded Manley's electoral defeat.

Conclusion

The 1970s witnessed the emergence of a quasi-regime of loosened norms and expectations replacing the traditional concession system. The end result has invariably been the transfer of formal ownership from foreign enterprises to state companies or local nationals. The dispossessed MNC generally received book value compensation, or less, and an ongoing relationship which preserved access to primary production for downstream operations. The real bargaining took placed over the conditions of that access.

As with IPC in Peru, cleavages within business and government impede a clear-cut vindication of either a statist or corporate preference model in explaining the U.S. government move toward accommodation. The key causal variable was systemic change, which had an uneven impact on different private and public actors. Treasury and the established firms (Exxon in Venezuela; Alcoa in Jamaica) held out the longest. The State Department pushed for a more tempered approach until it reasserted bureaucratic control of the issue in 1974. Further, the self-interests of firms in maintaining access to resources (SPCC in Peru; Kaiser and Reynolds in Jamaica) weakened any direct strategy of resistance. This, combined with OPEC's success, demonstrated the limits of leverage in preserving the traditional system. This eventually became clear even to those with the strongest stake in that system.

It is also difficult to disentangle the political and economic motivations behind this new strategy of accommodation. Krasner correctly notes that an important factor was the increasing political costs of economic pressure.[131] But nonintervention had economic rationales as well.

American policymakers redefined economic milieu goals regarding overseas resource investments. The traditional regime had been designed to protect corporate viability and national economic strategy. By the mid-1970s, it was clear that these aims were less threatened by nationalization than they were by market scarcities. Coercion could no longer maintain the old system and could possibly disrupt these traditional aims. As a result, nonintervention was functionally compatible not only with diplomatic aims, but also with the stability of a quasi-regime which preserved a role for foreign investments in an age of economic nationalism.

The United States could safely forego the traditional system because the quasi-regime still imposed significant limits on the sovereign discretion of LDC hosts. The ability of their state-owned enterprises to drive a hard bargain with the industry is a function of their ability to provide themselves with capital, technology, and market access.[132] The three cases examined in this chapter demonstrate how the structure of commodity markets and international finance constrain LDCs.

For example, Venezuela maintained its links to the foreign oil industry from the start to preserve the availability of modern technology and market access. Peru was compelled to deal "pragmatically" with Marcona because of the difficulty of moving iron ore in a glutted market and its need to maintain creditworthiness to private commercial lenders. Jamaica earned an initial windfall through the 1974 bauxite levy. But it steadily lost its share of the market because low barriers to entry in extraction enabled multinational aluminum companies to shift new investment and production to less expensive sources of supply.

One of the main factors that directly and indirectly magnified the constraints on nationalization strategies was the OPEC price increases. This is ironic because OPEC was strongly supported by the Third World coalition in the United Nations as a means of reducing stratification in the global economy. Its ability to assert sovereignty over natural resources and dramatically increase prices made it a model for emulation. By demonstrating the disunity of the North, it spurred other challenges to liberal economic regimes through nationalization and cartelization. It would also be used to place pressure on the North to be more forthcoming in concessions to the New International Economic Order.[133]

But OPEC's price increases also placed pressures on the South which weakened nationalization strategies. First, OPEC precipitated a serious recession in the North, the primary market for Third World commodity exports. This punched a hole in the demand for raw materials and pushed prices down. In the tighter market of the 1970s, sellers had considerable bargaining power. But as supply exceeded demand, this power evaporated. As exporters tried to challenge the existing system, they found themselves losing market access as they became suppliers of last resort. The difficulty Peru and Jamaica had in moving iron and bauxite ores provides a case in point.

Second, the quadrupling of energy prices imposed severe balance of payments difficulties on non–oil-producing

LDCs. With nationalization, LDCs relied more on private capital markets rather than MNCs to finance resource exploration and development. Compounding this with a staggering oil import bill, LDCs were faced with the alternatives of stagnation or mounting indebtedness. The latter implied increased dependence on international banks and the IMF. To maintain access to desperately needed credits, LDCs had to meet the performance criteria of these institutions, an important component of which is "pragmatic" treatment of MNCs.

For example, Peru was relatively successful in its economic strategies prior to October 1973. But the quadrupling of oil prices imposed enormous deficits which could only be financed through heavy borrowing. By 1975, Peru had difficulty servicing its debt. The conditions imposed by the banks and the IMF not only limted fiscal and monetary policies; they also served as a constraint in bargaining with foreign iron and copper companies. As one study of the Peruvian experiment concluded, Velasco's nationalization policies "aimed to reduce the influence of international corporations in the economy [but] only succeeded in changing which international corporate groups would have the most influence."[134]

Third, indebtedness impeded the ability of state enterprises to stabilize commodity prices through producer associations or international commodity agreements. Under normal conditions, commodity stabilization schemes are fraught with difficulties. A first prerequisite is that members have adequate financial reserves so they can limit output without curtailing essential imports. Yet OPEC created a desperate need for foreign exchange to import basic inputs and limit indebtedness. Such conditions make it extremely difficult for individual producers to resist short-term gains for long-term stability.[135]

For example, when Manley tried to play a leadership role in the IBA, the temptation of oil-importing producers, such as Brazil and Guinea, to "cheat" on the Caribbean to earn desperately needed export revenues was to great. Even Jamaica's Carbibbean "partners" increasingly defected to protect their share of the market. As a result, Jamaica was unable to translate majority ownership into control over pricing.

In sum, the OPEC's price increase produced the opposite of what it had promised. Rather than decrease stratification in the world economy, it increased it. By increasing indebtedness, it decreased host country bargaining power vis-à-vis multinationals, banks, and consumers. By precipitating a recession in the West, it decreased demand in the primary markets and pushed down prices. While OPEC may have shown the Third World the way, its unequivocal success in 1970s made even "modest" replications elsewhere extremely difficult.

Conclusion

If the State Department were asked to trace the evolution of United States policy toward expropriation, the reply would be that not much has changed. A screening of current legal documents and official pronouncements confirms this assessment. Public statements merely reiterate President Nixon's 1972 speech, and still defer to Cordell Hull's time-honored principle of "prompt, adequate, and effective" compensation. For the public record, the United States still flaunts itself as a hegemonic power trying to maintain the "rules of the game."

But if official policy has remained verbally intact, the manner in which it has been implemented has changed considerably. The United States has moved from a policy of regime maintenance, with emphasis on precedent and principle, to a policy of accommodation which accepts the *fait accompli* of host country ownership and focuses on short-term diplomatic interests and an ongoing relationship with the dispossessed firm.

A number of competing models have been put forward to explain this change. Each sets forth a parsimonious explanation of the decisive causal locus of policy determination and poses key questions to the researcher: Can anti-expropriation policy be deduced from the distribution of economic resources in the international system? To what extent is it limited by the need to reproduce the capitalist mode of production? Does it flow from a state pursuing an autonomously conceived national interest, or is it heavily influenced by corporate definitions of interest? Is it the consequence of a state behaving as a unitary actor, or of bargaining and compromise among various bureaucratic and societal groups?

Each approach provides a satisfactory explanation of some of the case studies in part 2. But no one model provides a satisfactory explanation of all cases.

Nor can we easily refute the competing approaches on the basis of this micro-level evidence. As noted earlier, each model establishes residual categories to explain deviant cases. Krasner invokes the concept of the "weak state" to account for cases where private economic actors successfully redefine public choices. Lipson excludes from his analysis intensely intersecting diplomatic issues where corporate preferences are less successful. Bureaucratic and interest group models concede that the state may act like a unitary rational actor in areas of "high" politics with intense presidential attention.

But understanding the conditions under which deviant cases occur can contribute to the cumulation of knowledge.[1] By probing into the circumstances of different forms of behavior one can generate contingent hypotheses and delimit the explanatory domain of various models. Such research is intended less to test and falsify particular paradigms or works than to develop a "sorting device" to generate from and explain the variance among the different explanations for each of the cases.

The research design below is intended to provide a framework for such an analysis. Each of the competing models is simplified into an "explanatory scheme" where it locates the modal causal explanation. A universe of cases is coded according to a number of attributes. These are correlated to the causal schemes to suggest conditions when different factors are decisive in influencing state behavior.

This framework is designed to overcome the major pitfall of case study analysis—the difficulty in generalizing from a single case.[2] Even with comparative case studies, there is a danger of selectivity bias. While the researcher strives for a representative sample, his decisions are based upon intuitive judgments of what is important. This can lead to the (conscious or unconscious) choice of cases that support a particular theory and the omission of others that pose troublesome anomalies.

Large-N studies have the advantage of allowing the researcher to cumulate the findings of a number of studies. In establishing a universe of events, Krasner's and Lipson's cases have been augmented by those from other studies and from the State Department' Bureau of Intelligence and Research reports on investment disputes.[3] In the State Department studies, the analysis is limited to include only those examples that involved significant raw material investments or elicitied high-level U.S. government attention. These include some nonextractive nationalizations that public and private decision makers feared would have externalities on all foreign investment, e.g., Brazil's 1962 nationalization of ITT's utility holdings.

This is not to argue that large-N studies are not problematical. Breaking down events into a finite number of categories cannot capture all the contexual richness of a case study. Hence, the skeleton is fleshed out with qualitative analysis from the case studies in part 2 to complement and give meaning to the correlations.

CLASSIFICATION OF THE DATA

The appendix classifies the events and disaggregates them in terms of type of response and locus of determination for three distinct periods. The data is mapped onto

three-by-three tables as a heuristic aid to understanding the
changing implementation of U.S. anti-expropriation policy and
the conditions under which different causal mechanisms are
most relevant.

   Types of U.S. Government Response. These can be
collapsed into three categories

   1. *Interventionary force* refers to the use of overt military
      or covert intrusions against a target state. The objective
      in such cases is the overthrow of an "undesirable" gov-
      ernment, either physically through armed force, or in-
      directly by destabilizing the system and/or conspiring
      with local political rivals.
   2. *Economic Reprisal* subsumes both formal and informal
      sanction. The former refers to legislative amendments
      regarding bilateral aid, voting in MDBs, and trade pref-
      erences; the latter, to unofficially deferring bilateral and
      multilateral assistance, impeding access to credits and
      markets, and discouraging new investments. The objec-
      tive is to pressure a target state into conformity with
      some set of political or economic norms or make an ex-
      ample of a violator to convince others that a price will
      be exacted for certain forms of proscribed behavior.
   3. *Accommodation* embraces inaction, intercession to me-
      diate a compromise, or encouragement of corporate ad-
      aptation by a refusal to proffer support. These outcomes
      are related to the state's unwillingness to exert coercive
      pressure to compel conformity to political or economic
      norms.

   The Locus of Determination. This refers to my judgment of which paradigmatic scheme best fits a particular case.
The taxonomy is divided into three variables, each representing a simplification of a particular theoretical perspective.

   1. Where considerations of the *diplomatic milieu goals* are
      dominant, the case most closely conforms to Krasner's
      statist thesis that the "broader interests of foreign pol-

icy" take precedence over the prerogatives of corporate ownership or regime maintenance. These contextual concerns are primarily defined by Cold War considerations, i.e., shoring up relations with allies, preventing the accession to power of or overthrowing ideologically heretical regimes perceived to be proxies of the Soviet Union.

2. *Economic milieu goals* refer to cases where foreign investment regime considerations are overriding. Such outcomes conform to Lipson's corporate preference model or, more accurately, Lindblom's theory of "the privileged position of business." In such cases, decision making is primarily concerned with maintaining stable international norms and expectations so that investors can confidently venture their funds overseas.

3. *Bureaucratic politics* becomes the decisive factor when it is not useful to trace foreign policy responses to a unitary purposive actor coherently pursuing hierarchically ranked national interests. Such an outcome is not exclusive of the first two categories; rather, it encompasses policies in which different agencies are divided between diplomatic and regime considerations and actual policy output is a function of bureaucratic bargaining and compromise. (*Note:* This category includes cases where there were not only interagency differences, but where tangible interagency differences produced conflicting operative proposals which substantively influenced policy outputs.)

Structural theories, such as the modified hegemonic model (see chapter 3), are incorporated by coding the events into three distinct periods, each reflecting the international position of the United States government and established industries with respect to the resources needed for regime maintenance:

1. *The period of a strong regime* (1938–1968), when relevant U.S. government and corporate resources were sufficiently concentrated to punish threats to, absorb the

costs of, and bribe medium powers into regime maintenance.

2. *The period of regime stress* (1968–1974), during which
   the dilution of American hegemony and corporate oligopoly allowed hosts to challenge the regime.
3. *The period of regime change* (1974–), during which private and public resources were no longer able to sustain
   the old order, and a quasi-regime of contractual flexibility emerged.

The variable of regime change is used as a "moderator variable" which influences the prevalence of the different explanatory schemes.[4] It is used to test how changes
in the international system mediate and influence patterns
of foreign policy decision making.

THE RESULTS

Table 3 organizes the data into a three-by-three table correlating type of U.S. government response with chro-
nological period. To incorporate examination of the central
locus of determination into the model, the tables are rear-
ranged (see tables 4, 5 and 6) to associate that variable with
type of response for each period. These devices will highlight
changes in policy implementation and the conditions under
which different causal schemes are most relevant.

Period One: The Era of American Hegemony. An examination of the cases of covert intervention during this (and
each) period reveals that they were undertaken only in response to Cold War diplomatic objectives, i.e., not to contain
economic nationalism, per se, but to abort or overthrow radical governments seen as proxies of the Soviet Union. This,
in part, conforms to Krasner's statist view that the sternest
measures were taken in cases where the decisive consideration was not only expropriation, but also politico-ideological
objectives, i.e., Mossadegh in Iran, Arbenz in Guatemala,
Castro in Cuba, or Allende in Chile.

One might fault Krasner for setting up too neat a dichotomy between "political" and "economic" interests, characterizing politico-ideological aims as nonlogical in terms of U.S. material interests.[5] Such an approach assumes that ideas are themselves determinants of policy.

Ideas, however, are not created and sustained in a vacuum. Ideology is not, as Krasner implies, a direct cause of policy or a substitute for interests when core needs are satisfied; rather, it is a filter which defines relationships between variables and interests. Thus conceived, opposition to revolution or radicalism was not cognitively unrelated to the expansion of overseas economic interest. As David Sylvan asks, was not the preservation of foreign investment incompatible, at least in theory, with the Communist's total state claim on the society?[6] This assumption may have been wrong, as recent corporate activities in China and Angola suggest. Nonetheless, it is still a perception of interest filtered through an ideological lens.

These interventions, moreover, were not entirely determined by autonomous state preferences. In the Iranian nationalization of AIOC, for example, the State Department initially opted for accommodation because the Mexican experience indicated the difficulties involved in economic coercion for rigid regime maintenance; some form of compromise was prudent. AIOC and the majors, however, refused to accept State's looser definition of regime rules and would not budge on their demands for rescission. They effectively conspired to boycott Iranian crude, destablizing their target politically and economically. By 1953, the perceived choices confronting the United States had been redefined: either intervention or increased Soviet penetration (via either a Mossadegh plea for Soviet aid or a successful Tudeh Party uprising.) While the decision to overthrow Mossadegh was ostensibly motivated by Cold War concerns, the United States was confronted with a situation that had been redefined by the more expansive regime considerations of the international oil industry.

The process by which state policies are shaped and constrained by private economic actors plays an important role in explaining responses during the hegemonic period. Krasner aptly observes the converse process that the state

Table 3. Types of United States Government Response by Period

	Interventionary Force	Economic Reprisal	Accommodation/ Inaction
1938–1968	Iran, 1953 Guatemala, 1954 Cuba, 1960 Brazil, 1964 (?)	Bolivia, 1938–40 Mexico, 1938–40 Mexico, 1945–50 Brazil, 1963–64 Ceylon, 1963–65 Peru, 1963–68 Honduras, 1962 Argentina, 1963–65 Iraq, 1961 Indonesia, 1960–65	Bolivia, 1940–42 Mexico, 1940–42 Venezuela, 1942–3 Saudi Arabia, 1950 Iran, 1951–52 Bolivia, 1952 Mexico, 1966–67 Chile, 1964–60
1968–1974	Chile, 1971–73	Peru, 1968–71 Peru, 1971–73 Bolivia, 1969 Libya, 1973 Guyana, 1970–71 Ghana, 1972–74 Bolivia, 1971 Ecuador, 1971–74 Venezuela, 1971–74 Algeria, 1971 Iraq, 1972	Zambia, 1969–73 Algeria, 1967–70 Libya, 1970 Persian Gulf, 1971 Persian Gulf, 1972 India, 1973–74 Nigeria, 1971
1974–	Nicaragua, 1979	Jamaica, 1974 Guyana, 1974 So. Yemen, 1975 Somalia, 1975 P.R. Congo, 1976 Uganda, 1975 Ethiopia, 1979	OPEC, 1974 Peru, 1974 Peru, 1975–76 Venezuela, 1975 Venezuela, 1976 Venezuela, 1977–80 Jamaica, 1975–76 Guyana, 1975 Indonesia, 1976 Malaysia, 1976 Nigeria, 1975 Costa Rica, 1975 Honduras, 1975 Jamaica, 1978

possesses the negative power to veer corporate strategies toward accommodation. Table 4 indicates a number of cases where State Department refusal to coercively support an intransigent bargaining position in disputes had induced affected firms to move away from a rigid regime maintenance stance. Recognizing that sufficient state support was not forthcoming, firms acceded to necessity. Therefore, the state possessed the power to rig the incentives so as to compel corporate managers to redefine their own interests in the direction of state objectives.

A closer examination of the data indicates, however, that cases in which the U.S. government opted for accommodation and exerted decisive influence over corporate strategy were almost exclusively limited to those involving critical national security considerations. In the pre–World War II cases (Bolivia and Mexico), the objective was to check the expansion of German influence in Latin America prior to and during the war. In the post–World II cases (Saudia Arabia and Chile), the possibility of radical nationalists or Marxists coming to power was the decisive consideration. In each case, a conciliatory policy emerged only when there was a perceived threat from a major imperial rival.

What then of cases where such primordial political objectives were not at stake? In almost every such case, economic reprisal was pursued routinely to defend the regime and was rarely modified by bureaucratic politics. Less pressing objectives, such as the Alliance for Progress, were subordinated to the principle of investment protection.[7]

This outcome is somewhat confounding to the statist paradigm because in the cases where loans were denied to Pemex in the late 1940s and aid to Latin America in the early 1960s, the actions contravened the initially articulated preferences of state actors. In the former case, the State Department urged the companies to contract with the nationalized state oil company because of the perceived need to reintegrate Mexican oil with the world economy. In the latter case, the Kennedy administration believed, after the Cuban revolution, that accommodation with Latin American economic nationalism was necessary to safeguard long-term political and economic interests in the hemisphere.

In both cases, the affected firms drew different lessons and believed their interests were ill-served by state priorities. In Mexico, the oil companies valued the reintegration of Mexican oil far less than they feared conferring upon the Mexican nationalization an image of success. In the Alliance for Progress cases, investors believed that political democracy and social reform threatened them with economic nationalism, and greater, not diminished activism was called for in investment disputes. In both instances, the more expansive corporate definitions of interest ultimately redirected the looser definitions of national actors.

The mechanism underlying this pattern conforms most closely to Lindblom's theory of the "privileged position of business."[8] That is, while the state possessed the negative

Table 4. Period of American Hegemony, 1938–1968:
Types of US Responses versus Dominant Mode of Determination

	Diplomatic Milieu Goals	Economic Milieu/ Regime Goals	Bureaucratic Politics
Interventionary Force	Iran, 1953 Guatemala, 1954 Cuba, 1960 Brazil, 1964 (?)		
Economic Reprisal	Egypt, 1961–65 Indonesia, 1960–65	Mexico, 1945–50 Brazil, 1962–1964 Ceylon, 1963–65 Peru, 1963–68 Honduras, 1962 Argentina, 1963–65 Iraq, 1961	Bolivia, 1937–40 Mexico, 1938–40
Accommodation	Bolivia, 1940–42 Mexico, 1940–42 Venezuela, 1942–43 Saudi Arabia, 1950 Iran, 1951–52 Bolivia, 1952 Mexico, 1966–67 Chile, 1964–69		

power to withhold support, it lacked the positive power to compel a specific response. It must persuade rather than command. Since the expansion of natural resource investment in the Third World was defined as an integral part of the national interest, and since this outcome depended upon the autonomous behavior of private economic actors, the state could induce performance only by "indulging" corporate concerns about expropriation and economic nationalism.

Turning back to the pre-1968 cases, this process is clearly discernible. In Mexico, the State Department defined regime requirements more loosely, but it could not induce the industry to compromise and contract with Pemex, and was consequently faced with the redefined choices of symbolically supporting a nationalized company without private participation or continuing the policy of containing nationalization. In the Alliance for Progress cases, a greater emphasis on nationalization issues was ultimately adopted because decision makers perceived that increasing expropriations would contribute to corporate noninvestment in Latin America and congressional threats (spurred by corporate lobbying) to the public assistance program. In each example, the state was compelled to adopt a more consistent policy of principle and precedent, more in conformity with corporate preferences.

In sum, except where cases impinged on the arena of "power politics," to borrow from Lowi's typology, U.S. anti-expropriation policy was measurably influenced by corporate desires for a tighter regime.[9] But the success of corporate interests in pushing the state toward a stronger regime maintenance orientation came not from their ability to impose their will on a passive state, as Lowi would contend; rather, it came from their ability to compel the state to incorporate their concerns, and their probable behavior (nonperformance) if those concerns were not met, into its decision calculus.

An important caveat in making this analysis is that the assumed connection between expropriation, corporate nonperformance, and the "national interest" was a perceived verity which may not have been wholly true. The view was reinforced by the pervasiveness of "liberal" economic beliefs which identified FDI and the traditional strategies of the MNC with its national interest and vision of world order. This world view was widely, though not universally, shared throughout the bureaucracy. The conventional wisdom was seldom challenged because of the absence of tangible costs and the apparent success of policy in enjoining deviant behavior.[10]

This world view also predisposed decision makers to deny or minimize the costs of coercive regime maintenance strategies to bilateral diplomatic relations. Since the benefits of FDI were considered axiomatic and self-evident, expropriation was not viewed as an economically self-interested act, but a challenge to the West. The perceived radicalism of the most prominent expropriators—Mossadegh, Arbenz, Castro, Nasser, Sukarno—reinforced the belief that the issue was a barometer of a regime's political coloration.[11]

A similar cognitive process was involved in minimizing the cost of economic pressures against democratic reformist regimes during the Alliance. As development was defined in terms of economic growth through private capital, many democratic regimes were viewed negatively for pursuing populist policies which scared off foreign business. Their replacement by the military was viewed positively for its contribution to a sound investment climate. Hence, the loss of social reform or constitutional government was no longer defined as a cost.[12]

Even those who advocated a more temperate approach still operated from liberal premises. Their policy preferences reflected an assessment that the costs of rigid regime maintenance were too great; corporate abuses may have existed in the era of "dollar diplomacy"; and the situation could be rectified through prudent renegotiation, thereby leaving intact a system of corporate ownership which benefited all parties. These "dissidents" still clung to an ideology of the "harmony of interests" oblivious to indications that structural differences between MNC and host generated conflicting interests and a rational dynamic toward increasing sovereign control. A notable exception to this ideological lacuna was Richard Funkhouser, whose comparison of nationalization to decolonization was twenty years ahead of its time.

But cases, such as that of IPC in Peru, gave evidence that the perceived connections may not have been as strong or as valid as initially believed—that nationalization need not subvert continued corporate investment, security of supply, or host country development. Events from 1968–1974 would lead many in the bureaucracy to question these traditional causal assumptions.

Period Two: The Era of Regime Stress. The period between 1968 and 1974 witnessed a dramatic change in the international economic system, highlighted by the American retreat from leadership in the global trade and monetary order. It was also a period of stress in international property relations as regime rules were challenged with increasing regularity and success. Natural resource firms began to slowly, reluctantly, and unevenly change course and adapt to economic nationalism. As might be expected during a pattern of systems flux, host countries challenged the rules more frequently to test the outer bounds of permissible behavior and the United States employed economic reprisals more frequently to test its level of control over change.

But while the number of reprisals increased, the policy became increasingly embroiled in intergovernmental conflict, as evidenced by the growing number of cases requiring a bureaucratic politics explanation (see Table 5). This scheme subsumes a greater proportion of the cases during this period primarily because elements of the bureaucracy were affected by systemic change in dissimilar, often contradictory ways, spawning divergent perceptions about the costs of regime change (or reprisal) and about probability of successful resistance.

As previously noted, Treasury called for renewed fidelity to an activist approach because of the effect of change on liberal economic principles and the American economy. This posture aroused opposition from State. This was because

sanctions impinged not only on the terrain of its regional bureaus, but also on two agencies reponsible for policy areas
that the regime had initially been designed to guarantee: the
Economic Bureau (the immediate investment climate), and
OFE (short-run security of supply). This represented a retooling of the instrumental assumptions underlying regime
maintanance policies.

   While expropriation policies from 1971–74 predominantly reflected Treasury's preference for a "presumptive"
policy, the severity and publicity of its application were tempered in bureaucratic bargaining with the relevant agencies
at State. Policy output reflected bureaucratic compromise between deterrent and pragmatic stances.

   From the evidence, it is reasonable to postulate that
bureaucratic politics becomes the most prevalent outcome
when the system is in flux, norms are less defined, and capabilities unclear. The only exceptions were the initial disjointed efforts to coerce Mexico and Bolivia to rescind the oil
nationalizations in the late 1930s. Prior to World War II, there
was considerable bureaucratic debate about the balance to be
struck between regime maintenance and hemispheric solidarity. In a global war, as in a polycentric order, the dominant power finds it difficult to act like a hegemonic power
vis-à-vis smaller powers. Since its core interest of security is
threatened and demands immediate attention, it must rely
more on cooperation through compromise rather than compliance through sanction.[13] The period before a global war,
like the period before hegemonic decline, is replete with uncertainty on the extent to which time-honored policies should
bend to change. Intragovernmental discord is likely to be more
prevalent.

   From 1968 to 1974, incidents of accommodation inaction were few. Locales were, for the most part, outside of
Latin America (Zambia, India, Nigeria), and American stakes
were relatively minor. A notable exception was the active encouragement of oil company adaptation to the pricing and
participation demands of the Persian Gulf states. The deter-

minative scheme was comparable to the pattern for accommodations prior to 1968: regime considerations and corporate solicitation were subordinated to Cold War aims. A prolonged confrontation over principle would generate immediate costs of potentially catastrophic magnitude, i.e., the disruption of critical energy supplies and the exposure of conservative Middle Eastern allies to radical nationalist rebellions and Soviet penetration.

Despite Treasury's preference for a more "aggressive" policy toward OPEC, this outcome was not a function of bureaucratic bargaining, but of unified governmental strategy. In most cases, Treasury's input was effectively excluded by highest-level executive branch involvement; adaptation nicely served the Nixon-Kissinger "grand design" of using Persian Gulf monarchies as surrogates for American power projection. Additionally, systemic changes (the proliferation of the independents, the disappearance of spare capacity, increased dependence on imported oil, OPEC cohesion, and consumer fragmentation) prevented Treasury from

Table 5. Period of Regime Stress, 1968–1974:
Types of USG Responses versus Dominant Loci of Determination

	Diplomatic Milieu Goals	Economic Milieu/ Regime Goals	Bureaucratic Politics
Interventionary Force	Chile, 1971–73		
Economic Reprisal	Ghana, 1972–74	Peru, 1968–71 Bolivia, 1969 Libya, 1973	Peru, 1971–74 Guyana, 1971 Bolivia, 1971 Ecuador, 1971–74 Venezuela, 1971–74 Algeria, 1971 Iraq, 1972
Accommodation	Persian Gulf, 1971 Persian Gulf, 1972 Algeria, 1967–70	Zambia, 1969–73 Libya, 1970 India, 1973–74 Nigeria, 1971	

translating its preference into the concrete alternatives needed to engage its bureaucratic colleagues in a bargaining contest. Therefore, policy most closely approximated a unified actor.

But prior to the oil crisis, there was no general movement toward accommodation with economic nationalism. Given both Treasury's strong bureaucratic position and the persistence of orthodox liberal beliefs, the United States was still wedded to the traditional system.

For example, as late as 1973, the United States was actively discouraging the development of new energy sources in Algeria (the El Paso LNG project) and Venezuela (the Orinoco Tar Basin) in deference to oil companies embroiled in disputes over ownership. That such options were disregarded on the eve of the world's worst energy crisis reveals the extent to which an ideological view of national economic security had become a substitute for independent evaluation. The liberal assumptions underlying the policy may have served American interests during the era of hegemony, but they produced dysfunctional outcomes once that era passed. By treating nationalization disputes as metaphysical confrontations between competing faiths rather than accommodations among self-interested parties, liberalism degenerated into an intellectual straitjacket which delayed adaptive responses to change.

Period Three: The Era of Regime Transformation. The post-1974 era witnessed the demise of the old order. The decentralization of public and private economic resources and the obsolescing bargain process sapped the foundations of the regime. A quasi-regime of wider sovereign discretion emerged in its place. The new system set forth looser norms and expectations. The modal outcome was formal state control, book value compensation or less, and an ongoing post-expropriation relationship, the terms of which became the real battleground for bargaining between firm and host.

Yet cognitive change does not necessarily flow smoothly in response to environmental change; it usually needs the stimulus of a catalytic experience imposing costs that can no longer be denied. That stimulus was provided by the OPEC price increases and embargo in 1973. The lesson generalized throughout the government was that the old order could no longer be maintained and attempts to do so would endanger resource supplies and overseas corporate viability. Adaptation became incumbent upon MNCs who wanted to operate in this new era.

In line with the lessons, Table 6 reveals that economic reprisal against expropriating hosts was almost exclusively reserved for states perceived as anti-Western or pro-Soviet, states to which aid was being phased down anyway. The only economic cases (Jamaica and Guyana over bauxite disputes in the summer of 1974), occurred early, were subject to strong bureaucratic dispute, and were of a magnitude insufficient to induce a settlement. In both cases, the modest exertion of pressure was subsequently withdrawn in favor of mediating compromise settlements which conformed to the norms of the new loosened order. Table 6 also reveals an increased number of cases of accommodation and a change in their composition. First, there was a greater sectoral distribution in Latin America, the sphere of the greatest U.S. interest and influence. In addition, accommodation was more prevalent for reasons other than pure Cold War considertions; it was clearly compatible with the new norms and expectations of the quasi-regime. A contrary policy would undermine the investment climate and security of supply, two objectives previously associated with the traditional order.

Pragmatism ultimately won out because systemic changes, which made themselves indelibly manifest in the OPEC revolution, demonstrated the costs and inefficacy of economic reprisal. Moreover, security of supply and continued corporate viability could be maintained through the loosened order of contractual flexibility. This awareness sufficiently persuaded high-level bureaucratic actors who were previously uncommitted or unconcerned with foreign economic matters to shift the bureaucratic weight on the side of pragmatism.

But the resultant policy was not as much a function of bureaucratic politics as it was of unified retreat. While Treasury held out the longest in defense of the traditional standard, systemic changes (and the unwillingness of most investors to play the old game) effectively invalidated its position. As in the OPEC cases, it had no concrete options to place on the table. This became increasingly obvious to Treasury officials, whose differences with their counterparts at State became more matters of bureaucratic turf fighting than of real operational differences. Changes in the international system rendered interagency differences meaningless and decisively influenced policy change.

This conclusion bears on the question of whether the source of U.S. and business pragmatism derived from state initiatives or corporate preferences. Krasner contends that

Table 6. Period of Regime Change (Post-1974 Quasi-Regime): Types of US Responses versus Dominant Loci of Determination

	Diplomatic Milieu Goals	Economic Milieu/ Regime Goals	Bureaucratic Politics
Interventionary Force	Nicaragua, 1981–		
Economic Reprisal	Somalia, 1975 Ethiopia, 1979 So. Yemen, 1975 Uganda, 1975 P.R. Congo, 1975		Jamaica, 1974 Guyana, 1974
Accommodation/ Inaction	Ethiopia, 1975 Somalia, 1978 Ecuador, 1977–79	Jamaica, 1975–76 Guyana, 1975 Peru, 1974 Peru, 1975–76 OPEC, 1974 Venezuela, 1975 Venezuela, 1976 Venezuela, 1977–80 Indonesia, 1976 Malaysia, 1976 Nigeria, 1975 Costa Rica, 1975 Honduras, 1975 Panama, 1975	

the corporate move toward pragmatism resulted from the state's unwillingness to use its coercive power to support aggrieved firms. Lipson, on the other hand, traces pragmatic state policies to changes in corporate ownership strategies toward accommodation with economic nationalism.[14] Each view is supported by some of the case studies: in the Peruvian case, the business community (except for IPC) was ahead of the state in recognizing the necessity of coming to terms with nationalism; in the Middle East oil cases, the reverse was generally true.

Each analysis portrays a part of the reality, but a clearer picture can be obtained through disaggregating public and private actors. The decisive causal force was systemic change, which imposed differential costs and opportunities on different segments of the bureaucracy and business community. A transnational coalition of LDC state companies, new entrants, and medium powers, whose interests were supported by contractual flexibility and/or threatened by economic reprisal, sabotaged the old system. The established firms and Treasury were most adversely affected by regime change and intensified their resistance. State's turf, on the other hand, was more threatened by reprisal and it increasingly sought to blunt Treasury's preference. Whether the public or private sector was more pragmatic was determined by which corporate or bureaucratic interests were activated in a particular case. This, in turn, was an epiphenomenon of deeper systemic causes.

Ultimately, all segments recognized that change was inexorable. Moreover, accommodation to nationalization did not preclude a continued corporate presence or destroy national interests associated with foreign investment. The real threat to those interests came not from host country control, but from market scarcities which enable LDCs to translate formal sovereignty into genuine economic clout.

Yet even in this retreat from traditional property norms, one is struck by the pervasiveness of the liberal economic paradigm in American thinking. The argument against traditional regime maintenance was that it did more to harm than help the investment climate by provoking nationalist animosity. Accommodation was still wedded to the assumption that private foreign investment provides a harmony of interests and that more is better. One can, however, discern the germ of an intellectual evolution, attributing greater legitimacy to LDC state intervention, i.e., an evolution from what Ruggie calls "orthodox" liberalism to an "embedded" liberalism which accepts a valid role for the state regulating the economy for public purposes.[15]

The same mind-set informs the new approach to national economic security. Despite warnings of the "threat from the Third World," the United States shied away from direct intervention in raw material markets.[16] The pragmatic approach was to encourage market forces to make higher prices unsustainable. The liberal defense of property and contract could be safely abandoned only because of the liberal faith in markets. To what extent the American political and economic system gives business a privileged position which constrains the state is difficult to measure. What is beyond dispute is its privileged position within the minds of American decision makers.

Appendix: Summary Analysis of United States Responses to Major Challenges to the Regime, 1937–1979

Case	USG Policy	Locus of Determination	Defining Features
Bolivia, 1937–1940 Standard Oil	Informal economic pressure	Bureaucratic politics	State/Treasury cleavage led to a fragmented policy of sanction and mediation.
Mexico, 1938–1940 Oil Industry	Informal economic pressure	Bureaucratic politics	State/Treasury divisions led to a disjointed strategy of pressure and mediation.
Bolivia, 1940–1942 Standard Oil	Accommodation	Diplomatic milieu goals	US withdrew support for Standard and mediated a compromise to shore up hemispheric position prior to World War II.
Mexico, 1940–1942 Oil Industry	Accommodation	Diplomatic milieu goals	US played an active role in encouraging oil company to compromise to solidify hemispheric position prior to World War II.

Case	USG Policy	Locus of Determination	Defining Features
Venezuela, 1942–1943 Oil Industry (Income Tax)	Accommodation	Diplomatic milieu goals	US encourages oil company compromise to support wartime interest in hemispheric solidarity and immediate security of supply.
Mexico, 1945–1950 Loans to Pemex	Economic pressure	Economic milieu goals	US refused to lend to Pemex to prevent precedent of state enterprise and nationalization.
Saudi Arabia, Income Tax 1950	Accommodation	Diplomatic milieu goals	US refused to support Aramco resistance to income tax to stabilize Saudi monarchy, minimize Soviet influence, and insure short-term security of supply.
Iran, 1951–1952 AIOC	Mediation	Diplomatic milieu goals	Initial US attempt to broker a compromise despite oil company boycott.
Iran, 1953 AIOC	Covert intervention	Diplomatic milieu goals	US concerns with political developments in Iran.
Bolivia, 1952 Tin Mines	Accommodation	Diplomatic milieu goals	US sees new Bolivian regime as anti-communist.
Guatemala, 1954 United Fruit	Covert intervention	Diplomatic milieu goals	Perception of Arbenz as a communist.
Cuba, 1959–1960 Socialization	Covert intervention	Diplomatic milieu goals	US concerns with Castro's Soviet ties. Decision to overthrow preceded the most serious nationalizations.

Case	Policy	Goal Type	Comments
Brazil, 1962–1963 ITT/AMFORP	Informal aid cutoff	Economic milieu goals	Goulart's failure to pay compensation seen as a dangerous precedent and a sign of economic irresponsibility.
Brazil, 1964 AMFORP	Covert intervention (?)	Diplomatic milieu goals	US sought alternatives to Goulart as he moves further to the Left.
Argentina, 1963–1965 Oil Industry	Informal aid cutoff	Economic milieu goals	Alliance for Progress aims subordinated to regime considerations.
Ceylon, 1963–1965 Oil Companies	Formal sanction	Economic milieu goals	Hickenlooper Amendment used in area of marginal material interest to show resolve in enforcing the regime.
Peru, 1963–1968 IPC	Informal aid cutoff	Economic milieu goals	Aid cutback to induce a favorable settlement with IPC.
Honduras, 1962 United Fruit	Threatened sanction	Economic milieu goals	Hickenlooper threatened to abort agrarian reform plan, which affected UFCO lands.
Iraq, 1961 Iraq Petroleum Company	Informal economic pressure	Economic milieu goals	USG assisted major company efforts to keep competitors out of Iraq.
Indonesia, 1961–1965 Oil & Rubber	Informal economic pressure	Diplomatic milieu goals	Perception of Sukarno as anti-Western.
Mexico, 1966–1967 Sulphur Companies	Inaction	Diplomatic milieu goals	Despite corporate requests for assistance, no action was forthcoming given Mexico's key geographic location.

Case	USG Policy	Locus of Determination	Defining Features
Chile, 1967–1969 Copper Industry	Accommodation	Diplomatic milieu goals	Bolstering of Frei to prevent Allende from coming to power.
Peru, 1968–1971 IPC	Informal aid cutoff	Economic milieu goals	Use of non-overt pressure to avert a precedent while limiting diplomatic damage.
Bolivia, 1969 Gulf Oil	Informal economic pressure	Economic milieu goals	Low profile economic pressure to avert a precedent and minimize political damage.
Guyana, 1970–1971 ALCAN	Overt informal pressure	Bureaucratic politics	Treasury pushes for abstention in IADB; US holds up new aid and credits.
Bolivia, 1971 Tin Mines	Overt informal pressure	Bureaucratic politics	Treasury opposes IADB loan. No new aid authorizations.
Ecuador, 1969–1974 Oil Companies	Non-overt informal pressure	Bureaucratic politics	US holds up new aid authorizations
Peru, 1971–1973 IPC	Overt informal pressure	Bureaucratic politics	Treasury influence in moving US policy toward a more overt and stringent policy.
Chile, 1971–1973 Copper, ITT	Covert intervention	Diplomatic milieu goals	Aim of overthrowing Allende precedes major takeovers.
Venezuela, 1971–1974 Oil Reversion	Informal economic pressure	Bureaucratic politics	Treasury pushes for hard-line through denying Venezuela hemispheric preferences.

Case	Action	Category	Notes
Zambia, 1969–1973 Copper Industry	Inaction	Economic milieu goals (quasi-regime)	No request for US involvement; Zambian actions compatible with corporate interests.
Ghana, 1972–1974 Union Carbide	Informal economic pressure	Economic milieu goals	US fears precedent of debt repudiation; Nationalization seen as part of the problem.
Peru, 1973–1974	Accommodation	Economic milieu goals (quasi-regime)	The company allowed the US mediate a compromise settlement.
India, 1973–1974 Oil Industry	Inaction	Economic milieu goals (quasi-regime)	Indian actions compatible with corporate interests; No solicitation of US assistance.
Nigeria, 1971 35% Participation in Oil Industry	Inaction	Economic milieu goals (quasi-regime)	Oil companies successfully adapt to equity participation.
Algeria, 1967–1970 US Oil Companies	Informal economic pressure	Economic milieu goals	US works to hold up new MDB loans and deny Eximbank credits.
Algeria, 1971 French Oil Industry	Informal economic pressure	Bureaucratic politics	US support France in IBRD and by delaying approval if El Paso LNG deal.
Libya, 1970–1971 Unilateral Price Hikes	Accommodation	Diplomatic milieu goals	US sought to avoid confrontation with new regime and recognized lack of leverage.
Persian Gulf, 1971 Teheran Pricing Accords	Accommodation	Diplomatic milieu goals	Bolster conservative Middle East regimes and ensure short-run security of supply.

Case	USG Policy	Locus of Determination	Defining Features
Persian Gulf, 1972 (Saudi Arabia, Kuwait, UAE, and Qatar) 25% participation	Accommodation	Diplomatic milieu goals	Bolster conservative Persian Gulf regimes and ensure short-run security of supply.
Iraq, 1972 Kirkuk Oil Fields	Overt informal sanctions	Bureaucratic politics	State opposes Treasury vote against IBRD loan.
Libya, 1973 51% Oil Industry	Overt informal pressures	Economic milieu goals	Pressure was ineffective because of disappearance of spare US capacity and dependence on Libyan crude for US domestic market
Persian Gulf, 1974 60% Oil Industry	Accommodation	Economic milieu goals (quasi-regime)	USG recognition of regime decay; Oil companies adapt; Short-term security of supply not threatened.
Peru, 1974 Greene Settlement IPC and others	Accommodation	Economic milieu goals (quasi-regime)	USG negotiates lump sum settlement that compromises with principle. Aim was to normalize bilateral relations and improve investment climate.
Peru, 1975–1976 Marcona Iron Mines	Accommodation	Economic milieu goals	USG mediates a compromise to facilitate debt refinancing and post-expropriation relationship.

Case	Response	Goal type	Description
Venezuela, 1975 Iron Ore	Inaction	Economic milieu goals	USG counsels adaptation to contractual relationships
Venezuela, 1976 Oil Industry	Inaction	Economic milieu goals	USG encourages adaptation to nationalization.
Jamaica, 1974 Bauxite	Informal non-overt pressure	Bureaucratic politics	State/Treasury division over withholding new aid to protest bauxite levy, participation, and rejection of ICSID
Guyana, 1974 Reynolds Bauxite Mines	Informal non-overt pressure	Bureaucratic politics	State/Treasury division over holding up new aid until Reynolds compensated.
Jamaica, 1975–6 Bauxite	Accommodation	Economic milieu goals (quasi-regime)	Aid pressures withdrawn as companies adapt and move new investment out of Jamaica.
Guyana, 1975 Bauxite	Accommodation	Economic milieu goals	OPIC mediates a compromise compensation package.
Ecuador, 1977–79 Oil	Accommodation	Diplomatic milieu goals	Carter administration subordinates minor investment disputes to aim of supporting return to civilian rule.
Venezuela, 1977–81 Oil Compensations	Inaction	Economic milieu goals (quasi-regime)	US uninvolved as companies face long delays over payment of compensation.
Somalia, 1975 Caltex	Formal sanction	Diplomatic milieu goals	Denial of GSP because of perception as Soviet client.
Ethiopia, 1975 Socialization	Inaction	Diplomatic milieu goals	Allow continuation of aid to wean new revolutionary regime away from USSR.

Case	USG Policy	Locus of Determination	Defining Features
Somalia, 1977	Accommodation	Diplomatic milieu goals	US removes sanctions as USSR switches sides to Ethiopia.
Ethiopia, 1978–79	Formal sanctions	Diplomatic milieu goals	US invokes Hickenlooper; Perceive as Soviet client supported by Cuban troops.
Uganda, 1975 General Socialization	Formal sanctions	Diplomatic milieu goals	Denial of GSP to regime considered politically repugnant.
People's Rep. of the Congo 1976	Formal sanctions	Diplomatic milieu goals	Denial to trade preferences to radical leftist regime.
Malaysia, 1976 Oil Industry	Inaction	Economic milieu goals (quasi-regime)	Oil companies adapt to new system
Indonesia, 1976 Oil Industry	Inaction	Economic milieu goals (quasi-regime)	Oil companies adapt; no request for assistance.
Nigeria, 1975 55% Oil	Inaction	Economic milieu goals (quasi-regime)	Oil companies adapt; no request for assistance
Honduras, 1975 United Fruit	Inaction	Economic milieu goals (quasi-regime)	Banana company adapts to role of marketer; no request for assistance.
Costa Rica, 1975 United Fruit and Standard Brands	Inaction	Economic milieu goals (quasi-regime)	Banana company adapts to role of marketer; no request for assistance.
Nicaragua, 1979 United Fruit, Asarco	Covert intervention	Diplomatic milieu goals	Perception of Sandinistas as anti-US Marxists; no corporate requests for assistance.

Notes

ABBREVIATIONS FOR UNPUBLISHED GOVERNMENT
DOCUMENTS USED IN NOTES

CIEP/FJB/NA   Records of the Council on International Economic Policy
               (1973–1977), Record Group (RG) 429, Fiscal and Judicial
               Branch, National Archives, Washington, D.C.
CIEP/NLM/NA   Records of the Council on International Economic Policy
               (1971–1972), Record Group (RG) 273 and 429, Nixon
               Library Materials Project, Office of Presidential Libraries,
               National Archives, Washington, D.C.
DDE/AWF   Ann Whitman File, Dwight D. Eisenhower Presidential
               Library, Abilene, Kansas.
DDI   Declassified Documents Index.
DOS/FOIA   Department of State, Freedom of Information Act.
DS/NA   Department of State Records, Diplomatic Branch, National
               Archives, Washington, D.C.
HST/PSF   Personal Secretary's Files, Harry S. Truman Presidential
               Library, Independence, Missouri.
JFK/POF   President's Office Files, John F. Kennedy Presidential
               Library, Boston, Massachusetts.
JFK/NSF   National Security Files, John F. Kennedy Presidential
               Library, Boston, Massachusetts.
LBJ/NSF   National Security Files, Lyndon B. Johnson Presidential
               Library, Austin, Texas.
LBJ/WHCF   White House Cental Files, Lyndon B. Johnson Presidential
               Library, Austin, Texas.

NSC/FOIA   National Security Council, Freedom of Information Act.
TD/FOIA   Treasury Department, Freedom of Information Act.

INTRODUCTION

1. Vernon, *Sovereignty at Bay,* pp. 46–59.

2. Wilkins, *The Maturing of the Multinational Enterprise,* p. 363; Bergsten, Horst, and Moran, *American Multinationals and American Interests,* p. 322.

3. For representative analyses of this observation, see Shafer, "Capturing the Mineral Multinationals"; Guasti, "The Peruvian Military Government and the International Corporations"; and Thomas Biersteker, "The Limits of State Power in the Contemporary World Economy," in Peter G. Brown and Henry Shue, eds., *Boundaries: National Limits on Autonomy* (Totowa, N.J.: Rowman and Littlefield, 1981).

4. The term "international regime" has been defined as a set of "explicit or implicit principles, norms, rules, and decision-making procedures around which actor expectations converge in a given area of international relations." See Krasner, ed., *International Regimes,* p. 2.

5. Friedrich Kratochwil and John Gerard Ruggie, "International Organization: A State of the Art on an Art of the State," *International Organization* (Autumn 1986), 40(4):759.

6. Jack Donnelly, "International Human Rights: A Regime Analysis," *International Organization* (Spring 1986), 40(3):601.

7. Kratochwil and Ruggie, "International Organization," p. 760.

8. Robert O. Keohane, "The Theory of Hegemonic Stability," pp. 134–138.

9. The structuralist argument for the need of preponderant powers to play a managerial role in world politics is put forward by Kenneth N. Waltz, *Theory of International Politics* (Reading, Mass.: Addison-Wesley, 1979), pp. 196–199.

10. Stephen D. Krasner, "American Policy and Global Economic Stability," in Avery and Rapkin, eds., *America in a Changing World Political Economy;* Keohane, *After Hegemony,* ch. 9.

11. John Ruggie notes that the norms underlying the Bretton Woods system were an "embedded liberal" compromise between liberalism and economic nationalism: "unlike the economic nationalism of the thirties, it would be multilateral in character; unlike the liberalism of the gold standard or free trade, its multilateralism would be predicated on domestic interventionism." See Ruggie, "International Regimes, Transactions, and Change," p. 209.

12. Jagdish N. Bhagwati, "Introduction," in Bhagwati and Ruggie, eds., *Power, Passions, and Purpose: Prospects for North–South Negotiations* (New York: Columbia University Press, 1984), p. 3; Krasner, *Structural Conflict,* p. 58.

13. Young, "Regime Dynamics," pp. 100, 108.

14. Lawrence P. Frank, "The First Oil Regime," *World Politics* (July 1985), 37(4):587; Lipson, *Standing Guard,* pp. 146, 191–192.

15. A good exposition of the need to combine structural and cognitive approaches in the study of international regimes is provided in Vinod K. Aggarwal,

Liberal Protectionism: The International Politics of Organized Textile Trade (Berkeley: University of California Press, 1985), pp. 19–20.

16. Ruggie argues that it is more appropriate to characterize the underlying principle of the postwar economic order as "embedded" rather than "orthodox" or laissez-faire liberalism in that it recognized a potentially constructive role for the state in regulating economic forces for political purposes (see n. 11). While this applied to North–North trade and monetary relations, Ruggie notes that the logic was not fully extended to North–South economic relations where more orthodox norms prevailed. See John Gerard Ruggie, ed., *The Antinomies of Interdependence: National Welfare and the International Division of Labor* (New York: Columbia University Press, 1983), pp. 428–451.

17. Packenham, *Liberal America and the Third World.*

18. Lipson, *Standing Guard*, pp. 203–215.

19. Adapted from Richard S. Olson, *Economic Sanctions in International Disputes: Three Expropriation Cases* (Ph.D. dissertation, University of Oregon, Eugene, Oregon, 1973), pp. 16–17.

20. On the role of economic surfeit in maintaining rules in the international petroleum regime, see Keohane, *After Hegemony*, pp. 167–174.

21. For a more state-centric view of regime strength, see Krasner, *Defending the National Interest*, p. 218; For the view that industry structure was the most important variable, see Stephen J. Kobrin, "The Nationalization of Oil Production, 1919–1980," New York University Faculty of Business Administration Working Papers (December 1982); see also Lipson, *Standing Guard*, ch. 5.

22. Smith and Wells, *Negotiating Third World Mineral Agreements: Promises as Prologue*, p. 9; Turner, *Oil Companies in the International System*, pp. 72–73.

23. Krasner, *Structural Conflict*, p. 179.

24. Young, "Regime Dynamics," p. 100–101.

25. Jeffrey Hart, *The New International Economic Order: Conflict and Cooperation in North–South Economic Relations, 1974–77* (New York: St. Martin's Press, 1983), pp. 33–35.

26. See n. 1.

27. Lipson, *Standing Guard*, pp. 153–162.

28. *Ibid.*, pp. 162–166.

29. Bergsten, Horst, and Moran, *American Multinationals and American Interests*, p. 137–138.

30. Theodore Moran, "Transnational Strategies of Protection and Defense by Multinational Corporations: Spreading the Risk and Raising the Cost of Nationalization in Natural Resources," *International Organization*, (Spring 1973), 27(2):273–287, and "New Deal or Raw Deal in Raw Materials," pp. 124–127. See also Feinberg, *The Intemperate Zone*, pp. 116–117, 120–121.

31. For interesting syntheses see Robert W. Tucker, *The Radical Left and American Foreign Policy* (Baltimore, Md.: Johns Hopkins University Press, 1971); Patrick McGowan and Stephen G. Walker, "Radical and Conventional Models of U.S. Foreign Economic Policy Making," *World Politics* (April 1981); 33(3):347–382; and Abraham Lowenthal, " 'Liberal,' 'Radical,' and 'Bureaucratic' Perspectives on United States–Latin American Relations: The Alliance for Progress in Retrospect," in Cotler and Fagen, eds., *Latin America and the United States*, pp. 212–235.

32. Krasner, *Defending the National Interest;* Gilpin, *U.S. Power and the Multinational Corporation.*

33. Krasner, *Defending the National Interest,* pp. 17–18.

34. Harry Magdoff, *The Age of Imperialism* (New York: Monthly Review Press, 1969), p. 14; Kolko and Kolko, *The Limits of Power,* p. 2.

35. Paul A. Baran and Paul M. Sweezy, "Notes on Theory of Imperialism," in K. T. Fann and Donald C. Hodges, eds., *Readings in U.S. Imperialism* (Boston: Porter, Sargent, 1971), p. 82.

36. Lipson, *Standing Guard,* p. 219.

37. *Ibid.,* pp. 27–28.

38. *Ibid.,* pp. 203–216.

39. For a discussion of these difficulties, see Joanne Gowa, "Subsidizing American Corporate Expansion Abroad: Pitfalls in the Analysis of Public and Private Power," *World Politics* (January 1985), 37(2):201–203.

40. Krasner, *Defending the National Interest,* p. 149.

41. Lindblom, *Politics and Markets,* pp. 170–188.

42. See Feinberg, *The Intemperate Zone,* p. 39; Stephen D. Krasner, "Domestic Constraints on International Economic Leverage," in Klaus Knorr and Frank N. Trager, eds., *Economic Issues and National Security* (Lawrence: Regents Press of Kansas, 1977), pp. 171–174.

43. Kudrle and Bobrow, "The Politics of Foreign Direct Investment," p. 357.

44. Krasner notes that the dispersion of power in the American political and economic system increases the salience of societal constraints on state autonomy. But the location of decision making for anti-expropriation policy was in the White House and State Department, weakening the effectiveness of corporate inputs. See Krasner, *Defending the National Interest,* pp. 17–20.

45. *Ibid.,* p. 31.

46. See Lipson, *Standing Guard,* pp. 223–224; a similar observation was made by David Sylvan in contrasting the radical model of Fred Block with the neomercantilist writings of Gilpin and Krasner. See Sylvan, "The Newest Mercantilism," p. 379; Keohane, *After Hegemony,* p. 42.

47. Graham T. Allison, *Essence of Decision: Explaining the Cuban Missile Crisis* (Boston: Little, Brown, 1971); For an application to investment protection, see Einhorn, *Expropriation Politics.*

48. Lowi, "American Business." For critiques limiting the explanatory power of this model vis-à-vis U.S. anti-expropriation policy, see Pastor, *Congress and the Politics of U.S. Foreign Economic Policy,* pp. 290–301; and Lipson, *Standing Guard,* pp. 219–221.

49. Krasner, *Defending the National Interest,* pp. 18–20.

50. Lipson, *Standing Guard,* p. 27.

51. Krasner suggests a typological analysis in arguing that the prospects for corporate or other societal frustration of foreign policy increase if decision making takes place in Congress. See Krasner, *Defending the National Interest,* pp. 18–19; this residual category, however, cannot account for corporate influences along the lines of the more indirect processes set forth by Lindblom.

52. The method approximates Alexander George's method of structured-focused comparison as a means of developing a "rich-differentiated theory." See his

"Case Studies and Theory Development: The Method of Structured, Focused Comparison," in Paul Gordon Lauren, ed., *Diplomacy: New Approaches in History, Theory, Policy* (New York: Free Press, 1979).

53. See Karen Mingst, "Process and Policy in U.S. Commodities: The Impact of the Liberal Economic Paradigm," in Avery and Rapkin, *America in a Changing World Economy;* Calleo and Rowland, *America and the World Political Economy;* Robert Reich, "Beyond Free Trade," *Foreign Affairs* (Spring 1983), 61(4):773–805; and Robert Heilbroner, "The Coming Invasion," *New York Review of Books,* December 8, 1983, pp. 23–25.

1. U.S. SUPPORT OF AN INTERNATIONAL PROPERTY REGIME: PRINCIPLES, NORMS, RULES, ENFORCEMENT

1. Arnold Wolfers, *Discord and Collaboration* (Baltimore, Md.: Johns Hopkins University Press, 1962), pp. 74–78.

2. U.S. General Accounting Office, "Nationalizations and Expropriations of U.S. Direct Private Investment: Problems and Issues," Report to the Congress by the Comptroller General of the United States, No. ID-77-9, (May 20, 1977), p. 1.

3. Krasner, *International Regimes,* p. 2.

4. U.S. Commission on Foreign Economic Policy, *Report to the President and the Congress,* p. 17. Hereafter cited as Randall Commission.

5. Smith, "The United States Government Perspective," p. 521.

6. U.S. Office of the President, President's Materials Policy Commission, *Resources for Freedom,* 1:64. Hereafter cited as Paley Commission.

7. Krasner, *Defending the National Interest,* pp. 48–51; Eckes, *The United States and the Global Struggle for Minerals,* pp. 15, 147–162.

8. *FRUS 1947,* 1:777–778; Eckes, *The U.S. and the Global Struggle for Minerals,* p. 158.

9. Eckes, *The U.S. and the Global Struggle for Minerals,* p. 161.

10. U.S. Senate, *Multinational Oil Corporations,* Report, p. 61.

11. Paley Commission, 1:3, 21, 66; Eckes, *The U.S. and the Global Struggle for Minerals,* pp. 177, 181; see also Wilkins, *The Maturing of the Multinational Enterprise,* p. 290.

12. Bergsten, Horst, and Moran, *American Multinationals and American Interests,* p. 128.

13. Paley Commission, p. 64; see also Eckes, *The U.S. and the Global Struggle for Minerals,* p. 149; Cook, *The Declassified Eishenhower,* p. 314; *FRUS 1950,* 5:85; and Report, Secretary of the Interior and the Petroleum Administrator for Defense to the U.S. National Security Council, "National Security Problems Concerning Free World Petroleum Demand and Potential Supply," NSC 138, December 8, 1952 (HST/PSF, DDI 1978/59C).

14. U.S. Senate, *Multinational Corporations,* Hearings, part 8, pp. 4–7.

15. Randall Commission, p. 40; see also Paley Commission, p. 67.

16. For an influential academic version of this argument, see Tannenbaum, *Ten Keys to Latin America,* pp. 232–237; for a critique of this view as it relates to U.S. foreign assistance policy, see Packenham, *Liberal America and the Third World.*

17. Dozer, *Are We Good Neighbors?*, p. 242; Wilkins, *The Maturing of the Multinational Enterprise*, p. 328; Baily, *The United States and the Development of South America*, p. 61.

18. Paley Commission, pp. 73–74.

19. Swansbrough, *The Embattled Colossus*, p. 98; Andreas Lowenfeld, "Reflections on Expropriation and the Future of Investment in the Americas," *International Lawyer* (January 1973), 7(1):117.

20. See Richard N. Gardner, "International Measures for the Promotion and Protection of Foreign Investment," *Proceedings of the American Society of International Law* (1959), 53:256; for a critique, see Packenham, *Liberal America and the Third World*, pp. 151–160.

21. Testimony of Charls Walker, U.S. House, Committee on Banking and Currency, *To Authorize the U.S. to Provide Additional Financial Resources to the Asian Development Bank and the Inter-American Development Bank*, Hearings 92d Congress, 1st Session, October 26, (1971), p. 141.

22. *Department of State Bulletin*, October 15, 1962, p. 578.

23. Richard M. Nixon, "Economic Assistance and Investment Security in the Developing Nations," *Department of State Bulletin*, February 7, 1972, p. 153.

24. *Department of State Bulletin*, July 30, 1962, p. 195.

25. *Department of State Bulletin*, September 22, 1946, p. 540.

26. *Department of State Bulletin*, August 6, 1962, p. 228.

27. Tannenbaum, *Ten Keys to Latin America*, pp. 233–235.

28. U.S. General Accounting Office, "Domestic Policy Issues Stemming from U.S. Direct Investment Abroad," Report to the Senate Committee on Commerce, Science, and Transportation by the Comptroller General of the United States, No. ID-78-2, January 16, 1978, p. i.

29. Gilpin, *U.S. Power and the Multinational Corporation*, pp. 149, 156–161.

30. Memorandum, Melville Blake, "Comments on Mr. Goodman's Papers on a More Active role for the U.S. Government on Expropriation Cases," U.S. Department of the Treasury, January 7, 1975 (TD/FOIA), p. 2.

31. Randall Commission, p. 18.

32. Cited in Wagner, *United States Policy Toward Latin America*, p. 159.

33. Cook, *The Declassified Eisenhower*, p. 341.

34. Richard N. Cooper, "Investment Flow in the International Economic System," Speech to the Council of the Americas, June 27, 1977, U.S. Department of State, Office of Media Services Bureau of Public Affairs, p. 1.

35. Nixon, "Economic Assistance and Investment Security," p. 153.

36. Cited in Gardner, *Sterling-Dollar Diplomacy*, p. 9.

37. *Department of State Bulletin*, May 11, 1959, p. 660.

38. Wilkins, *The Maturing of the Multinational Enterprise*, p. 329.

39. Marina von Neumann Whitman, *Government Risk-Sharing in Foreign Investment* (Princeton, N.J.: Princeton University Press, 1965), pp. 73–76; Lillich, *The Protection of Foreign Investment*, pp. 148–149.

40. Wilkins, *The Maturing of the Multinational Enterprise*, p. 288.

41. Blair, *The Control of Oil*, pp. 193–203.

42. Dozer, *Are We Good Neighbors?*, p. 244.

43. *Ibid.*

44. *FRUS 1938,* 5:674.

45. *Ibid.*

46. Schwebel, "International Protection of Contractual Arrangements," p. 269.

47. Becker, "Just Compensation in Expropriation Cases," p. 343.

48. FRUS 1938, 5:678.

49. *Ibid.; Restatement of the Law (Second): Foreign Relations Law of the United States* (St. Paul, Minn: American Law Institute Publishers, 1965), p. 563 (hereafter cited as *Restatement*); Marjorie M. Whiteman, *Digest of International Law,* 8:1143. But see Stanley Metzger's comments on the ambiguity of the phrase in Whiteman, *Digest,* p. 1164.

50. *Restatement,* p. 569.

51. *FRUS 1938,* 5:676.

52. White, *The Nationalization of Foreign Property* (London: Stevens and Sons, 1961), pp. 13–15; Smith, "The United States Perspective," p. 519; U.S. Department of State, "Statement on Standards of Compensation in Expropriation," undated draft (DOS/FOIA).

53. *Restatement,* pp. 569–571.

54. *Ibid.,* p. 569; White, *The Nationalization of Foreign Property,* p. 16.

55. Whiteman, *Digest,* 8:769–807.

56. *Restatement,* p. 562.

57. Whiteman, *Digest,* 8:697, 1035–1056.

58. See Donald R. Shea, *The Calvo Clause: A Problem of Inter-American and International Law and Diplomacy* (Minneapolis: University of Minnesota Press, 1955), pp. 17–19.

59. See James N. Hyde, "Permanent Sovereignty Over Natural Resources," *American Journal of International Law* (October 1956), 50(4):854–867; Weston, "The Charter of Economic Rights and Duties of States."

60. Baily, *The United States,* pp. 46–49.

61. Whiteman, *Digest,* 8:1026; Sigmund, *Multinationals in Latin America,* p. 50; Clair Wilcox, *A Charter for World Trade* (New York: Arnon, 1972), pp. 145–147.

62. Whiteman, *Digest,* 8:1027; Hyde, "Permanent Sovereignty," p. 854.

63. Hyde, "Permanent Sovereignty," pp. 856–860.

64. Akinsanya, *The Expropriation of Multinational Property,* pp. 52–53.

65. Stephen M. Schwebel, "The Story of the United Nations Declaration on Permanent Sovereignty over Natural Resources," *American Bar Association Journal* (May 1963), 49(5):463–464.

66. Akinsanya, *The Expropriation of Multinational Property,* pp. 57–58.

67. U.S. House, *Expropriation of American-Owned Property,* p. 30; Dozer, *Are We Good Neighbors?,* p. 247.

68. U.S. General Accounting Office (see n. 2), pp. 29–33; Seymour Rubin, *Private Foreign Investment* (Baltimore, Md.: Johns Hopkins University Press, 1956), p. 78; Lipson, *Standing Guard,* pp. 96–97; Shoshana Tancer, *Economic Nationalism in Latin America* (New York: Praeger, 1976), pp. 146–147; Lipson, *Standing Guard,* pp. 96–97.

69. Dozer, *Are We Good Neighbors?,* p. 242; Wilkins, *The Maturing of the Multinational Enterprise,* p. 332.

70. Paley Commission, p. 72.

71. Lipson, "Corporate Preferences," pp. 402–403; Wilkins, *The Maturing of the Multinational Enterprise,* p. 332.

72. Cited in Lilllich, *The Protection of Foreign Investment,* p. 211.

73. Lipson, "Corporate Preferences," p. 400; see also Pastor, *Congress and the Politics of U.S. Foreign Economic Policy,* pp. 290–293.

74. U.S. Congress, Senate, CFR, *Foreign Assistance Act of 1963,* Report, 88th Congress, 1st Session, October 22, 1963, p. 27.

75. Lillich, *The Protection of Foreign Investment,* pp. 127–128.

76. Lipson, "Corporate Preferences," p. 405.

77. *International Legal Materials* (1965), 4:458.

78. See Lipson, *Standing Guard,* pp. 216–218.

79. Cited in U.S. General Accounting Office (see n. 2), pp. 12–13.

80. U.S. Senate, *Foreign Assistance Act of 1962,* Hearings, pp. 27–31.

81. Mark L. Chadwin, "Foreign Policy Report: Nixon Administration Debates New Position on Latin America," *National Journal,* January 15, 1972, p. 104.

82. Testimony of Senator Russell Long, U.S. Senate, Committee on Finance, *Sugar Act Amendments of 1971,* part 1, p. 56.

83. U.S. House, *Foreign Assistance Act of 1964,* Hearings, p. 289.

84. Thomas O. Enders to William Eberle, "U.S. Expropriation Policy Review: Phase II," U.S. Department of State, December 6, 1974 (RG 429, CIEP/FJB/NA, File 7500263), p. 3.

85. U.S. Department of State, "Expropriation of U.S. Property," in U.S. Senate, *Foreign Assistance Act of 1962,* Hearings, pp. 557–558.

86. *Ibid.*

87. Lillich, *The Protection of Foreign Investment,* pp. 130–134.

88. U.S. House, *Foreign Assistance Act of 1964,* Hearings, p. 289.

89. Swansbrough, *The Embattled Colossus,* p. 194; Wilkins, *The Maturing of the Multinational Enterprise,* p. 333; Lipson, "Corporate Preferences," pp. 405–407. For a skeptical view of the effectiveness of the Hickenlooper Amendment and foreign aid sanctions in promoting favorable settlements in several cases in the early 1960s, see Lillich, *The Protection of Foreign Investment,* pp. 140–144.

90. For examples, see chapters 6 to 9; see also Lipson, *Standing Guard,* p. 213.

2. THE EROSION OF THE COGNITIVE BASES OF THE REGIME

1. Carr, *The Twenty Years Crisis,* p. 75; see also Harold D. Lasswell, *World Politics and Personal Insecurity* (New York: Free Press, 1965), p. 96.

2. Gardner, *Sterling-Dollar Diplomacy,* p. 102; Calleo and Rowland, *America and the World Political Economy,* ch. 2.

3. *Department of State Bulletin,* June 4, 1962, p. 915.

4. *Department of State Bulletin,* January 3, 1955, p. 21.

5. U.S. Commission on Foreign Economic Policy, *Report to the President and Congress,* p. 16. Hereafter cited as Randall Commission.

6. U.S. President, Materials Policy Commission, *Resources for Freedom,* p. 61. Hereafter cited as Paley Commission.

7. *Department of State Bulletin,* January 3, 1955, p. 20.

8. Quoted in Cook, *The Declassified Eisenhower,* p. 322.

9. Charles S. Maier, "The Politics of Productivity: Foundations of American International Economic Policy After World War II," in Peter J. Katzenstein, ed., *Between Power and Plenty: Foreign Economic Policies of the Advanced Industrial States* (Madison: University of Wisconsin Press, 1978), p. 27.

10. Richard M. Nixon, "Economic Assistance and Investment Security in the Developing Countries," *Department of State Bulletin,* February 7, 1972, p. 153.

11. *Department of State Bulletin,* September 22, 1946, p. 540.

12. Stephen H. Hymer, *The International Operations of National Firms: A Study of Direct Foreign Investment* (Cambridge: MIT Press, 1976); Charles P. Kindleberger, *American Business Abroad* (New Haven, Conn.: Yale University Press, 1969), pp. 66–72.

13. Cobbe, *Governments and Mining Companies in Developing Countries,* p. 12; Diaz-Alejandro, "International Markets for Exhausible Resources," pp. 13–14.

14. Cobbe, *Governments and Mining Companies,* p. 11.

15. Robinson, *International Business Management,* p. 12.

16. Diaz-Alejandro, "International Markets," p. 15.

17. Blair, *The Control of Oil,* pp. 81–83; U.S. Senate, *Multinational Corporations,* Hearings, part 8, pp. 529–533.

18. Cobbe, *Mining Companies and Governments,* p. 15; Barnet and Müller, *Global Reach,* pp. 157–159.

19. United Nations, Department of International Economic and Social Affairs, *Statistical Year Book: 1979/1980* (New York: United Nations, 1981), pp. 520–527.

20. Theodore H. Moran, "Policies of Economic Nationalism and the Evolution of the Concession Agreements," *Proceedings of the American Society of International Law* (September 1972), 66(4):218.

21. Wood, *The Making of the Good Neighbor Policy,* p. 276.

22. Tugwell, *The Politics of Oil in Venezuela,* p. 146; also see Barnet and Müller, *Global Reach,* pp. 162-166.

23. Vernon, *Storm Over the Multinationals,* p. 176.

24. *Department of State Bulletin,* June 4, 1962, p. 915; see also Bergsten, Horst, and Moran, *American Multinationals and American Interests,* p. 331.

25. Henry Kissinger, "Global Consensus and Economic Development," speech to the United Nations General Assembly, September 1, 1975 (U.S. Department of State, Office of Media Services, Bureau of Public Affairs), p. 2.

26. Vernon, *Storm Over the Multinationals,* p. 182.

27. *FRUS 1938,* 5:674–678.

28. Charles P. Kindleberger, "World Populism," *Atlantic Economic Journal* (November 1975), 3(2):1–6.

29. U.S. President, *Public Papers of the President of the United States: Richard Nixon 1970* (Washington, D.C.: GPO, 1971), p. 139; see also Swansbrough, *The Embattled Colossus,* p. 130.

30. Harry G. Johnson, "The Efficiency and Welfare Implications of the

Multinational Corporation," in Charles P. Kindleberger, ed., *The International Corporation* (Cambridge: MIT Press, 1970), pp. 50–53.

31. *Department of State Bulletin,* October 15, 1962, p. 578.

32. Nixon, "Economic Assistance and Investment Security," p. 153.

33. *Congressional Record,* May 13, 1962, p. 3922.

34. U.S. House, *Expropriation of American-Owned Property,* p. 40.

35. C. Fred Bergsten, "Coming Investment Wars?" *Foreign Affairs* (October 1974), 53(1):142.

36. *Congressional Record,* June 6, 1962, p. 9823.

37. Calleo and Rowland, *America and the World Political Economy,* p. 27; see also William H. Becker and Samuel F. Wells, Jr., eds., *Economics and World Power: An Assessment of American Diplomacy Since 1789* (New York: Columbia University Press, 1984), pp. 40, 73–74, 121–122.

38. Zuhayr Mikdashi, *The International Politics of Natural Resources,* p. 21.

39. Friedmann, *Law in a Changing Society,* p. 116; Sidney Fine, *Laissez-Faire and the General Welfare State* (Ann Arbor: University of Michigan Press, 1956), especially chs. 5, 7, 11.

40. Alan Wolfe, *The Limits of Legitimacy: Political Contradictions of Contemporary Capitalism* (New York: Free Press, 1977), p. 216.

41. This may be less true in the North–North sphere. See Ruggie, "International Regimes."

42. Calleo and Rowland, *America and the World Political Economy,* p. 5.

43. Stephen J. Kobrin, "Foreign Enterprise and Forced Divestment in the LDCs," *International Organization* (Winter 1980), 34(1):66.

44. *FRUS 1940,* 5:1010.

45. Schwebel, "International Protection of Contractual Arrangements," p. 270; Becker, "Just Compensation in Expropriation Cases," p. 344.

46. Alwyn V. Freeman, "Recent Aspects of the Calvo Doctrine and the Challenge to International Law," *American Journal of International Law* (January 1946), 40(1):125.

47. Louis Sohn and R. R. Baxter, "Responsibility of States for Injury to the Economic Interests of Aliens," *American Journal of International Law* (July 1961), 55(3):568.

48. Schwebel, "International Protection of Contractual Arrangements," p. 266.

49. Becker, "Just Compensation," p. 337.

50. Jorge Casteneda, "The Underdeveloped Nations and International Law," *International Organization* (Winter 1961), 15(1):39.

51. Akinsanya, *The Expropriation of Multinational Property,* p. 235; see also Sonarajah, "The Myth of International Contract Law," p. 188.

52. Schwebel, "International Protection of Contractual Arrangements," p. 272; Martin Domke, "Foreign Nationalizations: Some Aspects of Contemporary International Law," *American Journal of International Law* (July 1961), 55(3):594.

53. Carr, *The Twenty Years Crisis,* pp. 191, 189.

54. Friedmann, *Law in a Changing Society,* p. 125–126. See also Stocking, *Middle East Oil,* p. 130; Robinson, *International Business Policy,* p. 61; Henry Rottscaeffer, *The Constitution and Socio-Economic Change* (Ann Arbor: University of Michigan Press, 1948), pp. 173–177, 193–199.

55. Domke, "Foreign Nationalizations," pp. 594, 598; Schwebel, "International Protection of Contractual Arrangements," p. 272; Robinson, *International Business Policy,* pp. 66–74.

56. Robinson, *International Business Policy,* pp. 90–96.

57. Thomas O. Enders to William Eberle, "U.S. Expropriation Policy Review: Phase II," U.S. Department of State, December 6, 1974 (RG 429, CIEP/FJB/NA, File 7500263), p. 3. The first attempt to defray compensation as such was the Soviet Union's use of counterclaims for reparations for the Allied intervention (1917–1920) against compensation for nationalized businesses and repudiated debts. On the response of the international community to this, see Lipson, *Standing Guard,* pp. 66–70.

58. Friedmann, *Law in a Changing Society,* p. 129; Robinson, *International Business Policy,* pp. 63–64.

59. A. A. Fatouros, "International Law and the Third World," *Virginia Law Review* (June 1964), 50(5):802.

60. D. P. O'Connell, *The Law of State Succession* (New York: Cambridge University Press, 1956); for critiques, see Robinson, *International Business Policy,* p. 76, and Fatouros, "International Law and the Third World," p. 802.

61. Weston, "The Charter of Economic Rights and Duties of States," p. 456.

62. Bergsten, Horst, and Moran, *American Multinationals and American Interests,* p. 385.

3. THE EROSION OF THE STRUCTURAL BASES OF THE REGIME

1. Cited in Richard Stuart Olson, "Economic Coercion in World Politics: With a Focus on North–South Relations," *World Politics* (July 1979), 31(4):485.

2. Young, "Regime Dynamics," p. 100.

3. *Ibid.,* p. 108.

4. Jeffrey A. Hart, *The New International Economic Order: Conflict and Cooperation in North-South Economic Relations, 1974–77* (New York: St. Martins, 1983), p. 57.

5. Panel, "Mining the Resources of the Third World: From Concession Agreements to Service Contracts," *Proceedings of the American Society of International Law* (November 1973), 67(5):228.

6. Bergsten, Horst, and Moran, *American Multinationals and American Interests,* p. 134.

7. *Ibid.,* pp. 130–139; Vernon, *Sovereignty at Bay,* pp. 46–59; Theodore H. Moran, *Multinational Corporations and the Politics of Dependence* (Princeton, N.J.: Princeton University Press, 1974), ch. 7; Smith and Wells, *Negotiating Third World Mineral Agreements,* and "Mineral Agreements in Developing Countries: Structure and Substance," *American Journal of International Law* (July 1975), 69(3):560–590.

8. Barnet and Müller, *Global Reach,* p. 140.

9. Smith and Wells, "Mineral Agreements," p. 566.

10. *Ibid.,* p. 566f.

11. Smith and Wells, *Negotiating Third World Mineral Agreements*, p. 54.

12. Sonarajah, "The Myth of International Contract Law," p. 188.

13. Vernon, *Sovereignty at Bay*, p. 47.

14. Theodore H. Moran, "The Evolution of Concession Agreements in Underdeveloped Countries and the United States National Interest," *Vanderbilt Journal of Transnational Law* (Spring 1974), 7(2):315.

15. Barnet and Müller, *Global Reach*, p. 193.

16. Bergsten, Horst, and Moran, *American Multinationals and American Interests*, p. 379.

17. *Ibid.*, p. 132; Smith and Wells, *Negotiating Third World Mineral Agreements*, pp. 32–36.

18. Smith and Wells, "Mineral Agreements," p. 568; Vernon, *Sovereignty at Bay*, p. 54; Wilkins, *The Maturing of the Multinational Enterprise*, pp. 307, 317; Swansbrough, *The Embattled Colossus*, pp. 98–100.

19. Smith and Wells, "Mineral Agreements," p. 562.

20. Moran, *Multinational Corporations*, p. 169.

21. Mancur Olson, *The Logic of Collective Action: Public Goods and the Theory of Groups* (Cambridge, Mass.: Harvard University Press, 1965), pp. 33–36; Lipson, *Standing Guard*, p. 158.

22. Smith and Wells, *Negotiating Third World Mineral Agreements*, p. 9.

23. See pp. 150–162.

24. Vernon, *Storm over the Multinationals*, p. 81; Lipson, *Standing Guard*, p. 111–117.

25. See Lipson, *Standing Guard*, pp. 155–156.

26. Olson, *The Logic of Collective Action*, pp. 9–12.

27. Bergsten, Horst, and Moran, *American Multinationals and American Interests*, p. 135; Robinson, *International Business Management*, p. 358; Waddams, *The Libyan Oil Industry*, pp. 73–97, 117–134; Smith and Wells, *Negotiating Third World Mineral Agreements*, pp. 129–130.

28. See pp. 237–238.

29. Lipson, *Standing Guard*, p. 162.

30. Lipson, *Standing Guard*, pp. 162–163; Olson, *The Logic of Collective Action*, pp. 12–16.

31. Lipson, *Standing Guard*, pp. 147–149.

32. While the "politico-ideological" goals underlying the interventions were not unrelated to economic considerations, and the condition that led up to them was not wholly autonomous of societal forces, the United States, nonetheless, only intervened directly when the government in question was perceived as ideologically hostile. See Krasner, *Defending the National Interest*, chs, 7, 8.

33. Wood, *The Making of the Good Neighbor Policy*, pp. 41–47.

34. Robert O. Keohane and Joseph S. Nye, *Power and Interdependence* (Boston: Little, Brown, 1977), pp. 27–29.

35. Lipson, *Standing Guard*, p. 152.

36. Ernst Haas, "Why Collaborate? Issue Linkage and International Regimes," *World Politics* (April 1980), 32(3):357–358.

37. Lipson, *Standing Guard*, pp. 164.

38. Feinberg, *The Intemperate Zone*, p. 35.

39. *Ibid.*, pp. 17–18; John F. H. Purcell, "The Perceptions and Interests

of U.S. Business in Relation to the Political Crisis in Central America," in Richard E. Feinberg, ed., *Central America: International Dimensions of the Crisis* (New York: Holmes and Meier, 1982), pp. 107–113.

40. Stallings, "Peru and the U.S. Banks," p. 234.

41. Lipson, *Standing Guard,* p. 168.

42. Edward S. Mason and Robert E. Asher, *The World Bank Since Bretton Woods* (Washington, D.C.: Brookings Institution, 1973), pp. 746–747.

43. *Ibid.,* p. 748.

44. *Ibid.,* p. 338.

45. Krasner, *Structural Conflict,* pp. 139, 144–146.

46. *Ibid.;* The Treasury Department listed specific cases where IFI policy diverged from U.S. preferences in the following memoranda: Petty to Connally, "World Bank Policy on Expropriation," June 2, 1971, and Gonzales to Bradfield, "U.S. Votes on Loans in the IFI's and the Gonzales Amendment," July 27, 1973 (Both TD/FOIA); Confidential Interviews, Department of the Treasury.

47. David A. Lax and James K. Sebenius, "Insecure Contracts and Resource Development," *Public Policy* (Fall 1981), 29(4):417.

48. Sigmund, *Multinationals in Latin America,* p. 298.

49. T. Baumgartner and T. R. Burns, "The Structuring of International Economic Relations," *International Studies Quarterly* (June 1975), 19(2):126–159. For a view that contends that metapower strategies play a greater role in Third World demands, see Stephen D. Krasner, "Transforming International Regimes: What the Third World Wants and Why," *International Studies Quarterly* (March 1981), 25(1):119–148.

50. Robert W. Tucker, *The Inequality of Nations* (New York: Basic Books, 1975), p. 178.

51. Peter Gabriel, "The Multinational Corporation and the New International Economic Order," in Gerald and Louann Garvey, eds., *The Political Economy of International Resource Flows* (Lexington, Mass.: D. C. Heath, 1977), p. 71.

52. U.S. Department of the Treasury, "A More Active Policy for the USG in Investment Disputes," undated study (RG 429, CIEP/FJB/NA, File 7500263), p. 2.

53. Swansbrough, *The Embattled Colossus,* p. 194; and "The American Investor's View of Economic Nationalism," *Inter-American Economic Affairs* (Winter 1972), 26:66.

54. U.S. Council on International Economic Policy, "Survey of U.S. Business Perspective: U.S. Expropriation Policy" (written by James F. McClelland, III), November 1975 (RG 429, CIEP/FJB/NA, File 7600009), p. 3.

55. Smith and Wells, *Negotiating Third World Mineral Agreements,* pp. 24, 40–41.

56. Statement by Robert Frick, "Mining the Resources of the Third World," (see n. 5), p. 232.

57. Turner, *Oil Companies in the International System,* p. 117.

58. Moran notes that if there are low barriers to entry at the extractive phase, nationalization places LDCs in "an increasingly competitive and highly volatile impersonal market." They may only get an increasing share of a smaller pie. See Moran, "New Deal or Raw Deal," p. 126.

59. Swansbrough, *The Embattled Colossus,* pp. 207–210; Nathan Haver-

stock, "End to Retaliatory Legislation Sought," *Mexican-American Review* (November 1973), 41:13; Einhorn, *Expropriation Politics,* p. 51; Frank, *Foreign Enterprise in Developing Countries,* p. 127; *Congressional Record,* April 24, 1972, p. 14023.

60. Swansbrough, *The Embattled Colossus,* p. 210.

61. Bergsten, Horst, and Moran, *American Multinationals and American Interests,* p. 478.

62. Krasner, *Structural Conflict,* p. 178.

63. Moran, "New Deal or Raw Deal," p. 125; see also below, pp. 304–316.

64. See Michael Shafer, "Capturing the Mineral Multinationals," pp. 106–109; see also pp. 290–294.

65. Smith and Wells, "Mineral Agreements," p. 126.

66. Smith and Wells, *Negotiating Third World Mineral Agreements;* Albert O. Hirschman, "How to Divest in Latin America and Why," in *A Bias for Hope: Essays on Development in Latin America* (New Haven: Yale University Press, 1971).

4. EXPROPRIATION IN LATIN AMERICA, THE GOOD NEIGHBOR POLICY, AND WORLD WAR II: ESTABLISHING THE RULES OF THE GAME

1. Eckes, *The United States and the Global Struggle for Minerals,* pp. 35–37.

2. See Gordon Connell-Smith, *The Inter-American System* (London and New York: Oxford University Press, 1966), pp. 27, 42.

3. Wood, *The Making of the Good Neighbor Policy,* p. 166.

4. Walter Lippmann, "Vested Rights and Nationalism in Latin America," *Foreign Affairs* (April 1927), 5(3):362–363.

5. Lipson, *Standing Guard,* pp. 65–84.

6. Wood, *The Making of the Good Neighbor Policy,* pp. 41–47.

7. *Ibid.,* p. 7.

8. *Ibid.,* pp. 165–166.

9. Krasner, *Defending the National Interest,* p. 188.

10. *Ibid.,* p. 168; Ingram, *Expropriation of U.S. Property in South America,* pp. 107–113; Henrietta M. Larson et al., *History of the Standard Oil Company (New Jersey): New Horizons, 1927–1950* (New York: Harper and Row, 1971), p. 421.

11. Ingram, *Expropriation,* p. 113; Irwin Gellman, *Good Neighbor Diplomacy: United States Policies in Latin America, 1933–1945* (Baltimore, Md.: Johns Hopkins University Press, 1979), p. 49.

12. *FRUS 1937,* 5:286–288.

13. Ingram, *Expropriation,* p. 118.

14. Wood, *The Making of the Good Neighbor Policy,* p. 174; *FRUS 1937,* 5:292–294.

15. David Green, *The Containment of Latin America* (Chicago, Ill.: Quadrangle, 1971), p. 25.

16. Farish to Hull, November 13, 1940 (DS/NA, 824.6363 ST 2/495), p. 3; Palmer to Duggan, June 4, 1937 (DS/NA, 824.6363 ST 2/147).

17. *FRUS 1937*, 5:290–292.

18. George W. Grayson, *The Politics of Mexican Oil* (Pittsburgh, Pa.: University of Pittsburgh Press, 1980), pp. 4–5.

19. Sigmund, *Multinationals in Latin America*, p. 51.

20. Philip, *Oil and Politics in Latin America*, p. 203.

21. Sigmund, *Multinationals in Latin America*, p. 47.

22. *Ibid.*, pp. 55–56.

23. Gellman, *Good Neighbor Diplomacy*, p. 51; Philip, *Oil and Politics*, pp. 218–222.

24. *FRUS 1938*, 5:754.

25. E. David Cronon, *Josephus Daniels in Mexico* (Madison: University of Wisconsin Press, 1960), p. 207.

26. *Ibid.*

27. Krasner, *Defending the National Interest*, p. 186; Sigmund, *Multinationals in Latin America*, p. 59; Wood, *The Making of the Good Neighbor Policy*, p. 227.

28. Cole Blasier, *The Hovering Giant: United States Responses to Revolutionary Change in Latin America* (Pittsburgh, Pa.: Unviersity of Pittsburgh Press, 1976), p. 125.

29. Sigmund, *Multinationals in Latin America*, p. 59.

30. Wood, *The Making of the Good Neighbor Policy*, pp. 228–233.

31. Philip, *Oil and Politics*, pp. 56–57.

32. *FRUS 1938*, 5:742.

33. *Ibid.*, pp. 674–678.

34. *Ibid.*, pp. 754, 742.

35. *Ibid.*, pp. 741–742.

36. Cronon, *Josephus Daniels*, p. 193.

37. *FRUS 1938*, 5:732, 730.

38. *Ibid.*, p. 738.

39. Green, *The Containment of Latin America*, p. 33.

40. *FRUS 1939*, 5:328; See also Gellman, *Good Neighbor Diplomacy*, p. 53.

41. Green, *The Containment of Latin America*, p. 33; Gellman, *Good Neighbor Diplomacy*, p. 42.

42. Wood, *The Making of the Good Neighbor Policy*, p. 228.

43. *Ibid.*, p. 228; Blasier, *The Hovering Giant*, p. 123; Green, *The Containment of Latin America*, p. 31.

44. Howard F. Cline, *The United States and Mexico* (Cambridge, Mass.: Harvard University Press, 1963), p. 241.

45. Sigmund, *Multinationals in Latin America*, p. 61; Wood, *The Making of the Good Neighbor Policy*, p. 223; Cronon, *Josephus Daniels*, p. 190.

46. *FRUS 1938*, 5:735.

47. Krasner, *Defending the National Interest*, p. 183.

48. Wood, *The Making of the Good Neighbor Policy*, pp. 230–233.

49. Cronon, *Josephus Daniels*, p. 199; Allan S. Everest, *Morgenthau, the New Deal, and Silver* (New York: Kings Crown Press, 1950), pp. 90–91.

50. Cronon, *Josephus Daniels*, p. 200.

51. Wood, *The Making of the Good Neighbor Policy*, pp. 180–182.

52. *FRUS 1939*, 5:313, 320, and (on Mexico) 732; Wood, *The Making of the Good Neighbor Policy*, pp. 186–188.

53. Green, *The Containment of Latin America*, p. 47.

54. Wood, *The Making of the Good Neighbor Policy*, p. 244.

55. Green, *The Containment of Latin America*, p. 541; Gellman, *Good Neighbor Diplomacy*, p. 136.

56. Wood, *The Making of the Good Neighbor Policy*, p. 250.

57. Farish to Hull, October 8, 1941 (DS/NA, 812.6363/7353), p. 5; Farish to Hull, November 13, 1941 (DS/NA 812.6363/7430).

58. Wood, *The Making of the Good Neighbor Policy*, p. 255.

59. *Ibid.*, p. 249; Cronon, *Josephus Daniels*, p. 264.

60. Green, *The Containment of Latin America*, p. 55; Wood, *The Making of the Good Neighbor Policy*, pp. 252–258; Krasner, *Defending the National Interest*, p. 185.

61. *FRUS 1939*, 5:322.

62. Wood, *The Making of the Good Neighbor Policy*, p. 191.

63. *Ibid.*, p. 189.

64. *Ibid; FRUS 1941*, 7:473–476; Jenkins to Hull, "Subject: Standard Oil Case," April 28, 1941 (DS/NA, 824.6363 ST.2/542).

65. Wood, *The Making of the Good Neighbor Policy*, pp. 194–195; Memorandum of Conversation, "Bolivian Oil Deposits and the Standard Oil Controversy," February 25, 1941 (DS/NA 824.6363 ST 2/537); V. J. Hampton (American Ore Reduction Corporation) to Warren Lee Pierson (Export-Import Bank), "Re: Bolivia," February 6, 1941 (DS/NA, 824.6363 ST 2/537).

66. Welles to Farish, November 28, 1940 (DS/NA 824.6363 ST 2/495).

67. Green, *The Containment of Latin America*, p. 51.

68. Sigmund, *Multinationals in Latin America*, p. 228; Tugwell, *The Politics of Oil in Venezuela*, pp. 36–39.

69. Sigmund, *Multinationals in Latin America*, p. 229.

70. *Ibid.;* Tugwell, *The Politics of Oil*, p. 42.

71. Quoted in Wilkins, *The Maturing of the Multinational Enterprise*, p. 224.

72. Rabe, *The Road to OPEC*, p. 53.

73. *Ibid.*

74. Duggan to Welles and Hull, June 26, 1939 (DS/NA, 831.6363/1141), pp. 2, 7.

75. Rabe, *The Road to OPEC*, pp. 62, 65.

76. Wood, *The Making of the Good Neighbor Policy*, p. 274.

77. Rabe, *The Road to OPEC*, p. 75.

78. Memorandum, Satterthwaite to Walmsley and Bonsal, U.S. Department of State, August 12, 1941 (DS/NA, 831.6363/1249), p. 2.

79. Wood, *The Making of the Good Neighbor Policy*, p. 269.

80. Rabe, *The Road to OPEC*, p. 82.

81. Memo, Satterthwaite to Walmsley and Bonsal (see n.78).

82. Rabe, *The Road to OPEC*, p. 84.

83. *Ibid.*, p. 90.

84. Larson et al., *History of the Standard Oil Company*, p. 482.

85. *Ibid.*, p. 484.

86. Sigmund, *Multinationals in Latin America,* pp. 229–231.

87. *Ibid.*, p. 76; see also Lloyd Gardner, *Economic Aspects of New Deal Diplomacy* (Madison: University of Wisconsin Press, 1964), p. 206; and Gellman, *Good Neighbor Diplomacy,* p. 55.

88. *FRUS 1944,* 7:1337, 1346; *1945,* 9:1161.

89. David A. Baldwin, *Economic Development and American Foreign Policy, 1943–1962,* (Chicago: University of Chicago, 1962), pp. 20–21; Philip, *Oil and Politics,* pp. 77–78.

90. *FRUS 1948,* 9:619.

91. *FRUS 1944,* 7:1354.

92. *FRUS 1947,* 8:791.

93. *FRUS 1950,* 2:938.

94. *Ibid.;* Philip, *Oil and Politics,* p. 329.

95. *FRUS 1946,* 11:1015.

96. Philip, *Oil and Politics,* pp. 74–76, 334.

97. *FRUS 1948,* 9:612–613.

98. Krasner, *Defending the National Interest,* p. 178.

99. *Ibid.*, pp. 206–209.

5. REDEFINING THE PARAMETERS IN THE 1950s: OIL IN SAUDI ARABIA AND IRAN

1. See Lipson, *Standing Guard,* ch. 4.

2. Donald A. Wells, "Aramco: The Evolution of an Oil Concession," in Mikesell, ed., *Foreign Investment in the Petroleum and Mineral Industries,* pp. 217–219; Turner, *Oil Companies in the International System,* p. 47f; Stocking, *Middle East Oil,* p. 147.

3. Irvine Anderson, *Aramco, the United States, and Saudi Arabia: A Study in the Dynamics of Foreign Oil Policy, 1933–1950* (Princeton, N.J.: Princeton University Press, 1981), pp. 187–190; Zuhayr Mikdashi, *A Financial Analysis of the Middle East Oil Concessions, 1901–1965* (New York: Praeger, 1965), p. 148.

4. Anderson, *Aramco,* p. 190; *FRUS 1950,* 5:75–76.

5. *FRUS 1950,* 5:75–76.

6. U.S. Senate, *Multinational Oil Corporations,* Report, p. 81; memorandum, Richard Funkhouser, U.S. Department of State, *FRUS 1950,* 5:76.

7. Anderson, *Aramco,* p. 191; Funkhouser memo., pp. 88–90.

8. Anderson, *Aramco,* pp. 185, 189; Funkhouser memo., p. 86.

9. Funkhouser memo., pp. 89–90.

10. U.S. Senate, *Multinational Oil Corporations,* Report, p. 82; Funkhouser memo., p. 92.

11. U.S. Senate, *Multinational Corporations,* Hearings, part 4, p. 89.

12. *FRUS 1950,* 5:106.

13. *Ibid.*, pp. 106–108.

14. U.S. Senate, *Multinational Corporations,* Hearings, part 8, p. 346.

15. *Ibid.*, p. 347.

16. *Ibid.*, pp. 347–349.

17. *FRUS 1950*, 5:118, 121; Anderson, *Aramco*, p. 194; Stocking, *Middle East Oil*, pp. 150–151.

18. U.S. Senate, *Multinational Oil Corporations*, Report, p. 86.

19. *Ibid.*, p. 85.

20. Krasner, *Defending the National Interest*, p. 210.

21. U.S. Senate, *Multinational Corporations*, Hearings, part 7, p. 135.

22. *Ibid.*, p. 137.

23. Through classifying the United States government as a "weak state" that lacks positive power over private decisions, Krasner's model accounts for this apparent anomaly. See Krasner, *Defending the National Interest*, pp. 209–213.

24. U.S. Senate, *Multinational Corporations*, Hearings, part 7, pp. 137–138.

25. Benjamin Shwadran, *The Middle East, Oil, and the Great Powers*, 3d ed. (New York: Wiley, 1973), p. 90; Stocking, *Middle East Oil*, pp. 133–136; Mikdashi, *A Financial Analysis*, p. 77.

26. Mikdashi, *A Financial Analysis*, pp. 153–154; U.S. Senate, *Multinational Oil Corporations*, Report, p. 58.

27. Swadran, *The Middle East, Oil, and the Great Powers*, p. 90.

28. *Ibid.*, pp. 91–92.

29. *Ibid.*, pp. 94, 116; Barry Rubin, *Paved with Good Intentions: The American Experience in Iran* (New York: Oxford University Press, 1980), p. 61.

30. U.S. Senate, *Multinational Corporations*, Hearings, part 7, p. 298.

31. Stocking, *Middle East Oil*, p. 162; Blair, *The Control of Oil*, p. 79.

32. Shwadran, *The Middle East, Oil, and the Great Powers*, p. 124f; see also Amin Seikal, *The Rise and Fall of the Shah* (Princeton, N.J.: Princeton University Press, 1980), pp. 40–42.

33. U.S. Senate, *Multinational Oil Corporations*, Report, p. 58.

34. U.S. Department of State, Office of Intelligence and Research, "Iran and Its Potential Impact on Other Oil Concessions," Report No. 5563, June 28, 1951 (DDI 1979/77C), p. 17.

35. *Ibid.*, p. 15.

36. U.S. Central Intelligence Agency, "The Current Crisis in Iran," Special Estimate SE-3, March 16, 1951 (HST/PSF, DDI 1977/271A).

37. *FRUS 1950*, 5:615.

38. Dean Acheson, *Present at the Creation: My Years at the State Department* (New York: Norton, 1969), p. 506.

39. *Ibid.*, p. 505; U.S. Department of State (see n. 34), p. 13.

40. Funkhouser memo. (see n. 6), p. 82; Blair, *The Control of Oil*, p. 78.

41. Acheson, *Present at the Creation*, p. 505.

42. *FRUS 1950*, 5:156.

43. Richard Cottam, *Nationalism in Iran* (Pittsburgh, Pa.: University of Pittsburgh Press, 1979), p. 208; George S. McGhee, *Envoy to Middle World: Adventures in Diplomacy* (New York: Harper & Row, 1983), p. 391.

44. U.S. Department of State, Steering Group for Preparation for the Talks between the President and Prime Minister Churchill, Cover Memorandum, TCT D-14/4d, January 5, 1952 (HST/PSF, DDI 1978/80C).

45. U.S. Department of State (see n. 34), p. 9; Carl Solberg, *Oil Power: The Rise and Imminent Fall of an American Empire* (New York: Mentor, 1976), pp. 189–190; Turner, *Oil Companies in the International System*, p. 46.

46. Rubin, *Paved with Good Intentions*, p. 61; U.S. Department of State (see n. 34); National Security Council, "The Position of the United States With Respect to Iran," June 20, 1951 (DDI 1983/1293).

47. Turner, *Oil Companies in the International System*, p. 93; Blair, *The Control of Oil*, p. 79.

48. Testimony of George S. McGhee, October 10, 1951, in U.S. House, CFA, Selected Executive Session Hearings of the Committee, 1951–1956, vol. 16: *The Middle East, Africa, and Inter-American Affairs* (Washington, D.C.:GPO, 1981), p. 112; see also McGhee, *Envoy to Middle World*, p. 398.

49. David S. McClellan, *Dean Acheson: The State Department Years* (New York: Dodd, Mead, 1976), p. 390; Shwadran, *The Middle East, Oil, and the Great Powers*, pp. 102–103.

50. Shwadran, *The Middle East, Oil, and the Great Powers*, pp. 103–109; Cottam, *Nationalism in Iran*, p. 214.

51. McClellan, *Dean Acheson*, p. 391.

52. Shwadran, *The Middle East, Oil, and the Great Powers*, p. 111.

53. Acheson, *Present at the Creation*, p. 504.

54. U.S. National Security Council, "United States Policy Regarding the Present Situation in Iran," NSC 136/1, November 20, 1952 (DDI 1980/367C).

55. U.S. Department of State, Office of Intelligence and Research for Near East, South Asia, and Africa, Report No. 6126, January 9, 1953 (DDI 1979/79E), p. iv, 11; Rubin, *Paved with Good Intentions*, p. 76.

56. Rubin, *Paved with Good Intentions*, p. 56.

57. Cited in Cook, *The Declassified Eishenhower*, p. 184.

58. Shwadran, *The Middle East, Oil, and the Great Powers*, pp. 113–114.

59. *Ibid.*, p. 114.

60. *Ibid.*, pp. 114–115; *Department of State Bulletin*, July 20, 1953, p. 74; Outgoing Telegram No. 3295 to Am. Emb. Teheran from Eisenhower to Prime Minister Mossadegh, June 30, 1953 (DDE/AWF, International File, Folder: Iran, 1953–59, Box 29, DDI 1979/308C).

61. U.S. Central Intelligence Agency, "Comment on Tudeh Position in Current Iranian Situation," March 3, 1953 (DDI 1981/275B); "Tudeh Reportedly Orders Support for Mossadegh," April 7, 1953 (DDI 1981/276A); "Communists Demonstrate Impressively in Iran," June 21, 1953 (DDI 1981/276B). See also Cook, *The Declassified Eisenhower*, p. 106; Rubin *Paved with Good Intentions*, p. 88; Dwight D. Eishenhower, *Mandate for Change, 1953–1956* (Garden City, N.Y.: Doubleday, 1963), pp. 160–164.

62. See Burton I. Kaufman, *The Oil Cartel Case: A Documentary Study of Anti-Trust Action in the Cold War Era* (Westport, Conn.: Greenwood Press, 1978); Shwadran, *The Middle East, Oil, and the Great Powers*, ch. 7.

63. Kolko and Kolko, *The Limits of Power*, pp. 417–420; see also Mansour Farhang, *U.S. Imperialism: The Spanish-American War to the Iranian Revolution* (Boston: South End Press, 1981), pp. 1–4.

64. Krasner, *Defending the National Interest*, p. 119. For supporting arguments see Turner, *Oil Companies in the International System*, p. 44, and Rustow, *Oil and Turmoil*, p. 101.

65. U.S. Senate, *Multinational Corporations*, Hearings, part 7, pp. 137–138.

6. THE DECLINE AND RISE OF INVESTMENT PROTECTION DURING THE ALLIANCE FOR PROGRESS: BUSINESS ASSERTS ITS PRIVILEGED POSITION

1. Levinson and de Onís, *The Alliance That Lost Its Way*, p. 159.

2. See Immerman, "Guatemala as Cold War History," pp. 634–639.

3. Arthur M. Schlesinger, *A Thousand Days: John F. Kennedy and the White House* (Boston: Houghton-Mifflin, 1965), p. 196.

4. *Ibid.*, p. 195.

5. *Ibid.*, p. 789.

6. Actually this transformation began at the end of the Eisenhower administration. See Seyom Brown, *The Faces of Power*, pp. 131–136; and Walter LaFeber, *Inevitable Revolutions: The United States in Central America* (New York: Norton, 1983), pp. 126–144.

7. Swansbrough, *The Embattled Colossus*, pp. 124–125.

8. Schlesinger, *A Thousand Days*, p. 175.

9. Packenham, *Liberal America and the Third World*, ch. 5.

10. Schlesinger, *A Thousand Days*, p. 174.

11. *Ibid.*, p. 196; Theodore C. Sorensen, *Kennedy* (New York: Harper and Row, 1965), p. 539; Swansbrough, *The Embattled Colossus*, p. 115; Wagner, *United States Policy Toward Latin America*, pp. 174–175.

12. Levinson and de Onís, *The Alliance That Lost Its Way*, p. 141.

13. *Congressional Quarterly*, March 9, 1962, p. 419; *Department of State Bulletin*, July 30, 1962, p. 195.

14. Levinson and de Onís, *The Alliance That Lost Its Way*, p. 72.

15. Bruce Miroff, *Pragmatic Illusions: The Presidential Policies of John F. Kennedy* (New York: McKay, 1976), p. 121; see also Packenham, *Liberal America and the Third World*, pp. 112–123.

16. Emilio G. Collado, "Economic Development Through Private Enterprise," *Foreign Affairs* (July 1963), 41(4):712.

17. Swansbrough, *The Embattled Colossus*, p. 116; Levinson and de Onís, *The Alliance That Lost Its Way*, pp. 71–73.

18. Collado, "Economic Development," p. 709.

19. Sorenson, *Kennedy*, p. 537.

20. Abraham Lowenthal, "'Liberal,' 'Radical,' and 'Bureaucratic' Perspectives on U.S. Latin American Policy: The Alliance for Progress in Retrospect," in Cotler and Fagen, eds., *Latin America and the United States*, pp. 230–232.

21. Rusk to Am. Emb. Rio (Gordon), March 7, 1962 (JFK/POF, Countries, Brazil, 1962); Geneen to Kennedy, February 17, 1962 (JFK/NSF).

22. *New York Times*, February 18, 1962, p. 33.

23. Phyllis R. Parker, *Brazil and the Quiet Intervention 1964* (Austin: University of Texas Press, 1979), p. 16.

24. Richard Stuart Olson, "Expropriation and Economic Coercion in World Politics: A Retrospective Look at Brazil in the 1960s, *The Journal of Developing Areas* (April 1979), 13(3):252.

25. *Ibid.*

26. *Congressional Quarterly*, March 9, 1962, p. 419.

27. U.S. Senate, *Foreign Assistance Act of 1962*, Hearings pp. 30–31.

28. Collado, "Economic Development," p. 714.

29. *Wall Street Journal*, February 21, 1962.

30. Levinson and de Onís, *The Alliance That Lost Its Way*, p. 144; Lipson, "Corporate Preferences," pp. 403–404; Cobbe, *Mining Companies and Governments*, p. 160.

31. Lipson, "Corporate Preferences," p. 402.

32. *Congressional Record*, July 31, 1962, p. 1518F.

33. Lars Shoultz, *Human Rights and United States Policy in Latin America* (Princeton, N.J.: Princeton University Press, 1981), p. 98.

34. *Congressional Record*, October 2, 1962, p. 21618.

35. *Congressional Record*, June 7, 1962, pp. 9940–9942.

36. *Congressional Record*, February 20, 1962, p. 2616.

37. Testimony of Senator Russell Long, U.S. Senate, Committee on Finance, *Sugar Act Amendments of 1971, part 1*, p. 56; Thomas Schelling, *Arms and Influence* (New Haven, Conn.: Yale University Press, 1966), p. 37.

38. U.S. Senate, *Foreign Assistance Act of 1962*, p. 27; U.S. House, CFA, *Foreign Assistance Act of 1962*, 87th Congress, 2d Session, 1962, Hearings, p. 811.

39. U.S. Department of State, "Expropriation of U.S. Property," in U.S. Senate, *Foreign Assistance Act of 1962*, Hearings, p. 558.

40. *Ibid.*

41. *Ibid.*

42. U.S. Senate, *Foreign Assistance Act of 1962*, Hearings, p. 32.

43. Pastor, *Congress and the Politics of U.S. Foreign Economic Policy*, p. 286.

44. *Congressional Record*, October 2, 1962, pp. 21616–21221.

45. Pastor, *Congress and the Politics of U.S. Foreign Economic Policy*, p. 273; David Bell (AID) to President Kennedy, "House Debate on Foreign Aid Authorizations," August 15, 1963 (JFK/POF, Departments and Agencies, AID), p. 2.

46. *Congressional Record*, March 5, 1962, p. 3394.

47. Bell to Kennedy (see n. 45); see also Annex A, "Significant Committee Amendments," October 25, 1963 (JFK/NSF).

48. Bell to Kennedy (see n. 45).

49. U.S. House, CFA, *Foreign Assistance Act of 1964*, Hearings p. 289.

50. *Department of State Bulletin*, December 10, 1962, p. 899.

51. U.S. Department of Commerce, Committee of the Alliance for Progress, "Proposals to Improve the Flow of U.S. Private Investment to Latin America," March, 1963, p. 4.

52. Swansbrough, *The Embattled Colossus*, p. 119.

53. Edward S. Mason, *Foreign Aid and Foreign Policy* (New York: Harper and Row, 1964), p. 88.

54. *Congressional Record*, October 2, 1962, pp. 21615–21621; Miroff, *Pragmatic Illusions*, p. 129–130; Lipson, "Corporate Preferences," pp. 405–406.

55. Memorandum, Edwin M. Martin to President Kennedy, U.S. Department of State, undated (JFK/POF, Departments and Agencies, State, 8/62–12/62, Box 88, DDI R/502C), p. 4.

56. Cited in Swansbrough, *The Embattled Colossus*, p. 120.

57. Parker, *Brazil and the Quiet Intervention*, p. 35.

58. Memorandum, David Bell to John F. Kennedy, November 2, 1963 (JFK/POF, Departments and Agencies, AID, 1963), p. 2; see also Lipson, *Standing Guard*, p. 213.

59. *New York Times*, January 13, 1962, p. 64.

60. Richard Stuart Olson, "Expropriation and International Economic Coercion: Ceylon and the 'West', 1961–1965," *The Journal of Developing Areas* (January 1977), 11(2):208.

61. Memorandum, Rusk to Kennedy, "Case Study—Effect of the Hickenlooper Amendment on U.S.-Ceylonese Relations," U.S. Department of State, May 27, 1963 (JFK/POF).

62. *Economist*, February 23, 1963, p. 728; *New York Times*, January 6, 1963; *Asian Recorder*, February 12–18, 1963, 9(7):5037.

63. *International Legal Materials* (1963), 2:386–391.

64. *Economist* February 23, 1963, p. 728.

65. *Wall Street Journal*, July 25, 1963, p. 7.

66. Rusk to Kennedy (see n.61), p. 1.

67. Olson, "Expropriation and International Economic Coercion," p. 221.

68. Rusk to Kennedy (see n.61), p. 1.

69. *Ibid.*, pp. 2, 4.

70. Olson, "Expropriation and International Economic Coercion," p. 211; Teresa Hayter, *Aid as Imperialism* (London: Penguin, 1971), p. 31f.

71. Olson, "Expropriation and International Economic Coercion," p. 210.

72. *Ibid.*, pp. 214, 224.

73. *Ibid.*, p. 217.

74. Parker, *Brazil and the Quiet Intervention*, pp. 35–40.

75. U.S. Central Intelligence Agency, "Brazil, Situation and Prospects in," National Intelligence Estimate, NIE 93-2-63, July 2, 1963 (DDI 1976/4C), p. 18.

76. Parker, *Brazil and the Quiet Intervention*, p. 37.

77. Thomas E. Skidmore, *Politics in Brazil, 1930–1964: An Experiment in Democracy* (New York: Oxford University Press, 1967), p. 255; *Wall Street Journal*, February 6, 1963, p. 11 and April 23, 1963, p. 2.

78. Am. Emb. Rio (Gordon) to Rusk, April 9, 1963 (JFK/POF, Country Files, Brazil), p. 2.

79. Memorandum, "Background on the Current Situation in Brazil," U.S. Department of State, June 28, 1962 (JFK/POF, Countries, Brazil, Security, 1962 Box 112A, DDI R/338C).

80. Gordon to Rusk (see n. 78).

81. Ball to Am. Emb. Rio (Gordon), June 29, 1963 (JFK/POF, Countries, Brazil), p. 2.

82. Am. Emb. Rio (Gordon) to Rusk, June 2, 1963 (JFK/POF, Countries, Brazil), p. 2.

83. Levinson and de Onís, *The Alliance That Lost Its Way*, p. 88; Skidmore, *Politics in Brazil*, p. 323; Parker, *Brazil and the Quiet Intervention*, pp. 47, 92–93; Walter LaFeber, "Latin American Policy," in Robert A. Divine, ed., *Exploring the Johnson Years* (Austin: University of Texas Press, 1981), pp. 71–72.

84. Olson, "Expropriation and Economic Coercion," p. 256.

85. *Ibid.*, p. 260.

86. U.S. Central Intelligence Agency, Special National Intelligence Esti-

mate 93-2-61, December 7, 1961 (JFK/POF, Country Files, Brazil, DDI-1976/3E); U.S. Central Intelligence Agency, Office of Current Intelligence, "Communist Inroads in the Brazilian Government," September 27, 1961 (JFK/POF, Countries, Brazil, DDI 1976/3E).

87. Parker, *Brazil and the Quiet Intervention*, pp. 55, 69.

88. *Ibid.*, pp. 82–83.

89. Skidmore, *Politics in Brazil*, p. 325.

90. Parker, *Brazil and the Quiet Intervention*, pp. 75–78.

91. Gertrud G. Edwards, "The Frondizi Contracts and Petroleum Self-Sufficiency in Argentina," in Mikesell, ed., *Foreign Investment in the Petroleum and Mineral Industries*, pp. 158–164; Carl Solberg, *Oil and Nationalism in Argentina: A History* (Stanford, Ca.: Stanford University Press, 1979), pp. 166–168.

92. Laura Randall, *An Economic History of Argentina in the Twentieth Century* (New York: Columbia University Press, 1978), p. 206; Baily, *The United States and the Development of South America*, p. 101.

93. Randall, *An Economic History of Argentina*, p. 205.

94. Edwards, "The Frondizi Contracts," p. 166; Stephen R. Luce, "Argentina and the Hickenlooper Amendment," *California Law Review* (December 1966), 54(5):2084.

95. Edwards, "The Frondizi Contracts," p. 172; Am. Emb. Buenos Aires, Telegram No. 1000, December 2, 1963 (LBJ/NSF, Countries, Argentina, vol. 1, DDI 1976/46A); Am. Emb. Buenos Aires, Telegram No. 1016, for Harriman (LBJ/NSF, Countries, Argentina, vol. 1, DDI 1976/46B), pp. 1–2.

96. Economist Intelligence Unit, *Quarterly Economic Review: Argentina* (September 1964), no. 3, p. 9; Lillich, *The Protection of Foreign Investment*, p. 122; *Congressional Record*, November 13, 1963, p. 21761.

97. Baily, *The United States and the Development of South America*, p. 103.

98. Am. Emb. Buenos Aires, Telegram No. 1497, March 11, 1964 (LBJ/NSF, Countries, Argentina, vol. 1, DDI 1976/47B).

99. Am. Emb. Buenos Aires, Telegram No. 2070, June 22, 1964 (LBJ/NSF, Countries, Argentina, vol. 1, DDI 1976/172E).

100. Luce, "Argentina and the Hickenlooper Amendment," p. 2085; Baily, *The United States and the Development of South America*, p. 104; Outgoing Telegram No. 869 to Am. Emb. Buenos Aires, March 12, 1965 (LBJ/NSF, Countries, Argentina, vol. 2, DDI 1976/173C).

101. Baily, *The United States and the Development of South America*, pp. 102–103; McClintock, to Rusk, "Energy Policy: Resurgence of the Ultranationalists," November 9, 1963 (DOS/FOIA); Outgoing Telegram No. 1267 to Am. Emb. Buenos Aires, June 23, 1964 (LBJ/NSF, Countries, Argentina, vol. 1, DDI 1976/173A), p. 1; Am. Emb. Buenos Aires, Telegram No. 1497, March 11, 1964 (LBJ/NSF, Countries, Argentina, vol. 2, DDI 1977/112B); Am. Emb. Buenos Aires (see n. 99), p. 5.

102. Am. Emb. Buenos Aires (see n.98).

103. Correspondence with Ambassador Martin, September 1, 1981.

104. McClintock to Rusk, October 9, 1963, and Rusk to McClintock, October 8, 1963 (DOS/FOIA).

105. Outgoing Telegram No. 869 (see n.100).

106. Outgoing Telegram No. 1267 (see n.101).

107. Thomas L. Hughes to Dean Rusk, "Arturo Illía and His Program for Argentina," U.S. Department of State, Bureau of Intelligence and Research, July 12, 1963 (DOS/FOIA), pp. 3, 6.

108. Am. Emb. Buenos Aires, Telegram No. 1055, December 10, 1963 (LBJ/ NSF, Countries, Argentina, vol. 1, DDI 1977/46C); Am. Emb. Buenos Aires, Airgram A-632, December 28, 1963 (LBJ/NSF, Countries, Argentina, vol. 1, DDI 1976/ 46D); Am. Emb. Buenos Aires, Telegram No. 1016, (see n.95), Am. Emb. Buenos Aires (see n.99), p. 5; Outgoing Telegram No. 869 (see n.100).

109. *Wall Street Journal* September 22, 1965, p. 21; Rusk to Ball, November 17, 1965 (LBJ/NSF, Countries, Argentina, vol. 2, DDI 1976/173E), p. 1.

110. Am. Emb. Buenos Aires, Telegram No. 1866, from the Ambassador to Assistant Secretary Gordon, June 8, 1966 (LBJ/NSF, Country Files, Argentina, vol. 2, DDI 1976/256C); Memorandum, Ball to Johnson, June 29, 1966 (LBJ/NSF, Countries, Argentina, vol. 2, DDI 1976/256F).

111. Adapted from Levinson and de Onís, *The Alliance That Lost Its Way*, p. 88.

112. U.S. Central Intelligence Agency, Office of Current Intelligence "Survey of Latin America," Report No. 1063/1064 (LBJ/NSF, Countries, Latin America, vol. 1, DDI 1977/272C), pp. 5–9; see also LaFeber, "Latin American Policy," pp. 67–68.

113. LaFeber, "Latin American Policy," pp. 64–65.

114. The main exception to this pattern was accommodation toward Frei's Chileanization of the copper mines to prevent the Socialist Party under Salvador Allende from exploiting the issue in the 1970 elections. This is consistent with Krasner's argument that containment objectives tended to supercede economic milieu goals. See Krasner, *Defending the National Interest*, pp. 229–235.

115. Memorandum, U.S. Central Intelligence Agency, Office of Current Intelligence, No. 0748/65, January 15, 1965 (LBJ/NSF, Country Files, Latin America, vol. 3, DDI 1977/272D).

116. *Department of State Bulletin*, November 19, 1962, pp. 772–773.

117. U.S. Department of Defense, "Latin American Military Forces," Office of the Assistant Secretary of Defense for International Security Affairs, February 25, 1965 (LBJ/NSF, Countries, Argentina, vol. 3, DDI 1976/32B), pp. 1, 9.

118. *Ibid.*

119. *Ibid.*, pp. 50–52.

7. PERU'S EXPROPRIATION OF IPC AND THE ELEVATION OF U.S. ANTI-EXPROPRIATION POLICY

1. Krasner, *Defending the National Interest*, p. 238.

2. Lipson, *Standing Guard*, p. 215.

3. See pp. 295–296.

4. Einhorn, *Expropriation Politics*, pp. 12–13.

5. *Ibid.*, p. 13; Charles T. Goodsell, *American Corporations and Peruvian Politics* (Cambridge: Harvard University Press, 1974), pp. 121–122.

6. Goodsell, *American Corporations*, pp. 42–52; testimony of Richard Goodwin in U.S. Senate, CFR, *United States Relations with Peru*, Hearings, 91st Congress, 1st Session, 1969, pp. 86–88; Pedro Pablo Kuczynski, *Peruvian Democracy Under Stress: An Account of the Belaúnde Years* (Princeton, N.J.: Princeton University Press, 1977), p. 117.

7. Wilkins, *The Maturing of the Multinational Enterprise*, p. 359f.

8. Levinson and de Onís, *The Alliance That Lost Its Way*, p. 149.

9. *Ibid.*

10. Sigmund, *Multinationals in Latin America*, p. 187.

11. Ingram, *Expropriation of U.S. Property in South America*, pp. 56–59.

12. *Ibid.*, p. 60; Einhorn, *Expropriation Politics*, p. 15.

13. Levinson and de Onís, *The Alliance That Lost Its Way*, pp. 150–151; Einhorn, *Expropriation Politics*, pp. 60–63; Memorandum, Grant Hilliker to McGeorge Bundy, U.S. Department of State, July 6, 1965 (LBJ/NSF, Country Files, Peru, vol. 1, DDI 1977/340B); Briefing Memorandum, Benjamin Read to McGeorge Bundy, U.S. Department of State, February 7, 1964 (LBJ/WHCF, No. 234, DDI 1978/102B).

14. Einhorn, *Expropriation Politics*, pp. 33, 40; Testimony of Richard Goodwin in U.S. Senate, *United States Relations with Peru*, p. 96.

15. Special Memorandum No. 19–65, U.S. Central Intelligence Agency, Office of National Estimates, July 29, 1965 (LBJ/NSF, Countries, Peru, vol. 1, DDI 1977/174E); Am. Emb. Lima, Telegram No. 1287, to Mann from Neal, May 6, 1964 (LBJ/NSF, Countries, Peru, vol. 1, DDI 1977/339E).

16. Levinson and de Onís, *The Alliance That Lost Its Way*, p. 151; U.S. Central Intelligence Agency, Office of Current Intelligence, "Survey of Latin America," Report No. 1063/1064 (LBJ/NSF, Countries, Latin America, vol. 1, DDI 1977/272C), pp. 190–193.

17. Memorandum, Walt W. Rostow to Jack Vaughn, August 12, 1965 (LBJ/NSF, Countries, Peru, vol. 1, DDI 1977/340C).

18. Levinson and de Onís, *The Alliance That Lost Its Way*, p. 153; Einhorn, *Expropriation Politics*, pp. 63–65.

19. Goodwin testimony (see n.14), p. 93.

20. *Ibid.*, p. 89; see also Kuczynski, *Peruvian Democracy Under Stress*, pp. 122–125.

21. Goodwin testimony (see n.14), p. 85.

22. Am. Emb. Lima (Neal) to Mann, Telegram No. 1041, March 12, 1964 (LBJ/NSF, Countries, Peru, vol. 1, DDI 1977/339C), p. 2.

23. Wilkins, *The Maturing of the Multinational Enterprise*, p. 356.

24. *Latin America*, January 19, 1969, pp. 14–15.

25. Ingram, *Expropriation*, p. 62; Einhorn, *Expropriation Politics*, p. 45.

26. Levinson and de Onís, *The Alliance That Lost Its Way*, p. 150.

27. Goodsell, *American Corporations*, p. 132.

28. Krasner, *Defending the National Interest*, p. 243; "Investing in Peru—If Local Conditions Are Met," *Business International*, June 12, 1970, p. 189; U.S. Department of Commerce, Bureau of International Commerce, *Foreign Economic Trends and Their Implications for the United States: Peru* (March 1971), pp. 8–9.

29. Einhorn, *Expropriation Politics*, p. 35; John P. Powelson, "International Lending Agencies," in Daniel A. Sharp, ed., *United States Foreign Policy and*

Peru (Austin: University of Texas Press, 1972), pp. 148–149; Economist Intelligence Unit, *Quarterly Economic Review: Peru, Bolivia,* December 18, 1968, no. 4, pp. 7–8.

30. *Petroleum Press Service* (January 1969), 36(1):29; Economist Intelligence Unit, *Quarterly Economic Review: Peru, Bolivia,* July 30, 1970, no. 3, pp. 5–7.

31. Economist Intelligence Unit, *Quarterly Economic Review: Peru, Bolivia,* December 18, 1968, no. 4, p. 7; July 23, 1973, p. 4.

32. Einhorn, *Expropriation Politics,* p. 35; Economist Intelligence Unit, *Quarterly Economic Review: Peru, Bolivia,* July 23, 1973, no. 3, p. 4; July 30, 1971, no. 3, p. 6. *Petroleum Press Service* (July 1971), p. 253; (October 1971), p. 390; (November 1971), p. 431; (December 1971), p. 475; (February 1972), p. 71.

33. Einhorn, *Expropriation Politics,* p. 49–50, 70–74; Richard Stuart Olson, "Economic Coercion in International Disputes: The United States and Peru in the IPC Expropriation Dispute of 1968–71," *The Journal of Developing Areas* (April 1975), 9(3):411–412; Firms whose affiliates were taken over but opposed sanctions included Chase Manhattan, ITT, Cerro, and the Chemical Bank and Trust of New York. See U.S. House, Committee on Agriculture, *Extension of the Sugar Act,* Hearings, 92nd Congress, 1st Session, 1971, pp. 226–231, 235–238, 259–260.

34. Einhorn, *Expropriation Politics,* p. 49.

35. *Ibid.,* p. 65; U.S. House, *Extension of the Sugar Act,* p. 232.

36. Krasner, *Defending the National Interest,* p. 229–235.

37. *New York Times,* April 10, 1969; *Latin America,* May 13, 1969, pp. 149–150.

38. U.S. President, *Public Papers of the President of the United States: Richard Nixon 1969* (Washington, D.C.: U.S. Government Printing Office, 1971), p. 898.

39. Swansbrough, *The Embattled Colossus,* pp. 139–140.

40. Einhorn, *Expropriation Politics,* p. 62.

41. *New York Times,* March 10, 1969, p. 44.

42. Einhorn, *Expropriation Politics,* pp. 46, 53, 58.

43. Am. Emb. Lima (Jones) to Rogers, Telegram 1851, "March 17, 1969; Am. Emb. Lima (Jones) to Rogers," Telegram 2171, March 27, 1969; Am. Emb. Lima, (Jones) to Rogers, Telegram No. 2481, April 8, 1969; Am. Emb. Lima (Jones) to Rogers, Telegram No. 2482, April 8, 1969 (all from DOS/FOIA), supplied by Professor Paul Sigmund, Department of Politics, Princeton University, Princeton, N.J.

44. Am. Emb. Lima (Jones) to Rogers, Telegram No. 2036, March 21, 189 (DOS/FOIA).

45. Einhorn, *Expropriation Politics,* pp. 60–66; U.S. Senate, CFR, *United States Relations with Peru,* pp. 93, 125; U.S. House, *Extension of the Sugar Act,* p. 770. *National Journal,* January 15, 1972, pp. 103, 106; January 22, 1972, p. 149.

46. *Department of State Bulletin,* February 7, 1972, p. 154.

47. Graham Allison and Peter Szanton, *Remaking Foreign Policy: The Organizational Connection* (New York: Basic Books, 1976), p. 31; Stephen D. Cohen, *The Making of United States International Economic Policy* (New York: Praeger, 1977), pp. 46–50.

48. *National Journal,* November 13, 1971, pp. 2248, 2238.

49. U.S. House, CFA, *New Directions for the 1970s, part 2: Development*

Assistance Options for Latin America, 92d Congress, 1st Session, 1971, Hearings, p. 118.

50. Einhorn, *Expropriation Politics*, p. 89.

51. U.S. Department of the Treasury, "A System to Examine and Evaluate Pre-Expropriation Investment-Disputes," undated study (RG 429, CIEP/FJB/NA, File 7600405), p. 2; Also see Einhorn, *Expropriation Politics*, p. 91, and *National Journal*, January 22, 1972, p. 149.

52. Einhorn, *Expropriation Politics*, p. 96.

53. U.S. House, Committee on Interior and Insular Affairs, *Fuel and Energy Resources, 1972*, part 2, Hearings, p. 675.

54. Einhorn, *Expropriation Politics*, pp. 76–77.

55. Memorandum, Schmidt to Flanigan, "Treasury Dissent to Findings on Peru and Panama by the Chairman of the Interagency Staff Coordinating Group Under the CIEP," U.S. Department of the Treasury, June 14, 1972 (RG 429, CIEP/NLM/NA, File 7250745), pp. 2–3.

56. Einhorn, *Expropriation Politics*, p. 81; Jonathan Sanford, *U.S. Foreign Policy and Multilateral Development Banks* (Boulder, Colo.: Westview, 1982), p. 34.

57. National Security Study Memorandum No. 131, "U.S. Policy in Cases of Expropriation," June 23, 1971 (NSC/FOIA).

58. *New York Times*, June 28, 1971, p. 47.

59. *New York Times*, August 14, 1971, p. 3.

60. U.S. House, *New Directions for the 1970s*, pp. 111, 116.

61. *National Journal*, January 15, 1972, p. 106.

62. Einhorn, *Expropriation Politics*, pp. 30–31.

63. *Ibid.*, pp. 102–106.

64. Kubisch to Rogers, "Circular 175—Request for Authorization to Participate in Negotiations for the Establishment of an Inter-American Investment Dispute Settlement Mechanism," October 10, 1973, (DOS/FOIA).

65. *Department of State Bulletin*, February 16, 1970, pp. 182–183.

66. Quoted in Swansbrough, *The Embattled Colossus*, p. 143.

67. National Security Decision Memorandum No. 136, "Policy in Cases of Expropriation," October 8, 1971 (NSC/FOIA).

68. National Security Decision Memorandum No. 148, "Expropriation Policy in Multilateral Development Institutions," January 18, 1972 (NSC/FOIA); *Department of State Bulletin*, February 7, 1972, pp. 152–154.

69. Einhorn, *Expropriation Politics*, pp. 109–110.

70. *National Journal*, January 15, 1972, pp. 102, 106; January 22, 1972, p. 148; *Latin America*, January 28, 1972, p. 29.

71. Memorandum, Gunning to Rosen, "U.S. Policy Toward Peru," U.S. Council on International Economic Policy, October 9, 1972 (RG 429, CIEP/NLM/NA, File CIEPSM No. 23), pp. 1, 3.

72. U.S. Department of State, " Peru: Political and Economic Outlook Through Mid-1974," Annex to NSSM 158, September 6, 1972 (RG 429, CIEP/NLM/NA, File CIEPSM No. 23), p. 6; Rosen to Flanigan, "Review of U.S. Policy Toward Peru," October 2, 1972 (RG 273, CIEP/NLM/NA, NSC File 50806).

73. U.S. Department of State (see n.72), pp. 4–6; National Security Council, "Analytic Summary of NSSM 158/CIEPSM 23. Review of U.S. Policy Toward Peru" undated (RG 273, CIEP/NLM/NA, NSC File 50806), p. 4.

74. Goodsell, *American Corporations*, p. 133; Lipson, "Corporate Preferences," p. 415; *Latin America*, (December 3, 1971, pp. 389–390.
75. *Latin America*, April 7, 1972, p. 109.
76. *Latin America*, April 28, 1972, pp. 149–150; Einhorn, *Expropriation Politics*, p. 96.
77. See pp. 284–288.
78. Stallings, "Peru and the U.S. Banks," p. 234.

8. AMERICAN FOREIGN POLICY AND THE END OF THE CONCESSION SYSTEM IN THE MIDDLE EAST: THE CONFLICT BETWEEN THEORY AND REALITY

1. U.S. Senate, *Multinational Oil Corporations*, Report, p. 124.
2. Edith Penrose, "The Development of Crisis," in Raymond Vernon, ed., *The Oil Crisis* (New York: Norton, 1976), p. 41.
3. Blair, *The Control of Oil*, pp. 211–212; Rustow, *Oil and Turmoil*, p. 135.
4. U.S. Senate, *Multinational Oil Corporations*, Report, p. 122.
5. *Ibid.*
6. *Ibid.*
7. *Ibid.*, p. 125.
8. *Ibid.*, p. 123.
9. *Ibid.*, p. 125.
10. James E. Akins, "The Oil Crisis: This Time the Wolf Is Here," *Foreign Affairs* (April 1973), 51(3):471.
11. U.S. Senate, *Multinational Oil Corporations*, Report, p. 125.
12. Akins, "The Oil Crisis," p. 471; U.S. Senate, *Multinational Corporations*, Hearings, part 5, p. 12; Sampson, *The Seven Sisters*, p. 255.
13. U.S. Senate, *Multinational Corporations*, Hearings, part 5, p. 13; U.S. Senate. Multinational Oil Corporations, Report, p. 125.
14. Rustow, *Oil and Turmoil*, pp. 131–134; Confidential interview, former official, American Embassy, Tripoli.
15. *Oil and Gas Journal*, October 4, 1970, p. 71.
16. *Oil and Gas Journal*, January 4, 1971, p. 48.
17. U.S. Senate, *Multinational Oil Corporations*, Report, pp. 127–128.
18. U.S. Senate, *Multinational Corporations*, Hearings, part 5, p. 85.
19. *Ibid.*, p. 14.
20. *Oil and Gas Journal*, January 25, 1971, p. 82.
21. U.S. Senate, *Multinational Corporations*, Hearings, part 5, pp. 262–263.
22. *Ibid.*, p. 149; U.S. Senate, *Multinational Oil Corporations*, Report, p. 131.
23. U.S. Senate, *Multinational Corporations*, Hearings, part 5, p. 171; *Petroleum Intelligence Weekly*, April 22, 1974, p. 9.
24. U.S. Senate, *Multinational Corporations*, Hearings, part 5, pp. 158, 221, 224, 264.

25. *Petroleum Press Service* (March 1971), pp. 82–83; April 1971, pp. 122–123.

26. V. H. Oppenheim, "The Past: We Pushed Them," *Foreign Policy* (Winter 1975–76), 25:27.

27. Henry A. Kissinger, *White House Years* (Boston: Little, Brown, 1979), p. 1264.

28. *Petroleum Press Service* (April 1971), p. 143.

29. *Ibid.*

30. *Wall Street Journal*, April 16, 1971, p. 6; *Petroleum Press Service* (May 1971), p. 188; *Oil and Gas Journal*, April 19, 1971, p. 90.

31. *Wall Street Journal*, April 27, 1971, p. 13; *New York Times*, April 27, 1971, p. 31; *Petroleum Press Service* (June 1971), p. 204.

32. Zuhayr Mikdashi, *The International Politics of Natural Resources*, p. 173.

33. Hennessy to Bradfield, "Expropriation Policy—IFIs," U.S. Department of the Treasury, May 31, 1971 (TD/FOIA); Petty to Connally, "World Bank Policy on Expropriation," U.S. Department of the Treasury, June 2, 1971 (TD/FOIA).

34. *Oil and Gas Journal*, May 3, 1971, p. 61.

35. William Quandt, "Can We Do Business with Radical Nationalists? Algeria: Yes," *Foreign Policy* (Summer 1972), 7:124.

36. Memorandum (drafted by Philip Tresize) in Rogers, "SONATRACH-El Paso Project," U.S. Department of State, July 14, 1971 (DOS/FOIA).

37. *Ibid.*

38. *New York Times*, June 16, 1971, p. 1; *Wall Street Journal*, June 17, 1971, p. 14.

39. *New York Times*, July 1, 1971, p. 27; *Wall Street Journal*, July 20, 1971, p. 30; December 16, 1971, p. 19.

40. *Oil and Gas Journal*, May 10, 1971, p. 32; June 14, 1971, p. 52.

41. *Ibid.*, May 3, 1971, p. 61.

42. U.S. Senate, *Multinational Oil Corporations*, Report, p. 134.

43. *Ibid.*, p. 11.

44. Walter J. Levy, *Oil Strategy and Politics* (Boulder, Colo.: Westview, 1982), p. 186; see also M. A. Adelman, "Is the Oil Shortage Real?" *Foreign Policy* (Winter 1972–73), 9:84.

45. Sampson, *The Seven Sisters*, p. 277.

46. Cited in *African Diary*, October 22–28, 1971 11(43):5688.

47. Vernon, *Two Hungry Giants*, p. 25.

48. *Oil and Gas Journal*, November 1, 1971, p. 41; November 15, 1971, p. 106; U.S. Senate, *Multinational Oil Corporations*, Report, p. 135.

49. U.S. House, Committee on Interior and Insular Affairs, *Fuel and Energy Resources, 1972*, Part 2, p. 676.

50. Interview; U.S. Senate, *Multinational Corporations*, Hearings, part 6, p. 304.

51. Confidential correspondence.

52. Cited in *National Journal*, May 13, 1972, p. 815.

53. Testimony of Willis Armstrong, in U.S. Senate, Committee on Interior and Insular Affairs, *Oil and Gas Import Issues*, part 3, Hearings, 93d Congress, 1st Session, January 22, 1973, p. 839.

54. Testimony of William Casey, in U.S. House, CFA, Subcommittee on

Foreign Economic Policy and Subcommittee on Near East and South Asia, *Oil Negotiations, OPEC, and the Stability of Supply*, Hearings, 93d Congress, 1st Session, 1973, p. 131.

55. Testimony of James Akins, in U.S. House, Committee on Interior and Insular Affairs, *Fuel and Energy Resources, 1972*, Part 1, p. 157.

56. Oppenheim, "The Past: We Pushed Them," pp. 35–38; U.S. Department of State, "The United States and the Impending Energy Crisis," undated (unpublished State Department study supplied to me by Professor Joseph S. Szyliowicz, Department of Political Science, University of Denver, Denver, Colo.), p. 30.

57. *National Journal*, May 13, 1972, p. 814; Casey testimony (see n.54), p. 126.

58. Joseph S. Szyliowicz, "The Embargo and U.S. Foreign Policy," in Joseph S. Szyliowicz and Bard E. O'Neill, eds., *The Energy Crisis and United States Foreign Policy* (New York: Praeger, 1975), p. 216; U.S. Department of State, *The United States and the Impending Energy Crisis*, p. 30.

59. U.S. Senate, *Multinational Corporations*, Hearings, part 6, p. 304; *National Journal*, May 13, 1972, p. 814; Casey testimony (see n.54), p. 128.

60. *Petroleum Press Service* (April 1972), p. 118.

61. Akins, "The Oil Crisis," p. 476.

62. U.S. Senate, *Multinational Oil Corporations*, Report, p. 136.

63. *Petroleum Press Service* (September 1972), p. 340.

64. U.S. Senate, *Multinational Oil Corporations*, Report, pp. 135–136; *New York Times*, October 15, 1972, section 3, p. 1; *Petroleum Press Service* (February 1973), pp. 45–46.

65. Edith T. Penrose and E. F. Penrose, *Iraq: International Relations and National Development* (Boulder, Colo.: Westview, 1978), p. 260; *Wall Street Journal*, October 13, 1961, p. 28.

66. *Wall Street Journal*, December 13, 1961, p. 4.

67. Penrose and Penrose, *Iraq*, p. 268, Mikdashi, *The International Politics of Natural Resources*, p. 58.

68. Blair, *The Control of Oil*, pp. 85–88.

69. *New York Times*, April 7, 1972, p. 45.

70. Mikdashi, *The International Politics of Natural Resources*, p. 149; *Wall Street Journal*, June 6, 1972, p. 39.

71. Penrose and Penrose, *Iraq*, pp. 408–409; *New York Times*, May 18, 1972, p. 67.

72. *Petroleum Press Service* (July 1972), p. 238.

73. Cited in Penrose and Penrose, *Iraq*, p. 410. 9; *Wall Street Journal*, June 2, 1972, p. 2.

74. *New York Times*, June 21, 1972, p. 51; Mikdashi, *The International Politics of Natural Resources*, p. 59; Adelman, "Is the Oil Shortage Real?" p. 85.

75. *Wall Street Journal*, June 8, 1972, p. 30; U.S. Department of State, Bureau of Intelligence and Research, "Iraq: The IPC Nationalization," June 19, 1972 (DOS/FOIA), p. 7.

76. Penrose and Penrose, *Iraq*, p. 412; *New York Times*, June 19, 1972, p. 51; June 9, 1972, p. 49.

77. Penrose and Penrose, *Iraq*, p. 414; *Wall Street Journal*, March 1, 1973, p. 9.

78. *New York Times*, June 23, 1972, p. 47; *Wall Street Journal*, June 23, 1972, p. 5.

79. Memorandum Charls E. Walker to Treasury Secretary George Shultz, "IBRD Loan to Iraq," June 13, 1972 (TD/FOIA).

80. Memorandum, U. Alexis Johnson to Charls Walker, U.S. Department of State, June 14, 1972 (RG 429, CIEP/NLM/NA, File 7250745).

81. Walker to Shultz (see n.79).

82. Johnson to Walker (see n.80).

83. Waddams, *The Libyan Oil Industry*, p. 251.

84. *Wall Street Journal*, December 9, 1971, p. 4; December 13, 1971, p. 25; January 10, 1972, p. 3.

85. U.S. Senate, *Multinational Corporations*, Hearings, part 6, pp. 48–49.

86. *Ibid.*, part 5, p. 23; Memorandum, Moorhead Kennedy to William Mazzocco, U.S. Department of State, February 14, 1972 (RG 429, CIEP/NLM/NA, File 7250014), p. 5.

87. Waddams, *The Libyan Oil Industry*, p. 251; *Oil and Gas Journal*, June 19, 1972, p. 41.

88. U.S. Senate, *Multinational Corporations*, Hearings, part 6, p. 53; *New York Times*, March 5, 1972, p. 1; June 8, 1972, p. 69.

89. *New York Times*, January 18, 1973, p. 57.

90. U.S. Senate, *Multinational Corporations*, Hearings, part 6, pp. 52–56; *New York Times*, June 13, 1973, p. 63.

91. Waddams, *The Libyan Oil Industry*, p. 252. *Wall Street Journal*, July 19, 1973, p. 5; August 9, 1973, p. 7.

92. U.S. Senate, *Multinational Corporations*, Hearings, part 6, p. 317; *New York Times*, August 8, 1973, p. 55; *Oil and Gas Journal*, August 13, 1973, p. 54.

93. U.S. Senate, *Multinational Corporations*, Hearings, part 6, p. 56.

94. Turner, *Oil Companies in the International System*, p. 158.

95. *Wall Street Journal*, August 13, 1973, p. 43.

96. *New York Times*, August 17, 1973, p. 43.

97. Memorandum, George M. Bennsky, "Seven Sisters Strategy Re Libyan Oil," U.S. Department of State, August 15, 1973 (DOS/FOIA); Memorandum, "Libyan Oil Developments," U.S. Department of State, August 17, 1973 (RG 429, CIEP/FJB/NA, File 7315237).

98. *New York Times*, September 2, 1973, p. 1.

99. Memorandum, George M. Bennsky, "Substance of Oil Majors' Negotiators' August 20 Meeting with the Libyans," U.S. Department of State, August 22, 1973 (RG 429, CIEP/FJB/NA, File 7352660).

100. U.S. Department of State, Office of the Legal Adviser, *Digest of United States Practice in International Law 1975*, (Washington D.C.: Government Printing Office, 1976), pp. 489–490.

101. Cited in U.S. Senate, *Multinational Oil Corporations*, Report, pp. 138–139.

102. *New York Times*, September 13, 1972; confidential interviews, Department of State.

103. U.S. Senate, *Multinational Corporations*, Hearings, part 5, p. 45; part 6, p. 319–322.

104. U.S. Senate, *Multinational Corporations*, Hearings, part 5, p. 46; part 6, p. 321.

105. Memorandum, Willis Armstrong to Governor John Love, U.S. Department of State, October 9, 1973; Memorandum of Conversation, "Interest of Commonwealth Refining and New England Petroleum to Buy Libyan Oil," U.S. Department of State, September 13, 1973; Memorandum of Conversation, "Libyan Oil Developments," U.S. Department of State, September 13, 1973; Memorandum of Conversation, " 'Hot' Libyan Oil and U.S. Domestic Needs," U.S. Department of State, September 20, 1973 (all from DOS/FOIA).

106. Memorandum, Carlyle E. Maw and Sidney Sober to Mr. Sisco, "Protest to Libya on the Taking of the Remaining 49% Interests of Socal, Texaco, and ARCO in Libya," Department of State, June 6, 1974 (DOS/FOIA).

107. U.S. Senate, *Multinational Oil Corporations*, Report, p. 144.

108. *Ibid.*, p. 139.

109. *Wall Street Journal*, March 18, 1974, p. 2; April 17, 1974, p. 14.

110. *New York Times*, November 31, 1974, p. 47; February 19, 1974, p. 48; September 17, 1976, p. D3.

111. See Mikdashi, *The International Politics of Natural Resources*, p. 74–75.

112. U.S. Department of State, Briefing Paper, "Role of the International Oil Companies," undated (RG 429, CIEP/FJB/NA, File 7353183).

9. FROM PRINCIPLE TO PRAGMATISM: THE SEARCH FOR DÉTENTE WITH ECONOMIC NATIONALISM

1. Swansbrough, *The Embattled Colossus*, p. 194; U.S. Council on International Economic Policy, (CIEP), "Survey of U.S. Business Perspectives: U.S. Expropriation Policy" (written by James F. McClelland, III), November 1975 (RG 429, CIEP/FJB/NA, File 7600009), p. 3.

2. Commission on United States–Latin American Relations, *The Americas in a Changing World* (New York: Quadrangle, 1975), pp. 36–38.

3. Exxon *Annual Report* (1974), p. 2 as cited in Krasner, *Defending the National Interest*, p. 257.

4. Frank, *Foreign Enterprise in Developing Countries*, pp. 109–110.

5. Swansbrough, *The Embattled Colossus*, p. 194; CIEP, "Survey of U.S. Business Perspectives," p. 3.

6. CIEP, "Survey of U.S. Business Perspectives," p. 5; Frank, *Foreign Investment in Developing Countries*, pp. 127–129.

7. Swansbrough, *The Embattled Colossus*, p. 207; Lipson, "Corporate Preferences," p. 414.

8. Lipson, *Standing Guard*, p. 123; David G. Becker, *The New Bourgeoisie and the Limits of Dependency: Mining, Class, and Power in 'Revolutionary' Peru* (Princeton, N.J.: Princeton University Press, 1983), p. 99; Confidential interview, Department of State.

9. Philip, *Oil and Politics in Latin America*, pp. 118–119; Barnet and Müller, *Global Reach*, p. 87; *New York Times*.

10. Lipson, *Standing Guard*, p. 159.

11. *International Legal Materials* (1975), 14:255.

12. *International Legal Materials* (1974), 13:238–240.

13. *International Legal Materials* (1974), 13:746.

14. National Journal, October 25, 1975, p. 1481; Daniel P. Moynihan, "The United States in Opposition," *Commentary* (March 1975) 59(3):31–44.

15. *National Journal*, June 21, 1975, p. 922; Robert K. Olson, *U.S. Foreign Policy and the New International Economic Order* (Boulder, Colo.: Westview, 1981), p. 21.

16. Brown, *The Faces of Power*, pp. 424–432.

17. Michael Stohl and Harry R. Targ, "United States and the Third World: The Struggle to Make Others Adapt," in Philip Taylor and Gregory A. Raymond, eds., *Third World Policies of Industrialized Nations* (Westport, Conn.: Greenwood Press, 1982), pp. 115–117.

18. Memorandum, Eberle to Enders, "U.S. Expropriation Policy," U.S. Council on International Economic Policy, August 7, 1974 (RG 429, CIEP/FJB/NA, File 7453952).

19. Rogers, "Of Missionaries, Fanatics, and Lawyers," p. 15.

20. *Latin America*, November 8, 1974, p. 345.

21. Memorandum, Prickett to Smith, "USG Actions on Investment Disputes," U.S. Department of State (RG 429/CIEP/FJB/NA, File 7600405).

22. Rogers, "Of Missionaries, Fanatics, and Lawyers," p. 11; Richard J. Bloomfield, "The New Dialogue with Latin America and the Working Group on Transnational Enterprises," in Tom J. Farer, ed., *The Future of the Inter-American System* (New York: Praeger, 1979), p. 74.

23. Testimony of Charles W. Robinson, in U.S. House, CFA, *The Overseas Private Investment Corporation*, Hearings, 93d Congress, 1st Session, May 31, 1973, p. 76, Confidential correspondence, Department of State.

24. Memorandum, Stephen R. Bond to Richard Smith, "Standards of Compensation for Expropriation," U.S. Department of State, undated (DOS/FOIA), p. 5; Prickett to Smith (see n.21), p. 2; Confidential correspondence, Department of State.

25. Maresca to Erb, "Options Paper: Expropriation Policy," U.S. Department of the Treasury, February 9, 1977, (TD/FOIA), p. 4.

26. Testimony of Thomas O. Enders, U.S. Congress, Joint Economic Committee, *Outlook for Prices and Supplies of Industrial Raw Materials*, Hearings, 93d Congress, 2d Session, 1974, p. 179; Enders to Eberle, "U.S. Expropriation Policy Review: Phase II," U.S. Department of State, December 6, 1974 (RG 429, CIEP/NA/FJB, CIEP File 7500263), p. 2.

27. Memorandum, Miller to Eberle, "Talking Points on Expropriation Policy Item," U.S. Council on International Economic Policy, October 24, 1974 (RG 429, CIEP/NA/FJB, File 53817), p. 2; U.S. Department of the Treasury, "A More Active Role for the USG in Investment Disputes," (RG 429, CIEP/NA/FJB, File 7500263), p. 2; U.S. Department of the Treasury, "A More Active Role for the USG in Expropriation Negotiations" (draft), January 3, 1975 (TD/FOIA), p. 2.

28. U.S. Department of the Treasury, "Background For Expropriation Policy," (TD/FOIA), p. 3; U.S. Department of the Treasury, "Background State-

ment: U.S. Expropriation Policy," June 30, 1976 (RG 429, CIEP/NA/FJB, File 7600009).

29. Treasury, "Background For Expropriation Policy," p. 4.

30. U.S. Department of the Treasury, "A System to Examine and Evaluate Pre-Expropriation Disputes," undated (RG 429, CIEP/NA/FJB, File 7600405), p. 2; U.S. Department of the Treasury, "Expropriation Policy" (draft prepared by Richard Goodman), October 1974 (TD/FOIA), p. 14.

31. Treasury, "Expropriation Policy, (see n.30) p. 13.

32. U.S. Department of the Treasury, "Redirecting USG Expropriation Policy," June 15, 1976 (RG 429, CIEP/FJB/NA, File 7600009), p. 1.

33. Treasury, "Expropriation Policy" (see n.30), p. 21; Treasury, "A More Active Role for the USG in Expropriation Negotiations" (see n.27), p. 3.

34. Memorandum, Shapiro to Hufbauer, "Treasury Position at March 25 Meeting of Expropriation Group," U.S. Department of the Treasury, March 22, 1977 (TD/FOIA); Treasury, "Background Statement" (see n.28), p. 1.

35. Treasury, "Expropriation Policy" (see n.30), p. 18.

36. Treasury, "A More Active Role for the USG in Expropriation Negotiations" (see n.27) p. 14.

37. Memorandum, Einhorn to Bushnell, "Options Paper on U.S. Expropriation Policy," U.S. Department of the Treasury, October 11, 1974 (TD/FOIA), p. 2; Treasury, "Expropriation Policy" (see n.30), p. 6.

38. Hufbauer to Bergsten, "Expropriation Issues in Ethiopia," U.S. Department of the Treasury, June 8, 1977 (TD/FOIA), p. 1.

39. Ibid.; Goodman/Shapiro to Hufbauer, "Treasury Position at April 14 Meeting of Interagency Expropriation Group," U.S. Department of the Treasury, April 13, 1977 (TD/FOIA); Shapiro to Hufbauer, "March 25, 1977 Meeting of Expropriation Group," U.S. Department of the Treasury, March 31, 1977 (TD/FOIA).

40. David A. Gantz, "The United States-Peruvian Claims Commission Agreement of February 19, 1974," International Lawyer (Summer 1976), 10(3):392; Sigmund, Multinationals in Latin America, p. 205.

41. International Legal Materials (1974), 13:395.

42. Gantz, "The United States-Peruvian Claims Commission," pp. 396–397; Sigmund, Multinationals in Latin America, p. 206; that the final result was understood by the Peruvian government was confirmed by almost all of the U.S. government officials interviewed.

43. Sigmund, Multinationals in Latin America, p. 206; Economist Intelligence Unit, Quarterly Economic Review: Peru, Bolivia, 1974, no. 2, pp. 4, 8.

44. Business Latin America, February 27, 1974, p. 67; New York Times, May 1, 1976, p. 29; Becker, The New Bourgeoisie, p. 40.

45. Sigmund, Multinationals in Latin America, p. 207.

46. Economist Intelligence Unit, Quarterly Economic Review: Peru, Bolivia, 1975, no. 3, p. 13.

47. Ibid.

48. Sigmund, Multinationals in Latin America, pp. 212–213; Stallings, "Peru and the U.S. Banks," pp. 234, 232.

49. Stallings, "Peru and the U.S. Banks," pp. 238–239; New York Times, May 1, 1976, p. 38.

50. Sigmund, Multinationals in Latin America, p. 214; David A. Gantz,

"The Marcona Settlement: New Forms of Negotiation and Compensation for Nationalized Property," *American Journal of International Law* (July 1977), 71(3):479–480.

51. Gantz, "The Marcona Settlement," pp. 480–481.

52. *Ibid.*, p. 490; Treasury concurred in that the strategy was successful in "mov[ing] Marcona from an excessively high ($230 million) to a more reasonable opening position ($120 million), and eventually pressed the company toward a settlement of $65 million which, in fact, was fair value." Goodman to Hufbauer, "An Activist USG Role in Expropriation Cases," U.S. Department of the Treasury, June 3, 1977 (TD/FOIA), p. 1.

53. Economist Intelligence Unit, *Quarterly Economic Review: Peru, Bolivia*, 1976, no. 1, pp. 11–12.

54. Gantz, "The Marcona Settlement," p. 483; Am. Emb. Lima (Dean) to Kissinger, "Marcona—Meeting with Commission," Telegram 9304, November 11, 1975 (DOS/FOIA); Am. Emb. Lima (Dean) to Kissinger, "Marcona Negotiations—Monday Sessions," Telegram 2013, March 2, 1976 (DOS/FOIA).

55. *International Legal Materials* (1976), 15:1100–1104.

56. Nancy Belliveau, "What the Peruvian Experiment Means," *Institutional Investor* (October 1976), p. 148; Stallings, "International Capitalism and the Peruvian Military Government," p. 168; and Guasti, "The Peruvian Military Government and the International Corporations," p. 190.

57. Rogers, "Of Missionaries, Fanatics, and Lawyers," p. 7.

58. Gantz, "The Marcona Settlement," pp. 488–489.

59. Tugwell, *The Politics of Oil*, pp. 48–50; Luis Vallenilla, *The Making of a New Economic Order: Venezuelan Oil and OPEC* (New York: McGraw-Hill 1975), pp. 97–98.

60. Tugwell, *The Politics of Oil*, p. 54; Sigmund, *Multinationals in Latin America*, p. 231.

61. Vallenilla, *The Making of a New Economic Order*, p. 170; *Petroleum Press Service* (July 1971), p. 265.

62. *Latin America*, September 5, 1975, pp. 278–279; *Wall Street Journal*, October 14, 1975, p. 48.

63. Sigmund, *Multinationals in Latin America*, p. 240; *New York Times*, June 23, 1975, p. 43.

64. *New York Times*, June 19, 1971, p. 33; June 21, 1971, p. 41. Rabe, *The Road to OPEC*, p. 176.

65. Rabe, *The Road to OPEC*, p. 176.

66. Sigmund, *Multinationals in Latin America*, p. 236.

67. *New York Times*, January 10, 1975, p. 60.

68. Rabe, *The Road to OPEC*, p. 186; James F. Petras, Morris Morley, and Stephen Smith, *The Nationalization of Oil in Venezuela* (New York: Praeger, 1977), pp. 112–113.

69. Economist Intelligence Unit, *Quarterly Economic Review: Venezuela*, April 17, 1975, no. 2, p. 6.

70. *Ibid.*; *Wall Street Journal*, October 29, 1975, p. 15.

71. *Wall Street Journal*, January 7, 1976, p. 2; *New York Times*, January 7, 1976, p. 60.

72. *Business Week*, August 9, 1976, p. 47.

73. Am. Emb. Caracas (McClintock) to Rogers, June 29, 1971 (DOS/FOIA), p. 2; *New York Times*, June 9, 1972, p. 36.

74. Rogers to Am. Emb. Caracas, (McClintock), "Letter to F. M. Calvani," July 2, 1971 (DOS/FOIA), p. 3; Rogers to McClintock, "Petroleum Reversion," June 29, 1971 (DOS/FOIA).

75. Tugwell, *The Politics of Oil*, p. 134–135; Rabe, *The Road to OPEC*, p. 177; *Department of State Bulletin*, April 19, 1971, p. 526. *Latin America*, March 31, 1972, p. 104; February 18, 1972, p. 55.

76. *Latin America*, December 29, 1972, p. 413; Rogers to Am. Emb. Caracas (McClintock), "Western Hemisphere Preference," December 12, 1972, and Rogers to Am. Emb. Caracas (McClintock), "Suspension of Western Hemisphere Preference," December 14, 1972 (Both DOS/FOIA).

77. Devine to Secretary of State, "Possible Waiver of Western Hemisphere Preference on No. 2 Fuel Oil," October 4, 1971 (DOS/FOIA); Devine to Secretary of State, "Petroleum—Possible Waiver of Western Hemisphere Preference on No. 2 Fuel Oil," October 20, 1971 (DOS/FOIA).

78. Confidential interview, Department of State.

79. Tugwell, *The Politics of Oil*, p. 138; Rabe, *The Road to OPEC*, pp. 176–178.

80. Am. Emb. Caracas (McClintock) to Kissinger, "Reaction to OEP Statement on Hemispheric Preferences and Tar Belt," March 14, 1973 (DOS/FOIA).

81. Rush to Am. Emb. Caracas (McClintock), "Subject: WH Preference," May 23, 1973 (DOS/FOIA).

82. National Security Study Memorandum No. 203, "Review of U.S. Policy Toward Venezuela," June 10, 1974, (NSC/FOIA).

83. Enders to Eberle, "December 3 Meeting of the CIEP Interagency Coordinating Expropriation Group," December 20, 1974 (RG 429 CIEP/FJB/NA, File 7424823), p. 2; Am. Emb. Caracas (Shlaudemann) to Kissinger, "Oil Nationalization Status Report—the Final Month," Telegram No. 2615, August 21, 1975 (DOS/FOIA); Am. Emb. Caracas (Shlaudemann) to Kissinger, "Oil Nationalization—Price Remains the Issue," Telegram No. 13269, December 19, 1975 (DOS/FOIA).

84. Rogers, "Of Missionaries, Fanatics, and Lawyers," p. 9; see also testimony of Undersecretary of State Robert Ingersoll, U.S. House, Committee on Ways and Means, *Generalized Tariff Preferences*, Hearings, 94th Congress, 1st Session, May 13, 1975, p. 35.

85. Rabe, *The Road to OPEC*, p. 182, Petras, Morley, and Smith, *The Nationalization of Oil*, pp. 128–130.

86. U.S. Department of Commerce, Bureau of International Commerce, *Foreign Economic Trends and Their Implications for the United States: Venezuela* (December 1976), p. 4.

87. Petras, Morley, and Smith, *The Nationalization of Oil*, p. 123.

88. *New York Times*, June 30, 1975, p. 45; Rogers, "Of Missionaries, Fanatics, and Lawyers," p. 10; Memorandum, Hinton to Flanigan, "Expropriation Policy: Venezuela," The White House, May 3, 1974 and Memorandum, Flanigan to Scowcroft, The White House, May 3, 1974 (Both in RG 429, CIEP/FJB/NA, File 7453547).

89. Petras, Morley, and Smith, *The Nationalization of Oil*, p. 132; Confidential interview, Department of State.

90. *Internatioinal Legal Materials* (1976), 15:186.

91. Rabe, *The Road to OPEC*, p. 187; *Department of State Bulletin*, March 8, 1976, p. 321.

92. *Department of State Bulletin*, March 15, 1976, p. 328; March 22, 1976, p. 360. Ingersoll testimony (see n.84), p. 27.

93. Norman Girvan, *Corporate Imperialism: Conflict and Expropriation* (New York: Monthly Review, 1976), pp. 103–107; Dani Rodrik, "Changing Patterns in Ownership and Integration in the International Bauxite-Aluminim Industry," in Leroy P. Jones, ed., *Public Enterprise in Less-Developed Countries* (Cambridge: Cambridge University Press, 1982), pp. 193–194.

94. Girvan, *Corporate Imperialism*, p. 102.

95. Rodrik, "Changing Patterns," pp. 195–196; Vernon, *Two Hungry Giants*, p. 52.

96. Adam Boulton, "Jamaica's Bauxite Strategy: The Caribbean Flirts with the International System," *SAIS Review* (Summer 1981), 2:83; Sherry Keith and Robert Girling, "Caribbean Conflict: Jamaica and the United States," *NACLA Reports* (May–June 1978), 12(3):11; Michael Manley, *Jamaica: Struggle in the Periphery* (New York, Norton, 1982), pp. 44–47.

97. Ransford Palmer, *Caribbean Dependence on the United States Economy* (New York: Praeger, 1979), p. 7.

98. Manley, *Jamaica*, p. 99.

99. Boulton, "Jamaica's Bauxite Strategy," p. 84.

100. Manley, *Jamaica*, p. 98.

101. *New York Times*, June 18, 1974, p. 51; June 21, 1974, p. 53; June 24, 1974, p. 59. *Wall Street Journal*, June 18, 1974, p. 10.

102. *Wall Street Journal*, June 18, 1974, p. 10.

103. *Latin America*, August 2, 1974, p. 238.

104. C. Fred Bergsten, "A New OPEC in Bauxite?" *Challenge* (July–August 1976), 19(3):12–20.

105. Girvan, *Corporate Imperialism*, pp. 139–140.

106. *Wall Street Journal*, June 18, 1974, p. 10.

107. Miller to Eberle, "Redefining Expropriation Policy," U.S. Council on International Economic Policy, August 30, 1974 (RG 429, CIEP/NA/FJB, File 7453817), p. 3; Smith to Eberle, "July 10 Meeting of the Interagency Coordinating Group on Expropriations," U.S. Department of State, July 19, 1974 (RG 429, CIEP/FJB/NA, File 7453795), p. 1; Enders to Eberle, "December 3 Meeting of CIEP Interagency Coordinating Group on Expropriation," U.S. Department of State, December 19, 1974 (RG 429, CIEP/FJB/NA, File 7424823), pp. 4–5; Kissinger to Am. Emb. Kingston (Gerard), October 16, 1975 (DOS/FOIA), p. 3; Kissinger to Am. Emb. Kingston (Gerard), April 8, 1975 (DOS/FOIA), p. 2.

108. Ingersoll to Am. Emb. Kingston (Gerard), July 25, 1974 (DOS/FOIA), p. 2; Memorandum, Randy Jayne to Jamie McClaine, "Mr. Rush's Meeting with the Aluminum Industry," White House, June 13, 1974 (RG 429, CIEP/FJB/NA, File 7453599).

109. Smith to Eberle (see n.107); Enders to Eberle (see n.107), p. 5; Shapiro to Hufbauer (see n.39), p. 2; Memorandum, Julius Katz, "Meeting of the Expropriation Group," March 31, 1977 (DOS/FOIA), p. 2; Ingersoll to Am. Emb. Kingston (Gerard), September 4, 1974 (DOS/FOIA); Am. Emb. Kingston (Gerard) to Kissin-

ger, September 10, 1975 (DOS/FOIA); Kissinger to Am. Emb. Kingston (Gerard), August 7, 1975 (DOS/FOIA); Confidential interviews, Agency for International Development.

110. J. Daniel O'Flaherty, "Finding Jamaica's Way," *Foreign Policy* (Summer 1976, 31:154.

111. Am. Emb. Kingston (Gerard) to Kissinger, July 16, 1974 (DOS/FOIA), p. 2.

112. U.S. Agency for International Development, *U.S. Overseas Loans and Grants and Assistance from International Organizations*, 1977, p. 205; Economist Intelligence Unit, *Quarterly Economic Review: The West Indies*, June 25, 1975, no. 3, p. 7; Palmer, *Caribbean Dependence*, pp. 117–118; Confidential interviews, Agency for International Development.

113. *Business Latin America*, December 4, 1974, p. 387; April 9, 1975, p. 119. *New York Times*, November 21, 1974, p. 75; *Wall Street Journal*, November 21, 1974, p. 16.

114. *Business Latin America*, October 27, 1976, p. 344; Economist Intelligence Unit, *Quarterly Economic Review: The West Indies*, October 4, 1976, no. 4, p. 6.

115. Vernon, *Two Hungry Giants*, p. 44; Rodrik, "Changing Patterns," p. 196.

116. Edward Fried, "International Trade in Raw Materials: Myths and Realities," *Science*, February 20, 1976, p. 644.

117. *Wall Street Journal*, June 18, 1974, p. 10.

118. Theodore Moran, "New Deal or Raw Deal in Raw Materials?" *Foreign Policy* (Winter 1971–1972), 5:124–126.

119. Rodrik, "Changing Patterns," p. 205; *Iron Age*, January 24, 1977, p. 28; Robert J. Regan, "Caribbean Bauxite Loses Ground in U.S. Markets," *Iron Age*, March 6, 1978, pp. 30–32; Boulton, "Jamaica's Bauxite Strategy," p. 85.

120. Regan, "Caribbean Bauxite Loses Ground," p. 32.

121. Rodrik, "Changing Patterns," pp. 206, 201.

122. Gerard to Kissinger (see n.111), p. 2; Gerard to Kissinger, July 11, 1974 (DOS/FOIA); Jayne to McClaine (see n.108); Linwood Holton to Senator Henry Jackson, U.S. Department of State, Bureau of Congressional Relations, July 10, 1974 (DOS/FOIA), p. 1; Enders testimony (see n.25), p. 180; *Latin America*, August 2, 1974, p. 238.

123. Enders testimony (see n.26), pp. 181–186; Holton to Jackson (see n.122), pp. 2–5.

124. Girvan, *Corporate Imperialism*, p. 149.

125. Boulton, "Jamaica's Bauxite Strategy," pp. 86–88.

126. U.S. Department of the Interior, Bureau of the Mines, *Mineral Yearbook*, vol. 1: *Metals and Minerals 1977* (Washington, D.C.: GPO, 1980), pp. 178–179, and vol. 1: *Metals and Minerals 1980* (Washington, D.C.: GPO, 1981), pp. 122–123; See also Economist Intelligence Unit, *Quarterly Economic Review: Jamaica*, 1976, no. 1, p. 10, and 1976, no. 3, p. 6.

127. Robert J. Regan, "Windfall Profits Still Elude Caribbean Bauxite," *Iron Age*, April 21, 1980, p. 32.

128. U.S. Department of the Interior, Bureau of the Mines, *Mineral Yearbook*, vol. 1, 1980, pp. 118–120.

129. Anthony P. Maingot, "The Difficult Path to Socialism in the English-Speaking Caribbean," in Fagen, ed., *Capitalism and the State*, p. 278; Boulton, "Jamaica's Bauxite Strategy," pp. 85–86; O'Flaherty, "Finding Jamaica's Way," p. 144.

130. Economist Intelligence Unit, *Quarterly Economic Review: Jamaica* (1980), no. 2, p. 12; Boulton, "Jamaica's Bauxite Strategy," p. 88.

131. Krasner, *Defending the National Interest*, pp. 271–273.

132. Krasner, *Structural Conflict*, p. 178.

133. *Ibid.*, pp. 104–110.

134. Guasti, "The Peruvian Military Government," p. 181.

135. Shafer, "Capturing the Mineral Multinationals," pp. 104–105; Diaz-Alejandro, "International Markets for Exhaustible Resources," p. 22.

CONCLUSION

1. Bruce Russett, "International Behavior Research: Case Studies and Cumulation," in Michael Haas and Henry S. Kariel, eds., *Approaches to the Study of Political Science* (Scranton, Pa.: Chandler, 1970), p. 429.

2. For a recent debate on this issue, see Bruce Bueno de Mesquita, "Toward Scientific Understanding of International Conflict: A Personal View"; Stephen D. Krasner, "Toward Understanding in International Relations"; Robert Jervis, "Pluralistic Rigor: A Comment on Bueno de Mesquita"; and Bueno de Mesquita, "Reply to Krasner and Jervis," all in *International Studies Quarterly* (June 1985), 29(2):119–154.

3. U.S. Department of State, Bureau of Intelligence and Research, "Nationalization, Expropriation, and Other Takings of United States and Certain Foreign Property Since 1960" (RECS-14, December 1971); "Disputes Involving U.S. Foreign Direct Investment. July 1, 1971 Through July 31, 1973" (RECS-6, February 1974); "Disputes Involving U.S. Foreign Direct Investment: August 1, 1973–January 31, 1975" (RS-24U, March 20, 1975); "Disputes Involving U.S. Foreign Direct Investment, February 1, 1975–February 28, 1977" (Report No. 855, September 19, 1977); "Disputes Involving U.S. Private Direct Investment, March 1, 1977–February 29, 1980" (Report No. 1441, August 18, 1980). Other cases are drawn from Einhorn, *Expropriation Politics*; Sigmund, *Multinationals in Latin America*; Ingram, *Expropriation*; and Philip, *Oil and Politics*.

4. Robert Rosenthal, *Meta-Analytic Procedures for Social Research* (Beverly Hills: Sage, 1984), p. 13.

5. Krasner, *Defending the National Interest*, pp. 15–17.

6. Sylvan, "The Newest Mercantilism," p. 386.

7. The small number of cases between prior to 1960 should not indicate the absence of such an orientation. Rather, it suggests that the imbalance of bargaining power was sufficiently skewed so as to rig the incentive structure heavily against nationalization. The United States did not need to continuously coerce to ensure conformity. For a general analysis of this dynamic, see Young, "Regime Dynamics," p. 285.

8. Lindblom, *Politics and Markets*, ch. 13.

9. Lowi, "American Business."

10. Kudrle and Bobrow, "U.S. Policy Toward Foreign Direct Investment," p. 360.

11. For an example, see Immerman, "Guatemala as Cold War History,"

12. See chapter 6.

13. On the distinction between compliance and compromise models of decision making within international organization, see Beverly Crawford and Stephanie Lenway, "Decision-Modes and International Regime Change: Western Collaboration on East-West Trade," *World Politics* (April 1985), 38(3):380–384.

14. Lipson, *Standing Guard*, p. 225; Krasner, *Defending the National Interest*, pp. 220–221.

15. Ruggie, "International Regimes."

16. See Vernon, *Two Hungry Giants*, ch. 4; Secretary of State Kissinger's scheme for an International Resources Bank stands out as an exception to this overall approach. See Diaz-Alejandro, "International Markets for Exhaustible Resources," p. 28; and Krasner, *Structural Conflict*, pp. 175, 292–293.

Selected Bibliography

Akinsanya, Adeoye. *The Expropriation of Multinational Property in the Third World.* New York: Praeger, 1980.

Avery, William P. and David P. Rapkin, eds. *America in a Changing World Political Economy.* New York and London: Longmans, 1982.

Bailey, Samuel L. *The United States and the Development of South America, 1945–1975.* New York: New Viewpoints, 1976.

Barnet, Richard J. and Ronald Müller, *Global Reach: The Power of the Multinational Corporations.* New York: Touchstone, 1974.

Becker, Loftus E. "Just Compensation in Expropriation Cases: Decline and Partial Recovery." *Proceedings of the American Society of International Law.* (1959), 53:336–344.

Bergsten, C. Fred, Thomas Horst, and Theodore H. Moran. *American Multinationals and American Interests.* Washington, D.C.: Brookings Institution, 1976.

Blair, John M. *The Control of Oil.* New York: Pantheon, 1976.

Brown, Seyom. *The Faces of Power: Constancy and Change in United States Foreign Policy from Truman to Reagan.* New York: Columbia University Press, 1983.

Calleo, David P. and Benjamin M. Rowland. *America and the World Political Economy: Atlantic Dreams and National Realities.* Bloomington: Indiana University Press, 1973.

Carr, Edward Hallett. *The Twenty Years Crisis, 1919–1939: An Introduction to the Study of International Relations.* New York: Harper Torchbooks, 1964.

Cobbe, James H. *Governments and Mining Companies in Developing Countries.* Boulder, Colo.: Westview Press, 1979.

Cook, Blanche Wiesen. *The Declassified Eisenhower: A Divided Legacy.* Garden City, N.Y.: Doubleday, 1981.

Cotler, Julio and Richard R. Fagen, eds. *Latin America and the United States: The Changing Realities.* Stanford Ca.: Stanford University Press, 1974.

Diaz-Alejandro, Carlos. "International Markets for Exhaustible Resources: Less-Developed Countries, Transnational Corporations." New York University Faculty of Business Administration Working Papers (1976).

Dozer, Donald. *Are We Good Neighbors? Three Decades of Inter-American Relations.* Gainsville: University of Florida Press, 1959.

Eckes, Alfred E., Jr. *The United States and the Global Struggle for Minerals.* Austin: University of Texas Press, 1979.

Einhorn, Jessica Pernitz. *Expropriation Politics.* Lexington, Mass.: D. C. Heath, 1974.

Fagen, Richard R., ed. *Capitalism and the State in U.S.–Latin American Relations.* Stanford, Ca.: Stanford University Press, 1979.

Feinberg, Richard E. *The Intemperate Zone: The Third World Challenge to U.S. Foreign Policy.* New York: Norton, 1983.

Frank, Isaiah. *Foreign Enterprise in Developing Countries.* Baltimore, Md.: Johns Hopkins University Press, 1980.

Friedmann, Wolfgang. *Law in a Changing Society.* 2d ed. New York: Columbia University Press, 1972.

Gardner, Richard N. *Sterling-Dollar Diplomacy: The Origins and the Prospects of our International Economic Order.* Expanded ed. New York: McGraw-Hill, 1969.

Gilpin, Robert. *U.S. Power and the Multinational Corporation: The Political Economy of Foreign Direct Investment.* New York: Basic Books, 1975.

Guasti, Laura. "The Peruvian Military Government and the International Corporations." In Cynthia McClintock and Abraham F. Lowenthal, eds., *The Peruvian Experiment Reconsidered.* Princeton, N.J.: Princeton University Press, 1983.

Immerman, Richard H. "Guatemala as Cold War History." *Political Science Quarterly* (Winter 1980–1981), 95(4):629–653.

Ingram, George M. *Expropriation of United States Property in South America: Nationalization of Oil and Copper Companies in Peru, Bolivia, and Chile.* New York: Praeger, 1974.

Keohane, Robert O. *After Hegemony: Cooperation and Discord in the World Political Economy.* Princeton, N.J.: Princeton University Press, 1984.

Keohane, Robert O. "The Theory of Hegemonic Stability and Changes in International Economic Regimes, 1967–1977." In Ole R. Holsti, Randolph M. Siverson, and Alexander L. George, eds., *Change in the International System.* Boulder, Colo.: Westview, 1980.

Kolko, Gabriel and Joyce Kolko. *The Limits of Power: United States Foreign Policy and the World, 1945–1954.* New York: Harper and Row, 1972.

Krasner, Stephen D. *Defending the National Interest: Raw Materials Investments and U.S. Foreign Policy.* Princeton, N.J.: Princeton University Press, 1978.

Krasner, Stephen D. *Structural Conflict: The Third World Against Global Liberalism.* Berkeley: University of California Press, 1985.

Krasner, Stephen D., ed. *International Regimes*. Ithaca, N.Y.: Cornell University Press, 1984.

Kudrle, Richard T. and Davis B. Bobrow. "U.S. Policy toward Foreign Direct Investment." *World Politics* (April 1982), 34(3):353–379.

Levinson, Jerome and Juan de Onís. *The Alliance That Lost Its Way: A Critical Report on the Alliance for Progress*. Chicago, Ill.: Quadrangle, 1970.

Lillich, Richard B. *The Protection of Foreign Investment: Six Procedural Studies*. Syracuse, N.Y.: University of Syracuse Press, 1965.

Lindblom, Charles E. *Politics and Markets: The World's Political-Economic Systems*. New York, Basic Books, 1977.

Lipson, Charles H. "Corporate Preferences and Public Policies: Foreign Aid Sanctions and Investment Protection." *World Politics* (April 1976), 28(3):396–421.

Lipson, Charles. *Standing Guard: Protecting Foreign Capital in the Nineteenth and Twentieth Centuries*. Berkeley: University of California Press, 1985.

Lowi, Theodore J. "American Business, Public Policy, Case Studies, and Political Theory." *World Politics* (July 1964), 16(4):677–715.

Mikdashi, Zuhayr. *The International Politics of National Resources*. Ithaca, N.Y.: Cornell University Press, 1976.

Mikesell, Raymond F., ed. *Foreign Investment in the Petroleum and Mineral Industries: Case Studies of Investor-Host Country Relations*. Baltimore, Md.: Johns Hopkins University Press, 1971.

Moran, Theodore H. "New Deal or Raw Deal in Raw Materials." *Foreign Policy* (Winter 1971–72), 5:119–136.

Packenham, Robert A. *Liberal America and the Third World: Political Development Ideas in Foreign Aid and Social Science*. Princeton, N.J.: Princeton University Press, 1973.

Paley Commission, see United States Office of the President, President's Materials Policy Commission.

Pastor, Robert A. *Congress and the Politics of U.S. Foreign Economic Policy, 1929–1976*. Berkeley: University of California Press, 1980.

Philip, George. *Oil and Politics in Latin America: Nationalist Movements and State Companies*. Cambridge, England: Cambridge University Press, 1982.

Rabe, Stephen G. *The Road to OPEC: United States Relations with Venezuela, 1919–1976*. Austin: University of Texas Press, 1982.

Randall Commission, see U.S. Commission on Foreign Economic Policy.

Robinson, Richard D. *International Business Management: A Guide for Decision-makers*. Hinsdale, Ill.: Dryden Press, 1978.

Robinson, Richard D. *International Business Policy*. Cambridge: Hamlin Publications, 1963.

Rogers, William D. "Of Missionaries, Fanatics, and Lawyers: Some Thoughts on Investment Disputes in the Americas." *American Journal of International Law* (January 1978), 72(1):1–16.

Ruggie, John Gerard. "International Regimes, Transactions, and Change: Embedded Liberalism in the Postwar Economic Order." In Krasner, ed., *International Regimes*.

Rustow, Dankwart. *Oil and Turmoil: America Faces OPEC and the Middle East.* New York: Norton, 1982.

Sampson, Anthony. *The Seven Sisters: The Great Oil Companies and the World They Made.* New York: Viking, 1975.

Schwebel, Stephen M. "International Protection of Contractual Agreements." *Proceedings of the American Society of International Law* (1959), 53:266–273.

Shafer, Michael. "Capturing the Mineral Multinationals: Advantage or Disadvantage?" *International Organization* (Winter 1983), 37(1):93–119.

Sigmund, Paul E. *Multinationals in Latin America: The Politics of Nationalization.* Madison: University of Wisconsin Press, 1980.

Smith, David N. and Louis T. Wells, Jr. *Negotiating Third World Mineral Agreements: Promises as Prologue.* Cambridge, Mass.: Ballinger, 1975.

Smith, Richard J. "The United States Government Perspective on Expropriation and Investment in Developing Countries." *Vanderbilt Journal of Transnational Law* (Summer 1976), 9(3):517–522.

Sonarajah, M. "The Myth of International Contract Law." *Journal of World Trade Law* (May/June 1981), 15(3):187–217.

Stallings, Barbara. "International Capitalism and the Peruvian Military Government." In Cynthia McClintock and Abraham F. Lowenthal, eds., *The Peruvian Experiment Reconsidered.* Princeton, N.J.: Princeton University Press, 1983.

Stallings, Barbara. "Peru and the U.S. Banks: The Privatization of Financial Relations." In Richard R. Fagen, ed., *Capitalism and the State in U.S.-Latin American Relations.* Stanford, Ca.: Stanford University Press, 1979.

Stocking, George W. *Middle East Oil: A Study in Political and Economic Controversy.* Nashville, Tenn.: Vanderbilt University Press, 1970.

Swansbrough, Robert H. *The Embattled Colossus: Economic Nationalism and United States Investors in Latin America.* Gainsville: University of Florida Press, 1976.

Sylvan, David J. "The Newest Mercantilism." *International Organization* (Spring 1981), 35(2):375–393.

Tannenbaum, Frank. *Ten Keys to Latin America.* New York: Knopf, 1962.

Tugwell, Franklin. *The Politics of Oil in Venezuela.* Stanford, Ca.: Stanford University Press, 1976.

Turner, Louis. *Oil Companies in the International System.* 3d ed. London: Allen and Unwin, 1983.

United States, Commission on Foreign Economic Policy (Randall Commission). *Report to the President and the Congress.* January 23, 1954. Cited in Notes as Randall Commission.

United States, Congress House, CFA (Committee on Foreign Affairs). *Expropriation of American-Owned Property by Foreign Governments in the Twentieth Century.* Committee Print, 88th Congress, 1st Session, July 19, 1963.

United States, Congress, House, CFA. *Foreign Assistance Act of 1964.* Hearings, 88th Congress, 2d Session, 1964.

United States, Congress, House, Committee on Interior and Insular Affairs. *Fuel and Energy Resources, 1972* (parts 1 and 2). 92d Congress, 2d Session, 1972.

United States Congress, Senate, Committee on Finance. *Sugar Act Amendments for 1971* (parts 1 and 2). Hearings, 92d Congress, 1st Session, 1971.

United States, Congress, Senate, CFR (Committee on Foreign Relations). *Foreign Assistance Act of 1962*. Hearings, 87th Congress, 2d Session, 1962.

United States, Congress, Senate. CFR. Subcommittee on Multinational Corporations. *Multinational Corporations and United States Foreign Policy*. (parts 3–9, 11). Hearings, 93d Congress, 2d Session, 1973–1975.

United States, Congress, Senate, CFR. Subcommittee on Multinational Corporations. *Multinational Oil Corporations and United States Foreign Policy*. Report, 93d Congress, 2d Session, January 2, 1975.

United States, Department of State, *Foreign Relations of the United States*. Washington D.C.: GPO, 1956–1978. Annual Volumes, 1937–1950. Cited in the notes as *FRUS*.

United States, Office of the President, President's Materials Policy Commission, *Resources for Freedom*. vol. 1: *Foundations for Growth and Security*, June, 1952. Cited in Notes as Paley Commission.

Vernon, Raymond. *Sovereignty at Bay. The Multinational Spread of United States Enterprise*. New York: Basic Books, 1972.

Vernon, Raymond. *Storm Over the Multinationals: The Real Issues*. Cambridge, Mass.: Harvard University Press, 1977.

Vernon, Raymond. *Two Hungry Giants: The United States and Japan in the Quest for Oil and Ores*. Cambridge, Mass.: Harvard University Press, 1983.

Waddams, Frank C. *The Libyan Oil Industry*. Baltimore, Md. and London: Johns Hopkins University Press, 1980.

Wagner, R. Harrison. *United States Policy Toward Latin America: A Study in Domestic and International Politics*. Stanford, Ca: Stanford University Press, 1970.

Weston, Burns H. "The Charter of Economic Rights and Duties of States and the Deprivation of Foreign-Owned Wealth." *American Journal of International Law* (July 1981), 75(3):437–475.

Wilkins, Mira. *The Maturing of the Multinational Enterprise: American Business Abroad, 1914–1970*. Cambridge, Mass.: Harvard University Press, 1974.

Wood, Bryce. *The Making of the Good Neighbor Policy*. New York: Columbia University Press, 1961.

Young, Oran. "Regime Dynamics: The Rise and Fall of International Regimes." In Krasner, *International Regimes* (Ithaca, N.Y.: Cornell University Press, 1984).

INDEX